Groove Music

Groove Music

The Art and Culture of the Hip-Hop DJ

MARK KATZ

OXFORD
UNIVERSITY PRESS

Oxford University Press, Inc., publishes works that further
Oxford University's objective of excellence
in research, scholarship, and education.

Oxford   New York
Auckland   Cape Town   Dar es Salaam   Hong Kong   Karachi
Kuala Lumpur   Madrid   Melbourne   Mexico City   Nairobi
New Delhi   Shanghai   Taipei   Toronto

With offices in
Argentina   Austria   Brazil   Chile   Czech Republic   France   Greece
Guatemala   Hungary   Italy   Japan   Poland   Portugal   Singapore
South Korea   Switzerland   Thailand   Turkey   Ukraine   Vietnam

Published by Oxford University Press, Inc.
198 Madison Avenue, New York, New York 10016
www.oup.com

Oxford is a registered trademark of Oxford University Press

Library of Congress Cataloging-in-Publication Data

Katz, Mark, 1970–
   Groove music : the art and culture of the hip-hop DJ / Mark Katz.
     p. cm.
   Includes bibliographical references.
   ISBN 978-0-19-533111-0 (hardcover : alk. paper) — ISBN 978-0-19-533112-7 (pbk. : alk. paper)
1. Turntablism. 2. Rap (Music)—History and criticism. 3. Turntablists. I. Title.
   ML3531.K37 2012
   782.421649—dc23   2011031319

Publication for this book was supported by the Gustave Reese Endowment of the American
Musicological Society.

9 8 7 6 5 4 3 2 1
Printed in the United States of America
on acid-free paper

For Beth and Anna, and all the DJs.

ACKNOWLEDGMENTS

First, I must thank *all* hip-hop DJs. I thank you for your artistry, for sweeping dancers onto their feet and for transfixing audiences with your virtuosity. I thank you for your alchemy, for creating musical gold by mixing bits and pieces of song and sound in just the right measure. I thank you for your wisdom, for sharing your vast knowledge of music. This book is about you, and it is for you.

I mention many DJs in *Groove Music*, and I will start here by naming those I have been fortunate enough to interact with directly, whether by interviewing them, corresponding with them, hanging out with them, or all of the above. Some of these DJs are internationally famous, some are of more local renown, some come from the great cities of the United States, Europe, and Asia, and some from around the area known as the Research Triangle in North Carolina where I live. So let me take a deep breath, and say: A-Minor, A-Trak, Aladdin, Apollo, B-Side, Baby Dee, Afrika Bambaataa, Billy Jam, Bro-Rabb, Cash Money, Craze, Cutmaster Swift, Disco Wiz, Doc Rice, Food Stamp, GrandWizzard Theodore, Grandmixer DXT, Hapa, ie.MERG, Immortal, J.Dayz, Pete DJ Jones, Ken-One, Kid Koala, Killa-Jewel, King Britt, Kuttin Kandi, Kutzu, Maseo, Miyajima, Mista Donut, Neil Armstrong, 9th Wonder, P, Pone, Qbert, Quest, Radar, Revolution, Rhettmatic, Ivan "Doc" Rodriguez, Johnny "Juice" Rosado, Sarasa, Shadow, Shortkut, SK, SPCLGST, Steinski, Steve Dee, Swamp, Rob Swift, Ta-Shi, Tigerstyle, Trife, and Tyra from Saigon—I thank you for sharing your insights with me. There would be no *Groove Music* without you.

As central as DJs are to *Groove Music*, there are many others whose expertise informed and aided my work as well. I have been assisted by artists, filmmakers, and photographers; battle organizers, promoters, and entrepreneurs; engineers, producers, and a variety of other music industry professionals; scholars and journalists; archivists and librarians; and musicians of every stripe. (Some of these people—and damn them for being so multitalented—are DJs as well.)

Thank you, then, to Charlie Ahearn, Michael Beinhorn, Andrew Bernal, Lauren Bernofsky, Martin Bisi, Kool Lady Blue, Ann Marie Boyle, Laurent Burte, Michael Cannady, John Carluccio, Jeff Chang, Joe Conzo, Brian Cross, Cristina DiGiacomo, Phil Ford, Rayvon Fouché, Kim Francis, Fab 5 Freddy, Laurent Fintoni, Nicole Havey, Ellie Hisama, Catherine Hughes, Akitsugu Kawamoto, Adam Krims, Johan Kugelberg, Bill Laswell, Tim Lawrence, Stephen Levitin, Steve Macatee, Wayne Marshall, Robert Adam Mayer, Sally McLintock, Felicia Miyakawa, Mark Naison, Tony Prince, Katherine Reagan, Miriam Rezaei, Travis Rimando, Zane Ritt, Martin Scherzinger, Joe Schloss, Troy Smith, Jeremy Storch, Dave Tompkins, Roger Trilling, Oliver Wang, Tachelle Wilkes, Kimberly Williams, Raúl Yañez, Christie Z-Pabon, and Bernard Zekri.

In these days of blogging and self-publishing, it might seem that authors no longer need help to get their ideas to readers. All I can say is that *Groove Music* is a much better book for having been published by Oxford University Press. I must first thank my editor Suzanne Ryan. It only took me about two minutes to know that we would work well together. Cornering her at a conference, I pitched my idea for this book and then asked, a bit nervously, "So, do you think you might be interested?" She looked at me like I was an idiot, and responded, "Uh, *yeah*." That was more than six years ago, and since then she has helped me in so many ways, whether by pushing me to "lose the bowtie" when I indulged in too much academese in the manuscript, meeting DJs with me, brainstorming with me over meals, or giving me just the right amount of slack at just the right time. Thanks, too, must go to Adam Cohen, Gail Cooper, Anindita Sengupta, Norm Hirschy, Katie Hellier, Natalie Johnson, and Niko Pfund for their professionalism, thoughtfulness, and enthusiasm. I suspect that they all did more for me than I realize.

Although this next group of people is not connected to OUP, I also consider them part of my editorial team. Many people have read parts of this book in draft form, but I owe a special thanks to two who read the whole thing and gave me invaluable feedback: Christie Z-Pabon and Travis Rimando. Christie, a widely admired hip-hop promoter, publicist, and activist, is also one of the most careful and scrupulous critics I could want. She pulled me back when I wandered onto thin ice, checked my facts, and offered her valuable perspective throughout the process. Travis, also known as DJ Pone, has a deep knowledge of battle history, DJ equipment, and really all things turntablistic, and constantly proved himself to be a most perceptive, thoughtful reader. They deserve a tremendous amount of credit. Also working diligently behind the scenes were several UNC graduate students—Will Boone, Dan Guberman, Brian Jones, and Tim Miller—who helped me greatly by transcribing interviews, doing research, and assisting in a variety of other ways.

I wrote this book while teaching at the University of North Carolina at Chapel Hill, and I am grateful to many colleagues, administrators, and staff members for their support, including Bill Andrews, Tim Carter, Annegret Fauser, David Garcia, George Huntley, Jim Ketch, Dick Langston, Cary Levine, Carrie Monette, John Nádas, Don Oehler, Terry Rhodes, Sarah Sharma, Diane Steinhaus, Phil Vandermeer, Ken Weiss, and Susan Williams. I also owe a great deal to the literally hundreds of students who read parts of *Groove Music* in draft form, including those in my classes, The Art and Culture of the DJ, Capturing Sound, and Introduction to Rock. Special thanks go to the members of my seminar, Music, Technology, and Culture, who offered valuable feedback on nearly the whole manuscript: Karen Atkins, Chris Dahlie, Ryan Ebright, Ben Haas, Brian Jones, Erin Maher, Vanessa Pelletier, Chris Reali, and Kristen Turner.

Crucial institutional support also came from the National Science Foundation. In 2006, I was fortunate to receive, along with Rayvon Fouché, the National Science Foundation Award SES-0526095 for the project "A Comparative Investigation of Technological Transformation and Musical Expression." The award provided me with a semester's leave and funded a number of research trips, making it possible for me to interview many DJs in person and to visit several DJ academies.

The sound of scratching and looped breaks did not pervade my house when I was growing up, and I'm sure that my family never expected me to write a book about hip-hop. But no one in my family has ever questioned why I would do such a thing; to the contrary, they have been tremendously supportive. Thank you to my parents, Evelyn and Warren Katz; to my sister and brothers, Cheryl Anders, Ian Katz, and Michael Katz; and to my aunts, uncles, cousins, nephews, nieces, and in-laws: your love and support means so much to me. I especially want to thank my parents who, a few years ago, indulged me by letting me read a part of *Groove Music* to them. Their genuine interest and enthusiasm buoyed me, and gave me hope that there may be a general audience for this book.

I hope no one will begrudge me for saying that among all those I need to thank, there are two who deserve it most: my wife, Beth Jakub, and my daughter, Anna Katz. Beth, if I could find a nice word that rhymes with your name, I'd write a rapturous poem in your honor. It would be but a small token of my thanks for the more than twenty years you've been a part of my life, influencing me in the most positive ways as a person and as a scholar. It would the tiniest compensation for the suffering caused to you by the all-consuming project we semi-jokingly referred to as *Groove Music: Ruining Family Vacations Since 2006*. In lieu of that poem, I simply say, I love you and I owe you. Anna, you haven't yet read *Groove Music*, and that's okay, even though you're almost eight and can read just fine. Come to think of it, your mere existence often discouraged me from working on the book, since I'd always rather spend time with you than stare at a computer screen. So really, you haven't been much help, except that you bring such joy to my life that I find it easy to work through the night knowing that you're sleeping peacefully just fifteen feet away. That and the fact that you love to scratch vinyl with your daddy.

As I look back over the last several paragraphs, just seeing all those names arrayed in one place is humbling and awe-inspiring. I am very lucky to have had all these people on my side. So once again, thank you.

Carrboro, North Carolina,
November 2011

To the musicologists of the twenty-first century our epoch may not be known by the name of a school of composers or of a musical style. It may well be called the period of the phonograph. . . .

—ALAN LOMAX, folklorist and ethnomusicologist (1960)
"Saga of the Folksong Hunter," in *Alan Lomax,
Selected Writings 1934–1997*, ed. Ronald Cohen (New York:
Routledge, 2003), 173.

I don't even know what hip-hop is, to be honest with you. Do you know what hip-hop is? What is all this scratching of records?

—MILTON BABBITT, composer (2001)
Interview with Frank J. Oteri,
New Music Box, 1 December 2001,
www.newmusicbox.org

Records + Turntable + Scratching = Music

—D-STYLES, turntablist (2002)
Liner notes to *Phantazmagorea* (2002),
Beat Junkie Sound CD, PHAN-001

CONTENTS

ABOUT THE COMPANION WEBSITE

Oxford University Press has created a password-protected website to accompany *Groove Music*. The site includes nearly one hundred sound and video examples, as well as photographs, documents, and other materials. These audio-visual materials are all linked to specific parts of the book, and are indicated by a speaker icon 🔊. Since the art and culture of the hip-hop DJ is best understood by hearing and seeing DJs in action, readers are strongly encouraged to take full advantage of this site.

Groove Music

Introduction

A teenager walks into the Davidson Houses looking for his girl. As he wanders the maze-like hallways of the South Bronx housing development, he turns a corner and suddenly finds himself staring at a group of eight or nine young thugs drinking beer and smoking weed. They stare back menacingly, and start to move in. The boy is small and outnumbered—this will not be a fair fight. But then one of the stick-up kids, as they were called, recognizes him through the haze. "Yo, yo, it's the DJ!" he shouts, waving off the others. "Let him through, let him through!" They step aside, and the DJ lives to see another day.

The DJ was Theodore Livingston, and though just fourteen or fifteen, he was already making a name for himself as GrandWizzard Theodore. A prodigy on the turntables, he was known from the local block parties as the kid who came up with that record-scraping move that was later called *scratching*. It was 1977 or 1978, and a new cultural movement was brewing in the Bronx, one that combined music, dance, and painting. This brew came to be called hip-hop.[1]

The story of GrandWizzard Theodore is, in one sense, the story of the hip-hop DJ. Like many DJs of his time and since, he is a hardworking professional and musical jack-of-all-trades. Unlike those swaggering, jewel-encrusted rappers who capture the attention of the media, Theodore, like most DJs, is unassuming and quiet. Like most hip-hop DJs he is technologically savvy, having honed the necessary skills to assemble, disassemble, and repair turntables, mixers, and speakers quickly and under pressure. And like all good DJs, he holds a musicologist's knowledge of names, dates, tunes, and styles.

Yet Theodore is hardly representative of all hip-hop DJs. This is not so much because of his historical importance and extraordinary skills, but because there is no one type of DJ and no one way to spin records. Theodore is black, was born in the early 1960s and was raised (and still lives) in the Bronx, New York. But some of the earliest hip-hop DJs were Latino and a few were women. Later, Asian Americans and white Americans of various ethnicities became crucial to the development of DJing, and it wasn't long before DJs outside the United States played important roles in the art as well.

DJs differ not only in terms of race, gender, ethnicity, and geography, but in their approach to DJing. The hip-hop pioneers were mobile DJs—they toted their own equipment to every party, whether in apartment buildings or com-munity centers, on playgrounds or in school gyms. Later, some of them became club DJs, taking residencies in dance clubs, using the equipment provided for them. Some DJs worked at radio stations, employing their voices as much as their hands. Others teamed up with rappers, essentially becoming the rhythm section of a hip-hop group, and still others brought their craft to recording studios where they composed beats for rappers, and came to be known as pro-ducers. In the 1980s, turntablism emerged, in which DJs performed as self-sufficient instrumentalists. Turntablists did not simply spin songs, but created wholly new music through their complex manipulation of recorded sound. In the process, these DJs developed a host of new techniques, often testing and refining them in adrenaline-fueled competitions known as battles. To make matters more complex, these categories—mobile, club, and radio DJs, produc-ers and turntablists—are not mutually exclusive. Many DJs move from one to another and back in the course of a career or even a few days. And some DJs in the new millennium don't even use records or turntables, but employ CD players, laptops, or devices called controllers.

So what exactly is a "disc jockey"? At its broadest, a DJ is someone who plays recordings for an audience. The term was first used in the early 1940s to describe radio personalities who played phonograph records on the air—a novelty at a time when much music heard on the radio came from live broadcasts of per-formers.[2] DJs were not originally held in high esteem, and many saw them as a threat to the musicians whose livelihood depended on their live radio perfor-mances. As *Time* magazine noted in 1942, "Some stations merely hired 'disk-jockeys' to ride herd on swing records."[3] Imagine a caricature of a person straddling an oversized record, riding crop in hand, and you get a sense of this negative view of DJs. A 1946 article in the same magazine snidely defined a "disc jockey" as:

> A pitchman who knows how to change records. He exists because 1) radio prefers hot air to dead air; 2) some listeners like to hear their favorite musi-cians often, and an announcer and record library are much cheaper than the high-priced orchestras and entertainers.[4]

The taint of inauthenticity and inferiority never really dissipated, and still colors the way many regard DJs, and even how DJs view themselves. Hip-hop DJs, we'll see, often feel the need to defend what they do as more than simply playing records.

There are many types of DJs, but in this book I focus on what I call *performative DJs*, those who not only select recordings, but manipulate them in real time for audiences. This manipulation can consist of repeating fragments of a recording, mixing different records together, or distorting recorded sounds by pushing a record quickly back and forth—scratching. Their audiences can be dancers or listeners, spinning on their backs or bumping and grinding as couples, sitting at the judges' table at a DJ competition or lounging at home with headphones on. My focus on performative DJing means that we'll only peripherally encounter radio DJs and DJs who make beats, or producers, important as they might be.[5] My focus on performance is motivated by more than the need to keep this book to a manageable size. As I see it, performative DJing is the signal contribution of the hip-hop DJ to modern musical culture. Put another way, the purpose of this book is to chronicle and investigate the rise of a new type of musician—the DJ—who developed a new musical instrument—the turntable—and in doing so helped create a new type of music: hip-hop.

The story of the simultaneous rise of a new type of instrument, musician, and music is a complex one. Actually, there are many stories to be told, and although I have aspired to be thorough, I have had to be selective, and naturally, I write from my own particular perspective. So let me say a few words about how I have chosen to tell these stories and the perspectives from which I tell them.

I'm often asked how I became interested in this topic. Apparently, some think it odd that a not-exactly-young, not-exactly-hip white guy with a Ph.D. in musicology would spend years researching hip-hop, hanging out with DJs, going to battles, and even learning how to scratch. The assumptions underlying these reactions are based on misperceptions—of musicology, of hip-hop, and of me. Both musicology and hip-hop are more diverse than many outsiders realize. And in my own defense, I'm cooler than I look.

In any case, here is my story. The sound of record scratching first entered my consciousness in 1983; I was thirteen and had just heard the Herbie Hancock song "Rockit," featuring Grandmixer D.ST (now Grandmixer DXT) on the turntables. More than anything, it was the sound of D.ST's scratching that drew me. It was so vivid, so fresh, I could almost *taste* the sound—it was the sonic equivalent of biting into a crisp, tart apple. For me, a typical adolescent, my interest in scratching was intense but short-lived, similar to my desire to score red leather pants like the ones Loverboy's lead singer wore on the video of "Working for the Weekend," or to perfect my backslide (a.k.a. moonwalk) after seeing Michael Jackson's effortless glide on TV. Still, this strange sound lodged in my brain, and lay dormant for more than fifteen years before my interest in turntablism reawakened when I became an academic.

In 1999, I finished my doctoral dissertation on the impact of recording technology on the musical life of the early twentieth century.[6] I was thinking of new topics to explore as I expanded the dissertation into a book, and immediately thought of turntablism. At the time, scratching had returned to the mainstream and was surfacing in pop and rock songs on the radio. (Fondly or not, some readers will remember Hanson's "MMMbop," Sublime's "What I Got," or Kid Rock's "Bawitdaba.") Turntablism struck me as an obvious case study on the influence of sound recording; after all, this music simply wouldn't exist without the turntable and vinyl discs. So for four years, I researched the music and culture of the hip-hop DJ, attending battles, studying DJ videos, and interviewing DJs. The result was a chapter on DJ battles for my 2004 book, *Capturing Sound*.[7] This chapter planted the seed for *Groove Music*.

When I embarked on *Groove Music* in 2005, I imagined it as a series of case studies.[8] These case studies would have focused on issues of technology, race, and gender without regard to covering the whole history or scope of hip-hop DJing. But after talking with DJs over the next few years, I started to question this approach. I often ended my interviews by asking, "What would you like to see in a book about the hip-hop DJ?" One answer changed the course of this project. The answer, which came not from a single DJ but from many, was this: History. It's not as if the history of the hip-hop DJ had been completely neglected. *Yes Yes Y'all*, by Jim Fricke and Charlie Ahearn, Jeff Chang's *Can't Stop Won't Stop*, and *Last Night a DJ Saved My Life* by Bill Brewster and Frank Broughton, all covered hip-hop DJing as part of larger stories—and all, I want to state up front, deeply influenced this book.[9] But the DJs I talked to wanted to see something that hadn't been written: a book that focused solely on the rich, decades-long history of the hip-hop DJ. Some of the older DJs I knew lamented the fact that their younger colleagues knew little about who and what came before them; this generation, they told me, *needed* to know their history. As GrandWizzard Theodore explained in Doug Pray's documentary, *Scratch*, "You have to know where hip-hop's been in order to know where it's going."[10]

From the beginning, I knew that I wanted to reach a diverse audience of hip-hop fans, general readers, and scholars. But it was also important to me that DJs read and respect this book. I couldn't have written it without their help; the least I could do is write something they might want to read. So at the suggestion of many of the DJs I had met and because no book had yet focused on the history of the hip-hop DJ, I decided to make a fundamental change.

Groove Music is now a narrative of the development of hip-hop DJing, spanning the thirty-eight years from late 1973 to late 2011. Each of the book's eight chapters covers a cut of DJ history, a little less than four years on average, and each treats several developments, issues, or phenomena linked by a unifying theme. My change in approach did not mean, however, that I was setting out to write an exhaustive study of the hip-hop DJ. It would be impossible to give space to every notable figure, to explore every significant trend and event, or to range across the globe to hit every center of DJ activity. I could easily spend several more years doing research and still not capture it all. Inevitably, some readers will be disappointed by what they *don't* see in these pages—I can only hope that they understand why I have had to be selective, and find value in what they do see.

The story I am telling is largely an American one, and this, too, is part of my selective approach. I say *largely* American because I certainly acknowledge the international influences on the Bronx-born art form. I would be negligent if I didn't discuss the role of the Jamaican sound system or of the influence of Latin American music on the early hip-hop DJ. The French contribution to the internationalization of hip-hop, the British origins of the DMC battle, and the ubiquity of Japanese technology must also be recognized. But I am telling this as an American story not simply because hip-hop is American-born, but because the development of the hip-hop DJ helps tell the story of the United States. It's a story of technological innovation and do-it-yourself entrepreneurship, of race and gender relations, of the mainstream and the underground. The hip-hop DJ and the country of its birth are deeply intertwined, and although this book is not intended as a meditation on modern America, it offers a distinctive lens through which to view its culture and ethos.

Given my focus on the United States, I hope that others will write in depth about hip-hop DJing in all those places it has come to flourish over the last few decades. So, to the amazing DJs Switch and Woody (England); Fly, LigOne, and Netik (France); Rafik (Germany); Akakabe and Kentaro (Japan); and to the many others whose work I do not cover here, I apologize. Your stories need to be told and repeated.

Notice that I keep using the word *story*. This is no accident. The narrative mode feels right when discussing hip-hop DJs, for although audio recordings and videos as well as artifacts like flyers and posters help document their art and culture, it is the stories that DJs tell that truly make sense of their past. Stories are our most powerful conveyers of knowledge: they preserve traditions and reveal the values of a community, they connect us to the past and keep the dead in living memory, they illuminate the present and suggest possible futures. Throughout this book, I relate stories about sounds and songs, people and events. I retell the origins of hip-hop (Chapter 1); I untangle the story behind the ubiquitous "ah" and "fresh" sounds known to nearly all DJs (Chapter 3); I recount the legendary 1996 encounter between the X-Men and the Invisibl Skratch Piklz (Chapter 5); I even spin a tale about a hypothetical DJ preparing for and competing in a battle (Chapter 6). And woven throughout the book are stories about technology, about how DJs have reshaped turntables and mixers to suit their needs. As historian David Nye perceptively observed, "the meaning of a tool is inseparable from the stories that surround it."[11]

Storytelling has its pitfalls, of course. Chronology is often imprecise; names and places sometimes confused or forgotten. When different people talk about the same event, the divergences can be stark: a single innovation may be credited to multiple people, villains and heroes can switch places, important characters can be left out of the story, and completely distinct events may be conflated. I have been mindful of these problems, and whenever possible I have sought multiple accounts of a particular event and checked stories against verifiable facts.

Sometimes it's a simple matter to straighten out a story. DJ Steve Dee, for example, told me he first started developing the mixing technique that came to be known as beat juggling in either 1986 or 1987, but he couldn't (at least at that moment) be more precise. In telling his story, however, he recalled how he had just come up with a scratch called the Robocut, a name inspired by a movie he had recently seen, *Robocop*. *Robocop* was released on July 17, 1987, so Steve Dee's beat juggling couldn't have preceded that date. Similarly, I have used the release dates of songs—songs often figure prominently in the telling of DJ stories—to establish chronology. Some issues aren't so easily resolved, like the origin of the transformer scratch. As I explain in Chapter 4, multiple DJs claim that they invented the technique, and there's no clear consensus among the DJ community about who really was first. In this case I make no judgment, but simply relate the stories as clearly as possible. Although I would've liked to establish the facts definitively, the existence of competing claims turns out to be more interesting than a simple answer, for it reveals the high value DJs place on innovation and the differing roles of the individual and the community in the world of the hip-hop DJ.

My approach, then, is largely a combination of ethnography and history. To me, this is a powerful combination, for together they account for the importance of the stories of the practitioners as well as the social, cultural, and historical contexts in which they lived. Moreover, my approach emerged from my research and is tailored to my topic, rather than having been imposed upon it. In some academic scholarship the object of study serves to test, refine, or develop a methodology; I'm more interested in DJing than any theories that I might apply to it or derive from it.

That's not to say that I'm anti-theory. I bring academic theory into the picture when it helps make sense of the stories I tell. Most of the time theory lurks in the background, informing my thinking without (I hope) calling attention to itself. For the sake of scholars and other interested readers, however, let me say something about those lurking theories.

Technology scholars will recognize the influence of the social construction of technology (SCOT) approach and the concept of co-construction, both of which emerged from science and technology studies. The word *construction* here does not refer to physical objects, but is used metaphorically to describe the way *meanings* are created. SCOT holds that technologies do not determine their uses and meanings; rather, these are determined (i.e., constructed) in a social context by the people who invent, design, sell, and use the technologies. Co-construction is a related concept that focuses on the end-users or consumers of a technology and the often-unappreciated power of users to shape the tools and machines that play such an important role in their everyday lives. Therefore, when I spotlight the inventiveness of the DJs who tweaked, hacked, and even redesigned their turntables and mixers, I am both revealing the influence of, and offering case studies in, SCOT and co-construction.[12]

Scholars of race, ethnicity, and gender will recognize that I embrace the idea that identity is not inborn but—and here is that word again—constructed. I don't believe, for example, that men dominate the DJ battle scene because they naturally embrace all things competitive and mechanical, though these are common assumptions that represent what is called an *essentialist* view of gender. Rather, I see the dominance of men as a manifestation of the way boys are often pushed toward technical pursuits and encouraged to be overtly competitive, while girls are frequently given to believe that such things are unladylike and undesirable. I am similarly anti-essentialist when it comes to race and ethnicity. The African Americans and Latinos who created hip-hop didn't do it because of some essential blackness or brownness. That's not to say that their skin color and heritage were irrelevant; rather, they were factors—alongside time, place, class, economics, and the artistic contributions of certain individuals— that went into the creation of a new form of cultural expression in 1970s New York among marginalized working-class communities. Likewise, the Filipino Americans who helped make the San Francisco Bay Area the world center of turntablism in the 1990s weren't driven by their common connection to a distant archipelago. They, too, both shaped and were shaped by their environment.

Non-academics may find all this talk of constructivism to be, well, academic. Although I try to wear my academicism lightly, there's good reason for drawing attention to the idea of constructivism. I insist on the constructed nature of technology and identity because the idea explicitly recognizes the power that individuals and communities have in determining their identities, values, and aesthetics. Put this way, it may seem like a commonsense idea, but unfortunately there are equally common, but nonsensical, notions that propose otherwise. Take the old and noxious stereotype that African Americans are born with a good sense of rhythm and naturally take to singing, drumming, and dancing better than paler people. Here I'll paraphrase a rebuttal in the form of a thought experiment I once heard from the musicologist Guthrie Ramsey. Imagine an African American baby boy is raised to maturity in complete isolation from any music or community. Would he one day spontaneously break into a James Brown shuffle and belt out, "I've got soul and I'm superbad"? Essentialist views like the one Ramsey was refuting are not just illogical, they're insidious and disempowering. If black people are born with certain qualities or tendencies, then it's easy to dismiss or downplay their cultural achievements. It's as if their individual creativity and years of hard work are of no consequence. And of course, this is simply not true.

My anti-essentialism extends to other races and ethnicities as well, and yes, to white people, too. Just as blacks are sometimes thought to have been born with rhythm, white people are often said to be born without it. I guess no one told that to A-Trak or Z-Trip, Shiftee or Swamp, ie.MERG, Klever, Revolution, or Vajra—all incredibly talented DJs who have earned the well-deserved respect of their non-white peers. As I've mentioned, gender, too, is constructed, despite the fact that the biological differences between men and women are greater than those between people of different races. Yet the fact that men have parts that women don't, and vice-versa, does not explain why there are more male than female DJs. Although there is nothing about DJing that requires a certain amount of testosterone, plenty of people think otherwise. Several years ago I attended a DJ showcase where I ended up talking with a female college student, the lone woman in the crowd. Why, I asked her, did she think that so few women were DJs? Her answer concisely reduced women to their anatomy: "Women are pussies," she sneered. At the time I had been teaching at a conservatory, one filled with talented young classical musicians. During my years there I saw and heard plenty of evidence that women could outperform men as singers and instrumentalists. But for centuries, many thought that musicians of the "fairer sex" could never be the equal of men. There's no reason to think that the situation cannot change just as strikingly in the world of DJs, and there's good reason to think that it won't take centuries.

In explaining my approach, I have yet to say anything about music. It's possible to write a book about hip-hop DJs without delving into the music they play and create, but *Groove Music* is not that book. Here is where my background as a musician and a music scholar comes into play. I was drawn to this subject by a very specific sound—that *wicki-wicki*, that *zigga-zigga* that comes from pushing a vinyl record back and forth underneath the needle of a record player. (For the non-DJs out there, the needle is not dragged *across* the grooves but stays within the grooves. Scratching doesn't immediately ruin a record, though it does gradually wear out parts of a disc.) But there is, as I'll explain over the course of this book, much more than that *zigga-zigga* sound to the art

of the hip-hop DJ. In Chapter 1, I explore the musical nature of the short percussion solos known as *breaks* that the first DJs extracted from records and
extended in order to generate dance music for the b-boys and b-girls. (The "b"
is typically understood to stand for "break," but note that b-boys and b-girls
generally do not refer to themselves using the common term *breakdancer*.) In
later chapters I offer close readings of important songs, albums, and battle routines; for example, "The Adventures of Grandmaster Flash on the Wheels of
Steel" (Chapter 3) and DJ Shadow's *Endtroducing. . . . .* (Chapter 7).

My study of DJ music has involved not only my ears, but my hands. Before I
got my own equipment, I had played around on other people's turntables, and
even took classes at the New York, Miami, and Los Angeles branches of the
Scratch DJ Academy as part of my research (more on DJ schools in Chapter 8).
In 2007, I finally acquired my own gear: two Technics 1200 turntables (specifically, the SL-1200MK5 model) with Shure M44-7 needles and a Rane TTM-56
mixer, a semi-high-end but common setup among battle DJs. I'm still not very
good, but I've gained a new appreciation of the art I was studying. For one
thing, it's harder than it looks. Even the basic "baby" scratch requires finding a
particular part of a record and then holding the fingers and moving the arm in
just the right way. Once I learned how to scratch correctly, I became aware of an
almost physical bump when pushing a record back and forth across the attack,
or tip, of a snare hit. Done properly the result is a crisp and penetrating sound—
a "tight" scratch; done the wrong way the sound is barely audible, the rhythm
flabby. Trying to loop a beat—alternating between the same musical phrase on
two turntables—was the best way I could appreciate the exquisite timing and
control necessary to weave a seamless stream of music out of a brief fragment.
I also spent time searching for records to scratch and mix in record stores, thrift
shops, library sales, and the homes of friends and relatives. DJs call this *digging
in the crates*, the "crates" referring to the typical way records are stored. As I
discovered, it's called digging for a reason—it's tiring, hard on the back, and
often leaves the digger with dirty hands. But it can also be hugely rewarding,
and plays an important role in the education of DJs.

These hours spent handling vinyl have given me insights into the art and
culture of the hip-hop DJ that might have been lost on me if I had never gotten
my hands dirty. I understand why many DJs absolutely rejected the new breed
of CD players developed in the late 1990s that allowed scratching and mixing
through a simulated record platter. It's not that they were anti-digital or stuck in
the past: it's simply that these platters did not feel or handle like vinyl. I also
understand why many hip-hop DJs are perfectly happy to connect their turntables to laptops using the digital systems like Serato Scratch Live, Traktor, and
Torq that started coming on the market in the early 2000s. Laptops might seem
fatally inauthentic to hip-hop DJs, but as I explain in Chapter 8, these digital

systems are embraced because they allow DJs to use actual vinyl. If we understand the centrality of vinyl, we can understand why the community of hip-hop DJs has rejected one digital system and embraced another; more broadly, we can understand the values and aesthetics of these DJs.

In the end, this book is about a community—far-flung, yes, but one whose members often think of themselves as part of an extended family with common interests and values—and its music, technology, history, and culture. When I told the great DJ Cash Money that I was writing this book, his response came with the weight of this community behind him: "We need you to get this right."[13] Others will judge whether I've succeeded, but I can assure him and the rest of the DJ community that these words have guided *Groove Music* to its last page.

A NOTE ON THE INTERVIEWS

Because the dozens of interviews I conducted for this book form the single most important documentary source in *Groove Music*, I should contextualize this material. I conducted these interviews over the course of twelve years, from 1999 to 2011. Every interview was different—some were by phone or e-mail, but whenever possible I conducted them in person, typically near where the person lived at the time. The interviews tended to be in informal settings, and although I always had specific topics I wanted to discuss, they often turned into free-flowing conversations—more valuable, in my opinion, than formal interviews with set questions.

Each interview is identified in the endnotes, which indicate when and where the interview was conducted, or if the exchange took place by phone or e-mail. A separate list of the interviews is provided in the bibliography. Interviews before 2005 were conducted for my book *Capturing Sound*, though much of what is quoted from those interviews in this book did not appear in the earlier book; subsequent interviews were conducted expressly for *Groove Music*. All interviews that I quote were recorded with permission, and with a very few minor exceptions, all quotations from these interviews have been transcribed from recordings rather than reconstructed from my notes or memory. In transcribing these interviews I have removed "ums," "uhs" and the occasional repeated word (for example, one person I interviewed often said the word "like" several times in a row), but otherwise the quotations are as they were spoken. In most cases, I do not include my own questions or prompts, largely because my words would, more often than not, disrupt the flow of the text without illuminating the response.

Although my interviewees represent a wide variety of DJs and others, I wasn't able to speak with everyone I would have liked to interview. No one refused my request for an interview, but sometimes I was unable to make contact with a person, and occasionally a planned interview fell through. Fortunately, most of those I could not speak with have been interviewed before, and whenever possible I have drawn on these earlier sources. I'm especially grateful for *Yes Yes Y'all*, *Can't Stop Won't Stop*, *Last Night a DJ Saved My Life*, *Scratch*, John Carluccio's *Battle Sounds* documentary, and the interviews of Troy Smith and a few others, for filling in gaps for me.

The interviews I've conducted have been some of the most memorable experiences of my life, scholarly or otherwise. I interviewed GrandWizzard Theodore in his car while he drove me around the Bronx; Steve Dee in his boyhood Harlem apartment with his mother and daughter in attendance; Qbert in front of his turntables in his California home; Disco Wiz at a UNC basketball game; DJ Sarasa (a.k.a. Silverboombox) late at night at a Tokyo club; Grandmixer DXT on a bench in Central Park, and so on. I can only hope that their words are as vivid to readers now as they were for me when I first heard them.

The Breaks and the Bronx:
1973–1975

It's all about the break.

If you hope to understand the art of the hip-hop DJ—and even the very origins of hip-hop—you must understand the break. And to understand the break, you can hardly do better than to begin with James Brown. Though he's best known as the "Godfather of Soul," his music is also one of the crucial building blocks of hip-hop; Grandmaster Flash speaks the truth when he says, "no James Brown, no hip-hop."[1] So listen to Brown's 1970 opus, "Funky Drummer."[2] About four-and-a-half minutes in, Brown calls out to his band of nine: "I want to give the drummer some of this funky soul we got here. When I count to four I want everyone to lay out and let the drummer go. And when I count to four I want you to come back in." The groove continues for thirteen bars before Brown counts off, calling out to drummer Clyde Stubblefield to "Hit it!" The clouds part, and a ray of pure funk shines down, a simple but slightly off-kilter call and response between the bass and snare drums, the hi-hat keeping time in sixteenth notes. Brown can only keep quiet for two bars before he starts testifying, exclaiming, "Good God!" and "Ain't it funky!" All too soon, he counts the rest of the group back in, and the moment slips away. ◐

That moment was the break. A break is a brief percussion solo, typically found toward the end of a funk song, though it may show up anywhere in a song, and really, anywhere in music. The power of the break is in the way it moves people, literally, compelling them to "get on the good foot" as James Brown commands us in his song of the same name. And this power is only heightened by its contrast with its surroundings. It lays bare a short stretch of unadulterated rhythm as the singer and other instrumentalists abruptly drop out, and the effect, whether heard for the first or fiftieth time, is electrifying. "It's like all of a sudden the song took its clothes off," suggests the DJ and break connoisseur known as Steinski.[3] Steinski's metaphor works on two levels: it not only points to the stripping of the musical texture but also hints at the sexual tension generated by the bumping and grinding of full-contact dancing. The break was commonly known as the "get-down part" of a song, and it's no coincidence that "get down" had a double meaning in 1970s slang—to dance with abandon, or to have sex.

Although the breaks may have generated extra heat among the couples on the floor, it was solo dancers who made the breaks famous by bringing out their showiest moves during these percussive passages. These dancers called themselves *b-boys* and *b-girls*, their art later dubbed *breakdancing* by outsiders. (Most insiders reject *breakdancing* and refer to it as *b-boying*, and sometimes *b-girling*.[4]) This new style of dancing caused a sensation. In his 2008 memoir, pioneering hip-hop DJ Grandmaster Flash vividly described his first encounter with b-boying. It was 1975, and his friend Mike had come to see him in his basement, demanding to hear "It's Just Begun" (1972) by the Jimmy Castor Bunch.

> Mike was standing there with his arms crossed up, his head cocked to the side, and his Chuck Taylors spread about three feet apart. Told me to drop "Just Begun" by Jimmy Castor on the turntable. The music played but he kept standing there. I looked at him like he was crazy. BAM! As soon as the drums started [the percussion solo about two minutes into the song], Mike went nuts. He was movin' his feet and dancin' all fast, but not in any kind of steps I'd ever seen before.
>
> "What the hell was that?"
>
> "I just broke on you. And you can call me a b-boy."[5]

This new, exciting style of dance could not have flourished without the intervention of the disc jockey. This is for the simple reason that most breaks offer insufficient opportunity for getting down: they were simply too short.[6] But by laying hands on vinyl, a good DJ could breathe new life into the breaks. Here's how Breakout, an early hip-hop DJ from the Bronx, explained the DJ's job: "Say there's a lotta singin' on the record, and then the singin' stops and the beat [i.e., break] comes on. You gotta make that beat last for a long time to keep the b-boy keep dancin', 'cause once the words come on, he stops dancin'. So you gotta be able to catch that same beat, hit it, hit it, again and again."[7]

At first, DJs would hit the break by setting the needle down right at that point in the record, and then lift the tone arm and repeat it as desired. It's harder than it sounds. The DJ must know the exact location of the break by sight and needs a steady hand so as not to unleash the vibe-killing screech of a skidding stylus. An experienced DJ will even be able to look at an unfamiliar record and find the break; it's a darker band within the track, a sliver of groove music. Later, as we'll see in the next chapter, DJs like Grandmaster Flash developed more sophisticated ways of repeating breaks, using two copies of a record on two turntables and employing a mixer to switch quickly and seamlessly between the two discs.

Although the idea of repeating breaks for dancers may seem like a simple idea, it represented a crucial reconception of both the nature of the break and the function of the record and turntable. Hip-hop DJs (and the b-boys and b-girls they catered to) did not just hear breaks as tantalizing; they heard them as fundamentally incomplete, as fragments that demanded to be repeated. These DJs also, and perhaps in consequence, came to see the tools of their trade in a new light. Records were not inviolate; songs did not need to be played from start to finish. A turntable therefore was not simply a playback device but a means for manipulating sound.

It was the DJ's manipulation of recorded sound that formed the basis of hip-hop. If there is a Grand Unified Theory that underlies the arts of the DJ, the b-boy/b-girl, and later, the MC (or rapper), the break is the unifying force. Understand that in 1973 there was no separate musical category known as hip-hop. It was not yet a distinctive genre, but more a performance practice, a way of approaching other types of music. The performer was the DJ, and the practice was to isolate and repeat choice instrumental parts of popular songs—the breaks—at dance parties. Later, vocal parts were added over top these repeated breaks by MCs in the form of rapping. Eventually, what began as a practice became its own genre, one combining dance with instrumental and vocal music. Out of the collaboration between DJs and dancers, and in large part arising from the musical and technological ingenuity of these virtuosi of vinyl, a rich, new art form came into being.

BORN IN THE BRONX

In January 1973, the *New York Times* ran a four-article series whose lurid headlines painted a dire picture of the southern part of the city's northern borough:

"South Bronx: A Jungle Stalked by Fear, Seized by Rage"
"Gangs Spread Terror in the South Bronx"
"Rage Permeates All Facets of Life in the South Bronx"
"Future Looks Bleak for the South Bronx"

Twenty thousand residents had no running water, forced to carry buckets to the nearest working fire hydrant; thousands more had no heat. Forty percent of the residents were on welfare; thirty percent were unemployed. Among those living in the area's 600,000 substandard housing units were seven-year-old alcoholics and ten-year-old mothers. One Bronx district recorded an infant mortality rate more than sixty percent higher than the national average.[8] Merchants shuttered their stores at sunset, fearing the thugs and addicts who swarmed the neighborhoods. Arson was a daily occurrence, many of the fires set in dilapidated apartment buildings at the behest of slumlords who stood to reap the insurance payouts. (It only got worse. Some 30,000 fires were set in the South Bronx between 1973 and 1977—the most notorious occurring a mile from Yankee Stadium during the 1977 World Series. As the scene was captured on TV before an audience of tens of millions, sportscaster Howard Cosell famously deadpanned, "Ladies and gentlemen, there it is. The Bronx is burning."[9]) Crumbling schools came to resemble fortresses, though students were at times no safer inside them than out. Violence and addiction surged, disease ran rampant, buildings collapsed, and test scores plummeted; police and fire departments shrank, teachers were laid off, and city services withered. DJ GrandWizzard Theodore, a schoolboy of ten in 1973, could do little more than repeat one word when I asked him to describe the Bronx of his youth: *crazy*. "It was crazy, it was crazy because, see, back in the early '70s, you know, living in the Bronx—it's like, all the buildings were burning down. That shit was crazy, you know?"[10] Dr. Harold Wise, founder of a medical center in the Bathgate neighborhood, offered this bleak summation to the *New York Times* in 1973: "The South Bronx is a necropolis, a city of death."[11]

That summer of 1973, hip-hop was born. And it was born in the Bronx.[12]

The father was a hulking eighteen-year-old Jamaican-born DJ named Clive Campbell, better known as Kool Herc. ◐ The story, however, really begins with his sister Cindy. She wanted to throw a party, one that would raise money for some stylish new school clothes. For the price of admission—a quarter for the ladies and fifty cents for the fellas—partygoers got to hear the best new funk, soul, and rock records played on a powerful stereo borrowed from her father and manned by her older brother.

This was Herc's first party as DJ. It was held on August 11, 1973 in the low-ceilinged community room in the basement of his family's apartment building on 1520 Sedgwick Avenue, an address that has since come to be known as the birthplace of hip-hop ◐ (see Figure 1.1). Buzz was generated with invitations hand-written on index cards that listed some of the songs Herc intended to play, like James Brown's "Get on the Good Foot" (1972), or Mandrill's "Fencewalk" (1973). A few of these invitations still exist, and the childlike bubble lettering adorned with stars and hearts offers a vivid reminder that hip-hop—now a

Figure 1.1 1520 Sedgwick Avenue, the Bronx. The site of Kool Herc's first party and, to many, the birthplace of hip-hop. (Photograph by Mark Katz.)

multi-billion-dollar international and corporate enterprise—was started by school kids (see Figure 1.2).

It was a warm summer night, the temperature still hovering around eighty degrees after sunset, with the sweaty, tightly packed bodies of a hundred dancers generating an additional heat of their own. The party was a success, the revelry unmarred by the violence and desperation that permeated the borough. Herc had sought to create a safe space for the partygoers, and later, speaking in the third person, he explained the appeal of his parties in this way: "Hey, 'cross town on the West Side there's a guy named Herc, Kool Herc, giving parties, man. And it's nice, ya know. Girls is there, ya know. You could do

A DJ Kool Herc Party

★ ✶ BACK TO SCHOOL JAM ★ ✶

PLACE: 1520 SEDGWICK AVE. "REC ROOM"

DATE: August 11, 1973

TIME: 9:00 PM to 4:00 AM.

ADMISSION: $.25 LADIES ♡

$.50 FELLAS

GIVEN BY: Kool Herc

SPECIAL GUESTS: Coco, Cindy C., Klark K., Timmy T.

Figure 1.2 Invitation to Kool Herc's first party. (Reprinted from Johan Kugelberg, ed., *Born in the Bronx: A Visual Record of the Early Days of Hip Hop* [New York: Rizzoli, 2007], 70. Used by permission.)

your thing. All he asks is—don't start no problem in here, ya know. He's a big guy."[13] "Herc stood six and change," Grandmaster Flash noted, recalling the first time he went to one his parties. "With his Afro and the butterfly collar on his AJ Lester leisure suit turned up, he looked even bigger. He was a god up there, the red and blue party lights behind him pulsing away on that big thumping beat." Flash also marveled at how members of six rival gangs were in attendance, and yet "nobody was fighting . . . I mean *nobody* was swinging fists or pulling pistols."[14]

Herc continued to throw parties throughout the Bronx, and as his sound system grew more powerful and his record collection expanded, his parties and fame grew as well. His jams were held at the Cedar Playground (better known as Cedar Park) just up the hill on Sedgwick Avenue, at the Police Athletic League (P.A.L.) community center on Webster Avenue and East 183rd Street, and later at clubs like the Executive Playhouse. These jams drew hundreds and left an impression on visitors before they even arrived. Here's how Flash described his approach to a party Herc held in May 1974:

I was two full blocks from the park jam . . . but already it was loud. Really fucking loud. I could name the tune he was playin; it was "The Mexican" by Babe Ruth. And it was THUNDERING. BOOM-BOOM-BOOM! I had never heard sound—let alone music—that loud before in my whole life. And though the speakers made the ground shake, I could hear the highs of

the trumpets as clear as I could feel the boom of the bass coming up
through my Super Pro Keds.[15]

Herc so dominated the scene that for a time no sensible DJ would even plan
a party for the same night as one of his.

Herc wasn't the only DJ in town at the time, however. There were dozens of
others, though they focused largely on disco and played whole songs rather
than fragments. But in the Bronx River Houses, about three miles east of
Sedgwick Avenue, presided a kindred spirit to Herc, and in hip-hop mythology
he is the Godfather to Herc's Father (Figures 1.3 and 1.4). In 1973, the Godfather
of hip-hop was a sixteen-year-old ex–gang member who went by the name
Afrika Bambaataa, having been inspired by the proud and powerful African
warriors he saw depicted in the 1964 Michael Caine film *Zulu*.[16] ◉ Like Herc,
Bambaataa played only what he thought were the best parts of the record, but
his playlists were even more diverse. Bambaataa, known as "Master of Records,"
explained his approach this way:

> It might just be slammin', the people sweating, breaking, everything. And
> I would just stop in the middle of the thing and throw on "Sweet Georgia
> Brown," [theme song of the Harlem Globetrotters basketball team] and

Figure 1.3 Kool Herc, ca. 1979, at the T-Connection, an important early
hip-hop club in the Bronx. (Photograph by Joe Conzo, copyright
Joe Conzo Archives, 2011.)

Figure 1.4 Afrika Bambaataa, undated early 1980s
photo by David Corio. (Michael Ochs Archives/
Getty Images.)

then everybody'd just start doing that basketball-type dance. So when you
came to an Afrika Bambaataa party you . . . knew that you was going to
hear some weird type of stuff. I even played commercials that I taped off
the television shows, from Andy Griffith to the Pink Panther, and people
looked at me like I was crazy.[17]

Bambaataa's eclecticism wasn't simply a quirk; it set an example and shaped
the fundamental character of hip-hop, pushing DJs (and later producers) to see
all music as potential raw material. Grandmixer D.ST, a DJ from the earliest
days of hip-hop, but most famous for his scratching on Herbie Hancock's 1983
hit "Rockit," described the "master of records" this way: "Bambaataa was a
musical record connoisseur, he was a genius, he understood variety, he understood the genre-less concept of music—that's real hip-hop. And that's what he
taught all of us."[18]

And like Herc, "Bam," as he is often called, sought to create a safe space for his partygoers. Although he had run with the Black Spades gang, even rising to the level of warlord, he had always been more of a peacemaker than a fighter. As a high school student, he established an organization that later came to be known as the Universal Zulu Nation.[19] Drawing upon cultural movements and ideologies as diverse as his record collection—he has cited the Nation of Islam and the "flower power" of the hippies as influences—Bambaataa promoted "peace, unity, love, and having fun" through his massive dance parties.[20] Sha-Rock, one of the first women rappers, remembers, "There was nobody that could come into an Afrika Bambaataa party and start any trouble, because you had the Zulu Nation that made sure that there was no trouble whatsoever. So if you went to an Afrika Bambaataa party, you expect to be safe."[21] Ironically, this safety was ensured by the implicit threat of violence, apparent to all by the menacing ex–gang members arrayed in front of Bambaataa's sound system.

Not all parties were free of violence. "Back then it would happen for nothing," reports DJ Disco Wiz.[22] "You step on someone's sneakers and they'd fucking kill you, murder you right there." Wiz carried a gun and, like Bambaataa and others, was always accompanied by a security team. Remember that these DJs were what's known as "mobile DJs," and had to cart their equipment and records to every gig, often late at night and frequently on foot. They were vulnerable, so security and a fearsome reputation were necessities. DJ Baby Dee, a member of the Mercedes Ladies and one of the first women hip-hop DJs, kept a double-barreled shotgun with her to protect the group's sound system and records. Once she was DJing at a party when the audience, frightened by nearby gunshots, stampeded in her direction. She pulled the gun out from underneath the table and brandished it in front of the mob, which immediately switched course. She didn't have to fire it. "Crowd control," she called it.[23] A delicate balance between violence and peace thus existed in the early years of hip-hop, which Disco Wiz summed up in this way: "I know that a lot of people like to say that hip-hop was just this lovefest. Yeah, that was the premise to it, but at the end of the day, it was the Bronx."

"It was the Bronx." This simple fact remains a key to understanding the contributions of hip-hop's pioneering DJs and the rise of their unique style of DJing.[24] But before revisiting the subject of the Bronx as a shaping force in hip-hop, let's return for a moment to Kool Herc's party of August 11, 1973. Why is it invested with such deep significance that 1520 Sedgwick Avenue is practically a holy site?[25] The answer isn't obvious. There was no rapping at the party, there were no backspinning b-boys on the linoleum, and Herc wasn't scratching records, all things we might expect from a hip-hop jam. No one at the time knew this was hip-hop, and the music was not literally hip-hop as we know it today—it was largely funk, soul, and rock. Moreover, Afrika Bambaataa, one of the pillars of hip-hop culture, was spinning an eclectic mix over at the Bronx River Houses *before* Herc's first party, apparently as early as 1970.[26] He wasn't looping breaks, but then again, neither was Herc, at least at first.

So why exactly should Herc's party be considered the birth of hip-hop? One reason is practical: it has a specific date tied to it, and a flyer to back it up. Moreover, the components of hip-hop music—DJing, b-boying, and MCing—all coalesced around the practices witnessed at Herc's parties, and it's reasonable to look to this event as the beginning of it all. Finally, and this might be the most compelling point, the story of Herc's party is widely embraced as hip-hop's origin story. Origin stories aren't like birth certificates; their significance lies not in the facts they disclose but in the values they reveal. And what this origin story reveals is the veneration of the pioneer, the visionary who forges a new path. More generally, the story reveals a deep desire to claim for hip-hop a distinct identity. Hip-hop is more than dancing to funk breaks or rhyming over records. It is a unique art form and cultural phenomenon, and having a birth date proves that it is a living, growing entity.

Even if we can identify hip-hop's precise place and date of birth, we're still left with two important questions unanswered: how did the break-loving hip-hop DJ—and thus hip-hop itself—arise in the Bronx, and why in the early and mid-1970s? After all, if the only necessary ingredients were turntables, records, and poor people of color to play them, hip-hop would have arisen decades earlier. To answer the question we must investigate two broad forces, one musical and the other geographical. The first is a constellation of musical traditions whose songs, sounds, and practices shaped this emerging art. The second force is the Bronx itself, which DJs simultaneously resisted and celebrated through their sound systems.

THE MUSICAL INFLUENCES

It is a DJ's business to know music, and the best ones deploy a vast store of knowledge in their work. DJs are also some of the most broadminded of musicians; their creed might well be Duke Ellington's motto, "If it sounds good, it is good." I was initially surprised when, for example, GrandWizzard Theodore told me that Queen and Kiss—two white, gender-bending, glam-influenced rock groups—were among his favorites. But he simply loves the music, and for him, that is justification enough. When Grandmaster Caz was asked what he listened to when he was growing up, his list included not just James Brown, Al Green, and the Jackson 5, but Neil Diamond, Barry Manilow, Elvis Presley, the Osmonds, and Simon and Garfunkel. "I listened to everything," he explained. "I have an appreciation for music, period, not just black music."[27] Given that the

Bronx was awash in music of every sort, the early hip-hop DJs absorbed the
sounds and practices of many different traditions. But among them, four were
especially influential: funk, the Jamaican sound system, salsa, and disco. Rock,
soul, and just about every other type of music figured in some way as well, but
these four were essential ingredients in the making of hip-hop.

Funk

The most obvious place to look for musical influences would be the breaks
themselves. One might guess that all breaks come from funk. But just consider
some of the songs that supplied the classic hip-hop breaks. "Mary Mary" (1967),
by the Monkees, is bubble-gum pop. Aretha Franklin's "Rock Steady" (1971)
has its roots in gospel and soul. "It's Just Begun" (1972), by the Jimmy Castor
Bunch, is a slab of funk marbled with Latin percussion. Babe Ruth's "The
Mexican" (1972) mixes flamenco-infused progressive rock with the music of
Italian film composer Ennio Morricone. Bob James's "Take Me to the Mardi
Gras" (1975) has a smooth jazz vibe. Aerosmith's "Walk this Way" (1975), whose
opening drum solo DJs extracted years before Run-D.M.C. covered the song, is
blues-infused raunch rock. Then there's "Apache." This 1973 track by the
Incredible Bongo Band, which Kool Herc has called "hip-hop's national anthem,"
is hard to classify; it combines surf guitar, blaring horns, and a ponderous organ
with a reverb-drenched duet between rock drummer Jim Gordon and the
Bahamian conga and bongo player King Errisson. Even with this very partial
list we see just how varied hip-hop's source materials were, and can understand
why D.ST argues that hip-hop embodies the "genreless concept of music," and
why DJ Shadow contends that hip-hop should be understood as an *omnigenre*,
a genre of music that includes all others.[28]

Yet even if these songs sound quite different, there is a reason that their
breaks seem to come from funk. That's because they're all *funky*. Put more precisely, most of the breaks beloved by old-school hip-hop DJs exhibit a rhythmic,
textural, and timbral profile characteristic of funk. Rhythmically speaking,
they are usually anchored by a heavy downbeat emphasized by the bass (or
kick) drum—"the one," as it's often called—but are dominated by forward-
leaning syncopations that seem to propel themselves back to "the one." Over
the course of just a few seconds—usually two to four bars—a sense of stability
is constantly being undermined, reestablished, and undermined once again.
The result is a kind of musical perpetual motion machine; as music theorist
Anne Danielsen observes, a funk groove "does not stand still."[29] And this pro-
pulsiveness is infectious, keeping the dancer in constant motion as well. The
combination of downbeat and off-beat accents also imbues the break with a

sense of unpredictability, and can be repeated almost indefinitely without becoming tiresome. DJs often say that they can listen to their favorite breaks all day long, and this is surely why.

Although the rhythm of the break is its most defining characteristic, texture and timbre are important as well. Steinski, in defining the break as the moment a song "takes its clothes off," was pointing to the sudden thinning of the texture, the reduction of sonic density when just one or two instruments remain. When hearing, say, "Rock Steady," all the way through, the effect of the break comes from that unexpected change in texture. Yet that contrast is lost if the break is extracted and repeated. Nevertheless, the characteristically spare, transparent texture of a break draws the listener's attention and heightens the effect of the syncopation, which might otherwise be obscured by layers of competing musical lines. The typical timbral qualities of a good break also command attention. Timbre, or tone color, is what makes it possible to distinguish a piano from a guitar, or one voice from another, even when they are sounding the same pitch. The instruments usually featured on the classic breaks have penetrating timbres and sharp attacks—often percussion instruments struck with wood or metal, or smacked smartly with the hands. The snare drum is the most common, though cymbals, congas, timbales, and cowbells are often heard, too. The timbral qualities of these instruments become particularly advantageous when heard outside—say, at a park jam in the middle of the Bronx—for they cut through the noise of the street. Timbre is thus crucial. Imagine the "Funky Drummer" break played with brushes instead of sticks. Or plucked on a harp. Not so funky anymore.

Funkiness is what unites the classic breaks. Notice that I said funk*iness*, not funk. A great many breaks come from funk—as represented by James Brown, Bobby Byrd, George Clinton, Dennis Coffey, Lyn Collins, Isaac Hayes, Curtis Mayfield, Sly and the Family Stone, and others. (And here I should recognize some of the drummers who actually played the breaks, such as Greg Errico, Al Jackson, Zigaboo Modeliste, Bernard "Pretty" Purdie, John "Jabo" Starks, and the funky drummer himself, Clyde Stubblefield. There would be no breaks without them.[30]) Yet many breaks come from genres other than funk, although they contain, at least for a few seconds, an unmistakable funkiness. You know it when you hear it, and you know you're hearing it when your booty begins to shake without conscious effort. This funkiness is a defining quality of the best breaks, and a defining quality of hip-hop itself.

The Jamaican Sound System

Hip-hop's first DJ, Kool Herc, was Jamaican, coming to America from a land with a rich history of mobile sound systems. In the 1940s, a culture of mobile

DJing arose in Kingston, Jamaica's capital and musical center; these DJs, known as selectors, competed for listeners not only through their choice of records (which tended toward American rhythm and blues), but through the power of their sound systems. These systems were not simple, store-bought stereos, but were often homemade assemblages of turntables, amplifiers, speakers, and miles of cable. And they were enormous—some systems had as many as fifty speakers. Junior Lincoln, a Jamaican record producer, characterized the sound system in this way: "The amplifiers are huge. . . . They emphasize a lot on the bass. And they play sometimes twenty- or twenty-four-inch speakers. So it really thump, y'know. The bass line is really heavy. You've never heard anything so heavy in all your life."[31] Reputations were created and challenged in competitions, or "clashes," held at venues called dancehalls. Arriving hours early, a crew of "box men" would assemble the systems, which were often given names, like Trojan or Downbeat, at opposite ends of the dancehall. In the evening the clash would begin, with the selectors alternating sets and the winner determined by audience acclamation.[32]

Kool Herc's youthful encounters with these systems left a lasting impression. "[T]here was a lot of big sound systems they used to hook up and play on the weekends. I was a child, ya know, lookin', seein' all these things going on, and sneakin' out of my house and seein' the big systems rattling the zincs on the housetops and stuff."[33] As a young adult in the States, Herc assembled the most powerful system in the Bronx, quickly becoming the undisputed king of DJs in his new home.

The massive sound systems of the Bronx DJs—which featured bass-heavy speakers and sometimes included echo or reverb units—seem to replicate the Jamaican model. Some DJs had powerful "Jamaican bass bottoms," large speakers custom-built by Bronx-dwelling immigrants from the island.[34] DJs organized competitions known as battles, similar to Kingston's sound system clashes, and the shout outs, boasts, and disses of microphone-wielding DJs and MCs that evolved into rap are similar to the sound system practice of "toasting." Recent work by two ethnomusicologists posits further connections between the sound of hip-hop and Jamaican musical practices. Wayne Marshall suggests that Herc's choice of drum and bass-heavy breaks owes something to the "sparse, heavy grooves" characteristic of reggae, while Michael Veal identifies hip-hop's "tendency to strip prerecorded music to its purely rhythmic elements" as a "Caribbean-derived" practice.[35]

There is a danger, however, in overestimating the Jamaican influence on hip-hop. Hip-hop producer and historian Amir "Sa'id" Said reasonably suggests that although there are parallels between hip-hop and Jamaican practices, there is little hard evidence of any cause-and-effect relationship. As he points out, Herc was only twelve—and not a DJ—when he came to the United States, and notes that Herc himself downplayed the Kingston connection, once saying in an interview, for example, "I wasn't here reppin' Jamaica. I was just a kid."[36] Moreover, mobile DJs with large sound systems had been roaming the New York area for years before Herc's first gig. A *Discothekin* article from 1976 reports that mobile jocks Big John Ashby and Brother Q.J. Simpson were operating as early as 1959; certainly these much closer potential influences cannot be discounted.[37] In the end, it is impossible to quantify the Jamaican factor, though it is seems safe to say that hip-hop's strongest connection to the island came in the form of its famous sound systems and the practices surrounding them.

Salsa and the Latino Influence

Although people of countless nationalities, races, and ethnicities now embrace hip-hop, only one group other than African Americans was involved from the very beginning—Latinos, particularly those of Puerto Rican heritage. As cultural theorist Juan Flores points out, "while the relation of other cultural groups [to hip-hop] has been one of adoption and rearticulation, Puerto Ricans have been present as initiators and co-creators."[38] As examples, we can point to Prince Whipper Whip, an MC of Puerto Rican descent who rapped with many of the early hip-hop groups; or to renowned graffiti artist Lee Quiñones, who was featured in the 1982 hip-hop film *Wild Style*; or to the many Latino pioneers of hip-hop dance. The Latino influence on DJing was also considerable, and came in two forms: through the work of individual DJs and, more broadly, through the impact of Latin music.

Perhaps the two most important Latino DJs of the early hip-hop era were DJ Disco Wiz (Luis Cedeño) and Charlie Chase (Carlos Mandes). Disco Wiz makes a fair claim to being "hip-hop's first Latino DJ."[39] "I was probably the one who was going to do it," he reflects, "because you had to be really thick-skinned and tough."[40] Born in the Bronx of Cuban and Puerto Rican parents in 1960, and raised in what he describes as a broken home, he says gangs became his "extended family." At various times he was affiliated with the Savage Skulls and the Supreme Bachelors, though he was more of a freelance hoodlum. "I was a thug, straight up," he explains. "From the age of thirteen, fourteen, I always went around carrying a gun. I maybe had half-a-dozen arrests under my belt before the age of sixteen. If I had to rob a motherfucker I did it, you know what I mean? I had that level of danger to me."

After trying his hand as a graffiti writer and then a b-boy, Wiz became a DJ in the summer of 1974 at the age of fourteen. His partner and best friend, Curtis, was an African American teenager from the neighborhood. After only a few months of practicing on their parents' hi-fis, they started DJing at parties under the names DJ Louie Lou and Casanova Fly, though they soon became DJ Disco Wiz and Grandmaster Caz. Wiz encountered a good deal of resistance and prejudice as the only Latino among the population of black DJs. African Americans tended to express mostly surprise when discovering he was a DJ. "A couple of times I'd be going to a club with Caz and I'd be carrying records and the guy [the bouncer, an African American] would have a stupid look on his face, like, 'Fuck, it's a Spanish guy.' And Caz would say, 'That's my fucking DJ!' That's how it was." But he came in for worse treatment from other Latinos. "You trying to be black, you hanging out with black people?" he was often asked. "Stick to your kind, you're a disgrace," they told him. Wiz's toughness, his reputation as a "street cat," and his refusal to stick to his own kind may well have been necessary to his success in his pioneering role. None of this would have mattered, of course, if Wiz couldn't rock a party. He was particularly known for catering to the b-boys and b-girls: "I gravitated to the breakbeats. Being an ex–b-boy, I really embraced that. My sets were pretty intense and pretty violent. It was just one breakbeat after another . . . ."

Unfortunately, Wiz's violent ways halted a promising career as a DJ. In 1979, he started a four-year stint in prison for attempted murder; while Wiz was incarcerated, his former partner Caz went on to great acclaim as a rapper, becoming an MC for the Cold Crush Brothers, one of the seminal hip-hop groups. But this story has a rare happy ending, as Wiz reports in his 2009 memoir, *It's Just Begun*: after leaving prison he started a successful career as a chef, survived two bouts of cancer, and then rejoined the world of hip-hop as a DJ and activist.[41]

Charlie Chase, though older than Disco Wiz, arrived on the hip-hop scene a few years later. His parents had come to New York from Mayagüez, Puerto Rico, moving frequently from borough to borough. Born Carlos Mandes in Spanish Harlem, Chase lived most of his early life in Brooklyn and the Bronx. He had been a bass player before encountering hip-hop and was active in Latin music from an early age.[42] He later became a DJ, spinning mostly disco until 1977, when he stumbled upon some DJs looping breaks at a party in a Bronx community center.[43] Chase soon encountered and befriended Grandmaster Flash, who inspired his DJ name; he aspired to Flash's level of technical ability and decided to "chase" after this goal.[44] Like Disco Wiz, Charlie Chase encountered skepticism and prejudice. Dancers at his first gigs were sometimes shocked to see that the DJ who emerged from the shadows was Puerto Rican, not black, and early on he was frequently harassed at parties by security who assumed he didn't belong.

Yet Chase did not try to assimilate, and in any case he couldn't help but stand out among his African American colleagues in the Cold Crush Brothers (see Figure 1.5). At times he gleefully asserted his identity by playing salsa records at

Figure 1.5 Charlie Chase, prone, with the other members of the Cold Crush Brothers, at the Hoe Avenue Boys Club, 1982. (Photograph by Joe Conzo, copyright Joe Conzo Archives, 2011.)

his gigs. He recalls mixing in a bit of the song "Tú Coqueta," during one of his sets. "I'm jamming, I throw that sucker in, just the beat alone, and they'd go off. They never knew it was a Spanish record. And if I told them that they'd get off the floor." "You see," he explains, "what I emphasize is that I'm Hispanic in a black world. Not just surviving but making a name for myself and leaving a big impression. I had to be hip, I had to be a homeboy. But I also had to know how far to go without seeming like I was trying to kiss up or something, or 'he's just trying to be black.'"[45]

Disco Wiz and Charlie Chase may have been the first Latino DJs, but they weren't the last. Ivan "Doc" Rodriguez started DJing in Hell's Kitchen, Manhattan, in 1975; his experience on the turntables led to a career in the studio, and he went on to engineer and produce dozens of hit records, including two of hip-hop's most influential albums, Boogie Down Productions' *Criminal Minded* (1987) and Eric B. and Rakim's *Paid in Full* (1987). Johnny "Juice" Rosado grew up watching Kool DJ AJ and Grandmixer D.ST in the South Bronx, and later, after moving to Long Island in the 1980s, he became one of the main DJs for Public Enemy. Just a teenager when he auditioned for the group, he stood out, not just because of his skills: "I was the only Puerto Rican there, but I didn't give a fuck."[46] Apparently, neither did Public Enemy.

Rob Swift (Robert Aguilar), born in Jackson Heights, New York (in the borough of Queens), notes that "both my parents were born in Cali, Colombia, which makes me 100 percent Colombian."[47] Swift, who identifies himself as "Afro-Hispanic," is known for his work in the 1990s with the influential turntablist crew the X-Men (later the X-Ecutioners) and for his solo career, through which he has explored his heritage (e.g., his "Salsa Scratch"). Born in El Salvador, DJ Quest (Carlos Aguilar) became a prominent DJ in the San Francisco Bay Area starting in the early 1990s; his notable contributions include co-creating what was probably the first battle record and introducing the so-called hamster style of scratching. Nicaraguan-born, Miami-bred DJ Craze (Arist Delgado) is one of the greatest hip-hop DJs of all time, winning the DMC World Championship battle three years in a row (1998–2000); he later became a sought-after club DJ and producer.[48] We'll be hearing about each of these musicians as we move ahead.

However crucial the presence of pioneering DJs like Wiz and Chase and their successors may have been, the Latino influence on hip-hop is deeper and more pervasive than the contributions of any individuals. Latin music, particularly from Cuba and Puerto Rico, has been part of the Bronx soundscape since the 1940s.[49] A variety of styles and traditions could be heard throughout the borough, much of it coming under the umbrella of salsa, an imprecise and debated term introduced in the States to describe and market Latin popular music. Literally meaning "sauce," salsa can refer to a variety of Cuban and Puerto Rican–influenced dance music styles, like cha cha cha, guaracha, mambo, rumba, and so on, which were popular in New York City. Salsa ensembles typically consist of piano, trumpets, trombones, and bass; a large percussion section (bongos, claves, congas, cowbells, and timbales); and one or more vocalists. The music is fast and lively, driven by persistent interlocking syncopated rhythms, and typically featuring a *montuno* section that spotlights the instrumentalists.

Salsa could be heard throughout the Bronx—in gigantic ballrooms, like Hunts Point Palace; intimate clubs such as Tritons; and in churches, shops, and homes. But Bronx residents did not have to seek salsa to hear it; informal jam sessions—usually consisting of just a few percussionists—formed in the streets and parks, on stoops and fire escapes. It was literally in the air, often all day and all night. Consider the reminiscences of two African American residents of the South Bronx who have spoken of the ubiquity of the music. Back in the 1950s, Allen Jones heard a constant mashup of black and Latino music:

> Music was everywhere, coming out of people's apartments and played on outdoor benches. On one side of the street, you might hear The Temptations singing "My Girl," and on the other side of the street you could hear some brother singing along with a Frankie Lymon song. But the one constant, every night without fail, was the sound of Puerto Ricans playing their hand

drums in local parks and playgrounds. The steady beat of those drums became the background music to my living reality.[50]

Renee Scroggins, who later formed the musical group ESG with her sisters, had similar sonic memories from the 1970s. "Every summer in St. Mary's Park . . . you would have some Latin gentlemen in the park with some coke bottles, a cow bell and a set of congas playing the same thing, 'boom boom boom, tata ta boom, boom boom,' you know, and it was our summer sound."[51] Perhaps it's no coincidence that one of ESG's core members (and the only non-family member) was conga player Tito Labran.

Growing up in the late 1960s and early 1970s, the pioneers of hip-hop—like countless other Bronxites—encountered the sound of Latin percussion on a daily basis. They didn't have to be Cuban or Puerto Rican for it to lodge into their musical subconscious. And in one important way salsa is like much of the music the early hip-hop DJs played, in its predilection for hard-driving syncopations and percussion breaks. The salsa percussionists of the streets and parks of the Bronx were, in effect, playing one long break. Living in a musical soundscape saturated with breaks, it's no surprise that the early hip-hop DJs would have gravitated toward the types of popular songs, whether funk, soul, pop, or rock, that featured the same kind of naked percussion.

If, as I'm suggesting, the Bronx DJs were conditioned by Latin percussion, why didn't they just play salsa records? Perhaps they didn't regard it as *their* music. After all, African Americans dominated the scene, and tensions sometimes flared between the black and Latino communities. Remember that Charlie Chase insisted that if his audience thought he was playing salsa they'd leave the dance floor. Moreover, perhaps to them salsa just wasn't the hip music of the moment, and didn't exude the cool of James Brown or Sly and the Family Stone. Even a Latino DJ like Disco Wiz, who heard salsa at every family gathering, never played the music at his jams. It simply belonged to a separate sphere of his life. Yet, reflecting on his early days as a DJ, he speculates that the reason he was so drawn to the breaks was because of his early and frequent exposure to salsa. The music "hit me internally," he says.[52]

But even if DJs weren't spinning Tito Puente, many of the songs they did play were indebted to salsa. We hear the Latin influence, for example, in the percussion on "Apache," "I Just Want to Celebrate," and "It's Just Begun." In his song, "The Breaks" (1980), Kurtis Blow, an early hip-hop DJ and MC, makes the link to salsa explicit when he features the timbale playing of the great *salsero* Jimmy Delgado. Blow even raps about timbales and Delgado in his later song, "Juice" (1982):

The next to show was Kurtis Blow
With timbales in his hands

Well I'm known for rap and I play with snap
And I think you'll understand
Now I was taught to play in a different way
By a dude known as Delgado
He said listen to me and you soon will be
A timbale desperado.[53]

Musicians often speak of a "Latin tinge" in American popular music. The phrase, which apparently originated with jazz pioneer Jelly Roll Morton (though he referred to it as a "Spanish tinge"), is meant to acknowledge the Latin influence on a variety of styles, whether jazz, rock and roll, or R&B. With hip-hop, this influence is especially deep. Hip-hop's very breakcentricity—one of its strongest defining characteristics—owes a great deal to the salsified soundscape of the Bronx. The Latin contribution is not just in the tinge—it's at the core.

Disco

Hip-hop's early history is often recounted as developing in direct opposition to disco. According to Kool DJ AJ, what Herc was doing "was much different from the disco of the day . . . he played a lot of breakin' beats."[54] GrandWizzard Theodore says that "Everybody [else] was . . . listening to disco records—Van McCoy and the Village People and Donna Summer—and we were listening to, like, Kool and the Gang and James Brown and Earth, Wind and Fire and Rare Earth and Baby Huey and the Jimmy Castor Bunch and Sly and the Family Stone."[55] Grandmaster Flash calls disco "sterile," nothing like the records that Herc and others spun, music that "had soul to it."[56]

Hip-hop and disco: we'd be forgiven for thinking that these New York–based genres shared nothing more than the first two digits of a zip code. Yet the musical traditions have close ties. Both are DJ-centered genres that emerged in New York City in the early 1970s; both drew on funk, soul, and Latin music, catered to dancing, and created their distinctive styles by manipulating vinyl.

In the early 1970s, Manhattan DJs were spinning many of the artists and songs that we associate with the pioneering hip-hop DJs. Steve D'Acquisto pushed Curtis Mayfield at the Tamburlaine; David Mancuso spun Babe Ruth's "The Mexican" at The Loft before it became a b-boy anthem; Richie Kaczor and Michael Cappello featured B.T. Express—a favorite among Bronx DJs and later hip-hop producers—in their sets at Hollywood and Le Jardin in 1974 and 1975; and Francis Grasso, Nicky Siano, and, well, *every* disco DJ played James Brown.[57] And these were just the Manhattan DJs. There were also club DJs working in the Bronx and in Brooklyn who had a tremendous influence on the nascent hip-hop scene: among them were Pete DJ Jones, Grandmaster Flowers, Eddie Cheba, DJ Hollywood, Kool DJ Dee, Lovebug Starski, Ras Maboya, and DJ Plummer.

Moreover, many hip-hop DJs played *disco* records at their parties. As Afrika Bambaataa points out, "In the early days of hip-hop, all the hip-hop DJs played disco."[58] Grandmaster Flash spun the 1976 disco favorite "I Can't Stop" by John Davis and the Monster Orchestra at a b-boy battle.[59] Sheri Sher, an MC with the pioneering all-woman crew, The Mercedes Ladies, remembers that disco remained popular among hip-hoppers into the late 1970s and beyond. "Disco was still in at this time, so in between the routines, scratching and rhyming, a rap crew's DJ would play a few disco songs. 'Good Times' by Chic was considered a disco record, yet it was one of the hottest hip-hop beats for any MC to rock over."[60] Chic's 1979 hit, in fact, was incorporated into two landmark hip-hop recordings: The Sugar Hill Gang's "Rapper's Delight" (1979) and Grandmaster Flash's "The Adventures of Grandmaster Flash on the Wheels of Steel" (1981). (We'll return to both songs in Chapter 3.) And when Steinski started playing the first hip-hop records as a DJ in Brooklyn during the early 1980s, the first reaction of many of his listeners was that it was "disco with people talking over it."[61]

Hip-hop and disco DJs also shared a love of the break. Downtown DJ Walter Gibbons was known for seamlessly looping breaks at about the same time Grandmaster Flash was doing the same. As fellow disco DJ François Kevorkian has said, listeners "would never hear the actual song" when Gibbons spun two copies of Rare Earth's percussion-heavy "Happy Song." "You just heard the drums. It seemed like he kept them going forever, although I imagine it was actually about ten minutes."[62] Gibbons's handiwork was not unknown in the Bronx. "His style appealed to my Bronx sensibilities," John "Jellybean" Benitez says, noting that "Walter played a lot of beats and breaks, and I had never heard a disco DJ playing those kinds of records before."[63] Nicky Siano and Boston DJ Arthur Luongo also looped breaks, though not as often or as well as Gibbons.[64] To be sure, these DJs were outliers; most disco DJs weren't looping, and they definitely weren't scratching. But they didn't just play records, either. The best among the early disco DJs were matching the beats of different songs and segueing seamlessly between them; like their hip-hop colleagues, they can be classified as performative DJs, those who treat their turntables more like musical instruments than playback devices. The main difference is that when hip-hop DJs worked records, it was obvious, and intentionally so. Or as Bambaataa puts it, disco DJs had "that clean sound, where the hip-hop DJs were more rugged and rough."[65]

Disco and hip-hop began with some of the same basic materials and techniques, but by the end of the 1970s they had started to go their separate ways.

Hip-hop spent much of its time outdoors at block parties and park jams. The jams were anti-elitist and the dress code was casual; the dancing, too, was different. Not everyone at a hip-hop party would be breaking, but it was the b-boys and b-girls who drew the attention of the partygoers and the DJs. And even if some of the same records were being played in the discos, they didn't sound the same. The demands of the b-boys and b-girls encouraged the isolation of the breaks, and the hip-hop DJs did something that virtually no disco DJ would do, at least on purpose: they scratched records. The outdoor acoustics of the park and street jams favored a heavy funk beat to keep all of the dancers anchored; the longer wavelengths of the bass also carried greater distances, extending the DJ's reach farther into the neighborhood. Meanwhile, disco stayed indoors, and developed a seamless mix of songs that encouraged longer stretches of romantic couples' dancing.

Disco became a genre of its own sooner than hip-hop when producers started creating new dance music records. These new disco songs favored the swirling strings and high-flying diva vocals of soul records, while the syncopated rhythms were smoothed out into a simpler quarter-note bass drum pulse, or "four-on-the-floor" beat. When hip-hop started producing records of its own, the overall texture tended to be thinner but the beats were more complex and, of course, the vocals were anything but diva-like. One way to think about the relationship between disco and hip-hop is that, while they were both deeply influenced by soul and funk, the influence of soul more clearly shines through in disco, while hip-hop more obviously takes after the funk side of the family. Of course, disco was often funky, and hip-hop had soul, but there's no mistaking who takes after whom.

Disco is undeniably a part of hip-hop's history. Why, then, did they develop such a seemingly antagonistic relationship? First, there was disco's early rejection of hip-hop. Because discos often required patrons to pay a cover charge, dress up, and prove they were over eighteen, many of the early hip-hoppers never had a chance to dance at the hottest clubs. "We weren't socially accepted at disco joints," explains Disco Wiz, his name notwithstanding. "We were pretty much segregated."[66] GrandWizzard Theodore recalls that when he and his friends tried to get into some of DJ Hollywood's disco parties, "they would be like, 'Oh no. You have to have on suit jackets and [dress] shoes,' and all that. Sometimes we would get into the party and some of the guys would start b-boying and they would turn the music off and say, 'Oh, we don't do that in here.'"[67] Given this rejection, we can see why some of the Bronx hip-hop DJs in turn spurned disco. All the same, hip-hop flyers from the late 1970s and even into the 1980s reveal the influence of disco. Some feature a "No Sneakers" warning or depict stylishly attired dancers, with women in dresses and high heels and men in fashionable leisure suits.[68] Others explicitly use the word *disco*, as in these from the early 1980s: "An All Nite Thang Disco" (October 3, 1980, featuring Afrika Bambaataa); "Disco Tribute to James Brown and Sly and the Family Stone" (November 7–8, 1980, with Bambaataa, DJ Jazzy Jay, and DJ Red Alert); or "Super Pre-Summer Disco Jam" (May 2, 1981, Kool DJ AJ).[69]

In 1976 and 1977, while hip-hop remained a local phenomenon, disco became hugely popular, not just in New York, but globally, generating vast sums of money. This commercialization, and the watering down of disco that followed it, might also explain the disdain of hip-hop fans. "As the majors flooded the market with a glut of second-rate disco recordings just as the economy entered a deep recession," explains dance music historian Tim Lawrence, "disco was critiqued for being superficial, materialistic, and irretrievably commercial, and this caricature endured."[70] In the early 1970s, disco was cool and hip, but at the end of the decade my grandma was into disco, as was everyone else, and it was no longer so cool and hip. By the time of the July 1979 "Disco Demolition Night," when a near-riot ensued after a crate of disco records was blown up during a baseball game at Chicago's Comiskey Park, anti-disco fever was a nationwide phenomenon. Yet it was during the same summer of 1979 that Chic's disco song "Good Times" was a favorite track among hip-hop DJs, and the "Good Times"–based "Rapper's Delight" came out *after* Chicago's disco inferno. Hip-hop DJs may have turned against disco, but they weren't leading the way. Most of hip-hop's anti-disco rhetoric came years and even decades after disco peaked; the intense antagonism was really most pronounced in retrospect. So why the late dissing of disco? Disco never regained its mainstream popularity or its positive reputation, so it's understandable that hip-hop pioneers would be reluctant to embrace the music or acknowledge its influence. Homophobia could be another reason, given disco's close connection to certain gay subcultures. Homophobia actually became more pronounced in hip-hop in later years, so anti-gay sentiment doesn't explain why hip-hop took a different path in the 1970s as much as it explains hip-hop's more recent disavowal of disco. The larger point here is whatever its later reputation, disco played an important role in the early history of the hip-hop DJ. The two grew up alongside each other; as they developed their own identities they grew apart, but their shared history remains.[71]

URBAN INFLUENCES

If the musical traditions of the Bronx powerfully shaped the emergent hip-hop DJ, the city itself was no less of an integral force. As scholar Murray Forman has argued, the music of hip-hop "takes the city and its multiple spaces as the foundation of its cultural production."[72] Bronx DJs simultaneously resisted and embraced life in their city, and this complex relationship influenced their art in profound ways. Scholars, citing hip-hop's growth and development in decaying inner cities, have often described the music as a form of resistance or "oppositional culture."[73] The suggestion is that hip-hop is a form of protest music, a response to urban blight and the oppressive power structures that create it. Such a stance might be clear in the lyrics of overtly political rap, but if extracting a wordless drum break and pumping it through a sound system at a dance party can be seen as a form of resistance, then it is less obvious and more metaphorical than can be articulated through an MC's rhymes.

We might consider repetition as a form of resistance. When extending a break, the DJ defies physics, suspending the flow of time by creating an eternal present. The DJ forestalls the future, a future which, for those living in difficult conditions, promises little. As long as the break repeats, the dancing continues and the good times remain. (Ironic, because while time may stand still, the dancers do not.) The break was, indeed, a break, and provided respite from the tribulations of life in the city. "Break" has another relevant meaning here, as in "Them's the breaks," referring to the unexpected and often unfortunate turns that life brings. Kurtis Blow combined the different senses of the word in his song, "The Breaks":

> Breaks to win and breaks to lose
> But these here breaks will rock your shoes
> Breaks in love, breaks in war
> But we got the breaks to get you on the floor.[74]

Put another way, whatever may come, one can always seek solace in a good rump-shaking break.

Repetition was one way of resisting—if not overtly opposing—the harsh realities of life in the Bronx; sheer volume was another. Like all big cities, the Bronx is a noisy place, but because it is crisscrossed by major highways, the din is exceptional even compared to other urban areas (see Figure 1.6). In what is now considered a textbook case of disastrous (some say malicious) city planning, massive roads were cut through the borough in the 1950s and 1960s. The most controversial of these highways was the Cross-Bronx Expressway, built between 1948 and 1963 and overseen by the often-vilified urban planner Robert Moses. Designed not for the benefit of Bronx residents, it was a thoroughfare to transport cargo and commuters between Long Island and New Jersey. Construction of the seven-mile road required destroying an enormous swath of the heavily populated South Bronx. As Moses biographer Robert Caro explained, "The path of the great road lay across 113 streets, avenues and boulevards; sewers and water and utility mains numbering in the hundreds; one subway and

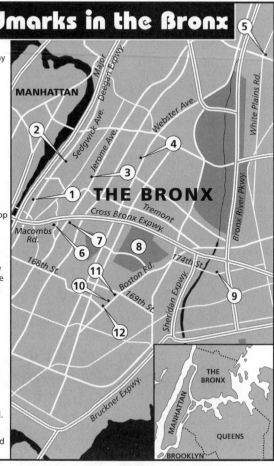

Hip-Hop Landmarks in the Bronx ⑤

1. Kool Herc's First Party
1520 Sedgwick Ave., considered by many to be hip-hop's birthplace.

2. Cedar Park
Sedgwick Ave., playground and site of early hip-hop jams.

3. The Hevalo
Jerome Ave., club where Kool Herc started spinning in 1973.

4. Webster Avenue Police Athletic League (P.A.L.)
Site of legendary hip-hop shows and battles.

5. The T-Connection
White Plains Rd., important early hip-hop club.

6. Ecstasy Garage Disco
Macombs Rd., hip-hop club.

7. The Executive Playhouse/The Sparkle
Jerome Ave., popular club, renamed The Sparkle.

8. Crotona Park
Site of early jams.

9. Bronx River Center
E. 174th St., apartment complex where Afrika Bambaataa reigned as DJ.

10. 63 Park
Playground for PS 63, site of early jams and battles.

11. The Black Door
Club where Grandmaster Flash presided.

12. Birthplace of the Scratch
1199 Boston Rd., home of GrandWizzard Theodore.

Figure 1.6 Highway map of the Bronx.

three railroads; five elevated rapid transit lines, and seven other expressways or parkways" (see Figure 1.7).[75]

Hip-hop historian Jeff Chang describes the Expressway as "a modernist catastrophe of massive proportions," one that destroyed a once "unbroken continuum of cohesive, diverse communities."[76] Construction of the highway displaced thousands of residents, and for those who remained, it left a legacy of noise. For much of its length, the Expressway is cut deep into the earth and lined with dozens of apartment buildings rising above high brick walls, all of which created what Caro described as "a gigantic echo chamber."[77] The incessant vehicular roar, made worse by the constant gear-shifting of large trucks trying to manage the Expressway's frequent grade changes, could be heard day

Figure 1.7 The Cross-Bronx Expressway. (Photograph by James Estrin/New York Times/Redux.)

and night from blocks away and was described over and again by residents as "unbearable."[78]

To live in the birthplace of hip-hop was to live near one of these highways. Kool Herc's apartment building and nearby Cedar Park, where he gave his first outdoor jams, practically sit atop the Major Deegan Expressway and are within hearing distance of the Cross Bronx Expressway. The Bronx River Houses, where Afrika Bambaataa ruled as DJ, are closely bordered by the Cross Bronx Expressway, the Bronx River Parkway, and the Sheridan Expressway. 🜨 Grandmaster Flash became a DJ while living just a few blocks from the confluence of the Bruckner and Sheridan Expressways. And not only did the apartment buildings of the Bronx absorb a great deal of sound, they generated their own noise as well. Consider Bambaataa's Bronx River Houses, a complex of nine fourteen-story buildings with more than three thousand residents. Standing in the courtyard is like standing at the bottom of a canyon, and the sounds emanating from the densely populated buildings can be all-enveloping. For the pioneering hip-hop DJs, merely to exist in the Bronx was to experience near-constant noise. But DJs did more than experience noise, they created it, and through their massive sound systems, they indelibly shaped the Bronx soundscape.

DJs may have been catering to their dancers, but the output of such extravagant volume can also be interpreted symbolically: both as a display of power and as a defense mechanism. It's not hard to understand how the booming sound systems could communicate power. Partygoers and passersby who heard—and felt—a sound system from afar were not just hearing music, they were witnessing a raw demonstration of the DJ's might and receiving a clear message: *you are entering my territory.* Grandmaster Flash put it this way: "Kool Herc had the West Side, Bam had Bronx River. DJ Breakout had way uptown past Gun Hill. Myself, my area was like 138th Street, Cypress Avenue, up to Gun Hill, so that we all had our territories and we all had to respect each other."[79] This respect was tied, in large part, to power—power expressed through the sonic output of their systems.

DJs not only used their sound systems to display power and claim territory; their music also sealed partygoers from the din of the city, almost physically separating them from the outside world. Musicologist Caroline O'Meara suggests that the sound systems of the Bronx could "conquer space, smooth over the rough edges of the city soundscape . . . finally overwhelming the ambient sound of the highways with music and accompanying pleasures."[80] If the repetition of breaks forestalled the future, the sheer strength of the sound systems kept the present at bay.

In an influential 1980 article, political theorist Langdon Winner posed the provocative question, "Do Artifacts Have Politics?"[81] His question was whether human-made creations could in some way be embedded or imbued with the ideologies of their creators or users. Could turntables and an array of speakers have politics as well? Whether DJs sought to keep an audience grooving, crush a rival, or create a safe space for partygoers, they generated and wielded a considerable amount of power. And in doing so they were denying the typical powerlessness of adolescence, defying the authority of adults, and resisting the poverty, despair, and decay that pervaded the Bronx. Against the ceaseless roar and echo of the city, they pitted their own. And if the DJs' use of sound systems does not seem to embody an explicit ideology, their reappropriation of noise and reclamation of territory suggests a clear oppositional stance. When I asked

Grandmixer D.ST if early hip-hop could be seen as political, he answered, "There was no agenda. It was sheer unadulterated, 'Let's do something else other than be in a gang.'" But then he paused, adding, "That's politics, actually."[82] If we want to see resistance in the actions of the first generation of DJs, then, it is the indirect resistance of choosing to express one's power and independence through music. "Express yourself!" the pioneering funk band Charles Wright & The 103rd Street Rhythm Band exhorted in their 1970 song of the same name: "You don't never need help from nobody else." Hip-hop DJs didn't just spin these words; they lived them.

Many of the early hip-hop DJs felt genuine affection for their city, taking deep pride in being a Bronxite rather than protesting its harsh conditions. In response to an interviewer who repeatedly asked about the desolation of the Bronx, Afrika Bambaataa—who considers himself a hip-hop activist—angrily retorted: "Why everybody keep sayin' abandoned buildings? They had some abandoned buildings, but you had a lot of buildings where people was livin' at. You had people who was nurses and doctors. You had construction workers. There was life there, you had people who was into drugs, you had people that wasn't into drugs, the same as anywhere else."[83] Sheri Sher of The Mercedes Ladies remembers how "everybody used to watch out for each other," especially the older neighborhood women who were unafraid to keep the kids in line. And as she points out, "you would be sure to find a church on every block along with the liquor store and the numbers spot."[84] Or note Grandmaster Flash's poignant reflection on his hometown, as he recalled a long walk through its streets in the mid-1970s: "I looked at my world . . . and I realized the Bronx was a beautiful place. It was so much more than a run-down, forgotten borough nobody cared about; it was everything that I was and the source for everything I would ever be."[85]

And let us not forget the DJ's prime directive: rock the party. Given that their most obvious goal was to promote the pursuit of happiness, we should be careful not to push the resistance/opposition model of hip-hop too far.[86] I have already suggested that the repetition of the break can be understood as creating an eternal present. And in extending what was recognized as the best part of the record, this eternal present becomes a world of eternal pleasure. It is easy to see why teenagers—and remember, most of these pioneering DJs were teenagers at the time—would seek instant and repeated gratification. The word "fun" comes up frequently when the pioneering DJs reminisce about the old days. "Little did anybody know that this thing was going to turn into a world-wide phenomenon, billion-dollar business and all that," says Kool Herc. "'Cause I wasn't looking at it like that back then. I love my music, I love my sound system, and I just love to see people havin' fun. Period."[87] Yet hip-hop was not purely escapist; fun was embraced as a force for good. As Afrika Bambaataa explains, hip-hop was all about "peace, unity, love, and having fun," a phrase that has become something of a mantra and philosophy among first-generation hip-hop DJs.[88] (A variation of this mantra—"Peace Love Unity Respect" or PLUR—later became central to rave culture, another DJ- and dancer-centered form.) Hip-hop was therefore as much an embrace of the positive as it was a rejection of the negative. "The music had a message in it," insists GrandWizzard Theodore, "and uplifted the people, and pretty much gave everybody hope."[89] Rare Earth's 1971 song "I Just Want to Celebrate"—a favorite among DJs for its funky break—articulated the hip-hop attitude. "I just want to celebrate another day of living," they chant over and over. And in so many words, that was what early hip-hop—and its unifying force, the break—was all about.

It is often said that hip-hop arose in part because there was little or no music instruction in the schools.[90] So, seeking other outlets, kids of the Bronx started DJing, breaking, or rapping. It's true that the schools were in dire straits throughout the 1970s; yet the argument goes only so far, and reveals further limitations of the opposition/resistance theory of hip-hop's development. Music never completely disappeared from the schools, and there's little to say that the kids who developed hip-hop would have participated in school music no matter how abundant the offerings. DJ Disco Wiz says he could have been a member of the school band had he actually wanted to. It just wasn't cool. As he put it, "I had enough trouble just walking down the street without a fucking trombone in my hand."[91] (Although my childhood had little in common with Wiz's, as someone who carried a violin to school for many years, I know exactly what he's talking about.) Moreover, school was hardly the only site of music-making—aspiring artists could develop their craft and receive instruction at the Casita Maria Center for Arts and Education, which had been serving the South Bronx since 1961. And of course, they could make and learn music in their homes and in the local parks and recreation centers, in their churches, or in the neighborhood clubs and bars. Nor is it necessarily the case that the pioneering DJs even thought of what they were doing as musical performance, and thus as an alternative to playing in school ensembles. Without minimizing the poor state of public schools in the Bronx at the time, or the importance of school music programs, it hardly seems that lack of opportunity was a prime motivator among DJs. In the end, what motivated DJs was not so much the absence of any one thing, but the presence of many things: imagination and ingenuity, drive and desire, turntables and records, and above all, music.

In the summer of 1973, a new, technologically mediated, break-based musical practice started to take shape, developed by teenagers, most of them African American, some Latino, living in the harsh environment of the Bronx. Much credit goes to those teenagers, whose creativity and persistence gave birth to hip-hop. But there were other protagonists, as well as a few antagonists, many of them unlikely characters in this story. There was the city itself, with its rumbling highways and crumbling schools, towering apartment buildings and teeming playgrounds. There were funk godfathers, soul queens, and disco DJs; street corner *salseros* and Jamaican sound system makers; menacing gangsters and hollow-eyed addicts; single-minded city planners and distant government officials. There were supportive but overburdened teachers, doctors, and religious leaders; and there were families, some of them broken, most of them loving. Amid all this, and shaped by all this, the DJs developed their craft. Their craft was more than simply a way of playing records. These young men— and a few women—generated both power and economic opportunity in an environment in which they had little access to either. In rocking parties they held sway over the moods and bodies of hundreds; in their sound system battles they fought for reputation and territory, establishing themselves within a hierarchy; through cover charges and booking fees at clubs, DJs could earn a decent and honest living, a rare combination at the time. In the space of just a few years, a distinctive musical culture arose out of the activities of the teenaged African American and Latino DJs of the Bronx. It was a culture of the turntable and of the break, a culture tied to its time and place, but one whose impact has been felt ever since and everywhere.

Mix and Scratch—The Turntable Becomes a Musical Instrument: 1975–1978

"When you have lived invisible as long as I have," muses the protagonist of Ralph Ellison's 1952 novel *Invisible Man*, "you develop a certain ingenuity." The unnamed character, a black man living in New York City, has just rigged up a secret display in his basement apartment: exactly 1,369 light bulbs covering every inch of his ceiling. He is literally fighting the power, diverting untold kilowatts from Monopolated Light & Power after years of being cheated by the utility. He is proud of his quixotic project, but only in part because he is resisting authority. It is his ingenuity that really pleases him. "Though invisible," he tells us, "I am in the great American tradition of tinkers. That makes me kin to Ford, Edison and Franklin. Call me, since I have a theory and a concept, a 'thinker-tinker.'"[1]

These lines—though written decades before the birth of hip-hop—capture the spirit and condition of the first generation of Bronx DJs. With their powerful homemade sound systems, they, like the Invisible Man, employed everyday technologies in ingenious ways. Like the Invisible Man, they often revealed an anti-authoritarian streak—they, too diverted electricity, tapping into light poles to power their sound systems for outdoor parties. Many DJs also spoke of their work in terms of concepts and theories, connecting themselves, consciously or not, to the great American inventors of the past. These thinker-tinkers of the Bronx brought a great many inventors to hip-hop in the mid- and late 1970s, but most important of all, they were responsible for two profound, and linked, developments: the transformation of the DJ battle from a display of power to a demonstration of skill, and the birth of a new musical instrument: the turntable.

THE EARLY BATTLE SCENE

Competition—aggressive, confrontational, obsessive competition—has always been at the core of hip-hop. B-boys and b-girls vied to outdo each other, their moves sometimes so aggressive that onlookers believed they were witnessing a brawl. MCs spat out fighting words, insulting other rappers in an attempt to render them speechless. Graffiti writers competed among themselves, too; those who had not established their territory or were deemed poor artists had their creations painted over, their identities symbolically erased. Competition was no less central to DJs. It motivated them, gave them direction, and structured their daily lives. DJs studied each other's equipment, records, and techniques, and spent countless hours working to assemble more powerful systems. One central vehicle channeled their competitive spirit: the battle. In battle, reputations were made and unmade, territory gained and lost, equipment tested and bested, techniques introduced and refined. Battles became the stuff of legend, and the stories of these clashes are retold to this day.

Because large, mobile sound systems were involved, battles didn't just erupt spontaneously, and required advance planning. Often one DJ (or crew of DJs) would approach another privately, and negotiate a time and place for the battle. Other times a DJ might come to a rival's party and throw down a challenge, and the battle would be announced in front of the crowd.

Before the battle, each DJ would marshal a crew of helpers and well-wishers. Consider the kind of crew connected with one of the more established DJs, such as Kool Herc or Afrika Bambaataa. The second in command—typically an experienced DJ—was the sound man, or hook-up man, who would assemble and test the equipment at the battle site. Tony Tone, for example, was the hook-up man for DJ Breakout and the Brothers Disco, and then went on to DJ with the Cold Crush Brothers (see Figure 2.1). Apprentices would buy vinyl for their DJs, hand them records during a performance, or carry the equipment. Friends and relatives were also enlisted for their support. Rahiem, an MC with the Funky Four Plus One and later with Grandmaster Flash, recounted a battle where a crew called the Little Brothers "had some girls walking around with picket-style signs saying 'Little Brothers,' and I remember saying to myself that this was kind of like a spectacle, you know?"[2]

Some DJs employed a security detail, usually beefy, unsmiling men, sometimes decked out in matching sweatshirts or jackets with "SECURITY" emblazoned on them.[3] A security team gave a DJ an aura of power and importance,

Figure 2.1 DJ and "hook-up man" Tony Tone atop part of his sound system, Hunts Point Palace, South Bronx, ca. 1982. (Photograph by Joe Conzo, copyright Joe Conzo Archives, 2011.)

but they were hardly just for show. "A lot of DJs had their parties shot up, got their stuff stolen, or [were] robbed at gunpoint, or beaten," remembers DJ Disco Wiz. But because he and his partner Grandmaster Caz had security—and were armed themselves—"people didn't fuck with us."[4]

The security also provided another service—they kept the curious from seeing the DJ's records. At this time DJs kept the identity of their more obscure records a secret, sometimes removing the labels on their most important discs or pasting them over with labels from inferior records. DJs even spied on each other while they were out buying records; in response, some took countermeasures, pulling second-rate discs to lead their watchers astray. In 1993, journalist Nelson George asked Kool Herc, Afrika Bambaataa, and Grandmaster Flash about their Spy Vs. Spy activity:

> NELSON GEORGE: Who was the first person to take the record in the bathtub and wipe the labels off?
>
> FLASH: That was me. People were getting too close, you know. I will give all due respect to my boys right here, but you know, other people.
>
> HERC: He put us on a wild goose chase.
>
> BAM: I had a way of telling things from the color of the album. Then I would try to see who it sounded like.
>
> FLASH: Hey Bam, I followed you on a Saturday with glasses on. I seen one bin you went to, pulled the same shit you pulled, took that shit home—and the break wasn't on the muthafucka.
>
> BAM: I used to tell people, "Do not follow me and buy what I buy," and I went into a record store and everyone was waitin' around to see what I pulled. So I pulled some Hare Krishna records. It had beats but . . .
>
> FLASH: You couldn't play that bullshit. I got a crate full of bullshit.[5]

In the late 1980s, the age of DJ spycraft more or less came to an end with the release of compilations that collected the songs with the best breaks (more on breakbeat compilations in Chapter 6). But at this time, there was almost nothing that DJs wouldn't do to keep their records secret.

Remarkably, almost everyone involved with these battles was under the age of eighteen. These teenagers were living in one of the most economically depressed cities in the country, where unemployment was rampant and job opportunities scarce. So they created their own opportunities, establishing complex organizations and arranging large-scale public events. "We were like young entrepreneurs," declares Afrika Bambaataa:

> We couldn't drive cars and all that, so we had to get older guys that would drive us around. We'd get the place, we'd rent it, then we had to get the fliers made, then we would have to get them back to the place where we were having the function and just flood the town with the advertisement of the event. And also sell what you'd call our album-cassettes. You would play from nine to about four in the morning, so you had some 60-minute or 90-minute cassettes that would become like your records. Everybody would wanna buy your tapes between the different areas and luxury cabs. Or you'd mail out tapes to your cousins and other friends in other places and they would make copies. It was a lot of work involved.[6]

They did this work largely without adult guidance or supervision. "We didn't have any teachers," says Charlie Chase. "Like everything else in this business of hip-hop, we learned on our own, nobody taught us."[7] Today we might marvel at how the hip-hop empires of Russell Simmons, Jay-Z, Master P, Sean Combs, and 50 Cent came to be built more or less out of nothing. This bootstrapping is a hip-hop tradition, a legacy of the first generation of industrious Bronx DJs.[8]

Let's now return to the battlefield and follow a typical event. With the help of their crews, the two DJs would set up their systems—roped off for security—at opposite ends of a playground, gym, or recreation room. Each DJ then played for, say, thirty minutes or an hour, with the challenger going first. There were no official judges; the winner was the DJ who drew the loudest cheers and the most dancers. Typically, the DJ with the better, louder system won. Skill—in terms of mixing and scratching—was not yet a decisive factor. According to Disco Wiz, "A lot of times guys won and they were wack DJs, but they had an awesome sound system and would drown you out. People loved that shit. If you had bullshit speakers, a bullshit system, but you were a good DJ, you lost."[9]

A DJ with a powerful system could even cut short a battle simply by playing over a rival. Rahiem explains how DJ Breakout ended a battle with the Little Brothers:

> The Little Brothers had their system up full blast. Breakout was listening to music in the headphones, and his sound system wasn't on yet—they were getting a sound check while the Little Brothers were doing their set. Breakout had a row of tweeters [high-frequency speakers] on strings going the width of the stage, and when he turned on the tweeters, it was deafening—high and loud, like a million bees in your eardrum at one time. Breakout is testing the highs in their sound system, and just by him turning up the tweeters, you couldn't really hear the Little Brothers' sound system. That wasn't good for them. So Breakout said on the mike, "Little Brothers, feel the highs," and the highs was kicking! Then he said, "Now here's the mid-range." He had some Electro-Voice horns on stands; they really projected the mid-range. Any record that he played, it was like the people who made that record were right there performing in your face. And when he turned up the bass, it was . . . you couldn't hear Little Brothers at all.[10]

The same thing happened to Breakout's partner, DJ Baron, who tells us how he was silenced by Afrika Bambaataa:

> Bambaataa was on one side of the gym, and we was on the other. The place was jam-packed. But Bambaataa had one up his sleeve: Disco King Mario

had loaned him a power amp. We were going back and forth, and all of a
sudden you couldn't hear us no more, 'cause Bam borrowed this amp from
Mario and blew us out of the water, just drowns us out totally. We lost the
battle.[11]

Bam got his comeuppance in a legendary encounter with Kool Herc. At one
point in the battle, while Bambaataa was spinning, Herc got on his microphone—run through an echo-generator for good effect—and thundered the
following command: "Bambaataa . . . turn your system down!" and then brought
the volume up on Babe Ruth's "The Mexican" until nothing else was audible.[12]
Bambaataa had no choice but to comply.

No one got rich battling, and in the early days money rarely changed hands.
Sometimes the winner would take—or at least try to take—the loser's mixer or
turntable, though DJs were always reluctant to relinquish the goods. Speaking
for Grandmaster Caz and himself, DJ Disco Wiz explained, "No one would take
our system even when we lost. [If they tried] they would probably walk out with
a hole in their fucking head."[13] Steve Dee, a Harlem DJ from a later generation,
was more apt to *break*—rather than take—the loser's turntable. "Instead of
keeping them, what I did was I would take the tone arm, and bend it back and
break it, and give it back to them." He was able to get away with such a confrontational move because, as he points out, "I'm a big guy."[14] Most often, however,
what was won and lost in battle was nothing so tangible as money or equipment. It was something more valuable: bragging rights. In the end, battles were
not so much about defeating rivals as they were about demonstrating power
and establishing one's place in the pecking order.

Despite the violence suggested by Disco Wiz's words and Steve Dee's actions,
battlers generally remained on good terms or at least granted each other due
respect, regardless of the outcome of the contest. Not all DJs were friends, but
neither were all rivals enemies. And when they lost, they learned from defeat.
In a 1977 battle with Afrika Bambaataa, Grandmaster Caz and Disco Wiz
opened by playing Queen's "We Will Rock You." Bam then played the same
record on his superior equipment, making the challengers' system seem puny.
Caz and Wiz tried again, but blew out their speakers; all they could do was to
start "unplugging shit." Caz continues: "Oh my god, it was one of the most
humiliating things. But it was one of those life lessons, man. And another thing
that we survived."[15] The defeated duo didn't leave, and they didn't cause any
trouble. They hung out with Bam and enjoyed the rest of the party. ◐

This was the hip-hop way, at least back then. By the 1990s, even before the
murders of rappers Tupac Shakur and The Notorious B.I.G. in 1996 and 1997,
hip-hop had a reputation for celebrating and promoting violence, one that
remains to this day. But in the earliest days, DJs, b-boys and b-girls, graffiti

writers, and MCs may have experienced violence, often on a daily basis, but their art didn't glorify it. Their battles and rivalries sublimated violence, channeling aggression into music, dance, and painting.

FROM SOUND TO SKILLS: THE BATTLE EVOLVES

DJs put huge amounts of time and energy into building their sound systems. Grandmaster Flash scoured the city's many vacant lots for any bit of abandoned equipment that he could cannibalize for his stereo. Jazzy Jay and his partner Superman sat for hours in Jay's basement, "covered with sawdust, 'cause we used to build speakers from the ground up."[16] Tony Tone, the hook-up man for Baron and Breakout, aspired to assemble a system that would rival even Kool Herc's:

> When we first started, it was two bass speakers, raw horns, and a guitar amp. And it was loud. But Herc had a real system. So people started trying to imitate his system. Everybody had their own little section of the town that they ruled, and at the top of the mountain is Kool Herc. We have to climb the mountain. So we made some money, and we went and bought equipment. We found out about crossover power amps; we tried to get more professional. We had 15-inch speakers made out of 55-gallon steel drums. The speakers faced down so you could get a bass reflex, and it would shoot out—you could hear it for at least ten blocks.[17]

Perhaps following Jamaican tradition, Tone gave his system a name: "The Mighty Mighty Sasquatch." (This wasn't the only named sound system: Herc's was dubbed "the Herculoids," Bambaataa's was "the Earthquake," and Flash at one point called his rig "the Gladiator.") "For us, for the first-generation pioneers," Disco Wiz explains, "it was always about acquiring that sound system. That was the quest. The awesome amp, the awesome turntables, the right mixer, and the right speakers towering—you wanted to emulate what Kool Herc had. That was the goal. All the other stuff just started happening as we went along."[18]

This "other stuff" that Wiz casually mentions constituted a major shift in the function of the DJ battle, and represented a turning point in the history of hip-hop. At some point—probably starting around 1976—battles began to change. No longer was power paramount; skill came to be the name of the game. Listen to Kevie Kev's description of a winning battle performance by GrandWizzard Theodore:

> Theodore . . . used to break out with the handcuffs. The other DJ, he's got his earphones on and he's got his hands loose. We'd take the earphones off

Theodore with the handcuffs on . . . and he used to tear it up and bring the house down. Everybody used to be shocked and amazed. We were just takin' it to another level because each time you'd do a performance they'd wanna see something different.[19]

This was no Kool Herc-style Voice-of-God victory. Rather than silencing rivals through sheer might, Theodore won by handicapping himself. He showed the crowd that he was so skilled that he could beat his opponents even when he was handcuffed; he wanted them to know that, unlike his rival, he didn't need headphones to mix records—he could set the needle in the right spot just by sight. What lay behind Theodore's victory was talent and hours of practice, ingenuity channeled not into his sound system, but into the techniques for extending the possibilities of the equipment. With this paradigm shift, DJs like Herc and Bambaataa—those with the best sound in the Bronx—came to be displaced by DJs who focused more on technique, especially Theodore and Grandmaster Flash. As DJ AJ noted, "Kool Herc couldn't draw a crowd after people saw Flash."[20]

What can account for the change in battle dynamics, the seemingly sudden shift to the skill-based contests we see in the mid- and late 1970s? Jeff Chang has pointed out that at hip-hop parties, "playlists became more standardized" after a few years, and suggests that DJs had to set themselves apart not by *what* songs they were playing, but by *how* they were playing them.[21] Improvements in technology were significant as well. In the earliest days of hip-hop, circa 1973 to 1975, stereo equipment just wasn't robust enough for what I call performative DJing, in which the DJ creates new music by manipulating recorded sound. However, when direct-drive turntables and mixers with more—and more rugged—controls became available in the mid- and late 1970s, DJs could start expanding their repertoire of techniques. Another contributing factor may be the decline in the importance of mobile sound systems and mobile DJs. As certain hip-hop DJs grew more popular (and not incidentally, came of legal age), some of them established residencies at dance clubs, where they used the house stereos. Freed from having to transport and set up their own equipment, they could collect more gigs—and more money—than ever before. Park jams and block parties, which demanded mobile systems, didn't disappear, but fewer DJs devoted themselves to constructing monstrous stereos, allowing those interested more in technique than in power a chance to shine. And this brings us to the most tangible and easily observed cause for the shift to technique-based DJing—the contribution of specific individuals. It is their contributions that most deeply shaped DJing during this period. It was because of them that hip-hop became less about playing other people's music and more about creating new performance styles and new music.

THE INSTRUMENT MAKERS: FLASH AND THEODORE

Kool Herc, Afrika Bambaataa, and Grandmaster Flash are often invoked as the "holy trinity" of pioneering DJs, the three who laid hip-hop's foundation. Herc set the cornerstone, a powerful, bass-heavy breakbeat; Bam, the Master of Records, supplied the bricks through his vast and eclectic selection of songs and sounds; and Flash (Figure 2.2), as we'll see, provided the mortar—the means of joining hip-hop's diverse sonic materials into a solid, unbroken structure. This is all true, but somewhat misleading. First, Herc and Bam came earlier, and had been spinning for at least two years when Flash arrived on the scene. Second, Flash's approach to DJing was markedly different—not only an extension of what came before but also a reaction *against* it. Flash, I believe, is better studied in conjunction with another DJ whose contributions are as crucial as the members of the so-called trinity: GrandWizzard Theodore. If Kool Herc and Afrika Bambaataa more or less invented hip-hop, Flash and Theodore transformed the turntable into a musical instrument, one of hip-hop's signal contributions to the history of music. As Bambaataa himself observed, "Grandmaster Flash brought the quick-mixing into the hip-hop culture. Then you had the scratching and needle dropping of GrandWizzard Theodore, and that's when the whole movement started changing."[22]

Figure 2.2 Grandmaster Flash, Crotona Park, South Bronx, 2010. (Photograph by Joe Conzo, copyright Joe Conzo Archives, 2011.)

The major innovation of Kool Herc and Afrika Bambaataa was to focus on musical fragments, playing only what they regarded as the best part of a record. They were less concerned with how those fragments connected with each other, and the result was often a jarring succession of distinct genres, tempos, timbres, keys, and moods. As Rahiem pointed out, "When you went to a Herc party, you would see the b-boys doing their thing, break-dancing or whatever, but there was always a lull, or a pause in the action. . . . Herc let his records play until you heard khhhhhh, khhhhh, khhh"—the sound of the needle hitting the end of a record.[23] Promoter and manager Van Silk said this about Bambaataa: "I'll be honest with you: I hated going to Bam parties. Bam would be playing the break-beats and then would jump off and start playing some calypso, or playing some reggae, or playing some rock. Bambaataa's mindset was that hip-hop was an open field of music. He'd take an Aerosmith record, 'Walk this Way,' and slow it, or speed it up."[24]

Flash was deeply influenced by both Herc and Bambaataa, but he, too, felt their jump-cut style was sometimes a liability. In his 2008 autobiography, he explained the problem, as he saw it, with Herc's approach:

> It was like Herc had a sixth sense for where one song reached out and a magic ear for the next perfect hook. But as monumental as Herc's insight was, there was something that bothered me about his style. He didn't care about keeping the actual beat locked in tight; he didn't make the switch from one song to the next in a clean cut that matched the beats, bars, and phrases of the two jams. [. . .] If you looked at the crowd in that moment between songs, everybody fell off the beat for a few seconds. They'd get back on it again, but in those few seconds you could see the energy and the magic start to fade from the crowd.[25]

Flash felt that the transition between songs was just as important as the tunes themselves, and he set out to develop a method of DJing that emphasized cohesion over fragmentation.

Born in 1958, Grandmaster Flash began life as Joseph Saddler. As he has explained in interviews and in his autobiography, he did not have an easy childhood. His father, a railroad worker and an amateur boxer, was a cruel disciplinarian. Mr. Saddler's prized possessions were his stereo and records, and just as surely as they were off limits to his son, the boy was irresistibly drawn to them. Joseph was fascinated by all things mechanical and musical, and the spinning turntable and shiny discs brought his loves together. As he put it, "Don't know which sent me higher—the music or the mystery of how it played."[26] But when he was caught touching the equipment, or worse yet, with a broken record at his feet, the punishment was swift and harsh. According to Flash, his father sometimes held his hand to a hot radiator, and on one occasion he beat his son into unconsciousness—the boy was not yet seven at the time. His mother protected him as best she could, but he was only safe when his father eventually abandoned the family. Unfortunately, life was hardly better under his mother's care. She became increasingly unstable when her husband left, and after she was repeatedly institutionalized for psychiatric care, Joseph and his sisters were left in the hands of foster families. He was later sent to the Greer School at Hope Farm, near Poughkeepsie, and after five generally happy years there he returned to the Bronx in 1971 at the age of thirteen.

Not long after his homecoming, Joseph became "Flash." He and a buddy were fans of the science fiction hero Flash Gordon, and since his friend was already named Gordon, Joseph gained the nickname Flash; being fast on his feet sealed it. ("Grandmaster" only came later. At his first park jams he was known as DJ Flash.) Like many hip-hop DJs, Flash had first tried his hand at graffiti and b-boying, but his heart and talent were more attuned to music and the technologies that brought his favorite tunes to life. His interest in all things mechanical and electronic only deepened during his years at Samuel Gompers Vocational Technical High School, where he unlocked the mysteries of stereo equipment, and even built a tube amplifier from scratch. But Flash still did not yet have his own stereo, and he couldn't afford to buy one. So he scavenged. For Flash the urban blight of the Bronx was a gift, and he roamed the junk-strewn streets with "a pair of wire cutters in one hand and a screwdriver in the other." "Fortunately," he says, "there were burned-out jalopies all over the place," and he stripped these abandoned cars of their wiring, resistors, capacitors, and the occasional stereo speaker. His great find, however, was a broken Thorens belt-driven turntable left for dead on the sidewalk. He soon had his first sound system.[27] It was the early 1970s, and Flash was still a high school student.

Flash took the same methodical approach to his DJing as he did to his equipment. His goal was to find a way to connect the breaks without ever losing the beat, so that listeners and dancers would never know when one ended and the other started. He already had the necessary equipment—two turntables, a mixer, and two copies of the same record. What he needed was a method.

The mixer was crucial to Flash's method. A piece of electronic equipment wired to the two turntables, the amplifier, and the speakers, the mixer has two basic functions: to control which turntable is heard through the speakers, and to allow the DJ to hear what is playing on the turntables, even if it can't be heard through the speakers. To control which turntable is heard the DJ usually uses the mixer's crossfader—in those days it was often a knob, though later, horizontal sliders became the norm. When the crossfader is turned or pushed to the left, the record playing on the left turntable (turntable one) sounds through the speakers; when pushed to the right, the right turntable (turntable two) is heard; and when in the middle, both sound at the same time. (Incidentally, another term for the DJ's set-up is "the ones and the twos." Another common term is "decks.") Using the crossfader, the DJ can switch smoothly between turntables without interrupting the flow of the music. Headphones plugged into the mixer make its second basic function possible. While one record is playing, the DJ can listen to another without anyone else hearing it, and thus cue it up—that is, locate a desired starting point on a disc. If you ever watch a DJ with a headphone cupped to one ear while putting the needle down or moving a record back and forth without ever interrupting the music coming from the speakers, this is the mixer at work. Much more is possible with a mixer than simply fading and cueing, but these two functions are what make a continuous flow, or mix, of music possible, or at least practicable. (See Appendix 1 for an illustration of a modern turntable and mixer set-up.)

I say practicable because it is actually possible to mix records without a mixer, and many early hip-hop DJs did just that. The DJ mixer was still a new technology in the early days of hip-hop. Introduced in 1971, the first commercially available mixer designed for club and mobile DJs (as opposed to radio DJs) was the Bozak CMA-10-2DL, a 25-pound monster that cost about a thousand dollars and was used largely by the most successful Manhattan discos. It had no crossfader and none of the slider-type faders we see in modern DJ mixers, but instead sported an array of nineteen rotary knobs mounted on the vertical face of the machine. The earliest ones were not sold in stores, and even if they had been, few DJs could afford them. Flash actually acquired a Bozak mixer in 1975, though he didn't buy it. As he explains, some admiring thieves stole one from the Hunts Point Palace ballroom in the Bronx and presented it to him at no charge, the only condition being that he "keep the park bangin.'"[28] Another coveted mixer was the Clubman 2, introduced in 1975, which had sliders rather than knobs, and even featured a horizontal crossfader.[29] Although not as expensive as the early Bozaks, it retailed at $425, making them largely inaccessible to most DJs. I say *largely* because, for example, Disco Wiz and Grandmaster Caz came to possess the Clubman on one chaotic night in the summer of 1977. "We got that in the blackout," Wiz explains.[30] Wiz, among others, has suggested that the price break, so to speak, afforded by the infamous blackout of 1977 greatly reduced the barrier to entry for aspiring DJs: "Before the blackout, you had maybe five legitimate crews of DJs. After the blackout, you had a DJ on every block. That blackout made a big spark in the hip-hop revolution."[31]

Before the blackout, most DJs didn't have fancy mixers and many didn't even have mixers at all. Through ingenious workarounds, however, they were able to mix records. Here's how Afrika Bambaataa did it:

You had one guy that was set up on this side of the room, and one guy that was set up on another side. We had a flashlight, so if he was playing the

Jackson Five, "I Want You Back," when his record was going down low, he would flash at me, and that would give me the time to put on "Stand" or "Everyday People" by Sly and the Family Stone. And that's how we started DJin' back and forth, before they came with the two turntables and a mixer.[32]

DJ Breakout had another method: "I had an old turntable. I had another turntable that had a radio on the bottom of it. So I took the wires, and I ran 'em together, and one would play, I cut that one, grab this one, and play the next record. There was no mixer. I just kept playin.'"[33] But even when mixers became more widely available, they were hardly the precision instruments that today's DJs take for granted. Horizontal crossfaders—necessary for advanced scratch techniques—weren't available on mixers until as late as 1975, when the Clubman Two came on the market. Stiff faders and unwieldy knobs, and in general their large size, also made quick mixing a challenge. GrandWizzard Theodore jokes that in the early days mixers (which usually sat in between the record players) were so big that he had to take a bus from one turntable to the other.[34] Ask old-school DJs about their first mixers and they often marvel at how they ever managed to rock parties with the equipment they had.

We will keep returning to the mixer, for its development in many ways parallels the development of the art of the hip-hop DJ. For now, let's return to Flash, hunched over his stereo in the basement studio he affectionately called "the sweatbox." Flash sequestered himself in the sweatbox for hours on end, determined to harness the powers of his equipment in the quest for a seamless mix. His central insight is reducible to a simple dictum: to best control the sound, you must touch the records. But this rule violated a taboo as old as the phonograph. "This was a major no-no," he points out. "You *never* touched the record with your fingers." For many, to touch a record is to defile it. One properly holds a disc only by the edges, keeping oily fingertips from making anything but the barest contact with the vinyl. Yet Flash realized that the best way to manipulate a break was to put "your greasy fingertips on the record." "I found a way to start the first record with my hand physically on the vinyl itself," he explains. "The platter would turn but the music wouldn't play because the needle wouldn't be traveling through the groove. However, when I took my hand off the record . . . BAM! The music started right where I wanted it."[35]

For the record to remain in place while the platter moved, he first had to remove the thin rubber mat that sat atop the platter. The purpose of this mat— which comes with all turntables—is to grip the record securely so it moves in tandem with the platter. Hip-hop DJs, however, replaced the rubber mat with what came to be known as a slipmat. Some DJs cut circles out of felt or from the plastic or paper sleeves that records came in, or really from whatever was at hand—"cereal boxes, curtains, anything you could cut a circle out of," is how GrandWizzard Theodore put it.[36] (Slipmats are now manufactured by a variety of companies that cater to DJs.) Whatever the material, the slipmat allowed the DJ to hold a record at a particular spot while the turntable platter moved beneath it. This meant that the DJ could keep the record in place without exerting much pressure and without working at odds with the turntable's motor. More importantly, when the record is released it starts up in exactly the right place and at full speed. This technique—which had already been familiar to radio and disco DJs—is known, appropriately enough, as slip-cueing.

Simply holding a record in place was not enough, however, because Flash also needed to know exactly where the break started and stopped. So once again, he touched his records. Taking a grease pencil he drew one line from the center hole to the edge of the label to indicate the beginning of the break, and another to show where it ended. From this he developed what he called the "clock theory." With the label facing up, he treated the cardinal points of the record as twelve, three, six, and nine o'clock. His pencil marks were like hour hands, and he could see at a glance that a break, say, started at two and ended at ten. It is a simple and effective system, and most hip-hop DJs to this day learn how to mix using some form of the clock theory.

Flash now had the means to repeat a break—or loop it, as DJs say—seamlessly and indefinitely. Here's the recipe:

- Put two copies of the same record on the turntables with the needles at the beginning of the break.
- Slide the crossfader to the left position so that only turntable one will sound.
- Using a marked label as a guide, start playing the disc on turntable one at the beginning of the break.
- While turntable one is playing, start turntable two, but hold the disc in place so the needle doesn't move through the grooves.
- Right when the break on turntable one ends, quickly slide the crossfader to the right side and let go of the disc on turntable two.
- While the break is playing on turntable two, manually rotate the disc on turntable one backwards (this is called backspinning) to the beginning of the break and hold the record in place.
- Right when the break on turntable two ends, quickly slide the crossfader back to the left side and let go of the disc on turntable one.
- Continue at your pleasure.

To watch a skilled DJ loop a break is to see a graceful dance of the hands—a quick pirouette to backspin the disc, a fluid sweep to slide the fader, another pirouette on the other turntable and back again to the mixer in the middle. ◐ This dance will produce no lag between breaks, no tempo fluctuations, no needle noise. It will sound to all like one perfect, unbroken beat. *If* it is performed with exact timing and precision, that is; if not, the mix will be sloppy, jarring. Like any musical technique, the more expertly it is executed the easier it looks and sounds. Many DJs, however—and Flash was among them—wanted their audiences to know exactly how hard they were working. They would raise the bar by spinning on their feet in between beats, moving the crossfader with their hands behind their back or under their leg or with their elbows or nose. DJs call these moves body tricks, and they're part of a long tradition of show-musicianship that connects Mozart, playing blindfolded at the piano, to Jimi Hendrix strumming his guitar with his teeth, to Grandmaster Flash sliding faders with his back.

Flash's method—which he called quick mixing—was not completely unprecedented. As I mentioned in Chapter 1, a number of disco DJs in New York had developed similar methods for manipulating records. One of them was Pete DJ Jones, whose technique Flash knew well.[37] Although Flash has derided the music as sterile, he often spun disco records and admired the seamless mixing of disco DJs. We might well understand Grandmaster Flash's lasting contribution as introducing the disco aesthetic of mixing to hip-hop. In other words, he made it possible to dance to breaks like others danced to disco: for long periods without missing a beat.

Quick mixing, which became the standard among hip-hop DJs, allowed b-boying to develop as it could never have before. Flash's mixing served not only the b-boys and b-girls, but the MCs as well. An endlessly looped break creates an unbroken instrumental beat for the rappers to rhyme over. But this came later. In 1975, when Flash was developing his method, rapping was not fully developed; it had not yet become the fourth element—after DJing, b-boying, and graffiti writing—of hip-hop culture.

For a time in 1975, Flash more or less lived with Gene Livingston, a Bronx DJ known as Mean Gene—so-called because, as Flash says, he was "the neighborhood bully and a real bastard."[38] Flash, who kept his equipment in Gene's apartment and spent long hours there, quickly realized that Gene was not the only DJ in the Livingston home. One day he noticed a small kid in the living room with a record player, picking up the tone arm and setting the needle down at the break with astonishing accuracy. The kid was Gene's younger brother, Theodore, and he was just twelve years old (Figure 2.3).

Theodore Livingston was already an experienced DJ at the time, and had advanced the art of needle placement—a technique that came to be known as the needle drop—further than perhaps anyone else in the Bronx.[39] Holding the tone arm between thumb and forefinger like a surgeon wielding a scalpel,

Figure 2.3 GrandWizzard Theodore, Scratch DJ Academy, Manhattan, 2009. (Photograph by Joe Conzo, copyright Joe Conzo Archives, 2011.)

he could set the needle down anywhere on a record and return to that exact spot over and again. ◐ He could repeat not only breaks, but single grooves with exquisite precision, and reconfigure any song by playing phrases from different parts of the track in quick succession. "I used to hate to wait for the break to come around," Theodore recalls. "I used to skip to the break part with my thumb. You watch the grooves, the thickest grooves are where the break part comes in. I watch the record go round and round, and then bam! It comes right in. I got this down to a science. I used to astonish myself."[40] Like Flash's quick mixing and body tricks, the needle drop was an impressive sight. DJ Charlie Chase remembers seeing Theodore for the first time at a jam with Flash at Arthur Park in the Bronx:

> Theodore was a kid I never even knew existed. He came out of nowhere, and he's only this big.... And what amazed me about Theodore was that he picks up the needles without having to spin back, and catches the beat, time after time after time after time. Throw a record on, pick up the needle, drop it. Continuously! And he's rocking this thing, he's just ripping this party up.[41]

The needle drop never quite caught on, probably because it is so difficult. Decades after introducing it, however, Theodore continues to perform the technique, often donning a blindfold—Mozart-like—to astonish audiences.

Theodore's most important contribution to hip-hop, however, was not the needle-drop. It was a technique and a sound that continues to be heard to this day, throughout the world and across the musical spectrum: the scratch. The specific day of discovery is no longer known, but we do know exactly where it happened. It was in a worn, but handsome South Bronx apartment building with stone columns and Corinthian capitals at the corner of Boston Road and East 168th street. This was the same apartment where Flash and Theodore first met, and given the history that was made there, 1199 Boston Road is perhaps as important an address in the history of hip-hop as 1520 Sedgwick Avenue, the site of Kool Herc's first party. ◐

One day, probably in late spring, Theodore was in his bedroom recording a set of songs from his two turntables to his tape recorder, making a mix tape to play in the Morris High School cafeteria during lunchtime. (Theodore was no troublemaker—he had gotten permission from his principal to do this.) At one point, he was cueing the record on the left turntable to a specific spot in the song, getting ready to segue to it from the record already playing on the right turntable. Theodore had his hand on the left record, ready to let it go. Then, at that very same moment, an agitated Mrs. Livingston appeared in the doorway. Here's how Theodore related the rest of the story:

> So, I'm in my house playing my music, playing the music really, really loud, and she comes in the room, she has that look on her face. I was like, "Oh shit, I'm gonna get my ass whipped," you know? So she gave me that look, like, "Look, either you turn the music down, or you turn the music *off*." So, while she was in the doorway, you know, getting ready to jump me, I had one record playing on my right side, and I was holding a record on my left side, not knowing that all the levels on the mixer [. . .] were up, because I was trying to keep the same groove that I was on. So while she was in the doorway screaming at me, I was moving the record back and forth, forth and back.[42]

Normally, a DJ wouldn't move the record like that, but Theodore didn't want to lose his place, and he also didn't want to hold the platter still, which could harm the motor. He also happened to have the volume up on that left turntable; normally, it would be down, heard only by the DJ through the headphones. So it was only under these unusual circumstances that one would hear that rasping sound against the beat of another song. Theodore liked what he heard and, as he explained, "when she left the room I just practiced it with different records, and it became the scratch, you know?"[43] He says that he publicly introduced the scratch at The Sparkle, a club on Mt. Eden just south of the Cross Bronx Expressway. The record he played was Thin Lizzy's "Johnny the Fox Meets

Jimmy the Weed," which not only contains one of the classic drum breaks, but a line that made the song especially popular among the record spinners: "They got some crazy DJ who will send you right up to Heaven."[44]

Theodore wasn't the first to create a scratching sound with vinyl. When DJs cued records they would often move the disc back and forth to find the right spot, and would hear a form of scratching in the headphones. So *every* hip-hop DJ knew that sound. But Theodore was the one who saw its musical potential and introduced it in public *as* music. And the hip-hop community largely agrees that he was the first to do this. Largely, but not completely. Some have claimed that Grandmaster Flash actually scratched before Theodore. Rahiem, who at one point was an MC with Grandmaster Flash and the Furious Five, argues: "[Flash] invented scratching, OK? There are other people who say other things, but Flash is the only person that I know who was scratching at that time."[45]

Flash himself hasn't helped clarify matters. In *Yes Yes Y'all*, he says, "Theodore came up with this style of adding rhythm to the rub, which was later coined as scratching."[46] (At first scratching was called rubbing, though it's not clear who gets credit for the term. "It was just [called] rubbin,'" Theodore told me. "It was pretty much just rubbin' the record, you know?"[47]) In his autobiography, however, Flash says hardly a word about Theodore or scratching. Instead, he suggests that he discovered scratching independently. Listen to how he describes mixing the Commodores' "Assembly Line" (1974) with "It's Just Begun" (1972) by The Jimmy Castor Bunch: "At one point, 'Assembly Line' fell off the beat for a split second and I dog-paddled the record backwards. . . . Then I punched it forward right on the break. . . . *Zuka-Zuka!* It sounded like a beat! But the drummer didn't play it, I did!"[48] Is *Zuka-Zuka* the sound of scratching? He doesn't say, and he seems to be the only DJ who uses that term—most DJs say *zigga zigga* or *wicki wicki*.

There's no doubt that that Flash made scratching sounds while mixing records, but notice that he doesn't use the word "scratching" to describe it, maybe to avoid asserting himself as its inventor. For his part, Theodore has suggested that Flash had conceived of the *possibility* of scratching, but without taking it any further: "He had a vision of scratching records, but he couldn't really present it to the people."[49] Presenting it to "the people" is exactly what Theodore did, and whoever might have made scratching sounds before him, there's little doubt that it was GrandWizzard Theodore who introduced this new musical technique to the world.

Yet there is some question about when exactly Theodore did this. Theodore has stated that he first scratched in 1975, and this date is widely repeated in the hip-hop literature. However, many of the records Theodore has said he first scratched hadn't yet been released in 1975. Passport's "Ju-Ju Man" and Ralph MacDonald's "Jam on the Groove" (which he has cited as records he had scratched in his bedroom), as well as Thin Lizzy's "Johnny the Fox Meets Jimmy the Weed," were all released in *1976*.[50] When I recently asked Theodore about the timing of his discovery, he was clear: "It was definitely 1975." He also mentioned the 1973 Incredible Bongo Band record "Bongo Rock" as one of the records he was scratching at the time.[51] Whether it was 1975, 1976, or even 1977, Theodore still has the strongest claim to have publicly introduced scratching. His profound influence on hip-hop is not in question. We have to remember that in its early years hip-hop was largely an oral tradition—any surprise at inconsistencies in the record, so to speak, should be at how few serious ones there actually are.

THE TURNTABLE AS INSTRUMENT

However important it is to establish an accurate historical record, it is more important to understand the bigger picture, the significance of these DJs' accomplishments. The significance is easy to state, and I repeat: Grandmaster Flash and GrandWizzard Theodore transformed the turntable into a musical instrument. But what exactly does this mean? How does this transformation take place?

Nearly anything can become an instrument. Take a partially filled jug, blow across the top, and you have a wind instrument. Hold a pair of spoons in one hand and strike them against your knee in rhythm, and you're playing percussion. Both spoons and jugs are, like the turntable, essentially "found" instruments associated with African American musical practices. The turntable presents a more complex case, however. Unlike jugs and spoons, it was intended and used to make music. But traditionally, it's not the person playing the turntable who is making the music—the music has already been made, and is simply *reproduced* by the turntable. And this is why it's often difficult for people to understand why some DJs claim that they are musicians, and that the turntable is a musical instrument. After all, anyone can put a record on a turntable, set the needle down, and press the start button. How does this make the turntable an instrument?

It doesn't. But Flash, Theodore and others were doing more than this. Like any instrumentalist, they were creating and manipulating sounds in real time. When Flash extracted a break, looped it, and segued to another break, or played one record while cutting rapidly to another record for a brief horn stab or snare hit—another of his techniques he called punch phrasing—he wasn't simply reproducing "Assembly Line" or "It's Just Begun." He was creating something new, and creating it in the moment. Theodore went even further; when he pushed "Ju-Ju Man" back and forth underneath the stylus, he was transforming it into something entirely different. It is because of this real-time manipulation that the turntable can be a musical instrument.

But there is a difference between an object that is treated like an instrument and one that is identified and accepted as an instrument. If I tap out the "Funky Drummer" break on my desk while pondering how to explain this distinction, I'm making music. But it's still a desk. The transformation of an object into an instrument involves not a single act, but a process, and this process requires not a single individual, but an entire community. There is no single test to determine instrumentality, but I would suggest that an object can be considered a musical instrument when:

- It involves real-time sound manipulation
- It has a body of techniques developed specifically for it
- It has its own distinctive sound
- The object itself is either specifically designed or modified for making music
- The sound it generates is considered to be music by a community of listeners.

I have already mentioned how DJs manipulated sound in real time. The turntable, just like all traditional instruments, also has its own catalog of idiomatic techniques. There's backspinning, slip-cueing, punch phrasing, and of course scratching. Scratching itself is subdivided into countless variations. The simple back-and-forth scratch that Theodore developed came to be known as the baby, but there are more advanced scratches such as the stab, the crab, the tear, the flare, and the transformer. Even the most basic scratches demand careful attention to hand position, a good ear, and lots of practice, and the techniques only get harder from there. Although the turntable need not be difficult to play in order for it to be an instrument, the fact that it *is* difficult helps make the case that it should be accepted among the ranks of traditional instruments.

The techniques of performative DJing create a distinctive sound that further helps define the turntable as a musical instrument. The sound of scratching is as strongly connected with the turntable as the sound of a snare hit or cymbal crash is associated with their instruments. Backspinning and the sound of rapidly decelerating music—created when the stop button is pressed while a record is playing—are also unmistakably connected to the turntable. Yet unlike other instruments, a turntable not only has its own sounds but can sound exactly like every other instrument, simply by playing recordings of those instruments. This is an asset, of course, but also a liability. When watching DJs it's not always clear which sounds they are creating or transforming, and which are coming straight from the records. There can be a disconnect between cause and effect, little evidence of that direct relationship between musician and instrument that is so clear when a guitarist strums strings or a pianist strikes keys. Ironically, it is the turntable's sheer diversity of sonic possibilities, its ability to sound like anything else, that not only makes it an instrument of infinite possibilities but also brings its very instrumentality into question.

Part of the turntable's image problem is that it did not begin life as a musical instrument. But not all musical instruments were created *as* instruments. Many started out as something else—cowbells and washboards, for example. And although cowbells and washboards could be played as instruments in their original state, musicians started to modify them or make new ones to suit their artistic purposes. A similar process took place with the turntable. At first, DJs simply made do with what they had. But then they started to make a variety of changes—they replaced rubber mats with slipmats, they weighted down tone arms to keep the needle from skipping while they scratched records, they altered speakers to emphasize the bass, they rewired equipment to make cueing easier. Later, manufacturers started adapting the equipment in response to DJ demands—controls were added to turntables, needles were adapted for scratching, mixers were completely redesigned, digital systems came to supplement the traditional analog machines, and so on. To the untrained eye, an Ortofon Qbert cartridge, a Numark TTXUSB turntable, or a Rane TTM 57 mixer might look more or less the same as equipment made for the home listening market. But make no mistake—these were designed and built for musicians.

Having idiomatic techniques, a unique sound, and specialized design is not enough to make the turntable a musical instrument, however. Jackhammers have all of the above and are not—at least to most ears—musical instruments. And this is what clinches something as a musical instrument—the ears of others. It is not simply through the actions of musicians that a new instrument comes to be; it is a community of listeners that renders the verdict. GrandWizzard Theodore made this point when he was asked how he knew that scratching was music. "I knew that it was music when people danced to it," he responded simply.[52] For decades now, people have heard the distinctive sounds of the turntable-as-instrument and have danced, bobbed their heads, or stood transfixed in awe, just like anyone might do in the presence of any other kind of music. They have thought of and experienced these sounds as music. And in the end, that's how we know that the turntable is a musical instrument.

Still, the turntable will always remain a complex case. If GrandWizzard Theodore puts a record on the platter and sits down to listen, his turntable is a playback device. If he feels inspired to scratch the record for a few bars before sitting down again, the turntable changes from a playback device to an instrument and back again in the space of seconds. If the turntable suffers from an identity crisis, it's because it actually has two different identities.

Given this schizophrenia, or perhaps schizophonia, it's amazing that the turntable has flourished as a musical instrument for decades, while dozens of other instruments introduced in the twentieth century have largely disappeared. Probably the most important reason for its success is its physical immediacy. The hand rests comfortably on the grooved, slightly tacky surface of the record. That tactility is enormously important to DJs, who often wax eloquent about the inimitable feel of vinyl. Pushing a record underneath a turntable needle, transforming the music held within its grooves, one has a sense of touching sound. Scratching a record isn't much different from playing traditional instruments that use friction to create their sounds. Johnny "Juice" Rosado told me that scratching reminds him of the sound of the cuíca, a Brazilian drum that creates its characteristic squeak by pulling a stick through the drumhead.[53] As I'm a violinist, scratching to me feels much like bowing. Grandmixer DXT sees the similarity as well, and has even taken to calling his instrument the *turnfiddle*.[54]

A second reason for the turntable's success is its simplicity. For the most part, the DJ chooses from among binaries: push or pull, sound on or sound off, turntable one or turntable two. But like many successful instruments, the turntable's simple interface yields an infinite number of musical possibilities. The turntable is, at heart, little more than a motorized platter, with relatively few small, moving, or delicate parts. Well-built machines, like the Technics 1200 (see Figure 2.4) or the best models from Vestax and Numark, are extremely robust, require little maintenance, and can take just about any abuse. Finally, the turntable has survived in part because it has been made in large quantities and is widely accessible; unlike many now-obsolete instruments, it hasn't had to depend on a few dedicated makers to handcraft them. While no instrument is guaranteed survival, a straightforward, flexible, and hardy one like the turntable stands a better chance than most.

A second question about the turntable's success returns us to the Bronx of the 1970s: Why is it that the turntable became a musical instrument when and where it did? It's sometimes said that the turntable was embraced because that's all that was available.[55] But that's not quite true. The Bronx was hardly awash in music classes, but as I've explained, traditional instruments and instruction were available in a variety of venues. And singing, of course, was always an option. It's also not the case that DJ-worthy turntables were so easy to come by. Yes, many Bronx families had record players, and those machines often figured prominently in the early lives of many DJs. Typically, however, these turntables were unsuitable for DJing, whether because they were poorly made, fragile, unwieldy, or simply off limits to children. DJs, as we know, went to great trouble to buy, find, modify, or make their *own* sound systems—witness the stories of Grandmaster Flash trolling vacant lots for components, or a sawdust-encrusted

Figure 2.4 The Technics SL1200 turntable was introduced by the Japanese electronics manufacturer Panasonic in 1972. Originally intended for consumers, it was quickly adopted by DJs for its sturdy, quick-starting and -stopping direct-drive motor and rugged case. Slight improvements were introduced over the years (especially with the SL1200 MK2 in 1979 and SL1200 MK5 in 2005), but overall it remained little changed from the 1972 model. To the dismay of DJs worldwide, the Technics 1200 line was discontinued in October 2010. (Photograph by Zane Ritt, courtesy of DJpedia. Creative Commons license CC BY-SA 2.0.)

Jazzy Jay building speaker cabinets. There were easier ways to get into music. So the mere presence of turntables cannot explain why DJ culture flourished. Furthermore, the assumption that necessity was the mother of hip-hop leaves little room for the creativity or even agency of individuals. This assumption, as Joseph Schloss rightly observes in his excellent book on hip-hop producers, *Making Beats*, "virtually precludes the possibility that people *chose* hip-hop's constituent elements from a variety of options and thus ignores the cultural values, personal opinions, and artistic preferences that led them to make those choices."[56]

DJ culture flourished because—and this should be an obvious point—something about the turntable appealed to a certain group of adolescent Bronxites. For one thing, the turntable's unlimited potential for sonic exploration provided a creative outlet for the musically adventurous. Another aspect of its appeal, as I've already mentioned, was its power. When connected to a gigantic sound system, the turntable placed a great deal of power at a DJ's fingertips. This was a multifaceted power—to crush rivals and establish territory, to shape tastes and demonstrate expertise, all of which would be attractive to adolescents, especially young men, who are often expected to prove their skill or might in one area or another.

In the hands of hip-hop DJs, the turntable could also be appealingly transgressive, both in the way DJs handled the equipment and through the sounds they produced with it. Merely touching the surface of a record was taboo, and DJs touched records in most inappropriate ways. Scratching was the ultimate expression of the DJ's transgression. To scratch a record is to damage it—it is a technique that violates its own medium. (Though scratching does not damage the record nearly as much as a needle being pulled *across* the grooves.) In a sense, scratching is, like its hip-hop cousin graffiti, an art of vandalism. It is a celebration of noise, and no doubt part of the pleasure it brought to DJs came from the knowledge that it annoyed the older generation. Perhaps scratching can also be understood as a celebration of the notoriously noisy city of the Bronx, for it transformed what could be considered sonic blight into music, an accompaniment for raucous, joyous dancing. Just as graffiti artists tagged their city with spray paint, DJs, using phonograph needles, etched their own signatures into the city soundscape.

DJS AS INVENTORS AND INNOVATORS

Is it going just a bit too far to call Grandmaster Flash and GrandWizzard Theodore instrument makers, to bestow upon them the title of inventor? The stories I've been telling don't sound much like those we hear about Edison's laboratory, and after all, how is scratching anything more than just ruining records? But these questions reveal a narrow conception of innovation and invention, one that tends to exclude the contributions of African Americans, Latinos, and other often-marginalized groups. As historian Rayvon Fouché has observed, when African Americans display technological creativity it is "regularly dismissed as cleverness, instead of being interpreted as smart, ingenious, or innovative."[57] Fouché, however, sees African American technological engagement differently, as what he calls "black vernacular technological creativity." This is a useful concept here because it illuminates the ways in which hip-hop DJs—of all races and ethnicities, in fact—have interacted with sound-recording technology.

Consider two modes of vernacular technological creativity: reconception and re-creation. As Fouché explains it, *reconception* involves deploying a

Figure 2.5 Kool DJ AJ spinning records at the Ecstasy Garage, 1980. Hunched over his machines and illuminated by a bare bulb, he could be mistaken for an inventor tinkering deep into the night. (Photograph by Charlie Ahearn.)

technology in a way "that transgresses that technology's designed function and dominant meaning," though without necessarily altering the technology itself.[58] Hip-hop DJs reconceived the turntable—originally designed as a straight-forward playback device—as a break-delivery mechanism and a musical instrument. We've already seen how Flash's mixing and Theodore's scratching demonstrate the turntable's instrumentality. An example of the turntable's reconception as a break-delivery mechanism comes in the form of the "plate" created by Grandmaster Caz and DJ Disco Wiz in 1977. Using a boom box that sat to the side of their sound system, they began recording their parties and battles, selling the tapes in their high school lunchroom. At one point they learned that it would be possible to record their tapes to disc, and they imme-diately saw an opportunity to do something entirely new. Instead of simply compiling their favorite songs, they painstakingly created a tape of their favor-ite breaks, sound bites, special effects, and scratches, and then had it made into a disc. (It was actually a ten-inch acetate, an aluminum test pressing with grooves on one side only.) They called the acetate their "plate," and used it as a "secret weapon" in their battles. "When it was time for our set," recalls Wiz, "we would put the plate on, turn off the lights, walk away from the set, leave the whole thing unmanned, and the plate would just play," sounding as if someone were deftly mixing a stack of records. "We would stand over on the side with our arms crossed, in the b-boy stance, and the plate would play for itself. And the opposing DJs would lose their minds when we did that. It was like a KO punch."[59] They would then return to the turntables to mix and scratch in real time, but by then the battle was usually already over. Rather than play short excerpts from longer records, Caz and Wiz created a new type of disc, and were years ahead of their time. Similar compilation discs, later known as battle records, proliferated in the 1990s and came to have a profound impact on the battle scene. In 1977, however, a battle record was shockingly unusual, and it may well be considered the very first hip-hop record, not to mention a prime example of the DJ's technological creativity.

DJs also *re-created* the turntable, physically altering it to meet their practical and aesthetic needs. As we've seen, they created slipmats, monkeyed with tone arms, and rewired components, all in the service of making certain techniques easier or simply possible. Here's another example. Manhattan DJ Ivan "Doc" Rodriguez wanted to be able to play records backwards to create certain sounds, but the turntables he had access to weren't equipped for it. So, taking one of his cheap record players, he removed the cartridge and glued it to the *top* of the tone arm so the needle was pointing up, not down. He then cut a cardboard toilet paper tube in half and put it over the turntable's spindle, using it to elevate a record above the stylus. Now when he raised the tone arm the needle played the record from *underneath*, which meant that it tracked counterclockwise through the grooves—that is, it played backwards. "It was innovative," he points out. "Now, you hit a button on the turntable and it goes backwards. Didn't exist [back then]. So I had to come up with ways to do it, and that's what I would do. I would always find a way."[60] Among DJs of the time, this kind of innovation wasn't rare. DJ Baby Dee of the Mercedes Ladies succinctly explained it this way: "The equipment wasn't made for what we wanted to do with it. So we urbanized it."[61]

Another example of technological alteration was the way DJs wired their sound systems into streetlamps, often a necessity during outdoor parties. "I'd break open a faceplate on the lightpole," remembers Grandmaster Flash, "and, thanks to what I'd learned at vocational school, I could split the wires, step the power down, and make it all work."[62] Flash wasn't the only DJ-electrician. On a hot summer night in the late 1970s, Grandmaster Caz and DJ Disco Wiz were battling a "local cat" named DJ Eddie in the Bronx when suddenly, as Wiz tells it, "the sound went dead and all the streetlamps started going, one after the other."[63] Since they had "hotwired the streetlamp" their first thought was that it was their sound system that had killed the power. The good news was that they had nothing to do with it; the bad news was that they were stranded in the dark with their expensive equipment at the beginning of the legendary New York City blackout of July 13, 1977. (Armed, Wiz and Caz were able to scare off potential thieves while they quickly moved the equipment to the safety of Wiz's nearby house.[64])

The concept of vernacular technological creativity helps us see the work of these early hip-hop DJs in a new light. What might be considered haphazard kludging is in fact nothing less than a radical reconception and re-creation of a century-old technology. These DJs were not accidental radicals, revolutionizing music and technology when all they wanted to do was play records. Hotwiring a streetlamp was about more than simply finding a power source. It was about bringing music out of the restrictive clubs and into the open, so everyone could dance. Creating an acetate of song fragments and sound effects was not about avoiding the need to switch from record to record while DJing. It was a cunning way of demonstrating mastery in battle. Reconfiguring a turntable to play records backwards served no *practical* end—it was all about creating a desired sound.

But wait: by applying the concept of vernacular technological creativity am I simply imposing academic theory where it's not needed or wanted? Or can it actually illuminate the reality of the lives of these DJs, the character of their ideals? Listen to the words of the DJs themselves. Grandmaster Flash calls his approach to mixing the clock *theory*, and recently remarked, "I'm a *scientist* before I'm anything."[65] GrandWizzard Theodore tells of testing and reworking his scratch technique until he "got [it] down to a *science*."[66] "Doc" Rodriguez boasts that his technological fixes were *innovative*. DJ Steve Dee describes beat juggling, a complex mixing technique he introduced in the late 1980s, in terms of *formulas* and *equations*, and calls the Harlem apartment bedroom where he developed it his *lab*.[67] When speaking of their art in general, DJs speak often of "taking it to the next level"—innovating beyond what is currently deemed possible—and "dropping science," or educating those who observe their work. For DJs, innovation is a central value, pursued through scientific concepts and theories. And technology—embodied by the sound system—is the vehicle through which they innovate. So to portray these DJs as a community of technological innovators, as I do here, is to fairly represent their values and ideals. Like the technologically savvy protagonist of Ralph Ellison's *Invisible Man*, the hip-hop DJs of the 1970s and beyond were tinkers *and* thinkers.

Out of the Bronx and into the Shadows: 1978–1983

With a simple repositioning of equipment, hip-hop changed forever. It was a gradual process, but in the late 1970s it became a common sight: microphone stands, and with them, rappers, or MCs, in *front* of the DJ. For the first half-decade of hip-hop's existence, you could go to any dance club or park jam and would probably see the MC off to the side, with the DJ holding the center of attention (Figure 3.1). But then crews started to form: The Mercedes Ladies in 1976, The Funky Four Plus One in 1977, Grandmaster Flash and the Furious Five as well as The Cold Crush Brothers in 1978. As the MCs came to outnumber the DJs, they naturally attracted attention. Dressed to impress with choreographed steps, simply the sight of three, four, or five MCs riveted partygoers (Figure 3.2). The DJs still tended to be the leaders of the crews—look at party flyers from 1978, 1979, and later, and the DJs usually get top billing (Figure 3.3).[1] But with this seemingly unremarkable shift in microphone placement, the relationship between DJs and MCs began to change. The DJ was no longer at the center of the hip-hop universe; a golden age of the DJ was coming to an end. 🎵

Although they were increasingly being supplanted by their MCs, this was also a time when DJs started to become known outside of the Bronx, some even gaining international renown. But the upward trajectory of the DJ was overshadowed—and slowed—by the meteoric rise of the MC. The story of these overlapping trajectories, and the growing independence of the MC and DJ, is best told through a phenomenon new to this era: the hip-hop song. Four songs in particular played important roles in the history of the hip-hop DJ: "Rapper's Delight" (1979), "The Adventures of Grandmaster Flash on the Wheels of Steel" (1981), "Change the Beat" (1982), and "Rockit" (1983).

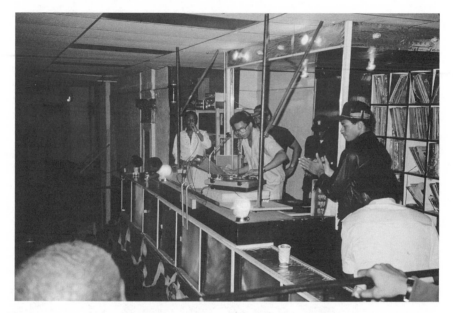

Figure 3.1 DJ Clark Kent on the turntables, with Busy Bee on the microphone, at the T-Connection in the South Bronx, 1980. (Photograph by Charlie Ahearn.)

Figure 3.2 The Funky Four Plus One at The Ritz, in Manhattan, 1981. Not visible are DJs Breakout and Baron. Compare the number and prominence of the MCs, and the invisibility of the DJs, to the photo in Figure 3.1. (Photograph by Charlie Ahearn.)

Figure 3.3 Flyer for DJ Breakout and DJ Baron party February 23, 1979. Note their top billing, and the lower billing of the MCs. Flyer by Buddy Esquire. (Courtesy of the Cornell University Hip-Hop Collection.)

But before we encounter those songs, let's take a closer look at the figure of the MC. Outsiders to hip-hop might wonder why rappers are called MCs. After all, the term MC, short for "master of ceremonies," usually conjures the image of a host or announcer, someone who might welcome an audience to an event, introduce acts at a variety show, or alert guests to mundane matters, like a car in the parking lot with its lights left on. At the earliest hip-hop parties, that's exactly what MCs did, and that's how they got their name. As Grandmaster Caz relates, the purpose of the MC was essentially to allow the DJ to focus on the music:

When I started out as a DJ, MC-in' as an art hadn't been formulated yet. The microphone was just used for makin' announcements, like when the next party was gonna be, or people's moms would come to the party lookin' for them, and you would have to announce it on the mike. The DJ was preoccupied with DJ-in', and he had whoever was in the crew . . . to start talkin' and make the announcements. Different groups started getting' their own personnel to do that so that it started growin' from there.[2]

But some MCs did more than just make announcements, and developed catchphrases to help stoke the energy in the room. Kid Creole was known for calling out, "Yes yes y'all, and you don't stop, to the beat y'all and you don't stop." Cowboy was probably the first to command dancers to "Throw your hands in the air and wave 'em like you just don't care.'[3] And like good catchphrases, they caught on, and became part of the hip-hop vocabulary. Certain MCs then started to do more, chanting brief rhymes to the crowd, and gradually their rhymes grew from couplets to stanzas to near epic-length poems. Their numbers expanded as well: often five rappers would stand before the crowd at a time, and crews of MCs, though still associated with a DJ, proliferated. A line had been crossed: announcers became artists, no longer assisting the DJ but commanding equal and often more attention from the crowd.

Grandmaster Flash explained the change from the earliest days of the MC— what he describes as the "Kool Herc style"—to the era of the DJ + MC crew. Here he refers to his group, Grandmaster Flash and the 3 MCs, which formed in 1977 and later grew to Grandmaster Flash and the Furious Five:

The Kool Herc style was basically freelance talking, not necessarily syncopated to the beat. The three of them—Cowboy, Creole, [Melle] Mel—came up with the style called the back and forth, where they would be MC-ing to the beat that I would play. Visually, it was an incredible sight to see. I'd keep the beat steady—I think probably the first song we did it to successfully, where we wanted the people to just stop and just look and just listen, was a song by Cymande. It's called "Bra." It's a funky beat, and it's real quiet. And they used to just do this thing, and it was so incredible.[4]

Note that the MCs were "an incredible sight to see," that Flash would "keep the beat steady" for them, and that the crowd would "just look and just listen." In other words, the spotlight was now trained on the MCs with the DJ working essentially as an accompanist, and the dancers had become, at least at times, an audience. DJs didn't immediately fade into the background, and hip-hop didn't become solely a spectator sport, but the place of the DJ within hip-hop, and hip-hop itself, was clearly changing.

Despite the relative suddenness of the change, rap didn't simply materialize out of nowhere. Similar kinds of musical speech had been part of African American music and cultural practices (and many African ones) for as long as anyone can remember. Precedents include the drum-accompanied chanting of West African *griots* and certain black oral traditions such as "toasting" and "the dozens." But there were influences much closer to home, and more familiar to New York DJs. Afrika Bambaataa has cited a just a few:

> Rap has always been here in history. . . . You could go and pick up the old Shirley Ellis records, "The Name Game," "The Clapping Song." . . . You could pick up Barry White with his love type of rap, or Isaac Hayes. You could get your poetry rap from Nikki Giovanni, Sonya Sanchez, the Last Poets, the Watts Prophets. You could get your militancy message rap from Malcolm X, Louis Farrakhan, Muhammad Ali. . . . And you could go back to the talks of Murray the K., Cousin Brucie, and all the other radio stations that was pushing the rap on the air or pushing the rock and roll. So rap was always there.[5]

Bam might have also mentioned the 1973 proto-rap of the spoken-word album, *Hustlers Convention*, large sections of which kids in many New York neighborhoods had memorized and could repeat at will. Moreover, throughout the 1970s, African American disco DJs like Eddie Cheba, Grandmaster Flowers, DJ Hollywood, Pete DJ Jones, and Lovebug Starski often spoke from behind the turntables in a kind of rap. Here's how Robert Palmer described Hollywood's patter in a 1982 *New York Times* article:

> He would begin by "signing on" with a rhythmic identification tag, something like "I'm D.J. Hollywood, and I want to be known / As a professional magician of the microphone." He phrased to the beat of a funk record and paced himself with a repeating refrain, usually either a variation on the nonsense formula "hip, hop, hip-hip-de-hop" or an audience participation gambit that began "Hey fellas!" or "Hey la-dies!"[6]

Given all the singsong rhyming that the hip-hop pioneers heard, it's hardly surprising that rap would arise.

But it's surprising just how quickly the MC came to dominate. Why did this happen? How is it that the DJ moved so far into the shadows that, in the public mind, rap came to be synonymous with hip-hop? Ironically, it was the DJ who created the need for the MC. Although hip-hop DJs never stopped playing whole songs at parties, many of them were isolating short phrases, looping instrumental breaks, or scratching. Consequently, vocals became scarcer and mixes moved further away from traditional song forms. Although this was the era of the break-loving b-boy and b-girl, most partygoers came to jams to dance socially, in couples or small groups, not competitively in cyphers. Many no doubt enjoyed singing along with their favorite songs as well. MCs, then, filled a void—one created by DJs—by bringing vocals and songs back into the spotlight. Rap reasserted the ancient primacy of the song in popular music.

The more DJ technique advanced, the farther it moved from its original purpose: to play songs for dancing. Go to a DJ battle today and it's easy to spot newcomers in the audience—they're the ones trying to dance. But the DJs aren't there to establish a danceable groove, and their routines often include frequent rhythm and tempo changes. This tension between advancing turntable technique and serving the needs of dancers has been one of the fundamental, even existential challenges for hip-hop DJs. As we'll see in later chapters, some DJs decided to leave the world of dance and vocal music behind, essentially becoming musicians who perform and compose instrumental music. Others have identified themselves strictly as party starters, body movers, and tastemakers. And yet others have sought to strike a balance between these worlds of DJing.

RAPPERS ARE DELIGHTED; DJS GET DISSED

The migration of microphone stands was only the beginning, a portent of the shifting fortunes of the DJ. The most dramatic change came when hip-hop moved into the recording studio. Ironically, it was the DJs, the very ones who helped create hip-hop by manipulating records, who were left out of the recording process. When in 1979 the Funky Four Plus One recorded 14- and 16-minute versions of "Rappin' and Rockin' the House," their DJs, Baron and Breakout, took no part. As Sha-Rock, the "Plus one" of the group and the first woman MC to join a hip-hop crew, relates, "When we'd perform live, our DJs was a part of our show, doing the mixes, the introductions, the records. But when we went into the studio with 'Rappin' and Rocking the House,' we used a live band; we didn't use a DJ. We never really used DJs in the studio; we always used live bands."[7]

Why were the DJs crucial for live gigs but excluded from the recording session? At parties, it was the DJ who was responsible for keeping the music going for hours on end. But the studio, with usually no audience other than engineers and producers, was a completely different environment. The focus was on the rappers, and the DJ would have little more to do than to keep a beat going. But the more crucial reason was money. A bitter Baron recalls how it went down with "Rappin' and Rocking the House," one of the first hip-hop records: "When we went into the studio, and they got their first payment of 600 dollars it was, 'Ha ha . . . we don't need Breakout and Baron no more. We got our own money. We let our records play for us.' That's how that went. That's how we faded away."[8] Naturally, the MCs' perspective was different—they saw a record deal as the opportunity for them to make the money they deserved. MC Jazzy Jeff (not to be confused with the DJ Jazzy Jeff who partnered with Will Smith in the 1980s), points out that before they started making records, "we had a salary of like $75 a party. That was for the MCs. It was about your sound system then. You couldn't do it without the system, so Baron and Breakout and [manager] Jazzy Dee made most of the money."[9] Money was also a concern for the record label. Hiring a drummer or small band was actually cheaper than securing the services of a well-known DJ. Moreover, by re-creating songs rather than playing records, they avoided having to pay mechanical royalties—money owed to the copyright holders of the record. In fact, many labels didn't pay royalties at all, either for the recording or for the underlying composition. When performed live with a DJ, "Rappin' and Rocking the House" used an instrumental section from Cheryl Lynn's 1978 song "Got to Be Real," but there's no mention of the song or its composers on the disc, released on Enjoy Records. The record lists six names—the five MCs plus their producer Bobby Robinson—as composers, with the note "Music by Pumpkin & Friends" added below.[10] Pumpkin was Errol "Pumpkin" Bedward, a drummer who played on this and several other important early hip-hop records; he was also a frequent and uncredited producer of many of those tracks, making him a seminal, but largely unknown, figure in the first years of recorded rap.

"Rappin' and Rocking the House" was just one of several songs recorded in 1979 in which crews brought their rhymes from the streets to the studios—without their DJs. But the biggest rap hit of 1979, "Rapper's Delight," used neither a DJ nor well-established MCs. In yet another irony of the time, the song that introduced the world to hip-hop had virtually no direct connection to those who pioneered the art form.

Anyone who went to even a few hip-hop parties that summer of 1979 would have heard Chic's "Good Times."[11] ◗ The 12-inch single has a three-minute long break featuring a thumping, rising-and-falling bass line, electronic hand-claps on the backbeat, and the quiet tsk-tsking of cymbals on top. The repeated four-bar pattern is distinctive, catchy, rhythmically rock-solid, and bare enough to serve as an ideal accompaniment to rapping. Simply put, the hit song was a gift to MCs. DJs loved it too, as Mercedes Ladies MC Sheri Sher relates: "DJs scratched the hell out of records like 'Good Times' by Chic, over and over, like 'good/good/*go-o-o-d* times/times/times.'"[12] "Good Times" may have been a disco song, but as Afrika Bambaataa explains, "it was a *funk* type of disco," and no one looked down on it.[13] "Good Times" was hot that summer, it only got hotter a few months later, when it metamorphosed into "Rapper's Delight."

One night in late 1979, Nile Rodgers heard some familiar music at the Manhattan dance club Leviticus. Rodgers, co-composer (with Bernard Edwards) of "Good Times," thought he was hearing his own song, but something was obviously wrong—someone was rapping over it. He confronted the DJ. "I just bought this record up in Harlem," the DJ told Rodgers. "What do you mean 'you bought the record'?" Rodgers demanded, "that's my song!"[14] ◐ Around that time, maybe that very night, Grandmaster Flash and his MC, Cowboy, were sitting in the VIP room in another club, the Bronx's Disco Fever, when they heard the same music. As Flash tells it: "I look at him. He looks at me. We're both thinking the same thing: *Who the hell is that?* The shit sounded familiar. At least the words did. But the voices weren't anybody we knew, and we knew everybody in the game. We go running downstairs and it ain't no live rappers, it's a 12-inch record! Who the hell made this song?"[15] DJ Disco Wiz heard it, too. He wasn't in a dance club, however—he was at the Coxsackie Correctional Facility in upstate New York, serving time for attempted murder. He recognized the rhymes immediately—they belonged to his former DJ partner Grandmaster Caz, who by then had become better known as an MC with the Cold Crush Brothers. "When I heard 'I'm the C-A-S and the O-V-A, and the rest is F-L-Y,' I almost hit the fucking ceiling. I knew all those lyrics from all of our routines in the parks." When he called Caz to congratulate him, his friend's answer puzzled him, "It's me but it isn't really me, you know what I'm saying?"[16]

Rodgers, Flash, Cowboy, and Wiz all recognized the instrumental part to "Good Times" on this record; Flash and Cowboy recognized the rhymes; Wiz recognized the author of the rhymes. None of them, however, knew the name of the song or its MCs. How could four people so intimately connected with the lyrics and music on this record be so mystified by it?

For the answer, we have to go to a pizza joint in Englewood, New Jersey, just a few months earlier. Henry "Big Bank Hank" Jackson was covered in flour when Joey Robinson entered the restaurant. Joey, son of Sylvia Robinson, owner of the Sugar Hill record label, was instructed by his mother to find some rappers to put on record. (The first commercial rap song, "King Tim III" by the Fatback Band, was recorded a few months before, and the astute Mrs. Robinson smelled a trend.) The MCs that Joey really wanted had turned him down, so on the advice of a friend he sought out Jackson. He wasn't actually an MC, but he managed the well-known Bronx MC and DJ Grandmaster Caz, then known as Casanova Fly. At the moment Robinson opened the door, Hank was making pizza, but more important, he was singing along to a practice tape Caz had recorded. Robinson liked what he heard and requested an audition, which meant having Hank Jackson rap along to a tape of "Good Times" while sitting in the back seat of Robinson's Oldsmobile, parked out front. Another amateur rapper, Guy "Master Gee" O'Brien, then walked by, heard the commotion, and wanted in. Now the two of them were rhyming in the Olds. Across the street, Michael Anthony "Wonder Mike" Wright stopped practicing his guitar to find the source of the muffled bass line that just wouldn't quit. Moments later, he squeezed into the car and he, too, was rapping along. With no more room in the Olds, they drove to Robinson's house to perform for "the Queen," as some came to call Mrs. Robinson. That Friday night, the Sugar Hill Gang was formed, and the next Monday, "Rapper's Delight," hip-hop's first hit record, was born.[17] 🔊

In the world of hip-hop, a "biter" is a plagiarist, someone who steals another's creative work. Hank Jackson's appropriation of Caz's words—really, his identity—may well be the most stunning and infamous example of biting in the history of hip-hop. After being introduced by Wonder Mike as "my man Hank," Jackson then calls himself Casanova Fly, the street name of the man who employed him as manager. Later in the song (11:19 in the full-length version), Hank has the audacity to relate a piece of advice his father purportedly gave him: "Whatever you do in this lifetime, you never let an MC steal your rhyme."

The situation was complicated by the fact that Hank had sought and received Caz's blessing to use some of the rhymes from that practice tape. Moreover, neither of them knew what would happen next. But given what did happen, the anger that remains with many in the hip-hop community is understandable. "To this day," Disco Wiz wrote thirty years later in his autobiography, "when I hear Hank spit those lyrics, I feel sick to my stomach."[18] What happened is that the song blew up. Given that rap was familiar to few outside the New York area, its success was remarkable. It rose to number four on the R&B chart and 36 on the pop chart, and even higher in Canada and England. It was selling 75,000 copies a week; millions overall. Radio DJs had to beg listeners to stop calling in with requests for the song, even though many would play it—all fifteen minutes of it—twice in a row. The hoopla generated mountains of money, but not a cent for Caz, nor for any DJ, nor, at least at first, for the composers of "Good Times."[19] But the millions of fans who loved "Rapper's Delight" knew nothing of the biting and the financial inequities, and probably never wondered why one of the MCs called himself Hank *and* Casanova Fly in the same song. Nor could they know how this song would change the future of hip-hop DJing.

THE ADVENTURES OF GRANDMASTER FLASH AND THE ORIGINS OF TURNTABLISM

DJs played virtually no role in the birth of recorded hip-hop. Yet on the streets and in the clubs, the DJs ran the parties, and the biggest names still had star power. The continued fame of these stars helps explain a few otherwise inexplicable absurdities—for example, that the best-known DJ of the time never played on many of the records that bear his name. The records may say "Grandmaster Flash and the Furious Five" on the releases of "Superrappin'" (1980), "Freedom" (1980), "The Birthday Party" (1981), and "The Message" (1982), but Flash did no more than "pace the studio like a coach" when these were being recorded, as Jeff Chang notes.[20] Flash, however, was not shut out completely, and in 1981, Sylvia Robinson granted his request to put out a solo record on her Sugar Hill label. Here's how Flash tells it: "After months of standing around the studio, letting live musicians play what I could be mixing on two turntables, and showing the engineers how to mix everybody's voice so the record sounds right, I finally got my own record. Finally got to punch-phase, cut, cue, spin back, rub, and zuka-zuka on wax."[21]

The result was "The Adventures of Grandmaster Flash on the Wheels of Steel," the first commercially produced solo DJ record, released by Sugar Hill Records in 1981. ◐ As Flash has emphasized, "Adventures" was a performance, not a studio creation. "When we decided to do it, Sylvia had to fly me and Melle Mel in, because we were on tour, we had one day to get it done and get back on the road. It had to be done live, because if I couldn't do it live, I wouldn't fake it to the people. So I might have taken three or four takes, but if I got one cut wrong, I wanted the tape rolled back from the beginning. I didn't want to punch [i.e., edit] it. I felt good about the record."[22] Flash had been performing it that summer, so it was ready to go when he got the call from Robinson. Among other places, he performed it in Manhattan when he and his Furious Five opened for the Clash (we'll hear more about this notorious concert later). One reviewer described the largely white audience as "bewildered" by the sight of a "single black man using nothing but two [possibly three] record players amid the cacophony."[23]

The presence of a DJ is clear from the first second of "Adventures." (See Figure 3.4 for a breakdown of how Flash incorporates and manipulates the different records.) Flash starts out by playing the opening of "Monster Jam," a 1980 collaboration between Spoonie G and The Sequence: "You say one for the trouble, two for the time, come on girls, let's rock that." But it takes five seconds for Flash just to get past "You say": he pulls the record back and releases it, and then does it again and again. Out of these two words he creates a rhythm and melody of his own (notice how the fourth "You say" is lower in pitch than its neighbors), and only after the seventh time does he let the full phrase spool out. We may not be able to see him, but we know without a doubt that what we are hearing was created by the hand of a DJ, fingertips lightly pressing down on the vinyl. ◐

While the opening sample makes it clear that a DJ is at work, the next record leaves no doubt about who that DJ is. The record is "Rapture," the 1980 hit by

Time	Record	Manipulation
0:00–0:10	Spoonie G and The Sequence, "Monster Jam" (1980)	Repeats "You say"
0:10–0:20	Blondie, "Rapture" (1980)	Repeats "Flash is fast"
0:20–0:25	"Monster Jam"	
0:25–0:34	Chic, "Good Times" (1979) (break)	Scratches
0:34–0:50	Incredible Bongo Band, "Apache" (1973)	Scratches
0:51–1:18	Queen, "Another One Bites the Dust" (1980)	Cuts up the first three notes (0:51–0:56); Scratches (1:05–1:18)
1:18–2:14	"Good Times" (break)	Cuts up bass line and string hit (1:51–1:56)
1:34–1:51	Grandmaster Flash and the Furious Five, "Freedom" (1980)	Cuts up "Grandmaster, cut faster"
2:09–2:44	Grandmaster Flash and the Furious Five, "The Birthday Party" (1981)	Scratches it over "Good Times" (2:09–2:14)
2:30, 2:34, 2:38	"Good Times" (break)	Cuts the word "Good" into "Birthday Party"
2:44–4:03	"Good Times" (break)	Scratching (3:23–3:28)
2:52–3:23	"Freedom"	Cuts in introductions of the Furious Five and their zodiac signs
3:33–4:03	The Hellers, "Life Story" (1968)	
4:03–4:33	Sugar Hill Gang, "8th Wonder" (1980)	Stabs (4:03–4:07)
4:26–7:10 (end)	"Good Times" (break)	Scratches it over top "8th Wonder" (4:26–4:34)
4:43–5:08	"Good Times"	Uses a second copy of "Good Times" to double and triple the handclaps
5:19–5:24	Unknown source, "Flash Gordon" announcement	
5:24–7:10 (end)	Unknown source, MC call and response with crowd	
5:57–6:01	"Good Times" (break)	Cuts in "Good"
6:02–6:05	Unknown source, "Hey Bro…"	
6:05–6:09, 6:14–6:18	"Good Times" (break)	Scratching
6:27–6:44	"Good Times" (introduction)	Loops 4 bars from introduction (guitar + piano)
6:31, 6:32, 6:34	"Good Times" (break)	Cuts in "Good"
6:59–7:01	"Good Times" (introduction)	Stabs
7:01–end	"Good Times" (introduction)	Two bars from introduction, then fade

Figure 3.4 "The Adventures of Grandmaster Flash on the Wheels of Steel."

the group Blondie. In it, lead singer Deborah Harry raps about guitar-eating Martians, Subarus, and Grandmaster Flash, among other things. Not long before the group cut the record, Harry saw Grandmaster Flash spin—an encounter that inspired her to record the line, "Flash is fast, Flash is cool."[24] This is the line Flash repeats several times early in his "Adventures."

After "Monster Jam" reappears for a few more seconds comes a fragment of a song that we'll hear more than any other in the seven-plus minutes of the Grandmaster's adventures. Yes, it is Chic's "Good Times." Flash scratches it, using both the back-and-forth baby scratch and the forward stab, a forceful staccato scratch with a silent backspin. He also loops the "Good Times" fragment, cuts it up, doubles and triples the electronic handclaps, and punches bits of it—usually the single word "good"—into other songs. But why did Flash choose to spotlight "Good Times," a song that, after "Rapper's Delight," might seem to have been played out? Was it because he had been cutting it up at his live gigs at the time, and had it ready to go when Sylvia Robinson called him in on a moment's notice?[25] Was it a reference to "Rapper's Delight," the biggest hit on the Sugar Hill label, and thus a gesture of respect to Robinson? Or was it a rebuke of the Queen, a display of what a DJ—as opposed to the house band that sidelined him—could do with the song? Maybe it was all of the above. But note that he used "Good Times" and not "Rapper's Delight," and that the Sugar Hill Gang song he did use, "8th Wonder," is an obvious reworking of the 1979 song, "Daisy Lady" by 7th Wonder. Flash may have thought it was politic to include some Sugar Hill Gang, but he didn't go out of his way to highlight their originality.

The first appearance of "Good Times" leads seamlessly into the most famous break of all, "Apache," which, other than the addition of a bar of sixteenth-note baby scratches, Flash largely leaves alone. Then comes the most brilliant section of the whole piece. Flash stutters a deep bass line in repetitions of three and then two notes, in a kind of instrumental response to his manipulation of "You say" in the opening. Given that he had just played "Good Times," we assume that he has returned to the Chic passage. But this bass line isn't quite the same— it has a two-note pickup, its contour is slightly different, and drums have replaced the electronic handclaps. It's actually the British group Queen, and the bass line is from the opening of their 1980 song "Another One Bites the Dust." After two bars, Flash joins the band, scratching along with the bass. In the Queen song, a crescendo—what sounds like a tape of a piano note being played backwards—leads to the first verse. But Flash has something else in store for us, and the climax of the crescendo is met, not by Queen's Freddie Mercury singing the first verse, but by Chic's singers calling out "Good times!"

When Flash first played "Good Times" it was as if he reached into his top hat and pulled out a rabbit—impressive, though only mildly surprising. He then reaches back into the hat and pulls out what we thought would be another rabbit—but this time it's a Guinea pig. He holds the animal in front of us, makes sure we can all see it, and then, with a quick wave of his hands, we suddenly realize that we're looking at the original rabbit. "Good Times" has turned into "Another One Bites the Dust" has turned back into "Good Times." We can read a sly commentary into this section, too. Much more effectively than could be done with words, Flash demonstrates just how similar the two bass lines are, perhaps suggesting that Queen, whose song came out while "Good Times" was still popular, was biting more than just dust.

Spinning ahead to about the midpoint of the track, we now hear Flash reach deep into his crates for what is the oldest, oddest, and most obscure song in the mix: The Hellers's "Life Story," from the 1968 album, *Singers ... Talkers ... Players ... Swingers ... & Doers*. In the fragment we hear on "Adventures," a man with a nasal inflection reminiscent of George Bush the Elder tells a group of children his life story, which began in Anamoose, North Dakota. The words don't seem to have any particular significance to Flash; rather, he was probably showing off his crate-digging skills by playing a record very few people had even heard of. Perhaps he also enjoyed the incongruity of dropping the voice of an obviously unhip man talking to children amid the raucous music, whoops, and chants that come before and after it. In any case, he seems not to take it very seriously. Before the man can finish his story, Flash cuts in with a series of stabs using the horns from the Sugar Hill Gang's "8th Wonder," noisily interrupting the gentle North Dakotan.

In the remaining three minutes, no new songs are introduced, only brief spoken-word fragments. One of these fragments is "Hey bro, I got something could blow your mind, man," which could have come from an album of the drug-addled comedy routines of Cheech and Chong. More notably, we hear another reference to Flash. At 5:19 the plummy voice of an old-time radio or television announcer intones, "The Official Adventures of Flash. . . ." This is an obvious reference to Flash Gordon, the fictional hero of comic books, radio, TV, and film. But in *these* "Adventures," it is DJ Flash who is the hero.

"Good Times" returns once again, and dominates the final two-and-a-half minutes of "Adventures." Once again, Flash uses it to his best advantage, looping, cutting, stabbing, and punch-phrasing. One new technique is introduced, too. Starting at 4:43, the handclaps in "Good Times" mysteriously multiply, sometimes doubled, sometimes tripled. Flash most likely managed this by switching back and forth between "Good Times" and a second copy of it playing slightly behind it on a second turntable. Amid this impressive demonstration we hear the general buzz of crowd noise punctuated by whoops and yells, as well as a call-and-response between an MC and a crowd—a party has erupted. Some of these sounds are part of the song "8th Wonder," which, like many early hip-hop records, was intended to sound like it had been recorded live at a local jam. And in this tradition, Flash adds to the hubbub, pressing one of his MCs (perhaps Melle Mel) to command: "Everybody say ho!" "Say disco!" "All the ladies in the house say ow!" "Everybody scream!" and so on. This doesn't seem to have been borrowed from a preexisting record, so it may well be that Flash organized this in the studio, or perhaps it was added later. The revelry continues as the music fades, giving the sense that we just left an all-night party in progress where Flash was basking in the adulation of thronged Bronxites, as he had been doing for years.

"Adventures" may *sound* like it's the collective creation of a DJ, MC, and partygoers, but it was the product of one person, working alone; and herein lies its real significance. Hip-hop DJs had always worked collaboratively, and their role had always been to serve the needs of dancers or MCs. "Adventures" represents a radical break from the status quo and presents a new role for the hip-hop DJ: that of self-sufficient artist. Although the term "turntablism" only came into wide use in the 1990s, the concept of DJing as a distinct art and the DJ as a distinct category of artist had existed before that, and we can see its origins here. We can also see how "Adventures" looks forward to digital sampling and the emergence of the hip-hop producer. Many of the techniques Flash uses here were later replicated in the digital realm when producers started looping and chopping snippets of recorded sound; we might even retrospectively call "Adventures" a work of *analog* sampling. In response to being dominated by MCs and relegated to a secondary role within hip-hop, Flash created a world in which DJs served no one but themselves. "The Adventures of Grandmaster Flash on the Wheels of Steel" may have been the personal statement of a single DJ, but we can also hear it as the DJs' Declaration of Independence.

DJs GO DOWNTOWN (AND ACROSS THE POND)

Although hip-hop was known in nearby Harlem, it was largely a Bronx phenomenon until "Rapper's Delight" hit in 1979. Even in downtown Manhattan, hip-hop was a mystery to most, more rumor than reality. Consider a small item in the July 1978 issue of *Billboard* magazine concerning a record shop near Times Square. The author, Robert Ford, Jr., who later became an important hip-hop producer, notes, "a funny thing has been happening at Downstairs Records." He continues:

> The store, which is the city's leading disco product retailer, has been getting calls for obscure R&B cutouts such as Dennis Coffey's "Son of Scorpio"

on Sussex, Jeannie Reynolds' "Fruit Song" on Sussex, and the Incredible
Bongo Band's "Bongo Rock" on Pride. The requests, for the most part,
come from young black disco DJs from the Bronx who are buying the
records just to play the 30 seconds or so of rhythm breaks that each
disk contains. The man responsible for this strange phenomenon is a
26-year-old mobile DJ who is known in the Bronx as Cool Herc.[26]

Although Kool Herc had been rocking parties for years by this time, in
Manhattan he was just one of a group of "black disco DJs" from the outer
boroughs. In our age of instantaneous information, it's amazing to think that
hip-hop could stay under the radar for nearly five years, attracting little more
than a one-column piece noting it as a "strange phenomenon."

Of course, "Rapper's Delight" changed that. Soon, millions across the globe
knew rap. But the song, which involved no turntables, did little to spread the art
of the hip-hop DJ south of the Major Deegan Expressway. Nor did DJs themselves do much toward that end. Although many of them had been scouring
Manhattan record stores for years, they tended to take their vinyl home and
keep it there, spinning it within their small fiefdoms. It was, in fact, the downtown hipsters who did the most to bring hip-hop south. Nile Rodgers, Chic's
guitarist and co-composer of "Good Times," was actually introduced to the
music he unintentionally influenced by two rockers, Deborah Harry and Chris
Stein of the group Blondie. "It was like the end of 1979, beginning of 1980,"
Rodgers remembers. "Debbie and Chris . . . said 'Hey Nile, you gotta come up
to a hip-hop with me,' which is what they called it. They said 'a hip-hop' and
when you went to a hip-hop, you'd go to some space . . . and a bunch of kids
would take it over with boomboxes, or sometimes they'd even have a proper
mobile DJ."[27]

Deborah Harry had learned about this music through a Brooklyn-born graffiti artist and occasional MC named Fab 5 Freddy. Freddy's place in hip-hop
history is assured for many reasons. Most broadly, he was instrumental in
bringing graffiti artists, MCs, DJs, b-boys and b-girls together, in the process,
promoting the idea of hip-hop as a four-pillared cultural phenomenon. He was,
in the positive sense of the word, a fixer. He introduced Bronx hip-hoppers to
downtown hipsters, visual artists to musicians, foreigners to locals. Moreover,
Freddy, despite not being a DJ himself, was a catalytic figure in the early history
of hip-hop DJing, and for these unlikeliest of reasons:

- He brought singer Deborah Harry to a party
- He encouraged filmmaker Charlie Ahearn to turn his talents to hip-hop
- He took English impresario Ruza Blue to a roller-skating rink
- He met French journalist Bernard Zekri and tried to rap in French.

The first I have already mentioned. Fab 5 Freddy, an unofficial liaison between the hip-hop world and the downtown rock/punk scene, took Deborah Harry to a Grandmaster Flash gig. She was deeply impressed and immortalized her experience in Blondie's 1980 record, "Rapture," with the lines, "Fab 5 Freddy told me everybody's fly / DJs spinnin,' I said 'My, my' / Flash is fast, Flash is cool." Flash, as we know, was flattered enough to mix "Rapture" into his "Adventures." More important was the exposure Blondie provided for Flash and for hip-hop in general. Between 1978 and 1980, Blondie was huge, scoring number-one hits across the world with "Heart of Glass," "Call Me," and "The Tide is High." Even "Rapture," for all of its weirdness, reached number one on the American pop charts, meaning that countless people came to know Flash's name, many of whom may never have encountered hip-hop otherwise.

Freddy's connections also gave Flash the chance to be on television and in film. When Blondie shot the video for "Rapture" in 1981, Flash was supposed to be shown behind the turntables, but on the day of filming he was missing in action. Freddy's friend and fellow graffiti artist Jean-Michel Basquiat took Flash's place. Flash didn't make the same mistake when filmmaker Charlie Ahearn invited him to be part of *Wild Style*, a film about hip-hop that Freddy had urged Ahearn to make, and a second reason for his influence on hip-hop (and DJing in particular).[28] Released in 1982, *Wild Style* is widely praised as the best film ever made on hip-hop, one that truly captures, as Jeff Chang puts it, "the ferocious energy, the feverish call-and-response, the phantasmic sense of possibility present in a hip-hop moment."[29] Its authenticity is attributed to the participation of many of hip-hop's pioneers; this was not the celluloid equivalent of "Rapper's Delight." As Charlie Chase pointed out, "there were no actors. Whoever was DJ-ing was a DJ. There was a graffiti writer in the movie, and he was a graffiti writer."[30] Chase, who appeared in the film, was just one of several DJs: DJ AJ, Grandmaster Flash, GrandWizzard Theodore, Grandmixer D.ST, and Tony Tone also had screen time. Flash takes part in a key scene toward the end of *Wild Style*, where he spins records (using not two, but *three* turntables) in a cramped kitchen while an implacably cool Freddy looks on through his trademark black sunglasses. He opens with the now familiar line, "The official adventures of . . . Flash" before mixing and scratching a beat. The scene is intercut with graffiti artist Lee Quiñones and a large team of helpers preparing an abandoned amphitheater for the film's climactic jam, where all the elements of hip-hop come together. ◑ Although *Wild Style* was not a huge commercial success, it exposed the art of the hip-hop DJ to a broader audience, and promoted the careers and reputations of the DJs who appeared in it. It also serves as a time capsule, offering a glimpse of a rarely recorded period of DJ history.

Film and television have been crucial for the broad dissemination of hip-hop, and *Wild Style* was just the beginning. A brief scene in the 1983 film

Flashdance, for example, helped transform b-boying into a global phenomenon. For DJs, the 1983 video to Herbie Hancock's "Rockit," the 1992 film *Juice* (which features a dramatic battle scene), and the 2001 documentary *Scratch* inspired three different generations of teenagers to seek out turntables.

We'll get to "Rockit" in a moment, but first let's return to Fab 5 Freddy. Freddy's influence also arose out of his friendship with Ruza Blue, or Kool Lady Blue, as Freddy and then everyone else came to call her. In 1981, the 21-year-old Englishwoman arrived in Manhattan, drawn by the New York punk scene. She first encountered hip-hop when Malcolm McLaren, former manager of the Sex Pistols and her employer at the time, encouraged her to check out a New York concert he was organizing for Bow Wow Wow, a New Wave act that he had put together a year earlier. "You need to come and check out the opening act," he told Blue. "I have this crazy act on before Bow Wow Wow."[31]

The crazy act was Afrika Bambaataa, whom McLaren had met during a recent visit to the Bronx. It was Bambaataa who introduced McLaren to hip-hop and inspired him to create "Buffalo Gals" with English producer Trevor Horn in late 1982, a track that in turn introduced scratching to British audiences and gave us the oft-sampled phrase, "All this scratchin' is making me itch."[32] But this came later; back in 1981, Ruza Blue took McLaren's advice and saw Bambaataa, who was joined by the b-boy group the Rock Steady Crew and Fab 5 Freddy. Her impression of that concert, held at The Ritz in the East Village on September 15, 1981, remains vivid. Here is how she recently recounted the experience:

> The sound and look of the show was very tribal and new—from the DJ who was ripping a mad selection of records apart, isolating beats and breaks and mashing them up to the b-boys spinning on their heads and dancing in ways previously unknown to man! The vibe was very funky, very fresh sounding, very DIY like Punk. I couldn't believe the spectacle . . . my eyes froze . . . what on earth was all this?! I had to get involved. I had no idea it was called Hip Hop at the time![33]

She introduced herself to Freddy after the show, and was soon accompanying him to Disco Fever in the Bronx to continue her hip-hop education. "I'd go up there and I'd be the only white face in the club, and that was wild, and I thought, 'Oh my god, I've got to bring all of this downtown.'"[34]

Blue started at Negril, a tiny East Village reggae club, where for four months she hosted a weekly event called "Wheels of Steel." Inspired by her experience at the Bow Wow Wow concert, she brought together the punk and hip-hop worlds: members of the Clash might be hanging out while watching the Bronx's finest hip-hop artists. She even managed to re-create the opening act that had made such an impression on her, bringing Bambaataa, the Rock Steady Crew, and Fab 5 Freddy to the basement club. DJ Jazzy Jay, who often performed with Bambaataa, saw their role not just as entertainers, but educators, introducing the downtown crowd to the uptown ways: "We was schooling them on our art-form. Bam would put these breaks on and drive them wild and then I'd get on the turntables and start cutting shit up and they'd be losing their minds. MCs get on, that was it. B-boys take the floor, it was like, yo!"[35] Blue's nights at the Negril were numbered, however—her overcrowded parties violated Fire Department codes, and in February 1982 she was forced to leave. She briefly moved her party to another club, Danceteria, but was still searching for a site whose size and potential matched her ambitions.

She soon found what she was looking for:

One night I was hanging out with Fab Five Freddy, who mentioned this roller rink on the West Side called the Roxy. I immediately took a liking to the sound of it since it was called The Roxy (an old punk hangout in London) so we went over there to take a look. I found a huge cavernous disco-lit roller rink with a great sound system. In my mind I had hit the jackpot—it was love at first sight. Fred thought I was crazy and said I would never be able to fill the space, it was far too big. But in my gut I knew one day the scene would explode into the universe![36]

The Roxy, an 18,000-square-foot former truck warehouse, opened to great fanfare in 1979 and was considered New York's classiest, most exclusive roller rink. (This was when "classy," "exclusive," and "roller rink" could occupy the same sentence without irony.) Anna Quindlen wrote of the Roxy in a 1981 *New York Times* review of the city's rinks:

Inside, there are beautiful people. It is evident from their figures that skat-ing is good exercise. The women at the Roxy seem to be divided into two types: models with their makeup off and models with their makeup on. Mick Jagger has been to the Roxy. So have Glen Campbell, Bjorn Borg and Lee Marvin. Dustin Hoffman held his daughter's birthday party there. It is the kind of place where Richard Gere can slip in quietly and no one watches him much. Those who want to skate and feel extremely chic at the same time should try the Roxy.[37]

Saturday nights belonged to chic skaters, but Blue was able to secure the Roxy for Fridays, and for about eighteen months starting in June 1982, the rink became New York's premiere hip-hop gathering spot. On skate nights, the Roxy oozed elitism. "Most skaters agree that the Roxy is to roller skating what

Studio 54 was to disco," Quindlen wrote, invoking the ultra-exclusive club that had had its heyday a few years earlier. But Blue's parties, which started Friday at 11:00 p.m. and ended Saturday at 6:00 a.m., brought a different attitude. To avoid any confusion between the Friday and Saturday night incarnations of the Roxy, Blue's opening-night flyer noted, "No Skating Just Dance Your Pants Off."[38] Steinski, a DJ whose eclectic mixes from the 1980s influenced countless DJs, praised the inclusive vibe. "The crowd at the Roxy was marvelously mixed. There was a lot of people from uptown, there was a lot of people from down-town, there were foreign people." He contrasted the openness of the Roxy with the "elitist bullshit" of Studio 54, where "you'd have some chump at a velvet rope looking over the crowd trying to figure out who looked good enough to get in. At the Roxy, everybody got in." The crowd tended to be—or at least look—a bit rougher, and security was tight. "Oh boy, they frisked you," Steinski remembers. "They knew more about me than my doctor. They were taking shit away from people. They were taking guns, knives, bottles of whiskey. . . ."[39]

But once inside, the atmosphere was friendly and celebratory, encouraged by the banner hanging out front: "COME IN PEACE THROUGH MUSIC."[40] Afrika Bambaataa saw Blue's Friday night parties as embodying the ethos of his Bronx jams. "The Roxy was truly a world club . . . everybody just partying all together under one roof. And the wilder we was onstage, the wilder the crowd was and the more the different races started coming to see us. It did its job—a little peace, unity, love, and having fun."[41] Art school student Ann Marie Boyle, who came to have a small but important role in the downtown hip-hop scene, described the Roxy as a "full-on collision" of distinct neighborhoods and cul-tures. But as she remembers it, the collision was anything but violent: "It was a love story."[42]

Although the DJs had been moving into the shadows over the previous few years, Blue wanted them to be literally at the center of attention. "It was unusual at the time to place the DJ on a riser in the middle of the dance floor—they were usually relegated to the DJ booth out of sight. The MCs were definitely starting to dominate the scene, but not in my club—the DJ was still the rock star there."[43] Roxy's rock stars included Afrika Bambaataa, Afrika Islam, Grandmixer D.ST, GrandWizzard Theodore, and Jazzy Jay, and while they spun vinyl, MCs spun their tales, and b-boys and b-girls spun themselves. The graffiti artist Phase II, in one of his forays into music, described the action in his 1983 song "The Roxy": "Wheels of steel, the DJ's spinning all night long / Everybody's in the party rocking strong / Rapping, breaking, cutting, taking on the night / Roxy is the place to be, it's out of sight."[44] These Friday night parties lasted little more than a year, but had a lasting impact on hip-hop.[45] The Roxy residency showed that hip-hop, far from being a novelty act or one-hit wonder, was a complex culture of music, dance, and painting unlikely to disappear anytime soon.

Think of the Roxy as an incubator—it was a temporary home, but its warmth and nurturing environment allowed hip-hop to take flight.

In fact, in November 1982, a group of Roxy artists winged its way across the Atlantic Ocean. "The New York City Rap Tour," as it was called, brought Freddy, Bambaataa, D.ST, as well as b-boys, graffiti artists, MCs, and even a girls Double Dutch jump-roping team to England and France.[46] As a way to promote the tour, the record label Celluloid put out five records by members of the touring contingent. One these records was Fab 5 Freddy's "Change the Beat."[47] And this brings us to the fourth unlikely reason that Freddy played a key role in the development of the hip-hop DJ. The key was this: he had a lousy French accent.

THE STORY OF "AH" AND "FRESH"

In the early 1980s, French journalist Bernard Zekri was living in Manhattan just as hip-hop was exploding downtown. (At the time he was writing for the cultural magazine *Actuel*, and later became an important figure in French media.) A regular at Kool Lady Blue's "Wheels of Steel" night at Negril, he quickly immersed himself in the scene, befriending many important players, including, naturally, Fab 5 Freddy. With Kool Lady Blue, Zekri was planning the 1982 New York City Rap Tour and was given $18,000 by a French radio station to create five 12-inch singles all by artists active in the downtown hip-hop scene. The idea behind the singles was to promote the tour and introduce France to hip-hop; given the audience, Zekri insisted that one of the songs would be in French, which he himself would write. This was "Change the Beat," and he wrote it for none other than Fab 5 Freddy. To get the record made, Zekri contacted fellow Frenchman Jean Karakos, head of the New York–based record label Celluloid. Karakos, in turn, called bass player Bill Laswell and keyboardist Michael Beinhorn, who had recorded for Celluloid as the band Material. Karakos asked the two musicians to create the instrumental tracks for the records in time for November's Rap Tour.

"Change the Beat" spins a not entirely flattering tale about a character named Freddy, a skirt-chasing, Adidas-wearing P.I., or *detective privé*.[48] (The original title was "Une Sale Histoire," French for "A Dirty Story.") The real Freddy's dark sunglasses, trench coat, and hat suggested to Zekri a hip-hop version of a character out of the hardboiled detective fiction of Raymond Chandler. "He had a strange look," Zekri recalls.[49]

The recording session—held in Brooklyn's OAO studio and engineered by Martin Bisi—did not go well at first, at least according to Trilling and Zekri. "It became apparent very quickly," says Roger Trilling, Material's manager, "that Freddy was not much of a rapper."[50] At least not in French. "He didn't really work very hard on his French accent," explains Zekri. "At the end of the recording session, I thought, nobody in France is really going to understand him. In America it would be OK, but if we want to have a chance in France the lyrics have to be more understandable." They needed another cut, a B side that would play in France.

Trilling had an idea. "Let the girl try it," he suggested. "The girl"—who nearly thirty years later still remembers her annoyance at Trilling for calling her that—was Ann Marie Boyle, at the time Zekri's wife and a student majoring in fashion illustration at the Parsons School for Design.[51] ("She seemed like some girl out of a prep school," recalls Beinhorn. "I had no idea what she was doing hanging around with Zekri."[52]) So Zekri dashed off a variation on the original lyrics. Boyle, a self-described "club kid," was not a rapper, nor had she ever recorded before. But she had a good voice and spoke French. In fact, she had been coaching Freddy on his French, and knew Zekri's rhymes well. So she recorded her part in just a few takes, and with this B side, a new rap artist was born.[53] In honor of her session-salvaging, she came to be known as BeSide, a *nom de rap* bestowed on her by Grandmixer D.ST.

Fab 5 Freddy, it should be said, asserts that it was his idea to record Boyle. "What I had found in working with [her] to learn my lyrics was that she sounded

Figure 3.5 Fab 5 Freddy and BeSide, "Change the Beat" (1982).

really great," he explains. "She sounded really sexy, she had this breathy, sexy kind of tone to her voice." So instead of putting an instrumental version of "Change the Beat" on the B side (which would have been the normal practice), "I'm like, 'I want to put her on the B side of my record.'" When I told Freddy how Trilling, Zekri and others told the story his response was unequivocal: "Bullshit, bullshit, bullshit—that's totally fucking wrong! That was never how it went down. No one came to me and said, 'Put her on the other side of the record.' That was *me*."[54]

Whoever had the idea for the B side, what's more important is what ended up on it. "The track turned into a mélange," keyboardist (and co-composer) Beinhorn explains, as they mixed in "a lot of diverse elements to see what would stick."[55] Responsible for two of these "diverse elements" was Trilling, who had arrived on the scene after a long subway ride from the Manhattan offices of Elektra Records. Two seemingly inconsequential details of his day turned out to be of particular significance. One was that he happened to be reading a book on Japanese film directors on the subway; the other was that he had just come from a meeting with Bruce Lundvall, an Elektra executive. Trilling didn't speak Japanese, but he took the book to the vocal booth, and in his best impression of Toshiro Mifune—the actor known for his Samurai roles—loudly declaimed film titles from the appendix. "Everybody was falling over themselves laughing," he remembers. His fake Samurai Japanese pops up in "Change the Beat" sporadically after the first minute, and includes the titles "Broken Drum" and "History of Postwar Japan as told by a Bar Hostess."[56]

The Lundvall connection figures in at the end of the track. Lundvall, an influential record man whom Trilling affectionately describes as an "ultra-über-WASP Connecticut yacht kind of guy," had a standard response after listening to a new recording he particularly liked. So Trilling did another impression, recording a brief line through a vocoder, a piece of electronic equipment popular in hip-hop at the time for making voices sound robotic.[57] This utterance came to be the most important sentence in the history of hip-hop DJing: "Ah, this stuff is really fresh!"[58]

Actually, it's just the first and last words that are important to DJs. Every scratch DJ knows "ah" and "fresh," even if the source is unfamiliar—the distinctive timbres are etched into their neurons, instantly recognizable. The two words, excerpted from the final four seconds of the song, were quickly adopted by DJs. ◑ In 1984, for example, Mix Master Ice scratched "ah" on UTFO's "Roxanne Roxanne," while Davy DMX was "fresh" on "One for the Treble (Fresh)." In 1985, Kurtis Mantronik also scratched "fresh" on Mantronix's "Needle to the Groove" as well as "ah" (oddly enough, given the title) on "Fresh is the Word." That same year DJ Cheese, as part of the group Word of Mouth, recorded the classic ode to scratching, "King Kut," showcasing his skills using both words. And speaking of cheese, a nineteen-year-old Andre Young rocked "fresh" on the 1984 song "Surgery," an amusing wedge of electro that sounds quaint next to his later, harder-edged, and better-known work. Unusually for a DJ, he rapped about himself as well: "I'm Dr. Dre, gorgeous hunk of a man / Doing tricks on the mix that no others can." Although the song may now elicit chuckles from first-time listeners, it inspired many DJs back in its day—DJ Apollo and DJ Shadow, among others, have cited its importance to them as young artists.[59]

Over the years, the two words have appeared on well over one hundred different songs, whether scratched or digitally sampled.[60] Moreover, "ah" and "fresh" show up on nearly every battle record ever made. (These are records that excerpt various breaks, beats, vocal phrases, and sound effects and are used by DJs at parties, shows, and battles. As we'll see in Chapter 6, they play a significant role in hip-hop DJ culture.) Sonically, the two sounds are ideal for scratching. The vocoder imparts a distinctive timbre that helps it stand out. The sound attracted Grandmixer D.ST, who says it had "just enough grittiness to it—it was dirty but it cut through clean."[61] Moreover, each word has its own distinctive qualities. "Ah" has a sharp attack, or "tip," good for short, fast scratches; and at just over one second long, it has a generous decay, or "tail," making a whole host of other scratches possible. The combination of the two means that a DJ can demonstrate a huge variety of scratches on a single sound. "Fresh," because it starts with the "fr" sound, doesn't have as clean a tip, but because it can be broken down into three different components—the two different consonant sounds in the beginning and ending, and the vowel in the middle—it offers DJs even more possibilities for manipulation.

The two words have come to be universally known "standards," sounds that DJs often use as a basic ingredient in their work, whether practicing, spinning at a club, or battling, and act as a basis by which the scratching of different DJs can be compared.[62] Some DJs scratch them both equally, others prefer one over the other. The Japanese DJ Miyajima, something of a purist, told me that when he DJs he only ever uses one sound: "ah." "Fresh" he considers too complex.[63] Qbert, on the other hand, prefers "fresh" for that very reason, though he points out that even with "ah" there are "infinite ways of using it."[64]

But wait: How in the world did this track, rapped in French, punctuated by broken Japanese, and topped off with vocodered English, come to play such an important role in the lives of hip-hop DJs for decades to come? Why didn't it languish in obscurity? It probably should have. As bassist Bill Laswell says, "It meant nothing, to be honest." His whole attitude was simply, "Let's bang this out for Karakos."[65]

In part, the answer for its longevity is that two well-known DJs started playing the record. Afrika Bambaataa, always on the lookout for unusual records, got a copy directly from Boyle, and played it at his parties in the Bronx. Apparently he didn't think it was too strange: "My audience was used to hearing me play off-key stuff," says Bambaataa, who had been spinning music with an "international flavor" for years.[66] Grandmixer D.ST, the one who came up with the name BeSide, spun it for the huge crowds at the Roxy. The record was never a hit, but it attracted attention at important hip-hop hot spots. (The attention also led to a brief career in music for BeSide, who went on to record several more tracks for Celluloid.) But this local exposure wouldn't have been enough to ensure the record's immortality. The main reason that "Change the Beat," or at least four seconds of it, lives on to this day is that in 1983 a DJ extracted a single word—"fresh"—and scratched it on a song that turned out to be a cornerstone of turntable music.

"ROCKIT:" THE SCRATCH HEARD AROUND THE WORLD

Ask any hip-hop DJ who was between eight and eighteen in 1983 how they caught the bug, and you'll probably get a one-word answer: "Rockit." In Herbie Hancock's hit track, with scratches by Grandmixer D.ST, a generation of nascent DJs heard the future and wanted to be a part of it. "Rockit" was their moon landing.

"Outer space music," was Qbert's first impression. "I didn't know it was a record or anything—I just knew it was going *wheesht wheesht whusht*. I didn't know it was vinyl, I didn't know what the hell it was. I just thought it was . . . weird."[67] The impact of "Rockit" came not just from its sound, however. Millions came to know the song through the video, which played in heavy rotation on MTV during the summer of 1983, or through televised performances, especially the February 1984 broadcast of the Grammy Awards. ("Rockit" won for Best R&B Instrumental Performance. See Figure 3.6) Mix Master Mike had encountered scratching before—he heard it on Malcolm McLaren's "Buffalo Gals"—but he didn't know what it was until he saw "Rockit" on the Grammy broadcast. "Where is that sound coming from—*zigga zigga*? What is that sound? So one day I turn on the TV and I see Grandmixer D.ST live in concert with Herbie Hancock. Oh, *that's* where that *zigga zigga* sound comes from, it's that turntable moving back and forth. And then I knew—that's what I was going to be one day."[68]

Among the many who were deeply affected by seeing and hearing "Rockit," one of them went on to write this book. I was thirteen at the time—about the same age as Qbert and Mix Master Mike—and it was the first time I encountered scratching. I became aware of the song through the MTV video, created by Godley & Creme, known for their innovative videos in the 1980s. The "Rockit"

Figure 3.6 Grandmixer D.ST in a performance of "Rockit" on the 1984 Grammy Awards telecast.

video is a creepy montage of mannequin legs stork-walking through a house and doing the can-can while pale humanoids, all missing various body parts, jerk robotically and in some cases erotically. The only human in sight is Herbie Hancock, playing keyboards on a television that crashes to the ground at the end of the video. ◐ Countless people of my generation, who would never consider themselves fans of turntablism or hip-hop, know "Rockit," and through it discovered the source of "that *zigga zigga* sound." "Rockit" marked the point at which scratching entered the mainstream.

Grandmixer D.ST (who since 1989 has called himself DXT) was a multi-instrumentalist from a young age, playing drums, keyboards, and turntables. Well before he was tapped to perform on "Rockit," he had been a huge fan of Hancock, and often tried to imitate him on his synthesizer. "I wanted to be Herbie Hancock," D.ST says.[69] He made his name in 1982 after Kool Lady Blue hired him to spin at the Roxy, and through this high-profile gig he was offered a contract with Celluloid Records. His first release was 1982's "Grandmixer Cuts It Up," which features him on synthesizers but, for some reason, not on turntables. He followed up with several more tracks for Celluloid, including "Crazy Cuts" (1983), "Mega-Mix II (Why Is It Fresh)" (1984), and "The Home of Hip-Hop" (1985), all of which do, in fact, feature Grandmixer cutting it up.

In 1983, Tony Meilandt, a manager for jazz keyboardist and composer Herbie Hancock, reached out to Bill Laswell to help create a new sound for Hancock's next release for Columbia. Laswell proposed something unusual: incorporating turntables. Hancock agreed, so Laswell sought out a DJ, one "who could really play in time, like a drummer."[70] He didn't immediately think of D.ST, even though he was part of the Celluloid family and a drummer as well; instead, he asked Afrika Bambaataa for his advice. Bambaataa suggested DJ Whiz Kid. Whiz declined, and recommended his protégé DJ Cheese, but Laswell worried the record company executives wouldn't take the project seriously with someone named Cheese attached.[71] (Both men, by the way, went on to become champions in the early DJ battle scene, and Cheese, as I mentioned, later scratched "ah" and "fresh" on "King Kut.") Laswell then went with the obvious candidate, and in 1983 he arranged a session with D.ST on turntables, Daniel Ponce on percussion, Michael Beinhorn programming the drum machines, and himself on bass. D.ST was paid $350 for his services. Hancock did not play in the first session, which took place in Brooklyn, and only later added the keyboard parts in a California studio.

"Rockit" was created over a period of a few weeks, largely assembled part by part.[72] First Beinhorn programmed the drum machine patterns using a new Oberheim DMX, whose sound can be heard in hip-hop tracks by Run D.M.C. and Davy DMX as well as new wave songs by New Order and Eurythmics. ("I didn't really know how to program it," Beinhorn admits.) Next, Laswell played the bass, the main melody of which (starting at 0:26) was adapted from the vocal line in Pharaoh Sanders's 1966 jazz piece "Upper Egypt and Lower Egypt" (starting in 14:34).[73] Then D.ST recorded his scratches. According to Beinhorn, he used three records: the previously mentioned 1982 Celluloid track "Grandmixer Cuts It Up" (D.ST scratching himself!), an unidentified drum hit, and most prominently, "Change the Beat."[74] They picked "Change the Beat" through a process of trial and error, with D.ST auditioning several discs by scratching parts of them. "We're going through the records," he recalls, "and finally I put 'fresh' on. And they all went, 'Oh, that's it!' Everybody said, 'That's it, that's the sound.'"[75] Once they settled on his records, he didn't take long to record his part. As Beinhorn explains, "He had very specific ideas about what he wanted to do and where he wanted to use the various sounds he scratched."[76] Wrapping up this first session, Daniel Ponce added three separate tracks using a set of Cuban double-headed *batá* drums. Beinhorn and engineer Bisi then took the tape to a studio in Manhattan, adding effects, some lines spoken through a vocoder, and a sample that very few people know is in the mix. The sample is a single guitar chord from Led Zeppelin's "I Can't Quit You Baby," a version recorded in 1970, but only released in 1982 on the album *Coda*. It first appears in its new home heard five seconds into the song, after the opening drum machine line. At the time, sampling was a time-consuming, difficult process, but that single chord added a nice bit of contrast to "break up the groove," which was largely electronic.[77]

A few weeks later, Hancock added his keyboard parts, recorded on three different synthesizers, at El Dorado studios in Los Angeles with engineer Dave Jerden. Although "Rockit" is known as a Herbie Hancock song, his participation was actually rather slight. For the most part he repeats a very simple line—two notes, pause, two notes, pause, then four notes and a brief tag. According to Bill Laswell, this line is a variation of a melody from "Chameleon," a track from Hancock's groundbreaking 1973 jazz fusion album *Head Hunters*, an album which, coincidentally, Bruce Lundvall—inspiration for the famous line in "Change the Beat"—helped bring to Columbia.[78] Only in the last forty-five seconds of the five-and-a-half minute studio album version does Hancock cut loose.

After the session with Hancock, Laswell and Beinhorn stopped at an electronics store on the way to the airport, and tested some speakers by playing the newly finished "Rockit" on a cassette. When the song was over, Laswell reports that he "felt a weird chill" and turned around to see a crowd of kids standing behind him, transfixed by what they had heard. Up until that point he had no idea that "Rockit" might be popular. "We just thought it was avant-garde stuff."[79]

It was D.ST's scratches that made "Rockit" more than just "avant-garde stuff," and although his part was just one of many, it would never have been a breakthrough without his participation. As the turntablist and battle champion Rob Swift puts it, Grandmixer D.ST "is a vital part of the song, and if you take his scratches out then something's missing. I always knew the turntable was a musical instrument, but to me he was the first one to prove it."[80] "Rockit" is a vehicle for the rhythm section—and in particular D.ST, who is almost always in the foreground and gets a minute-long solo in the middle of the track. D.ST's scratches are executed both vigorously and cleanly—he practiced incessantly in order to isolate only the sounds he wanted and eliminated any hint of a backspin, a telltale sign that a record was being manipulated. In fact, some of his fellow DJs doubted that he was using a turntable at all, and assumed he created the sound digitally with a sampler. "Jam Master Jay, bless his heart, was backstage at the Grammy Awards [before the performance of "Rockit"] and he comes up to me and goes, 'You didn't do that, you used the [E-mu] Emulator.'"[81] D.ST was, in a sense, transcending the very turntable-ness of the turntable, making it sound like something altogether different, to his ears the cuíca (sometimes called *guica*), the Brazilian frictional drum that produces a piercing squeak. In addition to the unique timbre and clean execution of the scratching, there is enough rhythmic and timbral variety to keep the listener's interest for more than five minutes. Sometimes he scratches straight sixteenth notes like a drum fill, sometimes he throws a few flourishes in on the off-beats, sometimes he imitates military-sounding drum rudiments.

Of course, the success of the song also depends on how D.ST's part fits into the broader texture. For the first twenty seconds, the turntable is part of the rhythm section, and the young D.ST is on an equal standing with the more seasoned musicians on the record. The rough, unpitched white noise of the scratches cuts through, demanding to be heard, but it also nicely complements the clear pitches and sharp attacks of the *batá*. As DJ Johnny "Juice" Rosado marvels, "It's like a synthesis of man and machine, because you don't know what's making what sound. And that's what makes it so beautiful."[82] Despite the fact that the instruments were recorded separately, there is an organic feeling to the song. (Credit for this goes to the producers, Beinhorn and Laswell.) The leisurely keyboard line balances out the busy scratching and drumming, and when the keyboard and turntables groove together at the end, we can easily imagine that the players are in the same room, feeding off each other's energy. (Later, that's exactly what they did—a newly formed "Rockit Band" toured the world in the wake of the song's popularity.) In other words, "Rockit" is a success not simply because of the scratching, but because it is a good song, effectively arranged and well performed.

Let's return to the link with "Change the Beat"—the "fresh" connection, so to speak. Listen closely to the album version of "Rockit," and you'll realize that you never hear the word fully articulated. For the most part, we hear "reh," without the beginning "f" or final "sh" sounds. ◑ According to D.ST, this was due to the state of mixer technology. At that time, crossfaders were designed to execute smooth and gradual transitions from one turntable to the other, meaning that if D.ST wanted to play the whole word "fresh" and then cut the sound off completely for the backspin he would have had to move the crossfader almost the complete length of the slider's track, perhaps four inches. This may not sound like a great distance, but it was too great to traverse as fast as D.ST wanted, especially given how stiff faders typically were at the time. So in order to cut as fast as he did, he had to position the crossfader closer to the middle, which would have decreased the distance he had to move but also truncated the word "fresh." (In the 1990s, new types of crossfaders made it possible to cut a sound off much more quickly, a technological advance that helped revolutionize turntable technique.) So given that D.ST was scratching less than a full word, one from a fairly obscure record at that, it seems odd that "fresh" (and "ah") would have caught on after the release of "Rockit." How would anyone not involved in the recording recognize the source of D.ST's scratches? "Word of mouth. This became the talk of the DJ world," D.ST explains, and eventually other DJs learned that D.ST was scratching "Change the Beat." Here an important difference between the album cut and the subsequent live performances comes into play. While we never hear a full "fresh" on the album, in the live performance at the 1984 Grammy Awards Ceremony (and in other concerts),

D.ST lets the word play in its entirety several times.[83] ◑ These live performances were seen by millions, and were probably better known and more
influential than the studio version. Keen-eared DJs listening to one of these
performances might well have discovered the source of D.ST's scratching.

"Rockit" was a modest hit in the United States, and sold even better abroad,
peaking in the top ten in several countries. The song garnered a Grammy, and
the video won several MTV awards. But "Rockit" did more than sell records; it
conferred upon the turntable both legitimacy and musicality. Legitimacy came
in large part through the figure of Herbie Hancock. Hancock was an influential
and highly regarded musician, having had a long and successful career as a
sideman with giants like Miles Davis and as the leader of his own groups. For a
musician of his standing to embrace scratching—something that most listeners
would not have even thought of as music—was to demand that it be taken seriously. (Hancock, of course, benefited as well, showing himself to be an innova-
tor up with the latest trends.) Hancock's presence also promised a high level of
musicianship, although it is the quality of the scratching and the arrangement
that truly stand out. Today, "Rockit" sounds a bit dated—the drum machine
and keyboard timbres have become sonic markers of the early 1980s. The significance of "Rockit," however, lies not in its timelessness, but in its timeliness.
It will always be associated with a time when musicians of various backgrounds
came together to create challenging, even experimental hip-hop, a period when
hip-hop, and hip-hop DJing, began to expand its horizons. ◑

* * * * *

In 1978, hip-hop was still little known beyond the borders of the Bronx and
nearby Harlem. DJs ran the show, though MCs were gaining more attention.
The music, born of records but created in real time, had yet to be committed to
vinyl. Hip-hop existed in the moment, and its natural habitat was the party,
whether it took place in a club, theater, community center, gymnasium, or playground. The deep influence of disco was still apparent, manifesting itself in the
DJs' choice of songs and the MCs' choice of outfits and choreographed moves.

A year later, with "Rapper's Delight," hip-hop had arrived. Stepping first out
of the limo, however, were the MCs. Some DJs remained famous, but their star
power was dimming. The influence of disco, too, was waning. It had been the
envied older sibling to hip-hop, the one with more money, better clothes, and
access to the best clubs. But then hip-hop met punk, and its encounter with the
downtown scene left it a bit embarrassed by the figure it had once tried to emulate. Consider the June 1981 New York shows in which Flash and his Furious
Five opened for the punk legends The Clash. Writing in the *Village Voice*, Robert
Christgau snidely remarked, "Their matching red soul-act suits (with piping for

contrast and green ribbons for unity) gave immediate notice that showbiz corn
was their vocation." The largely punk audience immediately loosed a barrage of
beer and derision, and the Bronx crew had to beat a hasty retreat. The next
night went over better. They reappeared, as Christgau reports, "wearing street
clothes instead of soul suits and making very clear that they'd been proving
their manhood in uptown facedowns since they were nine or so."[84] We can see
this moment as emblematic of a broader turning point. Hip-hop was starting
to change its image, attitude, and message. The rougher-hewn, stripped-down
look and sound embraced its gritty origins rather than seek refuge from it,
opening up space for groups like the Queens trio, Run-D.M.C., with their nearly
all-black outfits and their spare but powerful beats provided by Jam Master Jay.
In a 1984 homage to their DJ, "Jam Master Jay," they distinguish themselves
from groups like Flash's Furious Five; the rappers boast of themselves as "a crew
/ not five, not four, not three but two [MCs]," who recognize that "Jam Master
Jay is the one in charge."[85] ◐ The ascendancy of this new raw sound signaled
that the time had come for less flash and more clash.

By 1982, hip-hop had become firmly part of the downtown New York arts
scene. The expansion into those downtown Manhattan clubs opened up new
worlds. Mixing it up with the DJs were jazz and punk musicians as well as foreigners like Kool Lady Blue, Malcolm McLaren, and Bernard Zekri, all bringing
the art of the turntable to new audiences and new lands. Then came "Rockit" in
1983, firmly training the spotlight on the DJ, launching the careers of countless
DJs and introducing the world to a fresh new sound.

By 1983, hip-hop music was no longer solely an ephemeral phenomenon,
and had now been captured on millions of vinyl discs. Few of these actually
involved DJs, but a significant few of them displayed the mixing and scratching
of Bambaataa, D.ST, Flash, Theodore, and others. Although it was a difficult
lesson, DJs were learning that their artistry could exist apart from the MCs they
brought into the world, and with that realization they began to expand their art
into new realms.

Expansions: 1983–1989

Barely known beyond a few Bronx ZIP codes, hip-hop in 1973 hadn't yet been named, and few if anyone considered it—whatever exactly it was—to be a distinct art form. Ten years later, hip-hop was a household word and had an identity as a four-pillared artistic and cultural phenomenon combining music, dance, and painting. Millions of hip-hop records were funking up stereos across the world, while b-boying, MCing, and graffiti were known to millions more via newspapers, television, and film. Highbrow galleries featured the work of graffiti artists; national networks covered a b-boy battle staged outside Manhattan's venerable Lincoln Center.[1] Hip-hop was branching out, it was moving on up, and it was changing.

DJing was swept up in these changes as well, but the changes suggested conflicting possible futures for the art form. Some DJs were tremendously popular, holding forth at the hottest downtown New York venues or rocking audiences in Europe and Asia. The 1983 scratch vehicle "Rockit" made a star out of Grandmixer D.ST and showed the world that DJs could be instrumentalists in their own right. Yet these star DJs were outliers. More commonly, DJs of the early 1980s served to provide sonic support for MCs, at least those who weren't replaced by digital audiotapes. Introduced in 1987, the DAT (digital audio tape) allowed producers to record beats onto high-quality backing tapes, which could then accompany MCs in concert, leaving many DJs out of the loop completely. As hip-hop journalist Lefty Banks observed, "The DAT eliminated the cost and hassle of bringing DJs on tour, and let rappers bask solo in the glow of the marquee."[2] But back in the pre-DAT age of 1983 it was anybody's guess as to whether the art of the hip-hop DJ would flourish or fade.

In a sense the DJ both flourished *and* faded—faded from the mainstream, but flourished in the underground. These competing trajectories make it impossible to pull a single narrative thread through this part of our story. There is, however, a unifying theme: expansion. In the mid- and late 1980s, DJs expanded their territory and their technique. An emergent international battle culture pushed DJing to new heights of virtuosity. The art expanded geographically as well, taking root in Philadelphia, a city whose contributions to DJ history are both crucial and overlooked. And many DJs expanded their technique and territory simultaneously by moving into the recording studio and becoming producers, a type of hip-hop composer whose work is deeply influenced by the art of vinyl manipulation.

THE PHILADELPHIA STORY ●

Philadelphia is a city with a chip on its shoulder. Ever since 1800, when its ten-year run as the nation's capital ended, Philadelphians have felt that their hometown hasn't enjoyed its fair share of the spotlight. The city is home to one of the world's great orchestras, host of American Bandstand, and proud namesake of the renowned soul label Philadelphia International Records. Yet it's rarely considered the musical equal of New York, Chicago, or New Orleans. Nor are Philadelphia's contributions to hip-hop properly appreciated. In 1971, Philly was cited as "Graffiti Capital of the World," its aerosol artists—like Cornbread, generally considered the first of his kind—making names for themselves before many of the more famous Bronx figures were shaking Krylon cans.[3] (Coincidentally or not, the Krylon company was founded in Philadelphia.) Steppin,' a showy dance style, rose out of Philadelphia in the 1970s, and some claim that it anticipated and influenced New York's b-boying.[4] In 1979, the same year that "Rapper's Delight" was released, two Philly MCs made important contributions to recorded rap. Jocko Henderson's "Rhythm Talk" was the first rap disc made in the city, and proudly reflected its roots—the soulful strings of MFSB's "T.S.O.P. (The Sound of Philadelphia)" support Henderson's mellifluous rhymes—while Lady B's "To the Beat Y'all" was the first solo rap disc recorded by a woman.[5] Two other local MCs, Schoolly D and Will Smith, were among the first hip-hop artists outside New York to gain national prominence.

The real pride of Philly hip-hop is not its MCs, however, but its DJs. In particular, Philadelphia must be recognized for bringing into the world two of hip-hop's greatest and most influential DJs. As another accomplished DJ from the city of brotherly love, King Britt, puts it, "When you say Philly [you say] Cash Money and Jazzy Jeff."[6] Between the two of them, they won multiple world championship battles, introduced new techniques, inspired countless DJs to put needle to wax, and sold millions of records.

DJ Cash Money and DJ Jazzy Jeff were not the first or the only hip-hop spinners in the city. In the early 1980s they were just two of many locally renowned DJs who, like their counterparts in the Bronx, presided over small fiefdoms within the city. Philadelphia journalist A. D. Amorosi explained:

> Philly's world back in the late '70s and early '80s was separated into DJ and location. Cosmic Kev held down the fort for Mt. Airy and Germantown at the Wagner Ballroom; Lightning Rich had North Philly and the hall at Holy Souls High; Grandmaster Nell held South Philly. Cash Money was in Yeadon. If you were looking for Jazzy Jeff you went to the Wynne Ballroom. Other DJs like B Force, Disco Doc and E-Man Disco dotted the region.[7]

This is only a partial list of important early Philadelphia DJs: DJ Finesse, DJ Miz, DJ Tat Money, DJ Spinbad (a.k.a. the Original Spinbad), DJ Woody Wood, Grand Dragon KD, Grand Slam DJ Jam, and Too Tuff were also among the homegrown legends. Jeff and Cash have been quick to recognize the contributions of their colleagues. "There were people before us and there were people out [at the same time] who I think were just as good," Cash explains.[8] He cites Lightning Rich, for example, as one of the most original DJs of the era. "There was no telling what record he was gonna scratch or cut up. He was one of the top guys at the time."[9] Cash also gives enormous credit to Lady B. In addition to releasing "To the Beat Y'all" in 1979, Lady B was a radio DJ who brought hip-hop to Philly's airwaves before anyone else. She also championed local party DJs, promoting their careers beyond their neighborhoods. "I remember she seen me play at some club and asked if I could make a tape for her and she immediately put the tape over the air," Cash recalls. "I got so much response from that tape that she asked me to do another one and that's what made my reputation grow. She did the same for Jeff. She is the godmother to all of us."[10]

The biggest influence Cash Money cites, however, is Grand Wizard Rasheen. Around 1981, Cash started hearing cassette tapes of Grandmaster Flash imported from New York. He was amazed at the scratching and looping he heard, but he quickly discovered that there was a DJ living around the corner doing the same thing but, in his opinion, "to the tenth degree."[11] This was Rasheen, who ran a mobile DJ crew called Superbad Disco in Cash's Southwest Philly neighborhood. Cash often rode his bike straight to Rasheen's house after football practice to study with the older DJ. It was there that he learned a style that came to be known in Philadelphia as "rhythm scratching." Rasheen was inspired by Grandmaster Flash's practice of scratching one record along with an instrumental line playing on another, as when he scratches with Queen's

"Another One Bites the Dust" in "The Adventures of Grandmaster Flash." But instead of mimicking the exact rhythms of the track, Rasheen would throw in flourishes and faster notes, varying the phrases each time. As Cash explains, it's like "freestyling [in rap], ad-libbing with a scratch to an instrumental record."[12] What's also distinctive about rhythm scratching is the integrated use of the mixer; the complex patterns of rhythm scratching are really only possible when one can quickly cut the sound off and on through the various faders, especially the crossfader. ◐

Cash Money, who joined Superbad Disco as "the baby of the group," started DJing high school parties by 1984 or 1985, and was soon making a name for himself as a showman with superior technical skills. In 1987, he entered his first battle. It was not in Philadelphia, however—he claims the local DJs were "scared to battle me"—but in Manhattan at the 1987 New Music Seminar's Battle for World Supremacy. Given that it was considered (along with the DMC competition) one of the top venues for DJs seeking to prove themselves, it took some nerve for Cash to choose this for his debut. But as he says, "I'm a very competitive person, and I wanted to be known as the world's greatest DJ."[13]

When Cash arrived in New York he realized that the other DJs already knew about him, probably because of his mixtapes. "I guess my reputation was ahead of me 'cause [the other DJs] already knew everything about me and they were pretty much scared of me."[14] He's not boasting—in the first round he was introduced as the DJ "with the underground reputation that scares everybody."[15] He beat Jazzy Joyce—one of the only women battlers of the time—and then dispatched Easy G on his way to a memorable final round against L.A.'s Joe Cooley.

Cash went first, performing a riveting two-minute routine that manipulated the phrase "It's time" from Hashim's 1983 electro-funk song "Al-Naafiysh (The Soul)."[16] (In the 1980s, "It's time" became a standard scratching and mixing sample, and for a time was almost as popular as "ah" and "fresh" from "Change the Beat.") ◐ Cash thought he was "a shoo-in for winning"; that is, until Cooley came out with an inventive reworking of Kraftwerk's "Tour de France," also from 1983. "Yeah, he did that routine," recalls Cash, "and he made me say 'whoa.'"[17] Cash returned with Run-D.M.C.'s recent hit "Peter Piper" (1986)— itself a vehicle for New York DJ Jam Master Jay—schooling the audience on turntable technique using the lyric, "Not bad meaning bad, but bad meaning good!" Cooley went last, and whether it was a calculated gamble or his only remaining routine, he brought out his own take on "Al-Naafiysh." It's fascinating to compare the two. They both focus on the words "It's time," but whereas Cash tends play with whole words (e.g., rapidly spitting "It's time, It's time, It's time," or "It's It's It's It's It's…"), Cooley breaks down the individual words, often stuttering them, as in "ti-i-i-i-i-me," using the transformer scratch. Ironically, it is not Cash—as we'll see, one of the pioneers of the technique—that transforms more often. It's fair to say that Cooley's is the denser routine; there are more scratches per second on average than in Cash's performance, which has stretches where the beat is simply playing and few scratches can be heard. On the other hand, Cooley's routine ends abruptly, and not entirely satisfactorily. Yet both are astonishing performances. More than twenty years later, DJs continue to debate the judges' decision, though almost all agree: it was one of the greatest battles in the history of turntablism. 🜛

Even Cooley remembers it fondly. Writing in his blog in 2007, he explained,

> No matter where I go people ask me about this battle. . . . Honestly, it is totally amazing to me how many lives that were touched by this battle that took place 20 yrs ago! We both did our thang, DJ Cash Money and DJ Joe Cooley. The thing that is great is that Cash and I have remained friends over the years and it has been a pleasure to share such a moment in time. WE GAVE 'EM THE BEST BATTLE EVER! WE SET THE STANDARD THAT BATTLES ARE JUDGED BY! This was 20 yrs ago and no one had seen DJ's go at each other like this before, 2 minutes a piece 2 rounds. So I say thank you to all of you who have supported us over the span of our careers. It's HIP HOP HISTORY![18]

Cooley was right—the battle touched many lives, and became an important part of hip-hop history. Just consider a few examples of the lives it affected. A videotape of the battle found its way more than 7,500 miles to the east, and inspired a teenager in Okinawa. That teenager, DJ Ta-Shi, became one of Japan's top turntablists.[19] About 2,500 miles west of New York, in the San Francisco Bay area, the video blew the minds of two young virtuoso DJs, Qbert and Mixmaster Mike. "I saw that tape, and I'm like 'Goddamn, now that's some really advanced DJing right there,'" Qbert explains. "So Cash Money was my new superhero. That's how me and Mike would learn, watching the videotape. It was like . . . ," and here he makes the untranscribable sound of heads exploding. "That's how I got good, taking Cash Money's style."[20]

At the time of the battle, Cash Money was mostly known through his underground mixtapes. His name did end up on several commercial recordings, however. In 1986, he recorded "Scratchin' to the Funk," a one-take performance using Trouble Funk's "Pump Me Up"; he received $150, a limousine drive, and lunch for his trouble. This now-rare disc credits the team of Dr. Funnkenstein and Cash Money, though there was never a Dr. Funnkenstein. 🜛 Cash Money later hooked up with the Philly MC known as Marvelous, and the two released a popular single "Ugly People Be Quiet" in 1988 and a full album, *Where's the Party At?* that same year. The cover of the album shows Cash, standing front and center, surrounded by battle trophies and awards as he leans on the gold

Figure 4.1 Cover of *Where's the Party At?* (1988) by Cash Money and Marvelous. Used by permission of Phase One Communications.

turntables he won when he became DMC World Champion in 1988 in London and, as DMC founder Tony Prince put it, "took DJing to a whole new level"[21] (see Figure 4.1). ◑ This image points to his real legacy, not as any MC's DJ (Marvelous stands behind and to the side), but as one of the greatest turntablists of all time, one who inspired generations to come.

Cash Money was actually not the most famous DJ in Philadelphia at the time. That honor goes to DJ Jazzy Jeff, whose career took him to Hollywood with one of the biggest music (and later television and film) stars of all time. But he started in the same place as Cash Money, as a precocious teenaged DJ in Philadelphia. Jeff debuted on the tables at a neighborhood block party in 1979 before joining the Network Crew, a group from Southwestern Philly. Cash and Jeff came to know each other well. They even performed together occasionally, calling themselves "the Twins of Spin," and both often DJed parties at Central High School. The twins were hardly identical, however, with Cash's flashy routines, heavy with body tricks, contrasting with Jeff's technically impressive but less showy style. As Cash Money explains, "I had a completely different style to Jeff. He was basically very neat and precise and I have a bit more rhythm than he does and I was a bit faster."[22]

In 1985, Jazzy Jeff met Will Smith, a rapper with the Hypnotic MCs who performed as the Fresh Prince. Jeff's regular MC missed a gig, and Smith, who lived a few doors away, stepped in. "The chemistry was instant," remembers Jeff. "How did he know I was about to bring this record? How did I know his punchline was on the fourth bar and to drop out? Plus we were the biggest jackasses each other ever knew."[23] In 1986, the two released their first hit, "Girls Ain't Nothing But Trouble." It's a catchy, cheesy track that samples the theme from *I Dream of Jeannie*, and does little to showcase Jeff's talents. So when Jeff decided to enter the New Music Seminar that summer, the audience and the other competitors, who knew him as the DJ on "Girls," did not expect him to get very far. But they didn't know just how far his technique had advanced, and they didn't know about the secret weapon he carried with him in a little bag. "I came up there with my can of WD-40. Back then you get some WD-40 and shoot it into the crossfader and the crossfader's loose. So . . . I leaned over and took two shots to the crossfader cause it was gonna allow me to do the rhythm scratches and all of that. And then I started breaking records down with the syllables. After that everyone was just waiting to see what I was gonna do next."[24] What he did next was win the competition. 🔊

In the spring of 1987, DJ Jazzy Jeff and the Fresh Prince—this is how they billed themselves, with the DJ first—released their debut LP, *Rock the House*. One of the three singles was "The Magnificent Jazzy Jeff," a clever vehicle for the DJ. 🔊 DJs often say that they speak with their hands, and on this track Jeff manages to get a few words in edgewise against the voluble Fresh Prince. In the opening he "speaks" various words and phrases by playing them on disc. The bracketed words below are Jeff's.

Some DJs are [good]
Some DJs are [fresh]
Some DJs are even [def]
But here's a little something about my DJ
[The magnificent] Jazzy Jeff

The "good" and "fresh" samples should be familiar to us by now—they come from "Good Times" and "Change the Beat." Jeff later plays some classic breaks, including James Brown's "Funky Drummer," Herman Kelly's "Dance to the Drummer's Beat" (1978), and Billy Squier's "Big Beat" (1980); but he also cleverly slips in a line from the 1985 pop hit "Shout" by Tears for Fears—"I'm talking to you." Later in the song, the Fresh Prince directs Jeff to do some tricks, and he dutifully responds. One of his responses involves the appropriately named chirp scratch, which Jeff is generally credited with inventing.[25] The chirp involves pushing a record forward a short distance very quickly and cutting the sound off abruptly with the crossfader. Done in rapid succession, the scratch creates a high-pitched, rapid-fire effect that sounds, well, chirpy. A bit later in the song The Fresh Prince cleverly weaves a tale about his DJ transforming into an "autobot," which gives Jeff a chance to demonstrate the transformer scratch:

Now here's a story that should not be forgotten
About the day my DJ turned into an autobot
He got struck by lightning in an electrical storm
He got on the wheels of steel and began to transform

This was only one of the duo's DJ-centric tunes: later ones include "Jazzy's in the House," "D.J. on the Wheels," and "He's the DJ, I'm the Rapper," all from 1988, and "Jazzy's Groove" from the 1990 LP *And in this Corner....*

Given that Will Smith became one of the planet's biggest film stars, we may, in retrospect, be surprised that his DJ wasn't simply a sidekick. But Jeff always got top billing, and the cover of their most popular album, *He's the DJ, I'm the Rapper* (which went multi-platinum and won the first Grammy award for Best Rap Performance) also puts him in the spotlight. Jeff is pictured alone, with only Will Smith's outstretched arm in view; the rest of him can only be seen by turning the LP over or looking at the back of the CD booklet[26] (see Figure 4.2).

Figure 4.2 Cover of *He's the DJ, I'm the Rapper* (1988) by DJ Jazzy Jeff and the Fresh Prince.

We might interpret this cover image in a number of ways: as a nod to the historical primacy of DJs in hip-hop, as a gesture of humility and respect on the part of Smith, or perhaps as the recognition that, in Philadelphia, DJs came first.

When Smith left for Hollywood, Jeff followed, and there he did become a sidekick figure, though one with a role on a popular sitcom and a national audience. From 1990 to 1996, Jeff played the character Jazzy on forty-two episodes of *The Fresh Prince of Bel Air*. The two made a few more recordings, but when Smith started taking roles in major motion pictures, the duo split, and Jazzy Jeff moved back east to return to his roots. When asked why he didn't stay in Los Angeles, he replied, "Everything I got in life I owe in some way, some shape, some form to Philadelphia. And I'll be here till it's over."[27]

Our Philadelphia story is dominated by two names, Cash Money and Jazzy Jeff. The two of them put Philly on the DJ map by winning competitions on two continents, advancing turntable technique through rhythm scratching, chirping, and transforming, and by inspiring generations of DJs to come. But as I mentioned earlier, they were not the first important DJs in the city, and they were not the last. DJ Code Money, Schoolly D's partner, helped give gangsta rap its sound with his work in the mid- and late 1980s. King Britt, who heard Cash and Jeff play parties at Central High, later toured the world with the group Digable Planets (as Silkworm—King Britt is his real name), and then became a prolific producer and composer. Questlove (a.k.a. ?uestlove), is both a DJ and the drummer for the influential hip-hop group The Roots. Younger DJs include the internationally known club DJ Rich Medina, and the Illvibe Collective (made up of Statik, Panek, Phillee Blunt, Lil Dave, and Skipmode). The city is so rich with DJs, and takes so much pride in their accomplishments that in 2009 mayor Michael Nutter, himself a former DJ, declared September 24 "DJ Day," encouraging "all citizens to recognize the creative influence of Philadelphia's prominent disc jockeys on the rest of the world."[28]

Nutter's proclamation demonstrates just how crucial the figure of the DJ has become in the artistic and cultural life of this musical city. What should be obvious by now, too, is just how crucial Philadelphia has been to the art and culture of the DJ.

BATTLES GO NATIONAL (AND INTERNATIONAL): THE NEW MUSIC SEMINAR AND THE DMC

Ever since the earliest sound system showdowns shook the streets of the Bronx, competition has been part of the hip-hop DJ's DNA. The nature of this competition—and the DJ battle in particular—however, has continually evolved.

In the late 1970s, musicianship and manual dexterity became more important than sheer volume, and dance clubs like Executive Playhouse, Harlem World, and the T-Connection began sponsoring battles. Money started changing hands; audiences were charged admission, and winning DJs were awarded equipment or (less often) checks. Battles were still mostly a local phenomenon, with most competitors known to each other and coming from the same area or borough. Moreover, these battles did not solely feature DJs, but pitted combined crews of MCs and DJs against one another, with the rappers, not the spinners, getting the spotlight.

In the early and mid-1980s, the DJ battle scene expanded significantly. DJ-only battles became more common, and were often more formalized, with judges—and not audiences—crowning winners. Battles grew more complex, too, with multiple rounds leading to a final champion. Corporate sponsors began supplying equipment and valuable prizes. No longer just the stuff of legend, these new battles were recorded on audiotape and videotape, later heard and seen by fans and aspiring DJs thousands of miles from the battlegrounds. Over the course of the decade, the DJ battle became an international business, one that promoted the art of mixing and scratching vinyl across the globe. This was not simply the natural evolution of the battle, however. Although many hands directed this process, two individuals played a central role, and the battles they founded—the New Music Seminar Battle for World Supremacy and the DMC World Championships—transformed the scene.

Tom Silverman was an environmental science major at Colby College and a DJ at the school's radio station when in 1978 he started *Disco News*, a modest newsletter aimed at club and radio DJs that later became the influential trade magazine, *Dance Music Report*. Silverman had just become aware of hip-hop at the time, learning of it during a visit to Downstairs Records in Manhattan, the prime digging spot for Bronx DJs. Downstairs had a so-called B-Boy Room that sold an eclectic collection of break-harboring discs. He asked the staff how they knew all these records, and they gave him a name: Afrika Bambaataa. Intrigued, Silverman—then running a small independent label called Tommy Boy Records—went to see Bam spin at the T-Connection. "It was the weirdest mix of music I ever heard in my life, but it was amazing," Silverman later said.[29] Eventually he approached Bam about making a record. Their first, from 1981, was "Jazzy Sensation," which they followed with the huge-selling "Planet Rock" the next year.[30]

In 1980—a year before he met Bambaataa—Silverman and some partners launched the first New Music Seminar, an event that music critic Robert Christgau called "a mildly bohemian one-day affair in a friendly recording studio."[31] A few hundred musicians and industry types interested in dance music, punk, and new wave attended that first bohemian affair. The next year,

Silverman organized the Seminar's first DJ competition, the immodestly named Battle for World Supremacy. Not coincidentally, this came after Silverman first encountered hip-hop DJs at the T-Connection. As Jazzy Jay explains, "All of those contests, the battle of the DJs that's held at the [New] Music Seminar and all that shit, it started at the T-Connection. And that's where Tom Silverman got his whole idea from. . . . Tom Silverman and his wife would be the only two white people in the whole club. But they had mad juice, you know why? They were Bambaataa's guests."[32] It's possible that Silverman saw the March 1981 battle at the T-Connection where Bambaataa battled Herc and Jazzy Jay went up against Whiz Kid; regardless, it's fair to speculate that the impressive spectacle of these DJs manning the wheels of steel played a role in the birth of the New Music Seminar battle.[33]

The first battle, in 1981, featured just three DJs; Charlie Chase, Jazzy Jay, and the winner, Whiz Kid. The NMS got bigger each year, attracting several thousand conventioneers to the multi-day event, but the battle was always a highlight. At the 1982 Seminar, Malcolm McLaren—of Sex Pistols and "Buffalo Gals" fame—gave a keynote lecture in which he railed against the mainstream music industry but heaped praise on the hip-hop DJ. "The scratch DJ," he proclaimed, "exhibits the three S's of rock—sex, style, subversion—which make rock and roll both dangerous and yet magical, commercially viable."[34]

There was magic at every battle fought in the massive Marriott Marquis, where the competition soon moved. The NMS crowned some of the best-known and most respected hip-hop DJs, including DJ Jazzy Jeff (1986), DJ Cash Money (1987), DJ Steve Dee (1990), and Mix Master Mike (1992), all of whom we have encountered, or will encounter, in these pages.[35] The Battle for World Supremacy ran from 1981 to 1994, but its influence continued long after, in part through the many astonishing routines captured on video that still inspire DJs to this day. But it also helped spawn another battle series with worldwide reach, the DMC World Championships, whose battles have been central to the development of the hip-hop DJ for more than a quarter century.

DMC founder Tony Prince happily acknowledges the influence of the New Music Seminar. He attended the Seminar and its battles regularly and even used the name "Battle for World Supremacy" for his own competitions held across the ocean in England. "They planted the seeds," he says of the New Music Seminar, "and we took those seeds and grew them."[36]

Prince became a disc jockey in 1962 when he was asked to fill in for a no-show DJ at a party he was attending. This one-off gig marked the beginning of what came to be a successful and long-lived career. In 1965, he began a two-year stint as a DJ for the pirate radio station Radio Caroline North, living on a boat anchored off the Isle of Man and illegally broadcasting the latest hits to a pop-starved British public. (At the time, the British Broadcasting Corporation, BBC, had a monopoly on radio in the country and played little rock and roll.) Prince then left for Radio Luxembourg, a commercial station based in Luxembourg City that, like Radio Caroline, broadcast to the United Kingdom in circumvention of the BBC monopoly. During his sixteen years there, he rose to the level of program director, and it fell upon him to review audition tapes sent in by job-seeking DJs. One day in 1981 he got an unusual tape. "There was no voice, there was no speaking on it. It was just one track after another, and I thought, 'I've got a nutcase here.'"[37] Before throwing it out, he decided to give the tape a thorough listening during his drive home. "And it suddenly dawned on me, this guy is mixing tracks, one into another like I'd heard them doing in Studio 54 in New York, Paradise Garage, places like that. These were DJs who didn't want to talk after every record. In the UK up to this point a DJ in the club talked after every record. The [club] DJs tried to emulate radio DJs. And it kept breaking up the dance floor."

The tape was a revelation, and he invited the DJ who compiled it, Alan Coulthard, to create seamless pop mixes for the station. Soon Prince started getting letters from club DJs asking for copies to use in their gigs. The demand for Coulthard's mixes gave Prince the idea to make and sell cassette tape mixes of the latest songs to club DJs. The idea became reality in February 1983 when Prince launched Disco Mix Club—DMC for short—as a service for club DJs. Two years later Prince started an annual convention, which included, among other things, a mixing competition. The DMC battle was born.

The first competition was in 1985, and featured a roster of English and European dance music DJs. The battle, won that year by the British DJ Roger Johnson, was all about "concerted beat mixing" and "finding perfection" in the segueing of songs, as Prince describes it. But when Prince later traveled to New York to attend Tom Silverman's New Music Seminar, he saw a very different type of DJing, and DJ: "Black guys were scratching—it was really wild mixing," he recalls. The next year, New Jersey's DJ Cheese, who had previously won the New Music Seminar battle, brought some of that "wild mixing" to London.[38] He was the only one who scratched, manipulating Hashim's "Al-Naafiysh" and the 1982 go-go classic "Pump Me Up" by Trouble Funk. He also did something else unusual: he put the two turntables together with the mixer to his right, rather than having the mixer in the middle. When he had his right hand on the cross-fader and moved his left hand quickly back and forth between the two turntables, it was as if he was juggling two balls in one hand. Later he created recognizable rhythms out of his scratches, including Billy Squier's "Big Beat" and Queen's "We Will Rock You"; he even threw in some body tricks and, taking a page out of GrandWizzard Theodore's routines from back in the Bronx, hand-cuffed himself and continued without missing a beat. 🜨

The London crowd had never see anything like this; Cheese earned a standing ovation and won the competition. But not everyone was pleased. At the end of the battle, just as Tony Prince was announcing the new champion, the third-place winner, the Dutchman Orlando Voorn, yanked the microphone from the host's hands. Standing in front of the assembled crowd he demanded, "What is this, a mixing contest or a scratching contest?!" Voorn answered his own question the next year: his routine included scratching.

Cheese's routine marked the moment that hip-hop entered the DMC. And it never left. Thanks to the popularity of the "wild mixing," the competition moved to the famous 5,500-seat Royal Albert Hall (see Figure 4.3) and was for one year held in the even bigger Wembley Arena. In 1990, the sponsor Technics started awarding the winners gold-plated turntables (the Technics SL1200), which quickly became a symbol of the highest achievement possible in DJing. The battle allowed teams to compete in 1992 and 1993 and then added a separate team competition in 1999. The DMC Battle for World Supremacy started in 2000, the name taken from the defunct New Music Seminar battle. It featured shorter head-to-head elimination rounds in addition to the longer six-minute routines done showcase style, with each DJ playing successively. The battle simultaneously expanded geographically, and became truly global with regional competitions held in dozens of countries. The world champion was just as likely to be from Europe (e.g., France's Netik) or Asia (Japan's Kentaro) as from the birthplace of hip-hop. DMC expanded again in 2011, this time into cyberspace, when it launched its Online DJ Championship, in which contestants are judged by their two-minute uploaded videos. Video, however, had long been part of DMC's legacy—VHS tapes and then DVDs have been circulating the globe for

Figure 4.3 The DMC World DJ Championships at Royal Albert Hall, c. 1987–1989. Photograph courtesy of Sally McLintock and DMC.

years, serving as crucial study aids for battlers. When battle legend DJ Craze was asked to offer advice on how to succeed in competition, his top tip was simple: "Watch all the DMC videos."[39] ◐

The New Music Seminar and the DMC battles are only the most prominent competitions. Battles have also been organized or presented by the DJ crew The Allies, the music store Guitar Center, the International Turntablist Federation (ITF), the DJ equipment maker Vestax, and the Zulu Nation. Many of them stay close to the DMC or NMS model, while others have introduced novel variations. The World Series Turntable Championships (established 2003) was perhaps the first online battle; the Gong Battle (founded in 2006 by the late Roc Raida) sought to bring back some of the energy and chaos of earlier battles—and emulate the 1970s classic of daytime TV, *The Gong Show*—by having judges strike a large gong to eject poorly performing DJs. Only a few of these battles, however, have lasted for more than a few years.

The battle, writ large, holds a central place in the world of the hip-hop DJ. As DJ documentarian John Carluccio explains, battles are like a "turntablist almanac," a record of techniques, trends, and styles.[40] DJ A-Trak, the Canadian turntablist who won five world championships (the first when he was just fifteen) and later became a prominent producer, has touted the opportunities for musical and professional development that battles offer:

> I think the DJ battle is a great way for DJs to get their name out, to pay their dues and at the same time get some live experience. A lot of up-and-coming DJs can't really get gigs that easily, but if they're good enough then they can enter a battle and make themselves known that way. And when you're a DJ and you know you've got a battle coming up, it forces you to come up with new material. So when you're looking at the DJ community as a whole, the DJ battles are like a catalyzing element that contribute to raising the bar in DJing.[41]

Christie Z-Pabon, a longtime battle promoter in the United States, cites how these competitions are as much about developing community as about techniques or careers:

> A DJ battle brings together this artform's artists, enthusiasts, documenters, and others within the Hip Hop community, to witness new talent, the progression of the artform, meet each other, network etc. Ideally, the community gets to witness the artform as it progresses, with each DJ competing introducing new techniques, innovations, flavors, etc. Having Hip Hop DJ legends and pioneers present as judges and honored guests is also very important to the sense of community within Hip Hop DJ culture.

The newer DJs basically try to gain the approval from the "tribal elders" (as judges) and the elders in turn, who have long since retired from battling, give their blessings (bestowing championship status) to those who they feel best represent the artform.[42]

Competitive battling is a world unto itself. Only a small percentage of hip-hop DJs battle, and only a tiny minority of them rise to great renown in the battle scene. Yet, as A-Trak and Z-Pabon attest, what happens on the battlefield has a shaping role in DJ culture generally. The battle figures into every stage of DJ history, and we will revisit it often, but for now let's turn to explore how turntable technique—often formed in the crucible of battle—expanded in the decade of the 1980s.

TRANSFORMING TURNTABLE TECHNIQUE

By the turn of the 1980s, the technical vocabulary of the hip-hop DJ remained modest, comprising a handful of moves, including scratching, looping, needle-dropping, and punch-phrasing. But later in the decade, turntablist technique began to expand significantly, an expansion fueled by the growth of the battle scene and the circulation of recorded battle routines. DJs, competitive almost by nature, and now able to see and hear a wider array of styles and techniques, pushed themselves to impress audiences and outdo rivals.

The most important techniques that arose in this period were transforming and beat juggling. They became staples of the battle routine, but they also served as the building blocks for yet more techniques, broadening the turntablist's vocabulary. Their development is also significant because of the often-heated disputes about who deserves credit for them. These claims and counterclaims tell us more than who did what—this discourse opens a window into the hierarchical structure and value system of hip-hop DJs.

The transformer was probably the most important scratch developed in the 1980s. A DJ executes a transformer scratch by slowly moving the record back and forth underneath the needle while rapidly cutting the sound on and off to produce a stuttering effect.[43] 🔊 The cutting is typically done with the cross-fader, but DJs can also use volume controls or a phono/line switch, which changes the input from the turntable to another device, and can be used to mute and unmute the sound. Plenty of DJs have used the line switch to transform, but some consider it close to cheating because it's really no harder than flicking a light switch on and off. On the 1990 song "Funky Piano," EPMD MC Parrish Smith praises DJ Scratch for avoiding the line switch (and his hands altogether): "My DJ on the mix / No line switch, two transform cuts with his lips."

Transforming had a huge impact on DJs. As Qbert has said, "When transforming came out, it just flipped the whole scratching world around."[44] DJs often used
it in battle routines and in the scratch solos on hip-hop songs. Among the songs
that immortalize the transformer are "The Magnificent Jazzy Jeff" (1987) by DJ
Jazzy Jeff and the Fresh Prince, Public Enemy's 1988 "Rebel Without a Pause"
(with Terminator X and Johnny "Juice" Rosado on the decks), Gang Starr's "DJ
Premier in Deep Concentration" (1989), and any number of tracks by Florida's
DJ Magic Mike; for example, "Magic Mike Cuts the Record" (1989). The transformer also became the basis for new scratches, such as DJ Excel's twiddle scratch
and Qbert's crab scratch (more on these in the next chapter). Transforming even
inspired its own switch on some DJ mixers. The popular Rane TTM-56 battle
mixer, for example, made its phono/line switches more robust and labeled them
explicitly as "transform switches," while other mixers added transform buttons.

The importance of the transformer scratch to hip-hop DJing is unambigu-
ous. Its origins, however, are not so clear. Philadelphians Jazzy Jeff and Cash
Money have made directly competing claims. "I'm the one who invented it,"
Cash says, straight up. Here's how he explained it. Sometime in 1984 or 1985,
he saw a tape of DJ Spinbad, another Philadelphia DJ, executing what might
be called a proto-transformer. (This DJ, whom some call the Original Spinbad,
should not be confused with a younger DJ from New York who also calls himself Spinbad.) Spinbad was repeating the phrase "It's time," from "Al-Naafiysh";
he would play it, spin it back to the beginning it, play it again, backspin it again,
and so on, but—and this is the important part—he would cut the sound on and
off while he pulled the record back. The tape inspired Cash to take it a step further: he kept his hand on the vinyl and slowly moved it back and forth while
operating the crossfader. "I basically copied what he did and enhanced it to the
tenth power," he explains.[45] The name, he says, came from his MC, Kool Breeze
Steve, who heard it and quipped that he sounded like one of the robots from the
popular television cartoon *The Transformers*.

Now here's how Jazzy Jeff tells it:

DJ Spinbad let a record play, then pulled it back while he moved the volume
fader up and down. I loved the sound that made so I started experimenting
with it at my house. One part of the transform, or scratching in general,
is hand movement on the record, and the second part is hand movement
on the crossfader. For my version of the transform, I'd move the record
back and forward slowly while moving quickly moving the crossfader
from left to right. My friend was listening to me do it in my basement
one day and he said it sounded like the intro to the *Transformers* cartoon.
The name stuck. And the next party I played at the MC said, "Here's my
man Jazzy Jeff doing the transform."[46]

The scratch appears on at least two of his records, "Live at Union Square" (1986) and "The Magnificent Jazzy Jeff" (1987), in which his MC, The Fresh Prince (a.k.a. Will Smith), actually identifies the scratch. "That's DJ Jazzy Jeff on the transformer scratch!," he calls out in "Live at Union Square."

Cash and Jeff's stories are remarkably similar: both cite Spinbad as inspiration, both explain Spinbad's scratch in the same way, both describe their refinement of the earlier scratch in the same way, and both credit friends with coining the name. But let's muddy the waters even further: yet another DJ from Philadelphia claims to have been transforming before any of them. Grand Wizard Rasheen, Cash Money's mentor, has said that he had a scratch he called the "vibrator" which Cash saw and then made his own. As he told an interviewer, "I made lot of cuts up that a lot of people gave names to like 'Transformer' and all that. I showed Cash just the basics of tricks. Then from the basics of how to do the tricks, he invented his own rhythm. After he got his own rhythm and style, then he started making stuff on his own."[47] Now, to make things even more complicated, it seems that neither Jazzy Jeff nor Cash Money nor Rasheen was the first to record a transformer scratch: that was another Philly DJ, Grand Dragon KD, who used it on the 1986 Steady B song, "Bring the Beat Back."

As many as five different DJs—all from Philadelphia—could claim at least some credit for the transformer: Spinbad, Rasheen, Cash Money, Jazzy Jeff, and Grand Dragon KD. It simply may not be possible for an outside observer to determine the real circumstances of the transformer's origins. All we can say for certain is that the transformer scratch was developed in the mid-1980s and in Philadelphia. Jazzy Jeff has made this point himself: "Philly invented the transformer scratch. It wasn't just me, it wasn't just Cash, it wasn't just Spinbad. It was like what my mom used to say, "Ain't nobody invent nothing, it's just redone.'"[48] This bit of wisdom raises some questions we ought to ponder. Is what we call invention really just the act of tweaking something and giving it a new name? If that's the case, are all DJ techniques just slight variations on existing themes? And if this is true, is it meaningful—is it even *possible*—to assign anyone credit for these tweaks when they are just small changes made in the course of a long evolution of technique? We'll get back to these questions, but let's hold on to them for a moment as we consider a contrasting case study, the development of beat juggling.

In beat juggling the DJ plays two records (usually of the same song) simultaneously, but manipulates them to create wholly new beats. If the transformer can ultimately be traced back to GrandWizzard Theodore's scratch, beat juggling has its roots in Grandmaster Flash's looping. Like the transformer, beat juggling was one of the crucial technical developments of the 1980s and opened up vast new possibilities for DJs. It became a vital part of battle routines and also influenced hip-hop production in important ways. Beat juggling differs from transforming, however, in that it is not one specific move, but a method of mixing two records, the only real defining element being that it is not a straight-forward alternation between two records. Beat juggling is also different in that there is, in fact, general agreement that one person deserves credit for it—DJ Steve Dee—though even here there are competing claims, as we'll see.

Unlike many of the DJs we've encountered, Harlem-born and -bred Steve Dee came to the turntables fairly late; it wasn't until after high school in 1985 that he got his first set, a fine pair of Technics 1200s that he paid for with his earnings as a New York City parks worker. He learned quickly, and only a year later he was challenging more experienced DJs to battle and beating them soundly. He was brash and boastful, and on one occasion in the summer of 1987, his overconfidence got him into trouble:

> I was a cocky, headstrong, "I'll beat any DJ in the world" kind of guy. So, this one particular block party, I had a confrontation with another local DJ who happened to be a dude involved with the other side of the game, you know, the "urban pharmaceuticals." But I didn't know that. I thought he was a DJ like myself, wanted to do the same things, and I would go to his block and heckle him.[49]

He may have been cocky, but he wasn't stupid, so when he realized that the other DJ involved in the "confrontation"—that is, a fistfight—was a dangerous drug dealer, he holed himself up in his apartment in the Lionel Hampton Homes for a few days. It was there and then that he developed beat juggling. "I had to do something with my spare time," he quips.

At one point during his endless hours on the turntables, he was working on his doubling—something he knew of from other DJs like Cash Money and DJ Scratch—and put on his headphones so he could hear what was coming out of both turntables simultaneously. (Without headphones he would have just heard a doubled snare or bass drum.) To some the sound of two copies of the same drum solo playing a beat apart would be cacophony. Steve heard possibility. At the time he had already been working on a new scratch he was calling the "robocut," which, like the transformer, used the crossfader to manipulate the sound. Steve combined the rapid cutting of sound using the crossfader with the alternation between the two turntables and realized that he could do more than simply repeat beats—he could radically reconfigure them.

> Well, to me, what was different about it was that, say, if you wanted to add another snare into the loop, you could do it, as opposed to just letting it loop, you understand? I can add three kicks, or two kicks, where they don't even exist; if there's a word that comes in, I can chop that word up, and half

the word, so that it'll play in place of the snares, so I can add the word where the kick was, I can add the snare wherever the hi-hat was and you can come up with a rhythmic pattern, and it'll sound like you're remixing the record right before everybody's eyes.[50]

He distinctly remembers the song he was cutting when it finally clicked: "Just Rhyming with Biz," a 1987 B side from New York MC (and acquaintance) Big Daddy Kane.

Before the technique came to be called beat juggling, Steve dubbed it "The Funk," inspired by the innovativeness of some of his favorite musicians. "Like Bootsy Collins was on the next level, you know, Maceo [Parker] was on the next level. . . . I figured that what I was doing was similar to what they were doing, so I called it 'The Funk.'" But he also called it "The Mental Style," because he saw beat juggling not simply as a new musical technique but as an intellectual achievement. "Wait a minute, there's a science here," he realized when he discovered that he could create infinite permutations of beats that most people would simply regard as a fixed song. When he explains beat juggling, he sometimes invokes equations, mathematics, even quantum physics.

Once Steve was able to leave his apartment again, he continued to refine his new form of mixing and started using it in local battles. By 1990, he had more or less perfected it, and stunned the judges and audience at the New Music Seminar battle that year. Roc Raida described their reaction: "People were just fucked up, like all the judges that were on the panel. Like Richie Rich, DJ Scratch, all the popular DJs at the time were just fucked up. 'Oaawwww, what the *hell* is he doing?'"[51]

His routine at the 1991 DMC U.S. finals, which has been preserved on video, shows off his virtuosic beat juggling.[52] ◉ In one section he juggles the following lines from "I Know You Got Soul," Eric B. and Rakim's 1988 song: "This is how it should be done / This style is identical to none / Some try to make it sound like this. . . ." He chose these lines carefully—he fully intended to demonstrate exactly how beat juggling should be done. As we'll see in the next chapter, a DJ's "wordplay," as it's called, is a crucial part of a battle routine. But here, let's focus on how he chops up these lines in the first ten seconds of the routine.

This is how it should be done / This / This is how it should be / it should be / This is / This is how it should be / This is how it should be / This is how it should be / This is how it should be / This is how it should be / This is / how / how it sh / shou / should be done

This approximate transcription only hints at the richness and complexity of the routine. In certain parts he takes a short drum pattern and, mixing two copies of them together, produces an original, longer beat. At another point he slows the tempo from about 112 to 76 beats per minute while changing the rhythm from straight eighth notes to a swung pattern of dotted eighth and sixteenth notes. When he returns to the original tempo he doubles all the words so the effect is close to a tripling of the tempo. All of this he does in his trademark Superman T-shirt.

Steve Dee's beat juggling has been captured on tape many times, and his routines are well enough known that the technique is more closely associated with him than with any other DJ. Still, there have been questions about whether Steve was really the first to beat juggle. DJ Aladdin of Los Angeles juggled in his exhilarating routines in the 1989 New Music Seminar and DMC competition. He had a move he called the Aladdin Shuffle in which he would tap on the records to create a new beat in a slower tempo. Aladdin's shuffle isn't as intricate as Steve Dee's beat juggling, but video of it predates Steve's earliest footage of juggling.[53] Steve has a simple explanation: "In 1988, Aladdin and I were both on the same tour, and I showed it to him, and then everybody sees him doing it first in the '89 New Music Seminar. . . ."[54] When I asked Aladdin about his shuffle, he responded that he came up with it on his own while practicing in his North Hollywood studio. As far as the debate about who was first, he simply said, "I don't get into the political talk about the DJ world."[55]

Then there's the English DJ and 1989 DMC world champion Cutmaster Swift, who developed a technique similar to beat juggling that he called the copycat. The copycat began as a way to quickly repeat a sound by alternating between two copies of the same record, backspinning each one a short distance. Later he developed a more advanced version, where he wasn't simply doubling a sound but rearranging music in more complex ways, something that could fairly be called beat juggling. Moreover, he has audio and video of his copycatting from 1988 and 1989, predating Steve Dee's 1990 battle footage.[56] Does this mean, I asked Cutmaster Swift, that he should be given credit for introducing what came to be known as beat juggling? He didn't answer directly, but instead told me of how he first heard of Steve Dee, probably around 1990. "My partner, DJ Pogo, says, 'There's this guy in New York and he's doing your copycat!' "[57]

According to Grandmixer D.ST, he and others were beat juggling in the early 1980s, before Steve Dee *and* Cutmaster Swift. He points out that any time DJs would isolate and repeat the word "good" from the song "Good Times"—which they had been doing since the song came out in 1979—they were performing a kind of beat juggling. He notes how he first heard Flash do it, then Imperial Jay Cee do it, but faster, and then he himself did it even faster. As he suggests, there is an incrementalism in the development of DJ technique, making it difficult to identify a single originator.

Philadelphia's Cash Money has also said that he encountered juggling pre-Steve. "I heard beat juggling way before I heard Steve Dee do it. I'm gonna tell you, Grandwizard Rasheen was doing that stuff way before, but you know, Steve never heard of Grandwizard Rasheen, Rasheen never heard of Steve Dee."[58] So I asked Cash: should Steve Dee *not* get credit for beat juggling? Interestingly, Cash says, "No, he should definitely be given credit."

In the end, does it really matter who gets credit for new techniques—whether beat juggling or transforming—and can we even give a single person credit for their creation? The answers are yes, and maybe not. Credit for a new technique matters because innovation is a central value among hip-hop DJs.[59] However important it is to do something well, it is also important to have done it first. That is why, when the story of hip-hop is told, praise most high goes to the inventors, innovators, and trailblazers, those who introduced foundational techniques to the art form or in other ways influenced later generations of DJs.

The importance placed on innovation, however, tends to downplay the role of community, and the collaboration and exchange of ideas that happens within a community. There's a good reason that it's difficult to definitively answer the question of who invented the transformer scratch, and it's no coincidence that all those who have some claim to it were from the same city. We have not encountered a single DJ who was not influenced by another DJ, and most new techniques are in some way a variation on, or a pivot from, an earlier move. The concept of "taking it to the next level"—central in the world of the hip-hop DJ—embodies this tension between individual and community. A DJ cannot take it to the *next* level without there having been a *previous* level, one established by other DJs. Cash Money and Jazzy Jeff were inspired by Spinbad's scratching; Steve Dee, Aladdin, and Cutmaster Swift developed their mixing skills by observing other DJs. In other words, these techniques could not have existed without a community.

And it is the community that decides who gets credit for bringing a new technique to the world. The process by which these decisions are rendered is complex, rarely unanimous, and never truly final. A DJ will claim to have been the first; others will dispute or confirm the claim; community members of long memory offer their opinions. Not everyone's opinion is judged to be equally valuable, and the words of an elder or pioneer will carry more weight than those of a newcomer or marginal figure. Aladdin is right, this is "political talk," in part because reputations and legacies are at stake, and in part because there is rarely irrefutable evidence to appeal to. Because it may be impossible to verify who did what and when, invention is about more than being first. To be recognized as an inventor of a technique, it is crucial to have demonstrated it repeatedly and publicly, and to have influenced others through its dissemination. Who, then, should be credited with the transformer? When I asked Afrika Bambaataa whether it was important to decide this case, he responded, "I think it's very important to get the factology versus the beliefs, but if it becomes too much confusion you just add it all [together]."[60] Given the absence of hard evidence, and because of the recognized significance of these figures, this is exactly what has happened. The community has decided that Spinbad, Cash Money, and Jazzy Jeff should all get credit. Most descriptions of transforming, whether from *Last Night a DJ Saved My Life* or DJ Qbert's instructional videos, describe the transformer in more or less the same way: inspired by Spinbad, developed and popularized by Cash Money and Jazzy Jeff.[61] And what about beat juggling? Most sources cite Steve Dee. In this case, the attribution has as much to do with his recognized influence on other DJs and his general prominence in the community than on an established timeline of events. In the end, when it comes to techniques, the individual provides, but the community decides.

THE DJ–PRODUCER CONNECTION

Consider the following list: Dr. Dre, Just Blaze, Kid Capri, Marley Marl, Pete Rock, DJ Premier, Prince Paul, DJ Quik, DJ Scratch, and Hank Shocklee. What do they have in common? All are celebrated producers, responsible for some of the greatest and most influential records in hip-hop. And they were all DJs. This is not an incidental point, for hip-hop production—the creation of the instrumental tracks over which MCs rhyme—is intimately tied up with the techniques and aesthetics of DJing. In the mid- and late 1980s, hip-hop DJing spawned a new art, the art of making beats. In some ways the two are quite different—DJs perform live, manipulating records in front of audiences, while producers compose, often slowly and painstakingly, using digital samplers, drum machines, synthesizers, or computers. But there is a strong link between the two, and in the minds of many beat makers, the DJ begat the producer, simple as that. As producer Pete Rock explains in the documentary *Beat Kings*, "I started out DJing, *of course*. You know, it all stems from DJing. I'll always say that. Grandmaster Flash, GrandWizzard Theodore, D.ST."[62] 🔊

In the earliest era of hip-hop recordings, from 1979 to about 1985, DJs had little presence in the recording studio. At first DJs were replaced by live musicians; then drum machines, and to a lesser extent, digital samplers started to take their place. Two trailblazing records, Sugarhill Gang's "Rapper's Delight" (1979) and Afrika Bambaataa's "Planet Rock" (1982) are prominent examples of these early vinyl-free recording sessions. As far as hip-hop recordings were concerned, the DJ was drifting toward irrelevance. But then in 1985, a DJ from Queens named Marley Marl stumbled on a new use for the digital sampler that immediately made the DJ relevant again. The exact circumstances aren't clear, but apparently Marl, using an E-mu Emulator sampling keyboard, captured the sound of a recorded snare hit and then tapped out a new rhythm using that hit.[63] At this time, samplers typically came programmed with a variety of sounds and allowed users to sample and manipulate sounds of their own creation, but they were not designed to sample existing recordings. So Marl was coloring outside the lines, opening up an important new possibility for the sampler: the possibility of composing and recording a rhythm track out of prerecorded drum sounds just as vinyl-spinning DJs did in live performance. In 1986, he became the first hip-hop producer to sample and reconfigure a recorded drum break; using the beloved break that opens The Honeydrippers' 1973 single "Impeach the President," he created the instrumental foundation for MC Shan's rapping on "The Bridge."[64]

Soon, many of the techniques familiar to hip-hop DJs—looping, punch-phrasing, doubling, and beat juggling (producers call it chopping a beat)—directly or indirectly made their way into the work of producers and strongly shaped the sound of hip-hop for years to come. But so what? What else would one do with a sampler if not make loops and new beats? Pretty much anything is the answer. There was nothing about early sampling technology that necessarily led to the kind of beats we hear in hip-hop. In fact, Marley Marl's innovation can be considered a creative *mis*use of the technology. How one uses a technology is not influenced solely by its capabilities and limitations, but also by the history and aesthetics of the user or community of users.

When hip-hop producers first got their hands on samplers, they did not approach the technology as if it were a blank slate—there was already more than a decade's worth of DJ techniques to draw from. Moreover, the songs they sampled were often the same ones that DJs had been spinning for years. Consider what producer and veteran DJ Afrika Islam said of his production work on Ice-T's 1988 album *Power*. Referring to the E-mu SP-1200 sampler and drum machine, he explained, "I had never used an SP-1200 before. I knew all the beats that I'd have to program—I knew all the loops because I was a DJ who was down with Bambaataa. My supply of material was infinite. I just had to learn how to translate it onto that machine."[65] He could hardly be clearer—for him, and for many others, hip-hop production was a translation of hip-hop DJing. As sampling became prevalent in hip-hop, DJs started comparing their craft to the work of producers. Recall how Steve Dee explained that beat juggling could "sound like you're remixing the record right before everybody's eyes"; Shortkut describes Rob Swift, admired for his creative juggles, as "a human sampler."[66] DJ Evil Dee puts it this way: "Once you DJ ... it's like you automatically become a producer. When you take a record and you're cuttin' it up, when you're blending it, that's your interpretation of that record. You produced that interpretation of that record."[67] DJ Craze, who established his

reputation as a battler before going into production, sees the practices as mutually reinforcing: "Producing has definitely helped my DJing in that I know more
about sonics and what frequencies move people. DJing has helped my production in that I know what kind of music I wanna make for the clubs."[68]

Clearly, there are strong continuities between the art of the DJ and the art of
the producer. Most broadly, there's an aesthetic and practical continuity between
DJing and sampling. As a group, songs favored by the first generation of hip-
hop DJs and the first generation of producers share certain musical characteristics. These include a heavy kick drum, a tight snare, and rhythms that are usually
anchored by a strong downbeat—"the one." And these musical preferences are
all tied to a central function—to get bodies moving. Remember, hip-hop arose
out of the relationship between DJs and dancers; hip-hop sampling finds its
roots in that relationship.

Of course, not all DJing sounds like sampling or vice versa. Few producers
try to replicate, say, the shifting tempos and meters of Steve Dee or Rob Swift's
beat juggling or the insanely complex scratching of Qbert—it would be hard to
rap over. Likewise, there are many things that producers do that DJs generally
don't or can't do—for example, time-stretching, where the pitch stays the same
but the tempo changes. Certainly, there are differences between DJing and
producing, and their approach to manipulating music often differs. But to
acknowledge this does nothing to call into question the undeniable connection
between the two.

To probe this connection further I yield the floor to the producers, and will
let them explain four points of contact between these two hip-hop practices. I'll
begin with the words of Hank Shocklee, a member of Public Enemy's production team, The Bomb Squad. Here he touches on the aesthetics of producing
and DJing, and how he as a producer seeks to create a continuity between the
two in his own work.

> … because I'm a DJ, I want to make the DJ a part of the instrumentation.
> So, if you listen to all the records, a lot of the stuff that you are hearing is
> cut in with [i.e., played on] turntables. So you might hear a bassline just
> being cut in instead of sampling that bassline, because we didn't want that
> feel. There is a feeling when something is cut in as opposed when some-
> thing is played through the sample and it's another feeling when some-
> thing is played out live. I always wanted to make everybody feel the element
> of a DJ always being involved.[69]

Shocklee uses the word "feel" several times to explain why DJing is crucial to
him as a producer. As he points out, there's an important difference between
inserting a sound in a mix using a sampler and inserting it using turntables.

There's a distinctive quality to the sound of turntables that he wants listeners to be able to hear. Although he doesn't say this explicitly, his choice of words suggests that it is also important for producers to literally *feel* the connection to DJing by physically handling records and turntables, especially by scratching records. Scratching is the one DJ technique that many producers don't imitate through sampling. When producers want to incorporate scratching into their beats, they often do it themselves or bring in a DJ to do it. As Shocklee points out, the connection between DJing and producing is not just a matter of sound, but of the tactile qualities of vinyl and the physical sensation of turntable techniques.

A second view comes from Prince Paul. After starting his career as a DJ, he went on to produce albums for Stetsasonic, De La Soul, and Big Daddy Kane, and became one of the most highly respected beat makers in hip-hop. His words point out the important continuity between DJs and producers in terms of the music they share:

> People might know me as a producer for the most part. But DJing was always my first passion. I come from a DJ era and DJs play records. As a DJ I played [Billy Squier's] "Big Beat," [and] I sampled it. I played [The Honeydrippers] "Impeach The President" and I sampled it. A lot of us don't play instruments. But as far as hip-hop is concerned, it's based on two turntables and a microphone and that's it.[70]

The songs he mentioned are firmly part of the DJ *and* producer canon. "Big Beat" was being spun at parties in the Bronx by Grandmaster Flash and others and incorporated into countless battle routines; later it was sampled by dozens of artists, from Queen Latifah and Run-D.M.C. to Jay-Z and Dizzee Rascal. "Impeach the President" has been sampled even more widely, on well over a hundred songs.[71] Many other songs fit into this category. Consider just a few of the breaks most frequently played by DJs in the age before sampling: James Brown's "Funky Drummer" (1970), "Apache" (1973), by The Incredible Bongo Band, and "It's Just Begun" (1972) by the Jimmy Castor Bunch. Collectively, these three breaks have been sampled on literally hundreds of songs. This overlap in repertoire helps explain an apparent anomaly in which so many producers sampled songs that were popular before they were born. They were in fact sampling songs that were popular among the first generation of hip-hop DJs, and those DJs then passed the songs on to the later generations.

We now turn to Ivan "Doc" Rodriguez, the innovative New York DJ and later engineer and producer. In his long career he has worked on dozens of notable albums, including Boogie Down Productions' *Criminal Minded* (1987), Eric B. and Rakim's *Paid in Full* (1987), and all of EPMD's records. Here he points out the link between DJing and sampling in terms of musical knowledge and technique:

> You DJ long enough you start to learn the structure of a song. I've played millions of songs in my life. By DJing I learned how to count, I learned how to distinguish different instruments, it helped me learn how to mix records. Put it this way: if I didn't DJ I maybe would not even be doing this. And even if I did it would be different. I might be synthetic, I might be bubblegum, I don't know. I know that most of my background comes from the fact that I put a needle to a record.[72]

For Rodriguez and many other producers, DJing constituted their main musical education, through which they familiarized themselves with a huge range of music and learned how to disassemble and reassemble songs. Rodriguez also makes an interesting point about authenticity. If he hadn't been a DJ, and somehow still managed to become a producer, he believes he would have turned out to be "synthetic" or "bubblegum," in other words, an inauthentic producer. Rodriguez and others, however, are quick to point out that it's not absolutely necessary to have been a DJ to be a producer, and even a good one. Cut Chemist, for example, was once asked if he was bothered by the fact that a producer could have a career without ever having DJed. "Nah," he replied. "If he makes something dope, it's all good."[73] Still, for those producers who had been DJs, that history is tremendously important to their own work and self-worth as a producer.

And this brings us to a final quotation, from DJ Premier—longtime DJ and producer, half of the group Gang Starr, and the composer-performer of "DJ Premier in Deep Concentration" (1989), one of the great pieces of turntable music. Here, he talks about the importance of tradition:

> My DJ mentality is what made me and still makes me stay hot—and stay relevant to hip-hop the way I know it. The stuff that's on the radio now, anything that's current, top ten, I know what it is, I just don't do that style. Don't have to. I do traditional style. Somebody's got to do tradition; just like country music: you have to have the Hank Williams of the world, the Patsy Clines and all that.[74]

As Premier's words suggest, being aware of and staying true to tradition is a central value in hip-hop. It's a way to keep it real, to connect oneself to the founders of hip-hop and all that they represented. And given that the founders of hip-hop were DJs, the clearest way for a producer to be part of that lineage is to actually be a DJ. When ethnomusicologist Joseph Schloss asked producer

DJ Kool Akiem to explain the art of making beats, his answer was simple: "It's about playing records."[75] While beat making is its own musical practice, it bears the distinct influence of the hip-hop DJ, and the two draw on shared aesthetics, repertory, and history.

* * * * *

The birth of hip-hop production was only one of the ways in which DJing expanded its reach in the decade of the 1980s. DJing expanded geographically, as Philadelphia became a hotbed for the cultivation of vinyl manipulation, fostering champion turntablists and bringing influential new techniques into the world. Indeed, turntable technique was one of the decade's growth areas. Transforming and beat juggling, created between about 1985 and 1987, were foundational developments in the world of DJing. Their importance can be gauged by the contestations they generated, both in terms of disputes about who deserves credit for them and in terms of the countless battle routines in which they were deployed. The New Music Seminar's Battle for World Supremacy, and its English-born counterpart, the DMC World Championships, represented yet another expansion of the art of the DJ. Just a few years earlier, DJs sought to rule neighborhoods in the Bronx. Now they were seeking to command the planet. Ironically, these expansions did not bring most DJs great fame, power, or wealth. The world over which the best DJs reigned supreme was a small and shrinking one, a world that increasingly separated itself from the other elements of hip-hop and from mainstream hip-hop fans. But as we'll see, over the first half of the 1990s this near-hermetic world produced some of the most creative DJs and astonishing feats of turntable virtuosity that the larger world had, or has, ever seen.

Turntablism: 1989–1996

In 1995, Chris Oroc was a gas station attendant and a talented amateur DJ living in Southern California. One day as he was labeling homemade CDs, he unwittingly gave a name to an emerging musical movement. When he performed, Oroc was known as Babu, and on each CD he wrote "Babu the Turntablist"; later he called one of his tracks "Turntablism."[1] As a member of the Beat Junkies, a DJ crew that specialized in scratching and beat juggling, he had recently come to the realization that their whole approach to music had little in common with the work of traditional DJs. "I was telling my crew, 'You know, we can't even really call ourselves DJs anymore. There's guitarists, there's pianists, why not turntablists?' "[2] *Turntablist* came to designate a distinctive type of DJ, an instrumentalist who does not simply reproduce existing music but creates entirely new music out of records; *turntablism* is their art.[3] D-Styles, a fellow member of the Junkies, defined the art with a simple equation: "Records + Turntable + Scratching = Music."[4]

The "-ism" in turntablism was more than a simple suffix—it was a crucial signifier. Turntabl*ism* lent a sense of seriousness and cohesion to the art and even suggested something of a philosophy. To many, turntablism was a separatist movement, independent from dancers and MCs. The music of these DJs was meant for listening, not dancing, for head-nodding, not rump-shaking. The ideas behind turntablism, we know, were not actually new. The seeds were planted with "The Adventures of Grandmaster Flash on the Wheels of Steel" (1981), "Rockit" (1983), and the increasingly complex battle routines of the late 1980s. But it was not until the early and mid-1990s that a form of DJing, self-sufficient and largely independent from MCs, really flourished. Several crucial factors were at work: the rise of DJ crews, the growth of the battle scene, the simultaneous expansion of turntablism into California and the Filipino American community, and advancements in DJ technology. Taken together, these developments led to what many would consider to be the creative high point of the art and culture of the hip-hop DJ. Yet at the same time, this high point was the point of furthest remove from mainstream hip-hop and popular culture.

SCRATCH NEEDLES, THE HAMSTER SWITCH, AND THE CROSSFADER CURVE: DJ EQUIPMENT AND THE EVOLUTION OF TURNTABLISM

Try this experiment at home, or better yet, at someone else's home. Find an old turntable and a record. Turn the player on, set the needle on the record, and try to scratch. More likely than not, as soon as you start pushing the record back and forth, the stylus will jump the groove and skitter across the vinyl. Non-DJs often think of scratching as something anyone can do. But they're wrong, not only because it requires more skill than they realize, but because it requires the right—or properly modified—equipment. For most of the history of the record player, needles were made to track in one direction only, forward, and at a constant speed; in other words, they were not designed for scratching. But in the very earliest days of hip-hop these were the needles that DJs had at their disposal, and the state of their equipment affected how they worked their vinyl. DJ Disco Wiz remembers those days well:

> Not a lot of backspinning in those days, it was a lot of needle dropping. You have to understand that the equipment you had was nothing compared to what we have now. The needles had no tension on them, so you would tape pennies [to the cartridge] to give more weight. In the park [the tone arms] would just fly right off the record. There was really no traction.[5]

Many DJs simply used the cheapest needles they could find, often the Radio Shack brand, Realistic. The more expensive ones were sometimes the worst for mixing and scratching since the highest fidelity came from the lightest styli. Unlike audiophiles, hip-hop DJs weren't primarily concerned with "cleaner highs [and] more lucid texture," which is how a 1981 *Popular Mechanics* article described the virtues of a new Audio Technica cartridge. "I was originally using some HiFi Audio Technica stylus," British DJ Cutmaster Swift recalls of his early career in the mid-1980s; "they sucked but I made them work."[6] *I made them work*—phrases like this come up all the time in DJ discourse, especially about the early years of hip-hop. Rarely did the equipment do exactly what DJs wanted, but rarely was that a problem.

Occasionally, as in the example of the Technics 1200 series turntable, DJs happened upon equipment that seemed as if it had been tailor-made for them. This was also the case with two stylus models, both of which were introduced before the birth of hip-hop, but only became popular among turntablists in the 1980s and 1990s. One was Stanton's 500AL, originally designed for radio DJs who would have occasion to backspin (or back cue) a record while segueing between songs. "Meet the Stanton 500AL," opens an ad from 1970, "the cartridge that's tougher than disc jockeys. We designed the entire stylus assembly to withstand the rugged demands of back cueing and the kind of handling that would quickly ruin ordinary pick-ups."[7] It's not clear which hip-hop DJ or DJs "discovered" the 500AL, but it became popular among battlers and party-rockers alike in the late 1980s and early 1990s. "They were my favorites," DJ Craze says. "I used to put a dime on them and they wouldn't jump for anything!!"[8] Stanton responded warmly to Craze's enthusiasm, and in 2000 they introduced the Stanton 520-SK Craze. As Craze explains, "Stanton had approached me about sponsoring me and having my own needles. I told them that I loved the 500s and that I didn't wanna change a thing, I just wanted my name on it."[9] A glance at Stanton's website today reveals several different cartridges designated for turntablist use.[10]

In the mid-1990s, an even older needle came to the attention of turntablists, and it quickly became the needle of choice, favored even above the Stanton 500AL. This was the Shure M44-7, introduced back in 1963. The M44-7 was not especially popular, at least for its first thirty-three years. It was expensive, costing $44.50 when it was introduced, and didn't have an impressive frequency range: 20 to 17,000 Hz, compared to 10 to 25,000 Hz for more high-fidelity needles.[11] It had one singular virtue, crucial to turntablists but to few others: a high tracking force (the force exerted by the stylus on the sides of the v-shaped groove), three to four times higher than that of its hi-fi cousins. In other words, it was perfect for scratching because it stuck so resolutely in its rut.[12] Ironically, the famed scratch needle was originally touted by Shure in 1963 as "a no-scratch" stylus, but here they were proclaiming its resistance to jumping the groove and scratching *across* the vinyl.[13] For years, the M44-7 was difficult to find, and was even discontinued in the United States, Shure's home. But in 1995 or 1996, the Beat Junkies started traveling to Japan, and it was there that they happened across it. They quickly realized that they had found a needle that suited them even better than their Stantons. As Beat Junkie veteran DJ Rhettmatic told me, "When we started going to Japan we started buying [the M44-7] needles and bringing them back here," introducing them to the turntablist community at large. "We pretty much opened their eyes to it," he recalls.[14] The Beat Junkies also opened Shure's eyes. Shure recognized the potential of their near-dormant product, and in the late 1990s, they started marketing this "no-scratch" stylus directly to DJs, even featuring the Beat Junkies in full-page magazine ads. The Shure website now describes the M44-7 as a "turntablist record needle," one that is "engineered for scratch DJ's"[15] (see Appendix 1 for a close-up illustration of an M44-7 style cartridge and needle).

Shure and Stanton weren't the only companies to jump on the scratch needle bandwagon; Gemini, Numark, Ortofon, and others have as well. 〇 Ortofon, with its distinctive "Concorde" line of long, narrow cartridges, became especially prominent, in part because of DJ Qbert's endorsement and DMC's controversial "Ortofon Rule," which for a time (2005–2008), mandated the use of the Danish company's cartridges in its battles.

The relationship between DJs and needles reveals a common pattern. DJs at first either adapted equipment or found the equipment that suited them. It was only when DJs gained mainstream attention in the mid-1990s that the manufacturers took notice and started catering to DJs. At first, the DJs' approach to equipment was "to make them work," and only later did the equipment makers start to work for them. This pattern becomes even clearer, we'll see, in the case of the mixer.

The crab scratch is an impressive sight to behold. The DJ's mixer hand seems possessed, the fingers tapping the crossfader so quickly that one sees only a blur of swarming digits. Developed by Qbert in 1995, the crab is performed by essentially snapping each of the fingers against the thumb from the pinkie (or ring finger) to the index. This snapping is done with the crossfader in between the fingers, so that it's bouncing back and forth, cutting the sound off and on in quick succession as the DJ slowly moves the record back and forth with the other hand. The effect is hard to describe precisely, but if you've heard Porky Pig's stuttering send-off from the old Warner Brothers cartoons, "That's all folks!" then you have the idea. The crab, visually impressive and sonically distinctive, quickly caught on after Qbert deployed it in his battle routines, and it soon became a staple of turntablist technique across the world.[16] 〇

Why did the crab skitter into existence when it did? Part of the reason is that in 1995 Qbert saw the Welsh DJ Excel perform a new scratch he called the twiddle, in which the middle and index fingers bounce the fader off the thumb; Qbert tried it himself and then created a variation using all the fingers (which he actually found easier to execute).[17] But why hadn't someone else come up with the scratch earlier? Conceptually, it's not that different from the transformer, which had been around for nearly a decade. Qbert remembers the reaction of other DJs when he first crabbed in a battle: "Whoa, that's pretty damn fast transforming!" they said.[18] But there's a reason DJs didn't twiddle or crab in the 1980s: these new moves were nearly impossible to execute with the mixers available at the time. The roadblock was the crossfader.

Crossfaders, which didn't become common until the late 1970s, were originally used by radio DJs as an efficient way to segue from one song to the next.[19] Simply two faders coupled into one control, the crossfader simultaneously fades one channel out while fading the other channel in. The device made life easier for the DJ—whether on the radio or in the dance club—who could now use one hand to do what would otherwise require two hands operating separate controls. These early crossfaders were also designed to cut the sound in or out gradually, and the controls themselves offered a decent amount of resistance. Having a fairly stiff, gently graduated crossfader was perfect for DJs who put a premium on creating seamless segues and avoiding dead air.[20]

Yet what helped traditional DJs handicapped scratch DJs. Even into the late 1980s, DJ mixers were not made with scratching or even quick mixing in mind. With its wooden sides and VU (volume units) meters, the Gemini MX 2200 mixer popular in the late 1980s looks positively antique, and its wide profile and stiff fader were hardly conducive to performing virtuosic battle routines (see Figure 5.1). But comparatively speaking, the machine was a dream. Cash Money used it when he won the 1988 DMC World Championship battle, and actually brought his own Gemini to London, rather than use the even larger mixers DMC supplied.[21] Whatever equipment they used, scratch DJs of the time had to fight against their machines to create the sounds they wanted. As Shortkut put it, "Those faders—you've got to have muscles to scratch on those things, you know what I mean?"[22] Moreover, early faders were not designed to take the kind of abuse turntablists dispense. A radio or club DJ would use a crossfader maybe

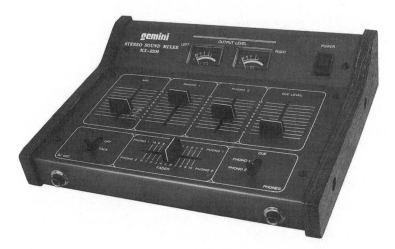

Figure 5.1 Gemini MX-2200 Mixer. (Photograph by Zane Ritt/Courtesy of DJpedia. Creative Commons license CC BY-SA 2.0.)

once every few minutes; a turntablist, on the other hand, might use the cross-fader *hundreds* of times in the same span. When they didn't simply break, over-used faders generated crackling or static (sometimes called "travel noise") and led to "bleeding," when both channels could be heard even when the fader was at one extreme or the other.

Without better mixers, turntablists of the late 1980s and early 1990s were reaching the technical limits of their art. But DJs have never waited for others to give them the features they sought, so they addressed the problems them-selves through a variety of workarounds and hacks. This attitude dates back to the very earliest days of hip-hop. Grandmaster Flash rigged his own cueing system; Bambaataa, Breakout, Disco Wiz, Grandmaster Caz, Kool Herc, and others found ways to mix records without even having a mixer. Some DJs avoided the crossfader altogether for certain scratches, such as the transformer, using the on-off line switch instead. Others liberated their crossfaders of the heavy grease they were packed in, using lighter, less frictional gun oil; Jazzy Jeff, remember, carried WD-40 with him to battles.[23]

One of the most interesting mixer fixes of the time was the so-called hamster switch. In the early 1990s, some DJs found that certain new scratches, like the crab and the twiddle, were easier to perform if the direction of the crossfader were reversed. This is known as "hamster style," the name coined by San Francisco's DJ Quest, a member (with DJ Eddie Def and DJ Cue) of a crew called the Bullet Proof Scratch Hamsters (later known as the Bullet Proof Space Travelerz). Quest stumbled upon the hamster style of DJing accidentally: when he got his first mixer (a Pyramid 4700) he wired it to his turntables incor-rectly, connecting the right turntable to the left turntable input on the mixer and vice versa. He liked the configuration and never changed back.[24] But not all scratches were best performed with the crossfader reversed, so ideally mixers would have a control that let the DJ change the fader direction on the fly. This is exactly what the hamster switch does, and enterprising DJs figured out how to install it themselves. Quest cites DJ Focus, "an electronics wizard" from Phoenix, as one of the first to create a hamster switch, which he attached to a small box connected to his turntables and mixer.[25]

Eventually the equipment manufacturers started paying more attention to turntablists, and responded by gradually adding the features DJs clamored for. Probably the first mixer specifically marketed as a scratch/battle mixer was the PMX-2, introduced in 1989 by the Japanese outfit Melos. It was used for a time as the official DMC battle mixer and even sported a decal with the DMC logo. Its uncluttered layout and smooth faceplate without jutting screws were designed to facilitate quick and efficient scratching and mixing, though it didn't have all the features battle DJs needed. Other mixers provided looser, smoother sliders as well as field-replaceable crossfader controls, so DJs could buy extra faders and swap them out on their own, which active DJs might have to do multiple times a year. And with Vestax's 1998 PMC-06 Pro, mixers started coming with hamster switches.[26] (On most mixers it is simply a button labeled "reverse.") That Vestax mixer, and a few others following it, were also narrower in width, meaning that DJs wouldn't have to reach as far when switching between turntables. Later machines, such as the Rane TTM-56 (introduced in 2001), were equipped with magnetic faders, which, as the manufacturer claims, eliminated bleeding and extraneous noise, and had a lifetime of over ten million operations.[27] (The mixer in Appendix 1 is drawn from a Rane TTM-56 model.) All these features directly addressed the needs of turntablists.

The most important change to mixers, however, and one that DJs couldn't easily implement themselves, was related to the crossfader curve, which refers to the distance the fader needs to travel before switching the sound from one turntable to the other. Traditional mixers had gentle crossfader curves for smooth, gradual transitions; practically speaking, this required that the slider be moved a relatively long distance, perhaps up to two inches, to effect a full fade. But turntablists wanted to be able to cut sound on and off quickly and with a minimum of motion. Mixer makers responded by creating a steeper curve, meaning that, in some cases, only a tenth of an inch, or 2.5 millimeters, separated full on and full off. In other words, the manufactures turned the fader into a highly responsive on-off switch, effectively removing the fade from the fader. Realizing, however, that sometimes DJs wanted longer fades, manufacturers also started offering multiple curve settings, so that DJs could change the shape of the curve at will. ◐ For example, the Vestax PMC-06 Pro, pictured in Figure 5.2, has a knob on the front called "C.F. Curve," which allows a variety of settings.

The Vestax PMC-06-Pro was designed with input from DJ Qbert, and built upon the PMC-05-Pro, which itself benefited from the suggestions of DJ Shortkut and DJ Rhettmatic. I spoke with each of them about their work with equipment manufacturers, and Vestax in particular, and what emerged was a fascinating picture of a new era in DJ technology, one in which turntablists came to play an ever-increasing role in the design stage.

In 1993, Shortkut was working as a convention DJ for a turntable and mixer manufacturer; it was his job to show off one of its mixers at the various equipment shows. The problem was, according to Shortkut, "it sucked."[28] "No disrespect to [the manufacturer] but I wasn't feelin' it. It had a small fader . . . so I couldn't really do beat juggles or mix or anything like that. So in the hotel room, I made a sketch on a napkin of a mixer that I thought would be nice. 'Cause, at the time—the best DJ mixer at the time was the DMC PMX-2, the official DMC mixer that you used in the battles. I was thinking something along those lines, but, you know, like a step up. A couple of features that that mixer

Figure 5.2 The Vestax PMC-06 Pro mixer. Its slim profile, variable crossfader curve settings, and reverse ("hamster") switch are all intended to facilitate advanced scratching. When first released, it came in a gold finish; the black finish came only with later models. (Images courtesy of Turntable Lab, www.turntablelab.com.)

didn't have." Most importantly, Shortkut wanted a hamster switch and a loose fader, and he wanted a simple design without any distracting, unnecessary features. When he showed his napkin to a company representative, the response was dispiriting. "He was like, 'Aw man, that ain't gonna sell. There's no features.' You know, that was during a time where all the mixer companies wanted to add some outrageous feature. I'm like, 'Simplicity is the best. As long as you have a solid fader, it doesn't [matter].' That was during the time where all faders bled. I was trying to tell them, 'I'm a scratch DJ and I would want to use this mixer.'"

While working at the annual NAMM convention, the enormous trade show for music products in Los Angeles, Shortkut and his friend DJ Rhettmatic visited the Vestax booth, and fell in love with their mixers. "My god, your faders are butter!'" Shortkut exclaimed. "Oh, wow!" was Rhettmatic's response.[29]

The Vestax reps, seeing that they had virtuoso turntablists and gear "geeks" (Rhettmatic's word) at their booth, asked them what they looked for in a mixer. Not long after this encounter, Shortkut was touring with Qbert in Japan, and had a chance to meet with representatives from the Osaka-based company. Vestax was responsive, and some of their people later met with him and DJ Rhettmatic back in California to discuss a new mixer, one that the DJs hoped would have all the best features of the Gemini, GLI, and Numark mixers combined into a slim machine that was, as Rhettmatic describes it, "basic, straight to the point, no bells and whistles." Vestax came out with a prototype and invited the two of them to Japan to showcase the new mixer. They were thrilled— "I was, like, 'Oh man this is it,'" says Shortkut. In 1995, the mixer was released as the Vestax PMC-05-Pro; it had a superior crossfader and a simple layout with the controls spaced far enough apart so a DJ would be unlikely to bump anything accidentally in the heat of battle. The only disappointment was that it did not have a hamster switch, at least at first. The two DJs had no formal business arrangement with Vestax, and were not paid for their work. Looking back, however, they have no regrets. "At the time we weren't thinking about money," explains Rhettmatic. "We wanted something for ourselves to use." Shortkut puts it this way: "I was like, what, 18 at the time. And I was more hyped that the company would actually listen to me. It was all good."

Qbert also worked with Vestax, and pushed them to add a hamster switch to the 05-Pro, which they included on a version they dubbed the Q-Bert Limited Edition I. Qbert had more input with the next line, the 06-Pro. "I drew a design, I gave it to Vestax, and they came out with [it]. When you see the 06, keep in mind that I drew that thing exactly to a tee."[30] Like Shortkut, he was not paid for his contributions and received no explicit credit from Vestax. "You motherfucker, that's my design!" was his immediate response when he first saw the finished product, "but [then] I was like, 'Ah, fuck it, whatever.'" He was unhappy about not receiving credit or payment, but like Shortkut he harbors no bitterness. "I mean, it's cool to have credit, but it's not really a big thing, it's like, whatever, as long as it makes the world a better place, then I'm happy, you know?"

Several years later, Akihiro Kaneko, chief design engineer at Vestax, explained the company's relationship with hip-hop DJs. Although Kaneko recognized their influence on Vestax's products, he seemed to view hip-hop DJs more as customers than as potential partners.

[F]or some reason, the hip-hop people are the ones who seem to be especially enthusiastic about our products. It may be partly because hip-hop DJs treat turntables more like musical instruments. They change a lot of things, and they complain a lot, too: "This does not work," and so forth.

House and techno people do not seem to complain as much. They are more concerned about choice of songs and mixing, but hip-hop DJs have, well, interesting personalities, stronger passion, and characters, and they tend to speak out to us "This is bad" and "That does not work," so we will know what was not good in our products. . . . We did not [at] first intend to make things for hip-hop, but since they voiced a lot of opinions to us . . . we have more products for hip-hop DJs.[31]

Note that he singles out hip-hop DJs among all others as being particularly outspoken and proactive when it comes to equipment, and that Vestax only started adding turntablist-friendly features at the prompting of this "most enthusiastic group."

Although we can criticize Vestax for exploiting young DJs who had no business experience or lawyers to represent their interests, it has long been sensitive to the needs of DJs, producing beloved scratch mixers for more than fifteen years. Whatever the details of the business relationships between Vestax and DJs might have been, a larger point emerges. We can see these stories as emblematic of a significant change in the world of the hip-hop DJ. In the 1970s and well into the 1980s, equipment manufacturers paid little heed to hip-hop DJs who, after all, didn't use the machines as intended and often positively abused them. These machines were not designed with the techniques and aesthetics of their most enthusiastic users in mind. But these users bent these machines to their wills and made them serve their needs. And then, after years of this tweaking and jury-rigging, the manufacturers finally began to make the machines the DJs had dreamed of. We can see this as the triumph of vernacular technological creativity, the crucial but oft-ignored innovativeness of marginalized communities.[32] In this case, the creative contributions of working-class African Americans, Latinos, and Filipino Americans led to nothing less than the reconception and redesign of a tool central to the work of the modern DJ.

This is not to say that DJs in the 1990s rested easy once they had the attention of the industry. The best DJs continued to fight with their machines, refusing to accept their limitations, and dreamed up new technological possibilities for their instruments. Kid Koala put it this way:

It's always about how the DJ can outthink the machine. Like after they developed a mixer in the '90s, with a short cut [i.e., steep fader curve] that made transforming a lot easier—well, then what happened? People said, now it's just second nature to do that, what else can we do with this new mixer? Then came the crab and things like that, you know? So it's really always that John Henry, man versus machine kind of thing at the root of a lot of scratch DJing.[33]

Whatever we call this—vernacular technological creativity, resistance to authority, or sheer stubbornness—it is the way of the hip-hop DJ.

BAY AREA TURNTABLISM AND THE "FILIPINO FACTOR"

In September 1972, Philippine president Ferdinand Marcos declared martial law. With Proclamation No. 1081, newspapers were shut down, tens of thousands of citizens were rounded up into military compounds, and the Congress was dissolved. Large numbers of Filipino families fled the country, seeking refuge across the world, many of them in the United States (which had recently opened the door to more immigrants with the 1965 Immigration Act). Marcos could not have realized it, but with the stroke of his pen he set into motion the flowering of DJ culture in a Filipino community that had settled in the San Francisco Bay Area, nearly 7,000 miles away.

Anyone with more than a passing interest in turntablism knows that Filipinos, especially Filipino Americans, are richly represented in the highest ranks of the art. The most famous are Qbert and Mix Master Mike, known well beyond the world of scratch DJs, but there are many others as well. These include Apollo, Babu, Celskiii, Deeandroid, Dexta, 8-Ball, Icy Ice, Jester, Kuttin Kandi, Neil Armstrong, Pone, P-Trix, Rhettmatic, Rocky Rock, Roli Rho, Shortkut, Sonny, Symphony, Vinroc, and Yogafrog; moreover, some of the most renowned DJ crews—the Beat Junkies, the 5th Platoon, and the Invisibl Skratch Piklz—are Filipino-dominated.[34] Not all of these DJs hail from around San Francisco— the Beat Junkies formed in Southern California, the 5th Platoon is a largely New York crew, Jester is a Texan, Dexta is an Aussie, and the Mega Team was actually based in the Philippines (more on them in a moment). But the Bay Area is unparalleled for its concentration of accomplished DJs, and the rise of a Filipino American turntablist scene there must be recognized as one of the key developments in the history of the hip-hop DJ, for it was the Bay Area Filipino American DJ community that, more than any other, spurred the rise and spread of turntablism.

The Filipino American turntablism explosion was a phenomenon of the 1990s, but to understand it we need some backstory first. A DJ scene emerged in the Bay Area in the late 1970s and early 1980s in the form of mobile DJ crews that hosted parties throughout the area. Although the scene encompassed the whole Bay Area, two pockets of activity are noteworthy for our story: Balboa High School, in the southern part of San Francisco, and Daly City, just a few exits down Interstate 280 in San Mateo County. Balboa can boast the first Filipino American DJ crew (Sound Explosion), as well as four of the other earliest crews and the first all-Filipina crew (the Go-Go's); Qbert was one of the school's graduates.[35] Daly City can claim Apollo, Mix Master Mike, Shortkut, and a host of popular crews. It was not long before the scene expanded. Sociologist and journalist Oliver Wang explains, "At its height, the DJ scene covered six counties and 7,000 square miles in the Bay Area alone, with well over 200 crews who had come and gone over a fifteen-year period."[36]

The first few generations of Bay Area crews, those active until the late 1980s, had little in common with the scratch-centric, breakbeat-loving turntablists who later made Filipino American DJs famous. In fact, hip-hop was for the most part not in the crates of these early DJs, who were more inclined toward soul or Hi-NRG, a fast, disco-influenced form of electronic dance music. Some DJs, like Qbert and Mix Master Mike, tried their hand at scratching at home after "Rockit" came out in 1983, but at parties it was rarely heard, and often drew glares rather than cheers from the dancers. Qbert, who started out with the Live Style crew, remembers, "When I first did it, people'd just be sitting down and they'd be like 'what the hell are you doing?' or, you know, 'just let the record play!'"[37] Shortkut and DJ Derrick D, both of the Daly City crew Just 2 Hype, also irritated partygoers with their hip-hop and their scratching. As Derrick says, "Me and Short would cut shit up . . . and people would be so mad at us but we didn't care."[38]

A turning point for the Filipino mobile DJ scene came in 1989, when Qbert faced Jazzy Jim in a high-profile battle held in Hayward. Jazzy Jim opened with a seamless segue of short song fragments in a demonstration of "quick-mixing," a traditional test of skills among DJs in the scene. Qbert went next, and stunned the crowd with a scratch routine based on the 1988 hip-hop hit "It Takes Two," by Rob Base and DJ E-Z Rock. John Francisco, one of the promoters of the battle, later described his impressions: "I was walking from one side of the hall to the other. I stopped dead in my tracks. I was like 'Jesus Christ, who the hell is this guy?' I mean, he was doing things to a record that I never heard before in my life. I mean I heard people scratching before, but not like that. He was like a damn madman up there."[39]

The judges faced a dilemma—how to compare two routines that demonstrated fundamentally different approaches to the turntables. In a hotly contested decision, they awarded first place to Jazzy Jim. Qbert may have lost, but his scratching portended the future of DJing in the Bay Area.

Scratching at Qbert's level does not emerge overnight; indeed, he had been developing his craft largely out of the public eye for years. As he admitted to me, when he started he had no idea what he was doing.[40] He actually thought that scratching involved dragging the needle *across* the grooves; when he realized that he was supposed to move the record, not the needle, he initially did it by rotating the label, like he was turning a knob or juicing an orange. His first "sound system" was a component stereo with a turntable, radio, and tape deck, and a lid that propped open, piano-style, with a small stick. He practiced by scratching along with the radio, and although he didn't have a mixer, he could use the volume knob to create a variety of scratches. Incidentally, Quitevis *hated* his DJ name, which originated as a childhood taunt inspired by the 1982 video game Q*bert, which featured an orange, roly-poly figure with a tubular nose. "I was short and fat, my last name [Quitevis] starts with a Q. It's like a really, really childish, immature nickname," he recalls ruefully. "When I became a DJ, I didn't want that to be my name. Then everybody was like, 'Hey that Qbert guy was pretty good,' and I was like, 'No! that's not my name!' I wanted to be something from a comic book, you know, Ripclaw or The Slasher."

A crucial point in Qbert's development came when Apollo introduced him to a kid of half-Filipino, half-German ancestry who later became known as Mix Master Mike. In their first encounter, Qbert showed Mike what he could do, and then, as Qbert tells it:

> Mike comes up and he's like, "let me try that," and Mike does a really fast, military scratch. I'm like "Aw, what the hell is that?" Mike had started like a month before I had, and he was doing all the "Rockit" scratches and everything. That was my first experience of what a real DJ is supposed to do. Mike was pretty much my mentor, but he didn't know that he was my mentor. I was just following him around, seeing, studying every show he did, every party he did.

The two became fast friends, schooling each other, but also learning from bootlegged videotapes of DMC and New Music Seminar battles, dissecting the routines of East Coast DJs like Cash Money, Jazzy Jeff, and Steve Dee.

Around the time of Qbert's 1989 battle against Jazzy Jim, the Bay Area DJ scene started to change. Crews had typically formed from groups of friends who lived in the same neighborhood or city, and the majority had just one DJ who could scratch, if that. But then likeminded scratchers from different crews across the Bay Area started to get together. In 1991, Qbert, after winning the U.S. finals of the DMC battle, joined Apollo, Mix Master Mike, and two MCs (FMD and H2) to form FM 2.0 (Furious Minds to Observe). This was perhaps the first group in the area to have multiple scratch DJs, and the three acted like a traditional band, with each member performing distinct roles. They soon left their MCs behind and, as the Rock Steady DJs, entered the 1992 DMC competition, which that year started allowing crews to enter. They made it all the way to the World Championships—and won.

Their winning routine was (after a slightly rough start) a well-oiled six-minute marvel.[41] It had its roots in a "Peter Piper" routine Apollo and Mix Master Mike had worked out several years earlier, but according to Apollo it was fully "composed" for this battle, and intended to show that three DJs could play together as a band.[42] As Mike explained, "We just had aspirations of playing like a band on the turntables instead of guitars and drums and stuff. We wanted to actually play all those instruments on the turntables together."[43] In the routine they perform distinct roles as drummer (Apollo), bass scratcher (Mike), and lead scratcher (Qbert).[44] Occasionally they scratch in unison, like a string quartet bowing together; they even take a dramatic grand pause for four beats before reentering. They dispense almost entirely with the antics common in battles of the time, as in the final routine that the 1992 Philippines DMC Champions The Mega Team (DJ M.O.D., DJ Sonny, DJ Ouch) brought to the battle that year. Their wigs, miming, and props made for an entertaining show, one that emphasized spectacle as much as sound.

The next year, 1993, Qbert and Mike competed at the DMC World Championships, this time without Apollo. (Apollo had joined Branford Marsalis's group, Buckshot LeFonque, and was unavailable.) They called themselves the Dream Team, the nickname for the American Olympic basketball team that had won the gold medal in Barcelona in 1992. The Michael Jordan and Scottie Pippen of the turntables dominated, now with an even more virtuosic routine that used only three turntables. Their technique had continued to develop since their last triumph in London. The routine features two-handed scratching with the fingers tapping the record like a bongo, and the furious use of the transformer switch; the two end with a crazed unison tremolo, an accelerated baby scratch called the scribble. With just a few recognizable words, the routine is almost abstract, largely a showcase of incredibly fast scratching on their trademark robotic bleeps. But they can't help closing with a recorded taunt taken from the popular 1991 video game *Street Fighter II*: "You Lose!"[45] 🌑

These years—1992 and 1993—were the only years that a crew won the DMC World Championships. The organizers apparently thought better of having teams compete against individuals, and it was not until 1999 that the DMC offered a separate competition for teams. But this wasn't the end for these Bay Area DJs; in fact, it was more of a prelude. In 1995, Qbert, Mike, and Apollo formed the Invisibl Skratch Piklz—the personnel changed over the years, with Shortkut, D-Styles, and Disk joining at various times; Yogafrog was a non-performing member who acted as the group's manager (see Figure 5.3). Until they disbanded in 2000, they were the best-known and perhaps the best group altogether, performing across the world and doing as much to bring attention to the art of the turntable as anyone since D.ST scratched on "Rockit" more than a decade earlier.

While the Piklz were becoming known as one of the premier scratch crews in the early 1990s, a distinctive turntablist culture was growing around them in the Bay Area. Turntablists were cutting it up in battles, clubs, basements, and

Figure 5.3. Members of the Invisibl Skratch Piklz. From left to right: Mix Master Mike, Shortkut, Qbert, D-Styles, Yogafrog. (Photograph by B+, courtesy of B+ and Raymond Roker.)

bedrooms, on the radio and TV—anywhere a DJ could lug two turntables and a mixer. The scene did not simply grow spontaneously out of all this DJ activity, however. Key venues and individuals played crucial role in establishing and promoting the scene: in particular, Billy Jam, Dave Paul, Alex Aquino, Cleo Fishman's Club Deco, and the home of DJ Qbert.

Billy Jam, born Billy Kiernan in Dublin, arrived in New York in 1979, quickly becoming an early champion of hip-hop as a radio DJ. In 1981, he left for San Francisco, and fell in love with the turntablist scene. Jam remembers when he first started hearing the virtuosic scratch routines from area turntablists. "I would literally get goose bumps. I was just so excited about it I just wanted more people to hear it and appreciate it."[46] Jam promoted local turntablism on a number of stations, but he often found himself in hot water for, among other things, violating FCC rules by playing obscenity-laced hip-hop songs on the air. So he became his own boss, setting up a pirate radio station (also in violation of FCC rules) in his house. There he started a series with the nose-thumbing name

Pirate Fuckin' Radio, which ran to more than 100 episodes and included the Shiggar Fraggar Show. Recorded between late 1994 and mid-1996, the five live all-turntablist shows featured members of the Invisibl Skratch Piklz and other important area DJs improvising routines. ◉ At about the same time he started filming other informal DJ jams in his house, calling the series *Hip Hop Slam TV*. Hip Hop Slam then became the name of Jam's record label, which released a variety of turntablist compilations, most featuring local artists, such as *Turntables by the Bay* and *Scratch Attack*.[47] Through his ardent advocacy as a DJ, a label owner, and a journalist, Billy Jam was a catalytic force in the Bay Area scene. More likely than not, if a DJ was scratching somewhere in northern California in the 1990s, Jam was probably there, recording it, filming it, broadcasting it, or writing about it, sharing the goose-bump-inducing experience with the world. The British journal *The Wire* aptly described his contributions in this way: "One gets the feeling that Billy Jam may one day be regarded as a sort of turntablist Alan Lomax (RIP), a field recording general who left no rockers unturned in his pursuit of the perfect scratch."[48]

Dave Paul, another important scratch impresario, started out as a mobile DJ in the mid-1980s, before he became a club and radio DJ and later founded the underground magazine *Bomb Hip-Hop*.[49] The magazine, whose first issues were made using a typewriter, glue, scissors, and a photocopier, was one of the few regional publications that focused on hip-hop, and featured articles, reviews, and interviews connected to the Bay Area scene. In 1992, he included in his magazine flexidiscs with music by producer Dan the Automator, DJ Peanut Butter Wolf, and MC Charizma; from this modest beginning the record label Bomb Hip-Hop was born. In 1995, Bomb Hip-Hop released *Return of the DJ*, the first all-turntablist album. Paul was motivated by what he saw as the disappearance of the DJ from the hip-hop scene. "When I came up with the concept of the first *Return of the DJ* in 1994," Paul explains, "I was disappointed with rap albums no longer featuring DJs scratching on them." He fondly remembered how DJs like Cash Money, Jazzy Jeff, Joe Cooley, and Mr. Mixx all had tracks spotlighting their talents when they spun for rappers (in these cases, MC Marvelous, The Fresh Prince, Rodney O, and 2 Live Crew, respectively). The idea behind the release, and the title, was to bring the DJ back into the spotlight. "So I decided to contact DJs that I knew and make a whole album of scratching music. I just told the DJs [to] make their tracks however they could, and try to keep it under five minutes." The idea was simple but unprecedented, and it made an unmistakable statement. On DJ Z-Trip's contribution, "U Can Get With Discs or U Can Get With D.A.T.," a voice proclaims: "Ignoring the disc jockey in hip-hop is like ignoring the guitar in rock and roll. You're either a D.A.T. jockey or a disc jockey." At the time, Z-Trip was a relative unknown, but he later became hugely popular—*DJ Times* declared him America's Best DJ in 2009.

The album features a number of up-and-coming turntablists, including Bay Area DJs (The Invisibl Skratch Piklz, Peanut Butter Wolf), but also Southern California tablists (Aladdin, Cut Chemist, the Beat Junkies), as well as DJs from New York (Rob Swift); Phoenix, Arizona (Z-Trip); England (Jeep Beat Collective); and Japan (Yutaka and Honda). David Paul's long-lived *Return of the DJ* series became a galvanizing force for turntablism, helping form and then enlarge the turntablist community, not only in Northern California, but throughout the world.[50]

Unlike Billy Jam and Dave Paul, Alex Aquino was not a DJ, though for many years he managed Bay Area turntablists, including Apollo, Mix Master Mike, Qbert, and Shortkut. His most important contribution to the world of the DJ, however, was his founding of the International Turntablist Federation in 1996. The idea behind the ITF was in part to fill the void left in 1994 by the discontinuation of the New Music Seminar Battle. The NMS featured head-to-head battles, favored by many turntablists over the showcase style used by the DMC, in which DJs performed for the judges but did not directly face other DJs. The ITF was also more focused on pushing turntable technique and less on reaching out to broad audiences than the DMC. Aquino explained the contrast this way: "The DMC thinks DJs doing handstands on turntables is the shit. And sometimes the crowd falls for it, because it's entertaining. Me, I'd rather hear a new scratching pattern. Some people just hear noise when these guys play. To us, it's music. It's percussion on a turntable."[51] The ITF also sponsored a team battle, something that DMC had flirted with but did not initiate formally until 1999. The first ITF competition crowned Total Eclipse of the X-Men (later X-Ecutioners) champion, after defeating Mr. Turntablism himself, Babu, in the final round. The next year the ITF introduced "Category Battles," specialized competitions that focused on either beat juggling or scratching, held in addition to the general "Advancement" battles, which were open to all types of "beat/noise manipulation."[52] That year Babu returned, defeating British DJ Tony Vegas in the scratching category battle. Some say that Vegas, the Brit with the American name, never stood a chance battling against a Californian and being judged by mostly American DJs. In subsequent years, the ITF battles became more internationalized with competitions held throughout the world, a development that addressed charges of bias.

With its focus on technique, the ITF helped advance the art of turntablism worldwide. At the same time, some felt that this specialization further isolated turntablism from mainstream DJing and hip-hop in general. DJ Pone (Travis Rimando), active in the Bay Area scene during the ITF's heyday, has mixed feelings about the category battles. "In a way," he suggests, "it encouraged the development of over-technical styles you see in abundance at DJ battles today."[53] The ITF sponsored battles for nearly a decade and was superseded by the

IDA: the International DJ Association. In its time, the ITF sponsored hundreds of battles throughout the world, acting as another global disseminator of turntablism while representing the hotbed of the art, the San Francisco Bay Area.

Arguably, ground zero of Bay Area turntablism during this time was a small club in San Francisco's seedy Tenderloin district. "Don't scan the tourist guides for Club Deco," advised the *San Jose Metro* in 1996, two years after founder Cleo Fishman opened it. "If it were any further underground, it would scratch the earth's core."[54] The club had two floors—those who patronized the upstairs came to dance; those who ventured down into "the dungeon," as some called it, came to scratch or watch others scratch. "Downstairs, the new breed of DJs gathers to jam," explained the *Metro* article. "Hip-hop culture looms large within this converted basement. Graffiti artists sketch tags in ringed notebooks. B-boys lean against I-beams, sucking on skinny joints. Humidity and weed smoke combine to give the scene a queasy, underwater feel."[55] Tuesday nights were for the turntablists—Apollo started the weekly gathering, first calling it Many Styles, then Beat Lounge. Lasting from 1995 to 1999, it served as a turntablism incubator where DJs would come to jam, to share, and to learn. It was remarkable for its openness—anyone could come in and sit just a foot or two away from some of the greatest DJs of the day, studying their technique at close range. And this was exactly Apollo's goal. "Our vision was to have a place where all the turntablists could just come in and do their thing—to sit in and play, like a jazz venue."[56] Qbert compared it to Minton's Playhouse, the legendary Harlem club where Dizzy Gillespie, Thelonious Monk, Charlie Parker, and others helped create a new form of jazz in the 1940s that came to be known as bebop.[57] The comparison isn't off the mark—both bebop and turntablism had roots in popular dance music, but became more complex and hermetic, appealing more to connoisseurs than to those who simply wanted to get their groove on.

The Beat Lounge had a smaller, even more underground counterpart—the home of DJ Qbert, which for years he regularly opened up for jam sessions. Gathering around a large table ringed with eight turntables—it's called the Lair of the Octagon, or just the Octagon—the musicians often "trade fours," to use a jazz term, with each DJ soloing for four bars; the music circles the table as each DJ responds to his or her neighbor, continuing and expanding the conversation. Even rank beginners and non-DJs are encouraged to get on the decks; few people who visit Qbert's home leave without making some noise.

I experienced this myself when I visited Qbert in March 2008. At the time, he lived in a handsome, well-appointed house in upper-middle-class Burlingame, California; a shiny black Range Rover with SQRATCH license plates sat out front. (He grew up in much more modest surroundings in the Excelsior district of San Francisco, living with his mother well into his twenties.) After talking for a while, we moved into the Octagon so he could practice for an upcoming gig. Qbert narrated his practice session, explaining that he was currently trying to incorporate drumming techniques in his music. He played some paradiddles and then more complex patterns in 5 and 7 in which both hands scratched simultaneously, each in a different rhythm. (He calls this the "brainsplitter.") At one point he paused and asked me if I scratched. A little, and poorly, I answered. So he gave me an impromptu lesson, at the end of which I was transforming and stabbing better than I had ever done before. Qbert was curious about my musical background, and we chatted about the similarities between violin playing and scratching, and how certain bowings might be translated into scratches. In one sense, there was nothing unusual about my experience—he had shared his time similarly with countless others before me. But my encounter with Qbert is extremely unusual in another sense. I can't think of another equally accomplished musician, whether DJ, rock guitarist, or concert violinist, whose home, techniques, and practice sessions are so freely open to others.

Qbert was not the only Bay Area DJ with such an open attitude, as Apollo's Tuesday nights at Club Deco demonstrate. But Qbert has always been the one who set the tone. As Billy Jam has said, "Everybody looks to him with awe and respect. He's truly an inspiration on all levels, as a human being and an artist." Fellow Filipinos (and especially Filipino Americans) look at him with a

Figure 5.4 DJ Qbert stands before the Octagon in his home in Burlingame, California, March 27, 2008. (Photograph by Mark Katz.)

particular sense of pride; he inspired them not just because he was good, but because he was one of them. As Rhettmatic told me, "He looks the same as I do, he's doing the same thing I want to do. [Maybe] he was just a dope DJ who happened to be Filipino. But from a Filipino point of view. . . ." Here, he went silent for a moment, and thumped his heart with his fist. "He was our Michael Jordan. He opened the door for us."[58]

Although I've been focusing here on the Filipino American turntablists in the Bay Area, they were not, of course, the only DJs active in the area at the time or since. A short list of other artists would have to include Dan the Automator, DJ Disk, Doc Rice, DJ Flare, Pam the Funkstress, Peanut Butter Wolf, DJ Quest, Mike Relm, DJ Shadow, Snayk Eyez, DJ Swift Rock, Tyra from Saigon, and the crews the Bulletproof Scratch Hamsters and the Supernatural Turntable Artists (some of whose members I've named here). These DJs are black, white, Latino, and (non-Filipino) Asian American, making the San Francisco DJ community perhaps the most racially and ethnically diverse anywhere. Yet it is impossible to ignore what Oliver Wang, in his study of the Bay Area DJ scene, calls the "Filipino Factor."[59] The phenomenal success of Filipino American DJs prompts a simple question: Why so many? What is it that has led a disproportionate number of Filipinos to the highest reaches of the turntablist world? Is there something, well, *Filipino*, about DJing?

Actually, no. There is no genetic predisposition toward scratching among any ethnic group, Filipino or otherwise. And there's nothing about the Philippines, its water, air, or food that makes Filipinos particularly good at the crab scratch. So what is it? Scholar Elizabeth Pisares suggests that Filipino Americans are driven by their near-invisibility in mainstream American culture. They are, she explains, "alienated from whites (for being nonwhite), blacks and Latinos (for being Asian), and Asian Americans (for being insufficiently Asian)—and resist invisibility by demanding they be acknowledged as Filipino American."[60] This is an important point that helps explain the cohesiveness of the Filipino American DJ community in the Bay Area. But why did the community cohere specifically around DJing? The answer, Oliver Wang suggests, may be rooted in "a very particular social structure that made it easier for DJ crews to get started, find gigs, and thus sustain themselves." Wang describes the Filipino American community as "deeply socially inter-networked," a community that supports "a preponderance of social events and festivities in which music plays an important role." These activities provided regular opportunities and great demand for DJs. "What made DJing so popular amongst Filipino Americans," Wang concludes, was "a special kind of social capital that these crews could draw upon in order to get started and stay DJing."[61]

In other words, the "Filipino Factor" is not a product of biology or nationality, but of space, place, time, and community. In this sense, the Bay Area DJ scene of the 1990s, dominated by Filipino Americans, was not so different from the African American- and Latino-dominated New York DJ scene of the 1970s. In both cases, a mobile DJ scene developed from the activities of self-taught DJs from working class minority communities. In both cases, as the scene developed it started spotlighting DJs as *musicians*, spawning skill-based battles and new techniques. And in both cases the scene flourished because of the industriousness, ingenuity, and entrepreneurial spirit of the DJs. When we consider two strikingly similar statements made by pioneers of both scenes, we realize that it is a spirit of resourcefulness and creativity that defines both, above and beyond their racial, ethnic, and economic particulars. The way GrandWizzard Theodore explains it, "Hip-hop came from nothing. The people that created hip-hop *had* nothing. And what they did was, they created *something* from *nothing*."[62] Now listen to words of Shortkut, a fellow DJ from a different generation, ethnic background, and coast. "That creativity of trying to make something out of nothing. That's just what the whole DJ essence is about."[63]

THE RISE OF TURNTABLIST CREWS

Hip-hop crews had existed since the 1970s. Crews might be populated with multiple MCs, "hook-up men," and various helpers—but most had a single DJ. There were some exceptions. The L Brothers had the three disc-spinning Livingston siblings—Cordio, Mean Gene, and GrandWizzard Theodore. The Mighty Force had Disco Wiz, Grandmaster Caz, Pambaataa (a woman DJ named after Bambaataa), and later DJ Mighty Mike and Starski. But their DJs always performed alone. Having more than one DJ simply allowed the crew to cover more parties or helped expand their equipment reserves. On the other side of the country, there were also crews of mobile DJs operating in the San Francisco Bay Area all through the 1980s, but there, too, DJs performed alone. Throughout the 1970s and 1980s, whether in New York, California, or elsewhere, the idea of having multiple DJs performing at the same time would have been a foreign concept. For the most part, a DJ's job was to get dancers moving or to provide the instrumental tracks for MCs. For this, only a single DJ was necessary.

The concept of the DJ crew as a performing ensemble, as the equivalent of a band, only made sense when the DJ could be accepted as self-sufficient, no longer understood primarily as a supplier of music to MCs or dancers. In other words, turntablism was a necessary precondition for the existence of turntable bands. At the same time, the success of these crews validated the whole idea of turntablism, proving that two, three, or four DJs performing together could create a rich new musical repertoire. Crews and turntablism existed in a symbiotic, mutually reinforcing relationship.

Two of the earliest and most important turntablist crews—I'll use this term to differentiate from the early DJ crews—were New York's X-Men and the Bay Area's Invisibl Skratch Piklz. They both had their origins at the turn of the 1990s, and came into prominence by mid-decade. Following not long after was the Beat Junkies (more formally known as the World Famous Beat Junkies), founded in Orange County, California, in 1992. Dozens of crews followed, but these were the three most prominent crews of the 1990s, and their stories are central to the history of turntablism.

The X-Men began as a group of DJs in Harlem, New York, in 1989. The crew, originally comprising Johnny Cash, Roc Raida, Sean Cee, and Steve Dee, took its name from the team of comic-book superheroes; the name was also something of a challenge to a rival group in Brooklyn known as the Supermen Crew, led by DJ Clark Kent. Rob Swift and his mentor Dr. Butcher, both from Queens, joined in 1991.[64] Steve Dee drifted away after going on tour as DJ for the hip-hop/R&B group Guy, and Dr. Butcher, Johnny Cash, and Sean Cee left as well. In 1992, the group was a trio—Roc Raida (the only remaining original member), Rob Swift, and Mista Sinista—and in 1996 Total Eclipse joined. This quartet remained stable for several years, and it was in this lineup that the X-Men became known as one of the premier turntablist crews in the world.[65] Each member was not only an experienced and successful battler, but they all worked with important hip-hop artists and groups. They were

Figure 5.5 Members of the X-Ecutioners (originally the X-Men). From left to right: Precision, Roc Raida, Rob Swift, Total Eclipse. (Photograph by Robert Adam Mayer.)

celebrated for their intricate juggling routines and charismatic performances, replete with body tricks, boasts, and disses.

In 1997, the group began recording albums, starting with *X-pressions*, and their move into the studio coincided with a new name: the X-Ecutioners. As Rob Swift explains it, the change was prompted by a lawyer who suggested that if they started selling CDs as the X-Men, Marvel Comics, owner of the name and the brand, would unleash their superhero attorneys on them.[66] As the X-Ecutioners, their fame increased as they released more albums and began to enjoy mainstream popularity. After their 2004 album *Revolutions*, however, Swift and then Eclipse left the group and eventually formed a trio, Ill Insanity, with DJ Precision. In 2007, the group reunited at Roc Raida's Gong Battle and toured on and off briefly afterward. Sadly, tragedy struck the group—and the DJ community as a whole—in September 2009, when thirty-seven-year-old Roc Raida died from injuries sustained while training in Krav Maga, the Israeli hand-to-hand combat system. He lived and died a battler.[67]

In 1991, the earliest incarnation of what came to be known as the Invisibl Skratch Piklz formed three thousand miles to the west. The original Piklz— Apollo, Mix Master Mike, and Qbert—were first known as the Rock Steady DJs; it wasn't until 1995 that they started calling themselves (for no good reason, apparently) the Invisibl Skratch Piklz. The personnel changed over the years, with Shortkut, D-Styles, Disk, and Babu joining and departing at various times. (In 1999, two former Piklz, Apollo and Shortkut, joined Vinroc to create Triple Threat DJs, and were still going strong a dozen years later.) The ISP style stood in stark contrast to their East Coast rivals'. The Northern Californians were famed for their complex scratching and tended to use more abstract sounds and noises than recognizable songs in their routines. They also looked and acted different. The West Coast Piklz were Filipino American, their onstage demeanor more lighthearted and their offstage interests tending toward the extraterrestrial—Qbert and Mix Master Mike speak often and to all appearances seriously about alien life forms.[68] By contrast, the Xs were African American (with some Latin roots—Swift, I've mentioned, considers himself "100 percent Colombian"), and presented a more menacing, streetwise personality. Their rivalry, which culminated in the legendary showdown at the 1996 ITF competition was purely an onstage one, however. Offstage, the two groups were friends, always quick to praise each other.

We'll get back to the friendly rivalry between these two crews, but first let's travel to Southern California, where the Beat Junkies took root. In the world of turntablism, Los Angeles has long been a second city to San Francisco, and its contributions to the art form unfortunately get less attention than they should. Simply the list of important L.A. hip-hop DJs who came up in the 1980s is impressive: battlers Aladdin and Joe Cooley; DJs-turned-MCs Egyptian Lover,

Dr. Dre, and Ice-T; renowned mobile DJs Rodger Clayton and DJ Bobcat (of the crew Uncle Jamm's Army); influential radio DJs Julio G. and Tony G. Other notable L.A. DJs of then and now include Cut Chemist, DJ Hapa, DJ M.Walk, DJ Muggs, DJ Nu-Mark, DJ Quik, P-Trix, DJ Pooh, DJ Revolution, Chris "The Glove" Taylor, Alonzo Williams, and DJ Yella.

Two forces in particular shaped the hip-hop DJ scene of greater Los Angeles: KDAY AM 1580 and the flourishing network of mobile DJ crews. KDAY was the world's first 24-hour hip-hop station, and with its team of popular DJs, the Mixmasters, it directly and indirectly launched the careers of many of the area's mixers and scratchers in 1980s. Aladdin, for example, became a battler just so he could get a show on KDAY. "I got into the battle scene by being a KDAY Mixmaster. You had to battle the radio DJs order to become a mix show DJ." From battling at local skating rinks, he later moved up to battling in DMC competitions, which required him to travel to what he calls "the Cold Hearted City of New York."[69] KDAY had a broader, more indirect influence on DJing as well. It was the station where most Angelenos got their first taste of hip-hop and first heard the sound of scratching. Rhettmatic grew up listening to KDAY, which turned him on to "The Adventures of Grandmaster Flash on the Wheels of Steel" and "Rockit" and other now-classic DJ tracks. "It's hard not to be influenced by that," he explains. "Any DJ coming from LA," he adds, "one way or another, was influenced by KDAY Mixmasters and KDAY in general."[70] And in trying to do what he heard on the radio, Rhettmatic—like many aspiring DJs of the area—discovered that there was an active mobile DJ scene full of crews waiting to be discovered, and to discover him.

It was out of this mobile DJ scene that the Beat Junkies emerged. The future Junkies were essentially the stars of their respective groups, and though many of the members had known each other in the 1980s, it was not until 1992 that J. Rocc, an Orange County DJ, founded the crew. Its original members also included Curse, Icy Ice, Melo-D, Rhettmatic, Symphony, and What?!. (Symphony was the only woman in the group.) Babu became part of the group in 1993, and several others came and went over the years, including Choc, D-Styles, Havik, Red-Jay, Shortkut, and Tommy Gun. (Both D-Styles and Shortkut also performed with the Piklz at various times.) Many of the Junkies were accomplished battlers—as a group they won the 1997 ITF team battle—and several also toured and recorded with MCs, including Dilated Peoples (Babu) and the Visionaries (Rhettmatic). In the late 1990s, the Junkies released three albums, *The World Famous Beat Junkies*, volumes 1, 2, and 3. In many ways the Beat Junkies can be thought of as a hybrid of the X-Men and the Invisibl Skratch Piklz. Their routines focused equally on scratching and beat juggling, and were influenced by both groups. The Junkies even *looked* like a combination of the X-Men and the Piklz. Several were Filipino, but J. Rocc is African American, and Melo-D is

Figure 5.6 Members of the Beat Junkies. Babu, foreground; others, left to right, J.Rocc, Rhettmatic, Shortkut, Melo-D. (Photograph by B+.)

Latino. Although they largely stopped battling and performing as a turntablist crew in 1998, they were intact more than a decade later, now focusing more on spinning at parties and clubs.

By the mid-1990s, the three crews were everywhere, traveling the world as they won battles and electrified audiences. During this period there was only one time that these DJs performed together. The event wasn't advertised, nor was it open to the public; few people today even know about it. The gathering took place in San Francisco on March 2, 1996, the night before the U.S. finals of the DMC. The Piklz were locals, and the other crews were represented in the battle—Babu and Melo-D from the Junkies, and Mista Sinista from the X-Men. In 24 hours these DJs would do battle, but until then there was no beef. As Rhettmatic puts it, "We got egos, but when it comes down to it, it's all about the music. That's why all us DJs get along for the most part."[71] So they gathered in a warehouse, set up several sound systems, and jammed. Andrew Bernal, the Junkies' manager, still marvels at the experience. "Just to see Qbert, Mix Master

Mike, Apollo, Rob Swift, Sinista in one room in a warehouse—everybody hangin' out and cuttin' it up—it was amazing."[72] The night after the warehouse summit, they battled to see which crew would leave with bragging rights. As it turns out, none of them did. In one of the great upsets in battle history, DJ Swamp of Cleveland took the crown.

The Beat Junkies, the Invisibl Skratch Piklz, and the X-Men helped legitimize the idea that a group of DJs could be a self-sufficient musical ensemble, and led the way for dozens of crews and turntable bands around the world, a short list of which would include The Allies, Birdy Nam Nam, The Bullet Proof Space Hamsters (a.k.a. The Bullet Proof Space Travelerz), C2C, 5th Platoon, Jeep Beat Collective, Kireek, The Scratch Perverts, and The Trooperz. But all of these groups can, in some way, thank the original three crews for paving the way.

Turntablism was the realization of a long-held goal among many DJs: independence. For DJs, independence meant the ability to create music that did not exist simply to serve the needs of b-boys, b-girls, and MCs, but could be enjoyed on its own merits. Independence meant technology advanced enough to free DJs from any mechanical constraints and the freedom to pursue their musical ideas wherever they might lead. Independence meant a physical space and a particular demographic—the San Francisco Bay Area and Filipino Americans— that allowed turntablism to flourish. Independence for DJs also meant a musical space—the battle—where they could explore the limits of their techniques. All of these factors—musical, technological, demographic, and geographic— were interconnected, and turntablism, perhaps the most profound development in the history of the hip-hop DJ, was the product of these many forces.

The Art of War—The DJ Battle: 1991–1996

So it is said that if you know your enemies and know yourself, you can win a hundred battles without a single loss.

—Sun Tzu, *The Art of War*, sixth century BC[1]

If I'm going to be in a battle [and] I know that your specialty is scratching, I'm going to practice a scratch routine to take you out, you know? It's almost like you're preparing yourself for combat. You come up with strategies; it's like a war. I want to practice it a certain way and be able to execute it every time the same exact way. If I go up against this DJ, I want to intercept whatever style he may come at me with. And when I go up against this other DJ, he DJs like this, so I need to be prepared for this and that and the third.

—Rob Swift, 2001[2]

By the mid-1990s, battles had spread across the world, inspiring a select segment of DJs to devote countless hours to the art of destroying rivals with vinyl. For these highly driven turntablists, battling was a way of life, occupying their waking hours and haunting what little sleep they managed. Their numbers were small, but their influence enormous, and during this period it was the battle, more than anything else, that pushed the growth and development of turntablism. To speak of an "art of war" here may seem grandiose, yet there *is* an art to battling, one that reveals itself in the preparation it demands, the techniques it inspires, and the music it creates.

RULES OF ENGAGEMENT, TOOLS OF WAR

Every battle is slightly different, but in general there are two types: head-to-head and showcase. The head-to-head format dates to the earliest days of hip-hop when battles typically involved DJs facing off against each other. In larger, more formalized head-to-head battles, DJs are paired and perform routines in alternation, after which a panel of judges (often several former battlers) selects one DJ to advance to the next round. These elimination rounds continue until one DJ is left standing. The first major battle series, established by the New Music Seminar, was organized around head-to-head elimination rounds, as was its successor, the International Turntablist Federation. By contrast, the DMC World DJ Championship featured the showcase style, in which DJs do not so much perform *against* each other as *for* the judges. (Later, DMC added a head-to-head competition.) Showcase routines tend to be longer (the DMC's are six minutes long), while head-to-head battle routines may be between one and two minutes long. Whether head-to-head or showcase, most battle organizers provide the turntables and mixers; DJs are expected to bring their own needles, slipmats, and headphones.

The first thing to understand about DJ battle routines at this time is that improvisation played almost no role, and this has largely remained the case. Contrast this with MC and b-boy and b-girl battles, where improvisation is common and crucial. Unlike DJs, dancers and rhymers keep all their weapons in their bodies; their armaments are instantly accessible and infinitely manipulable. The DJ's weapons, however, are records, tangible and fixed, a limiting factor that battlers must overcome. Most routines, therefore, are precisely planned compositions, created and memorized by the battler. As Rob Swift points out, however, the battle DJ still needs to be prepared for anything:

> You're dealing with a machine, and sometimes it can be faulty. There can be something wrong with it—the needles might skip on you or the sound may be messed up. So if you go to do a routine and you're not able to execute it the way you want you have to be ready to just improv, just do what comes natural while you're on stage, and hope that the crowd will like you, or hope that the crowd won't tell the difference . . . But when you're battling, you rarely improv because when you're battling, you're bringing to the stage set routines.[3]

All of this is to say that good battlers typically know *exactly* what to do once on the battlefield, even when they don't.

Every battle routine must be unique and original to the DJ performing it. No self-respecting battler would ever perform another DJ's routine or use the same selection of records, even if the routine itself was different. In DJ battles, originality is the highest virtue, while biting is beneath contempt. Here is how rule #4 of The Gong Battle explained it:

> 4. BITING, REPEATING ROUTINES AND OUTRIGHT WACKNESS: A DJ will be gonged if the judges think that he/she is biting or wack. It's OK to show influence but outright use of the same records (with the exception of a diss) and doing the same routine will be grounds for being eliminated by way of the gong.[4]

Most DJs know better than to perform someone else's whole routine, so actual instances of biting tend to be less flagrant—for example, using the same beat juggle pattern as another DJ and using the same records to do it. But DJs learn by watching and imitating others, and new techniques or moves are often variations on existing ones; there's a fine line between drawing inspiration from a DJ and biting that DJ's moves. As Shortkut says, "Without influence, there wouldn't be no change."[5] "Change" is the crucial word—to use someone's move without biting, there must be something new or different about it. Here's DJ Rectangle's advice: "If you're going to take someone's move, I would do it better than that person did it in the first place or slightly change it—put *your* style into it."[6]

Although all routines are, or at least should be, different, they usually share common elements. Most feature some combination of scratching and beat juggling, as well as a verbal element (wordplay), and a physical element (body tricks). We've encountered scratching and beat juggling throughout these pages, so let's focus on two aspects of battling that became more prevalent in the battles of the early and mid-1990s.

WORDPLAY

In battle, the biggest audience response often comes not from what the DJs are *doing*, but from what they're *saying*. But the DJs themselves rarely actually speak—their words come from their records, carefully chosen and juxtaposed to display their wit or intimidate their opponents.

Wordplay, as the verbal component of battling is often called, can appear at any point in a routine, but is often heard at the beginning and end, acting as a framing device. Wordplay can be about anything, but typically DJs use it to boast about their incredible prowess (musical and otherwise) or to diss, or insult, their rivals. The most memorable wordplay tends to be in the form of disses, and it's the disses that DJs and audiences remember years later. For example, in a single routine in the 1998 DMC U.S. finals, DJ Dummy used his wordplay to insult just about every one of his competitors; more than a decade on, Internet commentators talk about it as one of the best diss routines of all time.[7]

Disses can be mild, like "All you other DJs are a bunch of jerks" (from Marley Marl and MC Shan's "Marley Marl Scratch"), but they are often extravagantly obscene. DJs and fans of battle culture often cite DJ Noize's devastating disses as a model of the art, especially his 1993 New Music Seminar routine when he faced 8-Ball. Disses make up nearly every second of his one-minute routine, culminating in a *coup de grace* that plays on 8-Ball's name. Noize starts with a bit of Gang Starr, "And if ya don't like it and you wanna step up . . ." (from "Words from the Nutcracker") and then finishes the sentence with a fragment from N.W.A.'s "She Swallowed It," which sounds as if it were sampled from an X-rated how-to record: "Gently place the balls into the mouth," a well-mannered woman's voice instructs. An amateur video of the battle captures the audience roaring, leaping to its feet as Noize gestures to his crotch, then points to an offscreen 8-Ball.[8] In a move that mirrors the sexual violence of male prison life, Noize has made his opponent his "bitch," simultaneously dominating and emasculating him.

"That man was a beast," marvels DJ Craze, one of the most successful battlers of all time. "I was always scared to go up against him cause I knew he would diss me hard. What made his disses the best was that they made sense. He went in and would diss you on exactly what was wack about you."[9] This is exactly what Craze did in his 1998 ITF battle when he dissed England's First Rate using a record of old Looney Tunes cartoons. "What a dope, what a maroon," Bugs Bunny sneers, "You're going too fast . . . you're c-c-c-crazy!" Daffy Duck sputters. Craze gets high marks because he specifically mocked First Rate's scratching, which he illustrated by hunching over the records and flailing wildly as Daffy spoke.[10]

To outsiders, battle disses may seem cruel, but insiders accept that it's just part of the game. DJ Craze had to explain this to his mother, who was in the audience for his battle against First Rate. "I remember after the battle my mom came up to me and kinda told me off for being so rude to him. I explained to her that this was a battle and that anything goes. She just laughed it off and told me I killed it."[11] No doubt disses sting, but most DJs don't take them personally. It's easier to shrug them off when they're delivered via vinyl and other people's voices rather than directly from the other DJs. Lines can be crossed, however. Former battle champion A-Trak put it this way: "You want your disses to be a little bit personal, meaning that they're specific to the person that you're calling out, but you don't want them to be pointless in the context of a battle. So for example, to me, disses about your opponent being really fat are hard to pull off. It's stupid."[12] New York's DJ Fatfingaz actually thinks DJs should take *all* disses

personally. In a 2007 Internet discussion he wrote: "IF SOMEONE IS DISSING YOU
. . . TAKE THAT SHIT PERSONAL!! ALL THAT HAPPY SHIT GOT TO FLY OUT THE
DOOR! THIS IS A COMPETITION . . . NOT A FUCKIN' A.A. MEETING!"[13] DJs should
not laugh off disses so easily, he argues—it dulls the killer instinct.

Wordplay is just one of the battle DJ's tools, and like all tools—or weapons—
it can be used well or abused, and is subject to debate about how best it should
be deployed. The same can be said for another important tool that was also
widely used and sometimes abused by DJs in the 1990s: body tricks.

BODY TRICKS

Since the very earliest days of hip-hop, DJs have been bringing more than just
records to battles. They also brought moves: spinning in place in between beats,
moving the fader with their elbows, scratching while reaching under their legs,
using their feet instead of their hands—anything to add a bit of flash, a bit of
spectacle. Many early DJs were also (or formerly) b-boys or b-girls, and this
experience influenced their DJing, and the battle scene in general. Johnny
"Juice" Rosado, for a time one of Public Enemy's DJs and a fierce battler, was a
b-boy first. He speaks of some of his body tricks as *power moves*, a term used by
dancers to describe their most impressive techniques. One he called the Twin
Towers—this was before the September 11, 2001, terrorist attacks, of course—
where he would stand on the table that held his decks, straddle one of them and
reach down between his legs to scratch the record. He would then do a back flip,
landing right behind the turntables and resume scratching without missing a
beat. Never missing the beat is crucial—body tricks should have no effect on
the sound of the routine. They are handicaps imposed expressly for the purpose
of heroically overcoming them. It might seem odd that body tricks—seen but
never heard—should be so important to a musical art form. But DJing, and battling in particular, is not simply a sonic phenomenon. The sight of the DJ affects
our experience of the music, and can make the difference between a champion
battler and a runner-up.

Although most DJs recognize the value of body tricks, there's often debate
among DJs about when they become distracting and detract from the music.
Consider DJ David's winning 1991 DMC routine, which included the most
notorious body trick in battle history. The setting was London, the DMC World
Championships. Germany's DJ David, the reigning champion, began his final
six-minute routine with his turntables cloaked in a large banner. When he
unveiled his gear his decks were not sitting side-by-side, but were *stacked*, one
resting atop four aluminum soda cans placed at each corner of the lower turntable. It was simply an unusual set-up—which he soon dismantled—but it

clearly communicated his penchant for spectacle and foreshadowed his final trick. For the next four minutes he performed a number of standard body tricks, but he kept getting faster and faster, his motions accelerating to an almost superhuman speed. No one would still be talking about his routine, however, had he stopped there. With about thirty seconds left in his routine he picked up his still-playing right turntable and handed it to someone standing a few feet off to the side. Next he removed the record from the left turntable and placed a round object—about the size and shape of a snuff tin or a hockey puck—over top the spindle. Then in one fluid motion he put his right hand on the now-covered spindle and boosted himself aloft, his elbow tucked into his gut and the rest of his body parallel to the ground. Propped atop the platter and powered by the Technics 1200's beefy motor, he spun eight times while the other turntable accompanied him. He rotated, suspended several feet above the floor, accompanied by 1988 song "I'll House You"—"Here we go, round and round and round and round," the Jungle Brothers chanted. The crowd erupted. The dumbfounded host Tony Prince shouted hoarsely, "Wowww, I've never seen anything like that before that in my life!"[14] DJ David was crowned the first back-to-back champion in the history of the DMC competition, while runner-up Qbert looked on, stunned. ◐ "This was the greatest trick ever," Prince told me many years later. "It was absolutely brilliant!"[15] Others say it was simply a gimmick, that Qbert's performance was more musical, more technical, and more worthy of first place. Look at the hundreds of comments accompanying the YouTube videos, and even after twenty years there's no clear consensus.[16]

In the 1990s, body tricks started to change. They didn't disappear completely, but they became less outrageous and rarely involved the kind of props some earlier DJs used. The change was directly linked to the increasing complexity of battle routines. If, musically speaking, routines were to become denser, more sophisticated, and taken more seriously, then body tricks had to be minimized, and for some, they fell by the wayside.

BATTLE RECORDS

The growing frequency of wordplay in the 1990s and the relative decline of body tricks at the same time can be connected to a single development in the history of DJ competitions: the introduction and proliferation of the battle record. These are compilation discs created expressly for the needs of turntablists, and battle DJs in particular. Listen to one play for more than a few seconds and you get the impression of rapidly switching among radio stations, and odd ones at that. A looped drum break may be followed by the "ah" and "fresh" samples, followed by dialogue from a martial arts film, succeeded by a string of obscenities from a rap song. Arriving on the scene in 1992, the battle record was a major labor-saving device, giving DJs ready-made collections of sounds to scratch and beats to juggle as well as enough boasts and disses to populate their routines with wordplay.

The battle record did not appear out of nowhere, and it's worth backspinning in time to consider some precursors. Before the first battle records were released came the twenty-five-volume series called *Ultimate Beats and Breaks* (*UBB*), created by Lenny Roberts's Street Beat Records.[17] These were not battle records per se—they didn't extract parts of songs. Rather, Roberts, a record collector and amateur DJ, compiled whole funk, soul, rock, and pop songs that had the breaks beloved by hip-hop DJs; these discs are commonly called breakbeat records or breakbeat compilations. He issued the first volume in 1986, which included The Winstons' "Amen Brother" and its famous break. Other classics, like "Apache," "Big Beat," and "Dance to the Drummer's Beat," arrived in later volumes. The final installment came in 1991.

The *UBB* volumes were a godsend to many DJs as well as beat-making producers, saving them the time, energy, and money required to collect the records individually. They were especially useful for those who came up in the game when the breaks were getting harder to find. Among them was DJ Shadow, who attests that "they were the blueprint for what everybody was sampling from, from '86 to '91" and saw them as something to "absorb, digest, and spit out" in creating his own music.[18]

The series, however, didn't sit well with some among the generation of DJs who had discovered all those breaks. "For real collectors and DJs," reports DJ and producer Prince Paul, "it was traumatic. You know, you're there covering up your labels and all that, and those breakbeat records exposed a lot. To me, as far as beat collecting, breakbeat compilations ruined everything."[19] As Grandmixer D.ST puts it, these compilations, and *UBB* founder Lenny Roberts in particular, violated what he calls the "sacred crates":

> The sacred crates is what enable the hip-hop DJ to become a hip-hop DJ. [Y]our uniqueness . . . was your particular obscure records which made you different from the person over there. So we have to go to Grandmaster Flash parties because he has these particular beats that only he has. Everybody had records that the other DJs didn't have. That's what got people to come to your party.[20]

Lenny Roberts also went these parties, where D.ST often encountered him. "After the party, he would go, 'Hey man, what was the name of the record you was just playing? You gimme that one, and I'll give you that record that Bam plays that you don't have.'" To pry information out of tight-lipped DJs, he also offered to replace their favorite vinyl, knowing that, as D.ST explains, "we were wearing out these valuable, valuable records, and we needed to get new ones." D.ST believes that Roberts was just pursuing a business opportunity, and wasn't trying to change the culture of the hip-hop DJ. But that's what happened. "We compromised the whole code of secrecy. Before Lenny, you had to be really into hip-hop to have those records. He consolidated all our records. And that was the end of it." This was the end of an era in which knowledge—of records—was one of the highest forms of power that a DJ could wield. But it was also the beginning of a new era, one in which the secrets of hip-hop were no longer guarded by a select few DJs, but became available to a new generation.

Shortly after the final *UBB* volume was issued came the first commercially released battle records.[21] The first two were issued in 1992—*Hamster Breaks* by the Bullet Proof Scratch Hamsters and, a few months later, *Battle Breaks* by the Psychedelic Skratch Bastards (most likely an alias for Apollo, Mix Master Mike, and Qbert, before they became the Invisibl Skratch Piklz).[22] There are now hundreds of battle records to choose from. Favorites include Babu's *Superduckbreaks*, Flare's *Hee Haw Brayks*, Qbert's *Superseal Breaks*, Rectangle's *The Ultimate Battle Weapon*, and Ricci Rucker's *The Utility Phonograph Record*. A-Trak, Craze, ie.MERG, Swamp, and many other DJs have released battle records as well. Some even specialize: for example, *Hater Breaks*, a 2002 record from the late Roc Raida, is especially strong in disses, while *Bikini Wax*, a 2007 release by Shortee and Step1, is the first battle record created by women and, borrowing a women's deodorant slogan, claims to be "Strong enough for a man, made for a woman." Battle records are popular for many reasons. They save DJs time and money, eliminating the need to acquire dozens of records and protecting rare originals they already own. They allow battle DJs to scratch, juggle, and diss rivals without ever removing records from the turntables. DJs can save precious seconds and minimize mishaps, which in turn allows routines to include more scratches and juggles, and a greater variety of songs and sounds. Some battle records are also considered "skipless," meaning that each sound or phrase is repeated several times and occurs at the same position on the record; this way, the needle can jump a groove or two ahead or back without any noticeable change.

As with *Ultimate Beats and Breaks*, DJs have mixed feelings about battle records. Cash Money, for one, opposes them:

I think it's cheating. [Battling] is all about finding that break in the record real fast, faster than the next DJ. That's what made you special, you know? It's more than just scratching, it's about finding the record that suits you [and] being able to find that particular part of the record fast. You know, you take what Jazzy Jay and Theodore were doing with the whole needle dropping. That's actually hard to do.[23]

Another problem Cash Money sees is that battle records disconnect DJs from the music that created hip-hop. Battle records may include the famous breaks, but they never contain whole songs and don't identify the songs themselves; DJs who look no further may have no idea that "ah" and "fresh" come from "Change the Beat" or that the bongo sample on their record began life as "Apache." Cash recalls with disgust an encounter with an unschooled DJ. "I was playing something so basic as Herman Kelley 'Dance to the Drummer's Beat.' This DJ asked me, 'Hey is that from [the battle record] *Superduckbreaks*?'" To a veteran DJ this ignorance of music history is appalling.

Moreover, battle records rarely excerpt long sections of popular songs, meaning that they can't be used to create the type of routine that focuses on a single song and manipulates it. As Rob Swift advises, "When you're sitting at home creating your battle sets it's important to use records that your audience is familiar with. This way, when you manipulate these songs, the audience understands what you're doing to the record. How you're changing it from its original form into your own masterpiece."[24] Qbert, citing Swift as an example, concurs, and even blames himself for the near-disappearance of this approach.

> Rob Swift, he'll play a Biz Markie song, so it's like, "Oh, that's cool," and he all of a sudden flips it, it's like "Aw, man that's genius." I like that style better in battling. But all these DJs now, they're using trick records, you know, and I'm partially to blame for that, "cause I made a lot of trick records, but I actually really like the natural style. . . . It's like jazz—you know the song and then they're flipping it so that you know how they're flipping it.[25]

DJ Pone has offered an interesting philosophical objection to battle records. From one perspective, he points out, "Battle DJing should be about rearranging your original musical source to something which it wasn't intended to be. A battle record was intended to be scratched. And because it was made with that intention, it's doing part of the creative work . . . that the DJ should be doing."[26] So it's not just that battle records eliminate dues-paying, they eliminate part of the subversive element of DJing. From the beginning, hip-hop DJs have been treating records in ways they were never supposed to be treated, touching and scratching them, extracting and rearranging sounds as they please. Ironically, maybe the only way to subvert a battle record is to play it through without stopping or touching it.

Battle records have had unintended and far-reaching consequences. It's no coincidence that as they became more popular, collage-like routines built on snippets of sound became more prevalent. At the same time, one-song and two-song routines became less common. And so did body tricks, perhaps because the newer style of routine, dense with samples, left less time for extravagant physical displays. Although body tricks did not disappear, they tended to be shorter and faster as the 1990s wore on. Disses, on the other hand, proliferated, almost certainly because battle records put so many right in the hands of DJs.

With this introduction to the rules and tools of turntablist warfare, we can now drill deeper into the world of battling in the mid-1990s. We first head to New York for the battle that few DJs and fans can describe without adding the word "legendary."

THE LEGENDARY 1996 ISP *VS.* X-MEN BATTLE

In July 1996, the X-Men and the Invisibl Skratch Piklz squared off for the first time. The setting was Manhattan; the occasion was the Battle for World Supremacy, sponsored by the newly formed International Turntablist Federation. Since both crews had officially retired from battling, the event was billed as an exhibition, though no one called it anything other than a battle. According to Rob Swift, Crazy Legs, the pioneering b-boy from the Rock Steady Crew, suggested the idea to the crew over dinner after an X-Men show. At first they were reluctant—they hadn't battled since 1992—but they quickly relented: "Our egos didn't allow us to say no. No one wanted to come off as scared. At the time, we were the most respected DJs on the East Coast and they were the most respected DJs on the West Coast. We were known for beat juggling and they were known for scratching, and there was always this debate [about] which style was better."[27]

The battle was divided into two parts: the team battle and the individual rounds. First came the team battle, held in the Manhattan Center. Each group performed once, using three sets of turntables, but otherwise there seem not to have been any strict rules in place: the X-Men had five DJs (Diamond J, Mista Sinista, Rob Swift, Roc Raida, and Total Eclipse) and performed for seven minutes, while the Piklz used three DJs (Mix Master Mike, Qbert, and Shortkut) and played almost twice as long.[28] ◗

The X-Men started, with Sinista, Roc Raida, and Rob Swift first on the turntables. After a bit of wordplay, the three DJs combined short scratch patterns into a slow groove. The energy level stayed fairly low, and the routine only occasionally caught fire, as when Swift and Raida rotated on and off a single turntable in quick succession, keeping the beat rock steady, or during the animated sequence of body tricks toward the end. Overall, the routine was marred by a lack of cohesion and precision. This was not the X-Men at their best. (The routine comes off better in a version called "A Turntable Experience," which they later recorded for the 1997 album *Deep Concentration*.)

The Piklz routine opened with some wordplay directed right at the X-Men. It's hard to hear exactly, but it sounds like "No body tricks!" referring the X-Men's predilection for showy moves. The routine was precise and energetic, filled with tight, complex scratching. The three DJs seemed to become one with their machines, human pistons powering the faders and platters. They ran longer than necessary, and Mix Master Mike's mugging for the crowd was excessive, but overall it was a musical and crowd-pleasing performance.[29] The X-Men were going to have to step things up in the individual rounds, or this was going to be a one-sided battle.

The team competition took place earlier in the day; the individual rounds came later, and were held in the famed club Twilo, not far from the Manhattan Center. The actual ITF battle was won by Total Eclipse of the X-Men, with Babu the runner-up. Cash Money and Cutmaster Swift also performed showcases, so by the time the two crews came on again it was well into the morning. The individual battles went three rounds, the routines about two minutes each. This part of the ISP/X-Men showdown was the more exciting of the two parts, and demonstrated the very different strengths of the two crews.[30] 🌀

Roc Raida was up first, and set the tone by creating some personalized, crowd-pleasing disses. He used Gang Starr's "Mostly tha Voice" (1994), replacing certain words (struck through in the following excerpt) with the DJs' names (in brackets), which come from a record on the other turntable:

Then up steps ~~another~~ [Shortkut], he gets smothered
That's word to mother, or should I say moms
I drop bombs, scorchin niggaz like napalm
~~Sucka boy~~ [Qbert] get off my shit
[Qbert] Get off my dick

The rest of his routine consisted of ever-faster beat juggling, all the more impressive because Raida used his nose and chin instead of his hands at times and threw in a host of other body tricks. Watch the video and you'll swear that he has more than the usual number of limbs. Qbert was up next and fired right back with the diss, "Roc Raida can't scratch!" which he put together by reconfiguring lines from LL Cool J's "I Can't Live Without My Radio" (1985) and Egyptian Lover's "What Is a D.J. if He Can't Scratch?" (1984). He took the line, "Cut Creator, rock the beat with your hands" (Cut Creator was LL Cool J's DJ), chopped the words "Creator" and "rock" into "Roc Raida," and then added "can't scratch" from the Egyptian Lover song.[31] But other than the personalized disses, the two routines were completely different, with Qbert pitting his high-speed scratching against Raida's juggling. This battle was also one of the first times that Qbert's new scratch, the crab, was heard in public. The crowd was impressed.

The next pairing was Rob Swift and Mix Master Mike. Swift was clearly trying to intimidate the Piklz. At one point he worked the record with one hand while gesturing menacingly with the other—actually, he used only the middle finger. The music suddenly stopped as he left his equipment and strode across the stage toward the Piklz. He then pointed back at his turntables, and, as if by magic, the music started again. It was pure bravado, and the crowd loved it.

Mix Master Mike retorted with a masterful diss. Using two copies of Casual's "That's How It Is" (1993), he took these lines . . .

> But still I'm taxing, axing the competition,
> And any wack men, I stomp and diss 'em,
> Easily

. . . and by reconfiguring the words, he transformed it into this:

> But still I'm taxing, axing the competition,
> And any X-Men, any X-Men, any X-Men . . . I stomp X-Men, X-Men . . .
> and diss 'em,
> Easily

It's impressive how Mike turned "ax-" into "X" and made the line a diss without introducing another record. He then proceeded to put on a turntablism clinic, even using the same recording that Swift featured in "Rob Gets Busy," a track he released on the *Return of the D.J.* compilation a year earlier. Here we have an exception to the general prohibition against knowingly using the same records as another DJ in a battle routine. Mix Master Mike wasn't trying to copy Swift, he was trying to outdo him. He took straight tones and white noise and manipulated them in every possible way, his long-fingered hands bending and jerking like frenzied, giant spiders. At one point he actually bent one of his records while it was on the turntable and scratched the now-curved disc. Other times he tapped the records, creating staccato zips and zaps like he was firing laser guns. He stared into the middle distance, as if playing a video game in which he no doubt was the hero.

Mista Sinista and Shortkut took the stage next. Sinista's routine featured Steve Dee–like juggling as he slowed the tempo and brought it back to speed again. He threw in some body tricks, but overall, it seemed like a less impressive version of Raida's first routine. Shortkut brought out some old-school funk for the first time in the battle, playing James Brown's "Funky President" from 1974. But then, instead of breaking out a scratch routine as would be expected from a member of the Piklz, he started juggling. Shortkut cites as his main influence none other than one of the original X-Men, Steve Dee, who was actually standing on stage wearing his blue, red, and yellow Superman T-shirt. As a West Coast juggler, Shortkut was an anomaly. "I was just really, heavily influenced by the New York scene," he says.[32] After juggling the word "funky," he threw a curve ball, bringing in some New Wave music with the 1983 song "Beat Box" by The Art of Noise. It was a solid routine, and featured Shortkut's strobe juggle, his original contribution to turntablist technique, but it was not exactly riveting. Looking back on it, Shortkut reflects, "I could have done better. I could have landed my juggles a little cleaner. I could have been a little more charismatic."[33]

Two more rounds followed. Some highlights:

Qbert vs. Roc Raida, round 2: Qbert's routine was a tour de force created from a cymbal sound on one record and a kick and a snare on the other. At one point he was scratching two records in different rhythms at the same time—his brainsplitter move. Except for some brief wordplay in the opening, it was a purely abstract musical composition, with no recognizable songs, no lyrics, and no disses or boasts. It's probably his favorite routine, though he admits that "it kind of goes over people's heads."[34] Raida responded with a stinging diss of Qbert's musical style. Taking the line "all that tiggedy-tiggedy tongue-twistin' shit don't impress me" from "No Equal" by the Beatnuts, he replaced "tiggedy-tiggedy tongue-twistin'" with a caricature of Qbert's scratching, flailing goofily while using the same kind of squelchy sample that Qbert favors. He even wore his cap sideways like Q. In their next meeting, Qbert offered an updated version of an old-style scratch routine. He scratched "ah" and "fresh" against the electronic beat of "Jive Rhythm Trax 122 bpm," which Cash Money used in his 1987 New Music Seminar face-off with Joe Cooley. Qbert didn't like the routine, calling it "boring" in retrospect.[35] Raida also waxed nostalgic, using LL Cool J's "Rock the Bells" (1985), a favorite in routines years earlier. It's full of flashy body tricks, but not as tight as his earlier routines.

Finally, Mix Master Mike vs. Rob Swift: More clean, precise scratching from Mike. As in the first routine, he showed off his incredibly fast twiddle, a tremolo scratch in which the hand's motion is more like a vibration than a back-and-forth action. Swift came on and juggled brief snatches of James Brown, and then went even older-school with the Mohawks' "The Champ" from 1968.

It would have been a challenge to judge these battles. Although some routines were better than others, overall their strengths were so different that they were hard to compare. In terms of dissing and body tricks, and overall crowd appeal, the X-Men dominated. But the Piklz had the edge in the areas of precision and technical originality. The DJs have their own opinions about who won, and I had the opportunity to ask Shortkut, Qbert, and Rob Swift how they would have judged the outcome. (I spoke with them individually and didn't tell them what the others had said.) Surprisingly—or maybe not—they were unanimous. "You know what?" Shortkut said, "I definitely think that the X-Men got us really good on the individual battles."[36] Qbert agreed, saying that in the "one-on-one stuff . . . I think they took it in many ways."[37] As Shortkut pointed out—a fact that had surprised me—"Qbert's never been in a one-on-one battle . . . like a [New Music] Seminar-style battle." This could explain his reluctance to incorporate the kind of disses that win battles. But with the X-Men, battling was "their element," Shortkut said. "And they had it down. Down to the disses, to the stare-downs." Swift made the same point. "At the time our focus was battling one on one, which is why I feel the X-Men won the individual solo rounds. We lived for one on one battles. When we got bored we would battle each other, so going up there with the flair and showmanship of a boxer was second nature to us."[38]

The three DJs also agreed on the outcome of the team battle. Without hesitation, Rob Swift declared, "I can objectively say, they won the team battle. This was an area they mastered. We were new to the idea of creating routines that involved the [whole] crew." But this was nothing new to the Piklz, who had been creating well-tooled team routines since 1992, and had just come back from tour together. As Shortkut modestly explained, "I think we did a good job."

What may have been the most important battle in the history of turntablism ended in a draw. This is fitting, for it symbolizes the equally significant contributions both crews have made to the art of the DJ. They expanded the frontiers of turntablist technique, electrified the battle scene, and inspired a generation DJs to take to the decks, both as soloists and as part of crews. "At the end of the day, it wasn't about who won or who lost," Rob Swift says of the 1996 battle. "It was about two crews . . . help[ing] the art form grow."[39]

FROM THE BASEMENT TO THE STAGE: A PORTRAIT OF A BATTLE SEASON

To understand the preparation required of the most dedicated battlers, let's follow an American DJ in the months before a national competition in the mid-1990s. The story is a composite, drawing on and extrapolating from the experiences of a variety of battlers active at the time. I take this approach rather than simply reporting second-hand in order to communicate the visceral intensity of the battler's life, from the months of relentless preparation at home to the mere minutes onstage, where a single routine can shape a DJ's life for years to come.

June, 1994: Our battler is a man in his mid-twenties living in a medium-sized city on the East Coast. DJ X, as we'll call him, has been DJing for nearly a decade and battling for four years.[40] He works at a local copy shop to make ends meet, but he only works part-time so he can prepare for battles. As battle champion

DJ Slyce has said, "You gotta work constantly on your routine[s], don't think you can win while doing five other jobs. You gotta focus."[41] X has just returned from a national battle, having earned a spot by winning the preliminary regional battle in May. He's not unhappy with his performance—he made it to the second round—but he knows he can do better. May and June were exhausting, so he enjoys some down time in July and just gets on the decks long enough every day to keep from getting stiff.

During this down time, X spends countless hours studying videotapes of battles. He wants to familiarize himself with the strengths and weaknesses of potential competitors, and to draw inspiration for his routines. DJ Swamp did the same, watching eight years' worth of DJ battles in preparation for the 1996 DMC US finals in San Francisco. (Swamp is the Cleveland DJ who surprised everyone by beating heavily-favored battlers from the X-Men and the Beat Junkies.) When he would see a move that impressed him, he would ask himself, "Now, how can I take that to the next level?" For example, he saw Shortkut beat juggle with one turntable going forward and one going backwards: "So that's why [in the 1996 DMC battle] I did both in reverse, so I could one-up it," Swamp says. His "homework," as he called it, paid off. His final routine, a catalog of next-level moves, stunned the crowd and impressed the judges; no one had expected him to win.[42] ◉ Swamp's success in San Francisco gave a huge boost to his career; among other things, rock musician Beck invited him to be his DJ on tour and for his next album. This is the kind of success story that drives battlers, and it is this kind of success our DJ X dreams about during these long months of study and practice.

August arrives, and DJ X is ready to create some new routines. He likes to have a single song at the core of a routine, and after wading through his vinyl, he decides to use Gang Starr's recent track, "Code of the Streets." ◉ It appeals to him on several levels. Most broadly, X is a huge fan of Premier, Gang Starr's DJ/producer, and with his routine is offering a gesture of respect to one of his heroes. More specifically, the recurring, descending four-note line that runs through the song has a laid-back but slightly ominous feel to it, and he can scratch it and chop it in any number of ways. "Code of the Streets" also has some battle-appropriate lyrics that he can manipulate, like "If a sucker steps up, then I leave him bleeding," and "Nine times out of ten I win, with the skills I be wielding." Finally, "Code" is a hot track, and just the sound of the opening should get the crowd on his side.

By the time X steps onstage, every moment of his routine will be fixed, but at this point improvisation is crucial. Every day he puts a copy of "Code" on each turntable, trying out different scratches, experimenting with various ways of looping and chopping the beats. He does this for hours on end, discarding ideas, refining others, slowly building his routine. After a few weeks, the routine is taking shape. He'll start with the opening of "Code," letting the four-note pattern play twice unchanged. He knows the crowd will love the song, and he's counting on their cheers to pump him up. Then he'll slowly ratchet up the intensity and difficulty of the routine in a kind of theme-and-variation form. The first variation will be fairly simple—he'll replace the last note of each pattern with a scratch, doing that three times (each with a different scratch) before letting the last note drop. After this, things will get more complicated, and he'll move into some beat juggling—he's worked up one pattern that repeats, "Sucker . . . bleeding." He might incorporate another record or two for contrast or some other disses or boasts, but this is really a one-song routine. He likes to think that it will become known as "X's Code of the Streets routine," just like people refer to "Rob Swift's Nobody Beats the Biz routine" or "Babu's Blind Alley routine."

Although X's routine is an original creation—he's careful not to bite other DJs' moves—he's indebted to his idol, Steve Dee, for the shape of the routine and his overall strategy. So let's take a minute to hear directly from Steve Dee. "I would play the song," Steve explains, "get you familiar with the song, double up a couple of times, to let you see where I'm leading it, and then escalate up and up and up. I get you to that head-nod stage, and then I come down." Drilling down a level deeper, he explains further:

> I would probably play around with the kick or the snare, or if there's a word that I'm going to use, I would chop that up a little bit, then I would incorporate the beat, you know, the drumplay along with the wordplay and rearrange it and then change the tempo, slow it down. Or, you could change the speed of the record, and put it on 45 [rpm]—that has another effect—it's going real fast, but once you control it again, if you bring it down to a head nod, and everything is clean, you could actually call the authorities after that. 'Cause you just killed everybody.[43]

This mix of compositional savvy and complete badassery is exactly the one-two combination that X hopes to unleash on his opponents.

After finishing his "Code of the Streets" routine, X creates three others, each based on a single song. Single-song routines were popular in the late 1980s and early '90s, but soon new approaches started to emerge. Some DJs used large stretches of two songs and some composed medley-like routines with fragments of several tracks, while other DJ's routines weren't song-based at all, but more like collages of abstract sounds or effects. As we've seen, the single-song approach became less common as battle records started to proliferate; X does have a collection of battle records, and plans to use bits of two different ones in his routines, but he doesn't want to lean too heavily on them.

Our DJ also plans on seasoning his routines with body tricks. They've become somewhat less common since the backlash that followed DJ David's crazy stunt a few years back, but a few well-chosen moves will impress the crowd. X is on the short side, so some of the tricks favored by his long-limbed friends, like the under-the-leg scratch or behind-the-back, aren't for him. He does have some nice moves involving his elbows and shoulders—easier for him since he doesn't have to reach down very far. Once he has his routines whittled down to the required two minutes, he'll start incorporating his body tricks into his practice sessions.

It's now early 1995, and X is putting together three more routines. He doesn't know yet whom he'll be facing in the first round of this head-to-head battle, so he's crafting routines that should demonstrate his originality, command of technique, and crowd appeal, three areas that the best routines generally excel in. But his routines differ in some significant ways. Two of them are heavier on scratching, while two spotlight his juggling. One of them incorporates "tones," where the DJ fashions a melody out of a long-held note by manipulating the pitch adjuster. (It's a slider that actually changes the record speed, though the effect is heard as a change in pitch.) Battle records started including long, single pitches for this purpose, though originally DJs used actual test-tone records—specially made discs created for testing or calibrating audio equipment. At the time X is competing, tones have been popular for the last few years, the trend led by San Francisco DJ 8-Ball, who has played "Iron Man," "Frère Jacques," "Yankee Doodle," "Nuthin but a G Thang," and other tunes on the way to winning battles.[44] ◑ The tunes tend to be fairly basic because the calibrated pitch control on most turntables doesn't allow for a wide range—the standard Technics 1200 allows a plus or minus eight percent adjustment, though changing the platter speed from 33 to 45 rpm extends this range.[45] Simple they may be, but crowds always enjoy hearing these melodies, and our man plans on using tones in his "Code" routine to imitate the first four notes of the song.

Spring, 1995: battle season is just around the corner. Although X has been practicing regularly since the previous August, he now kicks it into high gear. Depending on his work schedule at the copy shop, he can usually put in four hours a day. This is hardly unusual among battlers. In the 1988 song "King Tech," MC Sway described his DJ (named in the track's title) this way: "Tucked away in his room you never see him for days / takin' skillful steps through a musical maze." Steve Dee often practiced eight or even ten hours a day when he was battling, though exactly how long depended on his mother's mood when she came home from work.[46] Rob Swift practiced five days a week after work at the house of his mentor, Dr. Butcher, for almost the whole year before the 1992 DMC.[47] For X, too, the days have become a succession of scratching, working, scratching, sleeping, and scratching. But mostly scratching. His social life blinks out of existence. This is a common affliction among turntablists, as DJ Beware has noted:

> Scratching damages your social life and your ability to function as a normal human being. You spend the whole day at home rubbing records and pushing buttons, while your friends are out there having fun. No matter how hard you try not to, all you end up talking about is scratching this and scratching that. Instead of brushing your teeth, the first thing you do in the morning is to put on records and scratch. . . .[48]

This is not to say that X lives a solitary life. He has a small network of DJ friends he practices with, and at least twice a week he meets with his mentor DJ Velvel, who taught him how to scratch when he was fifteen. Velvel, stopwatch in hand, circles his protégé as he practices, timing his routines while offering a running commentary on his scratches and juggles. Velvel is just what X needs: generous with his time, stingy with his praise.

It's the week before the regional battle—a preliminary step on the way to nationals—and his routines are ready to go. Life is now just about practicing and refining his routines. X is heavily favored to win—and he does. The battle's sponsor is a local sound equipment store, and he wins a gift certificate and a T-shirt. For him, the regionals are simply a steppingstone to the nationals, where his sights have always been set.

Two weeks now remain until nationals, and the list of competitors has just been posted on the Internet. X has his routines ready—as is common, he will recycle them from the regionals—but now it's time to start strategizing about which he will perform first. If he's lucky, he'll start out against a weaker DJ and can use his least impressive routine. But what if he draws one of the stronger DJs? Should he use his best routine to ensure that he'll get to the next round? Or should he gamble and save his best for the final round, hoping that he can dispatch other DJs without it? He also has to consider the particular strengths of each DJ. As Rob Swift explained in the quote that opens this chapter, "If I go up against this DJ, I want to intercept whatever style he may come at me with. And when I go up against this other DJ, he DJs like this, so I need to be prepared for this and that and the third." DJ X knows most of the entrants, and the ones he doesn't are probably new to battling. But he's smart enough not to assume anything, and he'll start asking around about the first-timers. After all, Cash Money was a first-time battler when he won the New Music Seminar in 1987.

There's yet another reason for identifying competitors as soon as possible: disses. X likes a good diss, but he doesn't live for them like some of his opponents do. So he'll keep them brief. He already has some generic disses ready, but the judges and crowd always enjoy hearing DJs insult each other by name.

In the days remaining before the battle he continues to practice, and when he can, he digs through his vinyl for personalized disses, all the while subsisting on little sleep and vast quantities of Mountain Dew.

The day before the battle, X checks into the cheap motel where the other out-of-town competitors are staying. As in most battles, the DJs pay their own way. Although everyone will use the equipment provided by the battle organizers, they all bring turntables and mixers and portable speakers so they can squeeze in a few more hours of practice; thumping bass and rasping scratches leak from each DJ's room into the sickly fluorescence of the motel's hallway. Even though they could practice with headphones, many DJs are there with friends or their crews—there's also a crew category in this battle—so they either want or need others to hear them practice. Despite the fierce competitiveness of most battle DJs, the atmosphere at the motel, and when tomorrow comes, at the battle itself, is surprisingly friendly and open. Enemy combatants even hang out in each other's rooms, and most wish their rivals good luck. Still, there's likely to be some trash talk and gamesmanship behind the scenes. Steve Dee, though friendly and well liked outside of competition, sees psychological warfare as an important part of battling. "I would really just come in there all loud mouth, and causing a ruckus, causing a scene. . . . I would figure out something to get under somebody's skin, throw their game plan off."[49] Fortunately for X, there are no Steve Dee-like tormentors prowling the motel's halls.

After a mostly sleepless night and some fitful naps the next day, X leaves for the venue, a small club with a tiny backstage. The battle organizer—a detail-minded woman in her late twenties who is liked by all DJs but takes grief from none—has instructed everyone to check in with her at 7:30 p.m. (Although most battle DJs are men, women have run many of the most important battles in the DJ world: prime examples including Christie Z-Pabon in the United States and Sally McLintock and Christine Prince in England.) Before the battle, a few renowned DJs who no longer compete will offer some showcases.

It's now 11:30 p.m., and the MC announces that the battle is to begin. The crowd, about 200 strong, inches toward the stage and starts to cheer. This being a typical American battle of the time, the audience is racially mixed, though with white men in the majority; most are between the ages of eighteen and twenty-five, and most wear T-shirts, baggy pants, and baseball caps. Sprinkled throughout the audience are young women and a handful of older folks, including some of the competitors' parents and a journalist or two.

X watches from the wings as the first two DJs perform, each standing before a set of turntables on opposite sides of the stage. He listens with an expert ear, at times nodding his head in admiration of a difficult and well executed scratch combination, at other times grimacing (or smiling) at a botched transition or unfortunate needle skip. Few in the audience are as knowledgeable, but there is a high level of connoisseurship here (and quite a few DJs in attendance). Many can identify the strengths and weaknesses of each routine, and even recognize when one DJ is biting someone else's routine. For spectators without this knowledge base, battles can bewilder. A harsh diss might be heard as a random fragment of a song; a complex juggle could pass entirely unappreciated. It might not even be clear how a DJ's motions are connected to the sounds booming from the speakers. A *New Yorker* review of the 1993 New Music Seminar makes this point: "The audience was enthusiastic and intent but highly discriminating. A d.j. whose set seemed spectacular to the uninitiated would receive polite applause, but other d.j.s were able to tap a mysterious current of excitement in the crowd, and hundreds of baseball caps would begin nodding to the beat, uplifted arms would begin waving, and hundreds of people would leap to their feet and cheer."[50] Although, as the critic points out, the uninitiated can enjoy a battle, the expertise required to fully appreciate a battle is a symptom of turntablism's insularity, an issue that would come to be of great concern and debate among DJs.

It's after midnight and X is up. He and his opponent step onto the hot, cramped stage. Crowded there are the DJs and the judges, the MC, the event organizers, and various hangers-on; several are standing right behind him, some of whom provide a running commentary during his routines. X takes the decks first, and goes with his third-best routine. He's up against DJ Krassen, not a particular threat, but solid overall. Too bad he hadn't gone with his weakest routine—one of Krassen's needles kept skipping, and although it shouldn't have been disastrous, he was thrown off his game. He missed his juggle routine completely and threw together some halfhearted scratch combinations to fill out the two minutes. Apparently, Krassen never got the advice that Velvel drilled into X: always expect equipment problems and *never* broadcast your mistakes. With the look on Krassen's face he might as well have just given up. The next two rounds aren't as easy, but X prevails, not simply because his routines were strong, but because of his relentless preparation. Even a sticky crossfader couldn't derail him.

He's now in the final round against DJ Boddicker, an experienced turntablist who specializes in complex juggle routines and clever wordplay. Fortunately, X has saved his "Code" routine. He'll need it. Although he's confident, this battle could go either way. He's up first, opening his routine with the beginning of "Code of the Streets." He recently tweaked his routine slightly, so instead of letting it play it out right away, he repeats the first note several times, bringing the volume up each time. The sound of the sample is so distinctive that people start to murmur in recognition, and by the time he lets the record continue, the crowd cheers with pleasure. Sweating underneath the spotlights, adrenaline coursing through his body, X performs the rest of his routine almost flawlessly.

The crowd loves his tones, and he coaxes them into a unison head nod during his juggles. However, he doesn't get much of a reaction out of the wordplay during his juggle—"sucker . . . bleeding." They've heard more than an hour's worth of dissing, and by now they need something stronger to stoke their enthusiasm. Still, by any criteria, the routine was a success and he feels good about his performance. There is nothing more for him to do except wait and watch. The moment he had been working toward for nearly a year has now passed.

During X's routine, Boddicker stood not fifteen feet away, slowly shaking his head, pretending to be disappointed at not having a more formidable opponent. Now it's his turn and he smirks as he hits the start button on his right turntable. X knows a nasty diss is coming, and his stomach turns sour in anticipation. It's worse than he thought. Boddicker obviously knows X's given name, a name that has always embarrassed him (and which only his mother is allowed to use). Floating out over the audience is a line of cartoon dialogue in which a woman sweetly calls to a baby with X's real name, cooing, "time to change your diaper." The crowd laughs as they turn toward X. Boddicker then isolates X's name, and then switches over to the other turntable to complete the diss: "I'll fuck your ass up!" booms out, courtesy of the Wu-Tang Clan's 1993 track, "Shame on a Nigga." He repeats the diss several times; worse, he expertly loops the records with one hand, so as to free the other to brandish a middle finger in X's direction. The crowd erupts, scores of young men gleefully jumping up and down. X usually doesn't mind even the nastiest disses, but this one takes him back to some of his least-pleasant childhood memories. He briefly fantasizes about beating Boddicker with a Technics.

Boddicker then continues to work "Shame." He brings the song back to the opening, a bouncy horn call and response sampled from Syl Johnson's 1967 R&B track "Different Strokes," and breaks it down, rebuilding it into a new rhythm. A few brief but inventive scratch patterns and some more choice disses create variety and keep the crowd hooting. All in all, it's a great routine.

The lights come up and the MC congratulates both DJs and tells the crowd not to wander far; the judges will have their decision soon. For what seems like an hour, but is more like ten minutes, X paces backstage, sweaty, jittery, and tense. Finally, he and Boddicker are called back. The spotlights are on them once again as the MC intones, "And the winner of the 1995 Battle for Global Domination is . . . DJ Boddicker!" Hearing this, X feels something collapse inside himself, his shoulders dropping visibly.

As runner-up, X wins a small pile of records, some slipmats, and two needles, which he accepts graciously but unenthusiastically. Some from the audience approach him afterward and say that he should have won the battle, and one of his friends speculates that Boddicker had one of the judges in his pocket.

Sure, X has seen his share of bad calls from battle judges, but he's not sure this is one of them. Boddicker's routine was well crafted and well executed, and the crowd loved it. Who knows, maybe X would have won if not for Boddicker's personalized diss. But where was he going to find "Boddicker" on record? He only later realized that Boddicker was named after Clarence Boddicker, the villain in *Robocop*. Still, he would have had a hard time getting the name from a VHS tape onto vinyl.

After the awards, the DJs go out for drinks. The sting of the loss is dulled by the alcohol and the friendly vibe—a lot of other DJs, Boddicker included, compliment him on his performances. After a late night, X heads back to the motel, where he collapses until the next morning, He can't afford to pay for another day, so he drags himself and his gear out to his car, cracks the windows, and sleeps for three more hours in the parking lot.

On the long drive home X reflects on the battle. He can think of a few places where his routines might have been stronger, and he definitely should have come up with better disses. Overall, though, he can't be too disappointed. He pushed himself and he tested himself, and in the end he was a better DJ for it. The steady march of white highway dashes lulls him into a reverie, and he starts to ponder his future. As he knows, most battle DJs only compete for a few years. The very best may garner lucrative gigs and sponsorships, and some make a decent living by touring and selling battle records. Others go on to make solo albums or become producers. But for those not at the top—and who may still be astoundingly good—battling can be financially ruinous. X spent a few hundred dollars just to compete this weekend, and thousands more on equipment and records over the past year, a period when he had cut back on his hours at work so he could devote more time to battling. For all who battle, the preparation is so intense, so time- and energy-consuming, that it is simply unsustainable for very long. So he has to make a decision. He can borrow some money and keep battling for another year, gambling that a few big wins will pay off. Or he can retire from competition, but still try to make a full-time living as a gigging DJ, spinning at clubs and restaurants and, if he can stomach it, the fraternity and sorority, bar- and bat-mitzvah, and quinceañera circuit. Or maybe he should just move on and recover his financial, physical, and emotional health. Whatever he does, he'll always look back on this period of his life with pride in his accomplishments and astonishment at his dedication to his craft. But for now, his future is uncertain.

For battle DJs—and our DJ is meant to be representative of his kind—complete dedication is necessary, while financial and personal sacrifices are common. And there are no guarantees. Months of preparation lead to just a few minutes in the spotlight, and all but a few walk away from the experience with an empty wallet to show for it. But most have no regrets. Thinking back on his battle career, Shortkut says, "I'm glad I did it. I'm glad I went through that hardship."[51] Or as Babu explains, "The battle experience was a big part of my development . . . having that tension in my life for like five years."[52]

WHY BATTLE? ISSUES OF GENDER AND IDENTITY

Why do they do it? Why would anyone willingly put themselves through such hardship and stress? When I put this question to DJs, they often use the same word to describe themselves: *competitive*. Battle DJs—successful ones at least— are at their best in high-stress, adrenaline-fueled competitions, and seek out arenas where they can prove themselves against others. Cash Money entered the New Music Seminar Battle because, as he said, "I'm a very competitive person [and] I wanted to be known as the world's greatest DJ." The adversarial nature of battling, however, was for him only a means to an end—improving his craft. "You know it's never been about beef or anything like that. I mean it's just being competitive. If someone beats you, you just go back to the drawing board and try to do better the next time."[53] Steve Dee's answer to the question, "Why battle?" is simple: "I'm a real competitive guy." Before he got into DJing, he was a serious baseball player, but unfortunately he never had the chance to prove himself. "I still feel to this day I would hold the single season home-run record," he told me. "My heart got like broken in the baseball realm, and so I put all my competitiveness into music."[54] Or consider the example of DJ Immortal from Miami. As a teenager he was inspired to become a turntablist after seeing the 1992 film *Juice*. Here's how he describes his reaction to a scene that depicted a DJ battle: "They were battling, they were throwin' down. I saw them going back and forth, fighting each other with turntables. The crowd was totally eggin' 'em on. It was just this awesome instrument that I was seeing, the turntable. Plus that competitive element, too, where you could just *destroy* someone. It was like a real sport."[55]

Like Steve Dee, Immortal sees a kinship between competitive sports and battling. These responses aren't surprising; after all, anyone who consistently enters battles must have a taste for competition. But there's something else that helps explain the draw of battling. This has to do with the obvious fact that most battle DJs are men. The reason for this, I believe, is that the institution of the DJ battle promotes a heroic model of masculinity that particularly appeals to many young men.[56]

A young man entering a battle does not enter as the unpopular teenager, the debt-laden single father, or even the well-adjusted, high-achieving university student. He enters with a new name and a distinct personality. Often DJs choose *noms de guerre* that hint at menace or extraordinary abilities—Craze, Daredevil,

Enferno, Homicide, Infamous, Lethal, Mista Sinista, Pimp, Ruthless, Troubl. Two early crews, the X-Men and the Supermen, were inspired by comic-book heroes, and Qbert, remember, wanted his name "to be something from a comic book," like "Ripclaw" or "The Slasher." Video games have also inspired DJs— British battle DJ Tigerstyle took his name from a character in *Street Fighter II*.[57] Yet whatever the name, coming armed with a moniker is a requisite part of battling. In fact, virtually no hip-hop DJs, battlers or otherwise, perform under their birth names. "I think it's corny when DJs use their real name," says DJ Quest, a turntablist from the Bay Area who battled between 1990 and 1996. "You want to create this other kind of identity. You want to come off as a super-hero."[58] Or as Johnny "Juice" Rosado puts it, many DJs want "to be superheroes, to rise above their mundane, everyday life."[59]

Taking on a heroic identity appeals to male DJs because, as they often admit, many fall into a category that is hardly heroic: the nerd. Although they inhabit the world of hip-hop, turntablists are not the bling-wearing, gun-slinging, macho ladies' men celebrated in gangsta rap lyrics and videos. Some turntablists even embrace the "nerd" label. Two of the most respected battle DJs, Craze and Klever, called their 2002 collaborative album *Scratch Nerds*; DJ Revolution has a track by the same name on his 2008 release *King of the Decks*. And the renowned DJ Qbert proclaims, "I am a nerd. Fuck yeah! Proud of it!"[60] In Japan, some turntablists jokingly refer to themselves or their colleagues as "scratch *otaku*," *otaku* being a general term that describes someone who obsesses over a particular hobby or activity, like comic books or video games.[61] At the same time, these self-proclaimed nerds are drawn to DJing because it allows them, at least for brief periods, to stop being nerds. Kid Koala's 1995 track "Tricks 'n' Treats," where he plays with dialogue from the beloved 1966 animated special, *It's the Great Pumpkin, Charlie Brown*, illustrates this perfectly. It's Halloween, and after visiting each neighbor's house to gather treats, Charlie Brown and friends peek inside their bags. "I got a chocolate bar!," "I got a quarter!," "I got five pieces of candy!," the other kids exclaim. But poor Charlie Brown, what did he get? "I got a rock," he moans. Koala takes this line, stutters it a few times and adds a heavy breakbeat beneath it. In the process he transforms a lament, "I got a rock," into an imperative, "I *gotta* rock." Each time the line returns we can almost hear the boy's voice gain confidence. As Kid Koala demonstrates, given a set of turntables and some dope beats, even the Charlie Browniest of DJs can rock.

This transformation is only possible because of the mediation of technology. It's no small matter that DJs battle each other not only from behind assumed names and identities, but literally from behind a table full of machinery, which Kid Koala likens to "a suit of armor."[62] This technological distancing allows them to be cleverer, and more confident, intimidating, and powerful than their non-battle selves. Shortkut, one of the great battlers, points this out himself: "I'm a really quiet guy, but when it's battle time, I want to be, like, awesome, you know what I mean?"[63] Peanut Butter Wolf, a fellow DJ from the Bay Area, is even blunter. "Here I was, this little white boy, this funny-looking ugly dude, and I wound up beating a lot of people."[64] In battle, these normally quiet guys and awkward dudes can be heroes and even claim global conquest by winning international competitions.

Of course, women can also be battle heroes, but they rarely even enter these competitions. It's astonishing just how few there are. Among the thousands of DJs who have entered DMC battles, perhaps no more than a dozen have been women, and only one—Kuttin Kandi—has progressed to the U.S. finals.[65] Even those who follow the scene would be hard-pressed to name more than a few women battlers; in addition to Kuttin Kandi these might include Jazzy Joyce and Pam the Funkstress, representing an earlier generation, and more recent figures such as Killa-Jewel and DJ Sparkles. To put this in a broader perspective, women (at least in United States) are *much* more likely to become construction workers and coal miners than battle DJs.[66] The reason for this scarcity, however, does not seem to be direct discrimination. "I never saw one incident where a woman was discouraged from battling," battle organizer Christie Z-Pabon has pointed out. "In fact, the battle DJ scene, though male dominated, is very supportive of women battling."[67] There are surely subtler forms of prejudice affecting active or aspiring women battlers, but discrimination itself cannot explain the dearth of women.

There *are* barriers to women in the battle world, but they are erected well before any female DJ considers entering a competition. Even today, in many societies girls are not often encouraged to embrace technology or enter techni-cal fields. Nor are they typically socialized to be aggressively and loudly com-petitive, and when they do act in this way, they are rarely rewarded or excused for it; there is no "girls will be girls" pass for that kind of behavior. In other words, the defining characteristics of DJ battles have been enough to keep most women out, even if the men truly do want them to be included. There's nothing to say the battle scene cannot become more female-friendly, however. In fact, there have been women-only DJ competitions, but these are more recent phe-nomena that we'll consider in the final chapter. Still, even in 2012, the scarcity of women battlers is striking, just as it was in 1995 and in the two decades before that.

Battling has been central to hip-hop DJ culture since the very beginning, but there was something exceptional about the scene of the early and mid-1990s. The period was unparalleled in the number of battlers and the international scope of battling, in the technical innovations in scratching and beat juggling, and in the artistry and virtuosity of the music making heard at these competitions.

To many, it was a golden age of battling and of turntablism in general. As Los Angeles–based DJ Revolution put it, the battle scene of the mid-1990s "was like the jazz scene in Harlem in the 1920s. Cats would come from all over to see what was going on, hear the new songs, learn the new tricks."[68] There has never been, and may never again be, a period in which competition was such a driving force in the world of the hip-hop DJ.

Golden ages rarely last long, however, and often plant the seeds of their own decline. The more turntablist technique advanced and the more intense the competition became, the more insular the battle scene turned. As the 1990s wore on, battle routines became ever more complex, sounding less and less like anything mainstream hip-hop fans could sing along with or dance to. Even to many hip-hop fans it was a closed world.

Some turntablists themselves wondered if things had gone too far. Z-Trip sees the problem in historical terms, tracing the separatist mentality in turntablism to the marginalization of DJs by MCs in the 1980s: "We got so tired of the MCs—'Fuck you, guys, we're going to do our own thing'—but now we're kind of screwing ourselves because we're doing what the MCs were doing."[69] DJ Quest, an active battler in the 1990s, believes that turntablism became too technical and got too far from "the dance element." He claims that he can only listen to pure scratching for about fifteen minutes at a stretch. "I can only take so much of that shit," he says in all seriousness.[70] Apollo, a founding member of the Invisibl Skratch Piklz, laments the split among hip-hop DJs into different camps. "There was a separation at one point. Turntablists just wanted to be turntablists, and party-rocking DJs just wanted to be party-rocking DJs. There wasn't a mutual respect between them. I think everyone should support each other." He also thinks overspecialization can be a DJ's downfall. "DJs should encompass as many different aspects of DJing as they can. It's only right. It's only right as a musician."[71] His own post-ISP career has embodied these sentiments. In 1999, he, Shortkut, and Vinroc formed Triple Threat DJs and promoted themselves as DJs who could fill a dance floor but also perform mind-blowing scratch routines.

To some DJs, the pendulum had swung too far. No one wanted to return to the fallow years of 1989 and 1990, when DATs were threatening the existence of DJs and when crucial advances in mixer technology still lay in the future. The artistic independence that turntablism achieved was inarguably a major accomplishment, but some DJs sought a broader acceptance of their art as well. As we will see, they got their wish, but they could not have foreseen the consequences of this newfound acceptance.

Legitimacy: 1996–2002

Two turntablists face each other from opposite ends of a large room. One launches a flurry of scratches and then points at the other, daring him to do better. The second DJ gestures dismissively and scratches right back. All the while, an attractive woman dances behind a third set of turntables positioned in between the two men, swinging her hips. The music stops and she purrs, "My first love—boys who scratch."

This should be the point when the DJ wakes up suddenly, a smile on his face. But this is no nocturnal fantasy. The setting is an August 2001 television commercial for the clothing retailer, The Gap.[1] The battlers are the celebrated turntablists Shortkut and Rob Swift, and the woman is Shannyn Sossamon, a former DJ turned actress. The fact that all three are clad in denim is no coincidence: this is a jeans commercial. ◐

Though only thirty seconds long, the commercial speaks volumes about the state of the hip-hop DJ at the beginning of the new millennium. The Gap spot was just a part of broader changes taking place at the time. Starting in the mid-1990s, DJs were collaborating with pop, rock, jazz, and classical musicians, bringing the sound of scratching to new audiences. As soloists and as crews, DJs were recording albums, collectively demonstrating that they could be composers capable of creating cohesive, long-form works; a handful of DJs even developed notation systems in order to preserve their art and to claim for it a place in high culture. In 2000, DJs from around the world gathered in San Francisco for Skratchcon, an event billed as "The world's first conference dedicated to the education and development of skratch music literacy."[2] Hosted by the Invisibl Skratch Piklz, this one-day program of public seminars revealed a growing consciousness among turntablists of their history and a growing desire to demonstrate the richness of their art. Two well-regarded documentaries, *Battle Sounds* by John Carluccio (1997) and Doug Pray's *Scratch* (2001), exposed turntablism to those who thought it was little more than ruining records, and were embraced by many DJs as a validation of their culture. The common theme here is legitimacy. At the turn of the millennium, hip-hop DJing was becoming part of the mainstream and at the same time making a bid for artistic significance, seeking—and gaining—acceptance in new realms. ◐

SCRATCHING GOES MAINSTREAM

DJs were becoming scarcer in the mainstream hip-hop of the late 1980s and early 1990s. DATs of prerecorded beats had been replacing hip-hop DJs both on tour and in the studio, and gangsta rap, which was becoming a dominant form of hip-hop at the time, seldom featured scratching. Rarely would a hip-hop album devote a track to its DJ as had been common in the 1980s, and those that did often came from lesser known or underground groups. Some MCs still worked with DJs—the Beastie Boys and Mix Master Mike being a notable example—but even so, scratching was just not a prominent feature of 1990s hip-hop.[3]

It was left to musicians outside of hip-hop—boy bands and heavy metal groups, indie acts and jazz ensembles—to embrace the DJ. In the early 1990s, DJs were featured in the music of Britain's Pop Will Eat Itself, the American funk metal band Living Colour, and a variety of projects from bassist, composer, and producer Bill Laswell, who had been intimately involved with "Change the Beat" and "Rockit."[4] But these were early, somewhat exceptional examples. Only later in the decade did scratching once again catch the ear of the general listening public.

There was no 1990s equivalent to "Rockit"; no single song propelled the DJ back into the spotlight. Rather, the return of the DJ was part of a broader phenomenon at work. Hip-hop in the 1990s was bigger than ever, and was now practically synonymous with American youth culture. In part this was because legions of white kids loved hip-hop. As journalist Charles Aaron wrote from the vantage point of 1998, "White fans no longer listen to hip-hop on the sly or surreptitiously rhyme in front of the mirror; they form bands and rhyme on MTV. [Hip-hop is] simply how kids communicate."[5] With the mainstreaming of hip-hop, its musical signifiers started to float freely, showing up in a variety of genres. One of the most recognizable of these signifiers is scratching, and just as it was becoming less popular in its native genre, it started popping up with ever greater frequency on radio-friendly songs outside of hip-hop in the mid- and late 1990s. ◐

The friendliest of these songs arrived in April 1997. The group was a trio of young brothers from Oklahoma named Hanson; the tune was "MMMbop," a double-platinum-selling song that reached number one in almost a dozen countries.[6] "MMMbop" is bubblegum pop, but there is one tiny bit of grit in this otherwise perfect pink confection—scratching. Just below the surface of the chorus, a medley of *mmmbops, doos, wops,* and *dops* that bounces along irresistibly, is something few listeners at the time expected to encounter—a short burst of high-pitched *wicki wicki wickis.* No pop music fan today would think anything of it, but at that time scratching was an incongruity in a non-rap song. I remember hearing it for the first time and wondering, what was *that* sound doing in *this* song? *Wicki wickis* and all, "MMMbop" was beloved by millions, and brought the sound of scratching to a new generation and a new audience.

"MMMbop" was just one of dozens of tracks from the 1990s that featured DJs. DJ Marshall Goodman performed with the Southern California group Sublime on its three studio albums, including their most popular track, "What I've Got" (1996). The best-known songs by the quirky genre-defying American musician known as Beck—"Loser" (1993) and "Where It's At" (1996)—boast brief bouts of scratching.[7] More popular than either of Beck's songs were the 1999 hits "Every Morning" and "Someday" by Californians Sugar Ray and DJ Homicide. On the other side of the ocean, a down-tempo form of electronic music was developing in England that came to be called trip-hop, and the sounds of scratching punctuated moody tracks by Massive Attack, Morcheeba, Portishead, Tricky, and UNKLE.

In the mid- and late 1990s, a subgenre of heavy metal called nu-metal or rap-metal came into prominence, and one of its hallmarks was its hip-hop borrowings. Several of the biggest nu-metal songs of the decade mixed the sound of scratching into a texture of heavily distorted guitars and voices; the combination was fresh at the time, appealing to millions of kids who enjoyed both hip-hop and metal. "Down," a metal-rap-ska hybrid by the Nebraska group 311 with vocalist S.A. Martinez doubling on the turntables, rose to number one on the *Billboard* Modern Rock Tracks chart in the summer of 1996. Kid Rock featured Uncle Kracker on the turntables for his 1998 hit "Bawitdaba." In 1999, Limp Bizkit's "Nookie" gave listeners a dose of DJ Lethal, the Latvian-born Leor Dimant. Earlier, Lethal had been a member of the Boston hip-hop group House of Pain; he also served as Sugar Ray's first DJ and acted as guest DJ for a variety of other acts, making him one of the busier and more versatile DJs of the 1990s. The DJ known as Mr. Hahn was a permanent member of Linkin Park, performing on the group's signature song "One Step Closer" (2000) and still scratching with them more than a decade later.

Finally, although the rap-metal band Rage Against the Machine did not have a DJ, we should bestow the title of Honorary DJ on RATM's guitarist, Tom Morello. This innovative musician, clearly influenced by hip-hop, expanded the realm of guitar sound by imitating scratch techniques. In "Bulls on Parade" (1996), for example, he has a full twenty-second "scratch" solo where he rubs

the strings with the fingers of his left hand over the pick-ups while rapidly toggling the pick-up selector switch with his right hand to cut the sound on and
off, just like DJs might use the line switch on a mixer to do the transformer
scratch. "[Hip-hop] changed the way I looked at music," he explains. "I started
studying . . . DJs rather than guitar players and trying to emulate them."[8]

In almost all of the songs I've mentioned, the DJ plays only a minor part. The
scratches in "MMMbop" serve to enhance the texture more than anything else.
In "Bawitdaba" the DJ and guitarist interact in a brief call and response, the
scratches acting like drum fills. In "Down" the scratching is subtle; in "Nookie"
it's barely heard. For many of these groups, scratching served mostly as a sonic
signifier of hip-hop, and often the DJs functioned mainly as *visual* signifiers in
their concerts and videos, seen more than heard.

There were some exceptions. Marshall Goodman's four-bar scratch solo at
the end of Sublime's "What I've Got" is more prominent and sophisticated than
what was usually heard at the time, and his manipulation of R2D2-like bleeps
reveals the influence of Qbert. The rock band Incubus actually released a
DJ-only track, "Battlestar Scralatchtica" (1999), showcasing the group's resident
turntablist DJ Kilmore with guest scratchers Cut Chemist and Nu-Mark from
the hip-hop group Jurassic 5. Most bands, however, treated scratching like
musical seasoning, more spice than meat, and rarely featured advanced turntable techniques. But this doesn't have to be a criticism—take the scratches out
of many of these songs and they're not as appealing or interesting.

In the mid- and late 1990s, the reach of the hip-hop DJ expanded into
almost every corner of popular music, whether bubblegum pop, ska, alternative
rock, heavy metal, or trip-hop. Even groups without regular DJs jumped on
the bandwagon and brought turntablists with them on tour; DJ P, for example,
toured with both Garbage and Lit.[9] For the most part this music offered
listeners only a taste of the musical possibilities of turntablism, which in turn
colored their perception of the art and culture of the hip-hop DJ. As it turns
out, just because the masses might have enjoyed a sprinkling of scratches
on their music did not mean that they would eagerly embrace turntablism in a
less-adulterated form.

THE DJ ALBUM

While mainstream pop groups were embracing DJs on a rather superficial
level and mainstream hip-hop acts were shying away from them, there was one
group of DJs that continued to deepen and expand the art. These were the turntablists, who had been striking out on their own since the early 1990s. A crucial
milestone in this journey was the advent of the all-DJ album. As we saw in

Chapter 5, the first album devoted solely to turntablism was Bomb Hip-Hop's *Return of the DJ*, released in 1995. Other compilations followed. The Bill Laswell project, *Altered Beats: Assassin Knowledges of the Remanipulated* (1996), teamed Bootsy Collins with DJ Disk and DJ Krush, Grandmixer DXT (formerly D.ST), Rob Swift, and members of the Invisibl Skratch Piklz, among others. The next year Om Records released the first volume in its series *Deep Concentration* with a roster that included Cut Chemist, Eddie Def, Peanut Butter Wolf, Prince Paul, DJ Radar, and members of the Beat Junkies. Although scratching was a familiar sound on the radio by the time these albums were released, the art of turntablism, in all of its complexity, was not widely understood. Brian Coleman, reviewing the two Bomb Hip-Hop releases in *CMJ New Music Monthly* in 1997, described turntablism to his readers as a "somewhat mysterious, insular, and highly underground art."[10]

All of the albums I just mentioned were multi-artist compilations, but starting in 1997 with the X-Ecutioners' *X-Pressions*, a new type of DJ album arose: the single-artist or single-group release. The work of the X-Ecutioners offers a revealing case study of the challenges facing turntablists as they ventured into the studio, and aspired to leave the underground for the mainstream.

In 1996, the four members of the X-Ecutioners (at the time they were still called the X-Men) were either performing alone or as a group in small venues or touring with MCs. But they wanted more. As Rob Swift relates in the documentary *As the Tables Turn*, "We made a conscious effort to . . . really try to build an identity beyond us being battle DJs, build an identity in the world of music and make an impact."[11] So they each left their rappers and focused on creating what is considered the highest form of artistic achievement in the world of popular music: the album.

When the X-Ecutioners signed with the respected San Francisco independent label Asphodel, their world changed. Swift explains: "We went from [being] battle DJs to signing a recording contract and getting a check. And our first check was for $20,000. That was our first signing check, and to us that was like we were millionaires."[12] *As the Tables Turn* includes a charming amateur video recorded in the showroom of a BMW dealership. Swift is probably behind the camera, and we see Sinista and Total Eclipse sitting in a shiny new convertible, while Roc Raida stands nearby, flashing cash. Sinista grins at the camera and says, "This is how we roll." "Word up," concurs Raida, who then pretends to drive off.[13] Never mind that the $20,000—split four ways—wouldn't go far. They had signed with a label and felt rich for the first time in their lives.

In moving from the stage to the studio, the X-Ecutioners faced a serious challenge. The problem is that most turntablist routines are not designed for recordings—they're designed to make an immediate impression on live audiences. There are two related issues here. One is that DJ routines are usually not structured in a way that would make them easy to listen to repeatedly on a recording. Think of a typical song, which has repeating melodies and harmonies and a certain consistency that makes it easy for listeners to follow along. However, routines, especially in battle, tend to avoid repetition; the whole point is to show every facet of the DJ or crew's art in a short time. In a routine, twenty seconds of one beat might be followed by a completely different beat in a new tempo and key; a scratch segment might cut suddenly to a juggle, neither to return. The other issue is that the *visual* aspect of turntablism—lost in the transfer to recording—is crucial to the experience and understanding of the music. DMC founder Tony Prince, who has probably seen more live battle routines than anyone else in the world, has made this point forcefully. "With turntablism, with all the crabs and flares and all the excitement that's going on with the hands on the mixer and the vinyl, it *looks* great. In fact, I always say, if you just listen to a six-minute mix that a guy's done in a live competition, it will sound [like] crap. But if you watch him doing it, you'll understand what he's doing."[14]

Conscious of it or not, the X-Ecutioners seem to have accounted for the difficulty of moving from the stage to the studio. Most noticeably, they included vocalists, whose singing and rapping provide an obvious coherence to their tracks. But there are also subtler touches, like the stereo panning between left and right that gives a sense of movement, simulating the DJ's switching between one turntable and the other. The best cuts on *X-Pressions*, to my ear, are the ones that address both the repeatability and invisibility factors of recording.[15] "Mad Flava," is a good example. One of only three tracks in which the crew performs together, it has a clear sense of structure, and the smooth segues between the sections help hold the track together. Overall it's an example of a strong *recorded* turntablist composition. ◐

X-Pressions received positive reviews, but the group still flew below the mainstream radar. Their fortunes changed dramatically with the second X-Ecutioners album, *Built from Scratch*. Released in 2002, it enjoyed success unprecedented for a group of DJs.[16] The album sold more than 500,000 copies, and its popularity led to a worldwide tour and major television appearances (including the *David Letterman Show* and MTV's *Total Request Live* and its Video Music Awards). Why the sudden fame? It was a single song, and the addition of two musicians, that made all the difference.

The song was "It's Goin' Down," and the guests were singer Mike Shinoda and DJ Mr. Hahn of Linkin Park. ◐ As it turns out, when the Xs floated the idea of a collaboration, the members of Linkin Park were already fans. As Shinoda told *Vibe* in 2002, "These guys were some of the artists who gave us inspiration to be the musicians we are today. Plus, they have an open ear for musical evolution and aren't afraid to experiment."[17]

"It's Goin' Down," opens as straight metal, guitar distortion coalescing into a jagged riff. But then a quick scratch fill from the hip-hop DJs announces that we're hearing a hybrid, which seems to be the subject of the song's lyrics:

> The rhythm projects 'round the next sound
> Reflects the complex hybrid dialect now
> Detects the mesh of many elements compressed down
> The melting pot of a super-futurist style.

For much of the song, the scratching is less prominent than the rhyming or the guitar thrashing, but the DJs have an interlude to themselves after the first chorus, and the forty-second outro is an energetic scratchfest. Toward the end, the DJs cleverly manipulate the song "The Year 2000" by labelmate Xzibit, re-arranging his words to make him say "X-Men about to blast off worldwide." Unlike many of the tracks from *X-Pressions*, this song has a traditional rock form: an intro and outro with verses and a recurring chorus. This traditional structure not only made it wear well as a repeatable recording but also helped it go down easy with mainstream listeners. The "hybrid dialect" of virtuosic scratching and hard metal made for a potent combination, appealing to more listeners than the X-Ecutioners had ever reached.

"It's Goin' Down" turned out to be a mixed blessing for the X-Ecutioners. The album owes much of its success to the song, but it set up expectations the group couldn't fulfill. Although *Built from Scratch* lists "It's Goin' Down" as "featuring Mike Shinoda and Mr. Hahn of Linkin Park," it's really more of a Linkin Park song with guest scratches by the X-Ecutioners. Rob Swift admits as much: "My role on that song was just more of a supporting role."[18] Fans of the song liked it because it had the X-Ecutioners *and* Mike Shinoda—but Shinoda wasn't part of the group. So, as Swift explains, "We'd show up at places and it would be like, 'Yo, is Mike Shinoda here? Are you going to perform 'It's Goin' Down?' And after, like, hearing that a thousand times we tried to figure out ways to perform 'It's Goin' Down' without Mike Shinoda and that didn't work. It never worked."[19] "The album," laments Swift, "revolved more around who we collaborated with and it didn't really shine a light on us artistically."[20]

Then there was the issue of the audience. Most of those who came to see the X-Ecutioners in concert were white. "It is sort of bittersweet to see all these white kids into our music," Swift told *Vibe*. "I'm on clouds right now regardless of which audience appreciates us. But it's like, damn, if you're not up there with platinum jewelry, then you can't reach the kids you really want."[21] When I first interviewed Swift in 2001, before the release of *Built from Scratch*, he was already concerned about the demographics of his audience. It's not that he didn't want white fans, but he missed seeing black and brown faces in the audience.

"Whites and Asians predominantly make up the fan base of the whole turntable movement," he explained, "[but] I wish we could play at crowds where there was more Latinos and more blacks."[22]

The X-Ecutioners faced an existential crisis in the early years of the millennium. They had achieved success beyond their greatest aspirations, but that success was based on a narrow representation of their artistry. Worse, when new fans discovered that the X-Ecutioners were serious instrumentalists and not simply sidekicks to rappers and rock guitarists, they tended to drift away. Their most enthusiastic fans were not the fans they had expected to attract, and those they hoped to appeal to showed little interest. "What was so special about the X-Ecutioners?" Swift wonders. "Was it that we made good music with other bands or was it that we were these DJs using the turntable as musical instruments? What was our niche?"[23] After the 2002 release of *Built from Scratch*, the X-Ecutioners never experienced the same record sales or media exposure. But they continued to make music, together and separately. Two X-Ecutioners records followed *Built from Scratch*, while Rob Swift has released more than a dozen albums both as a solo artist and as a member of the crew Ill Insanity. After a brief and not entirely happy moment in the spotlight, these turntablists found a productive niche.

CULT FAVORITES: ALBUMS BY QBERT, KID KOALA, D-STYLES, AND DJ SHADOW

"Cult favorite" describes what I would consider some of the most significant turntablist releases of this, or any, period: DJ Shadow's *Endtroducing.....* (1996), Qbert's *Wave Twisters* (1998), Kid Koala's *Carpal Tunnel Syndrome* (2000) and *Some of My Best Friends Are DJs* (2003), and D-Styles's *Phantazmagorea* (2002). Unlike the X-Ecutioners, these artists did not collaborate with high-profile rappers or rock musicians, and, not coincidentally, sold far fewer records. On the other hand, they avoided the problems that the X-Ecutioners faced with *Built from Scratch*: they were not crowded out by better-known guest artists, and their albums did not project a narrow view of their artistry. If *Built from Scratch* broadened the appeal of turntablism, these four albums expanded the musical possibilities of the art form.

Wave Twisters

Think of Qbert's *Wave Twisters* as the turntablist equivalent of a rock opera.[24] *Wave Twisters* plunges us into an epic struggle involving a hero known as the

Inner Space Dental Commander, the villains the Red Worm and the Octopus People, spaceships, and lots of noisy laser guns. An animated film was created to accompany the album and released in 2001, but even without the film, the music seems to be the soundtrack to a futuristic and demented Saturday morning cartoon. Qbert clearly had television in mind—the cover is dominated by a large television set, the opening track is called "Turntable TV," and the music is marbled with clips that sound like old-fashioned television commercials.

Although the music seems chaotic, there is more than Space Invaders–style sound effects to hold *Wave Twisters* together. Of the seventeen tracks, numbers 1–3 and 13–16 frame the album, acting as prologue and epilogue. (The final track is an anomaly; more on it in a moment.) The middle tracks come in two forms, which I will call *recitatives* and *arias*. (I'm borrowing these terms from the language of opera.) Traditionally, recitatives are musical numbers that are dominated by monologue or dialogue and help push the plot forward. Arias, on the other hand, are self-contained songs that tend to express a particular emotion or mood—these are the showstoppers, the songs with the memorable melodies.

The first "aria" in *Wave Twisters* is the third track, "Inner Space Dental Commander." The song is set as a duet between a dentist (our hero) and his patient. Instead of simply telling his patient to "Say ah," he speaks the choppy, stuttered language of scratching: "Say ah-ah-ah-oh-ah-ah-oh-ah," he instructs his patient, who dutifully replies "Ah-ah-ah-oh-ah-ah-oh-ah." Note the witty insider reference with the common DJ sample, "ah," from "Change the Beat." *All* turntablists say "ah." In between two call and response sections we hear virtuosic scratching from Qbert and virtuosic shredding from the guitarist Buckethead. This is—along with the two other "arias," "Invasion of the Octopus People" and "Razor Blade Alcohol Slide"—one of the most musically satisfying tracks on the album. It's catchy, clever, and holds together nicely as a stand-alone composition.

Most of the other tracks (except for 1–3 and 13–17) are like recitatives. Recitatives are typically much talkier than arias, the point of them being to disclose important plot information. The same is true in *Wave Twisters*, though as is the case throughout the album, the information we get is often fragmentary. The first recitative, "Red Worm," however, is fairly explicit. It begins with one voice asking, "Who are you? Where do you come from?" and another voice answering "I am the Redworm!" and the rest of the vocal snippets suggest the first meeting of two enemy spaceships. Some of the dialogue is not related to the plot, especially the last track, "Aphrodisiskratch." It opens with the sound of quickly changing television channels before settling on one that combines fragments from an old sex-education record with copious amounts of pornographic moaning. The final words of the album confirm that the track really is out of place, at the same time affirming the TV-centricity of the whole project: "Oops, wrong channel."

The *Wave Twisters* animated film came out in 2001, created by the team of Doug Cunningham, Syd Garon, and Eric Henry. The film is as freaky—or freakier—than the album alone, but it also fleshes out the plot, bringing some coherence to the loose-limbed story suggested by the music. Through various images and text insertions the following story comes somewhat into focus. The setting is "inner space"—all of the action takes place in a tiny galaxy resting on a single hair attached to the posterior of a microscopic flea-like insect that lives on the tip of a turntable needle. (This is a visual reference to the name of the label that released the album version of *Wave Twisters*, Galactic Butt Hair Records.) The villain is crime boss Lord Ook, an oversized baby with a red worm living his navel. Ook has imposed a reign of terror over the people of Quasar 16.33.45.78, forbidding them to practice the Lost Arts—the four elements of hip-hop, DJing, MCing, b-boying, and graffiti. In this galaxy, turntables are supremely powerful, armed with decapitating laser beams; the evil Ook has not only confiscated them but uses them to keep the citizenry in line. However, the deadliest of weapons—a wristwatch with a tiny turntable attached known as the Wave Twister—is missing.

Enter our hero, the Inner Space Dental Commander, an incompetent nitrous oxide-huffing dentist who wreaks bloody havoc on his un-anesthetized patients (see Figure 7.1). While operating on a hybrid shark-alligator-man he finds in its gullet a severed hand with the mysterious and powerful Wave Twister attached to it. Soon Lord Ook discovers that the Wave Twister has resurfaced, and he captures the Dental Commander and his associates, among them the midriff-baring, gun-bearing Honey Drips and the robot known as Rubbish. In the end, the ragtag gang overcomes the evil Lord Ook and his henchmen and restores the once lost arts of hip-hop to the good folk of Quasar 16.33.45.78. (The numbers refer to the standard record playback speeds).

The film perfectly captures the off-kilter wit and humor of the album, which it leaves virtually untouched. There seems to be no added music or dialogue. The only noticeable difference is that it omits the final track, "Aphrodisiskratch," which even the filmmakers couldn't sensibly incorporate. It would be accurate, but not complete, to call this an "animated" film—still photographs and occasional bits of live-action film complement the garishly colored characters and scenes. A retro aesthetic prevails, invoking many of the images and cultural phenomena of the late 1970s and early 1980s, the period of Qbert's youth. Atari joysticks and the video game Asteroids, Transformers robots and Playmobil figurines, eight-track tapes and computer monitors with green on black displays all populate the film world of *Wave Twisters*. It's enough to make anyone

Figure 7.1 From the film *Wave Twisters*. The Inner Space Dental Commander uses his powerful turntable watch, the Wave Twister, to defend himself against an aggressive octopus.

who grew up during those years, especially slow-maturing men, nostalgic for a simpler and cheesier time.

The film also nicely reinforces the aesthetics and values of turntablism. The many pop culture references provide a visual analogue to crate digging, while the editing style often imitates (and accompanies) scratching by scrubbing the image back and forth. *Wave Twisters* also embodies the heroic masculinity of the DJ battle. Turntables are not just metaphorical weapons, they actually fire death rays, and the struggles of the hip-hop DJ are inflated to galactic proportions, where the welfare of entire civilizations depends on the skillful manipulation of vinyl. Clearly, however, the filmmakers (and Qbert, too) don't take themselves too seriously. After all, the world in which our heroes live is small enough to fit onto a hair on a flea's ass.

Carpal Tunnel Syndrome and *Some of My Best Friends are DJs*

Qbert and the Canadian DJ known as Kid Koala are kindred spirits in many ways. Both are highly skilled turntablists who share an offbeat sensibility, impish sense of humor, and a love of jazz and kitsch. But their music differs in striking ways. Qbert is a scratch virtuoso whose music tends toward the abstract; Koala is more of a mixer who, rather than deconstructing records into an untraceable *zigga-zigga*, constructs original music out of myriad recorded fragments. To put it another way, Qbert takes something simple—the syllable "fresh," for example—and creates a complex musical world out of it. Kid Koala, on the other hand, takes bits of completely unrelated records and stitches them into nearly seamless, deceptively simple songs.

Koala grew up practicing classical piano while immersing himself in his parents' record collection, which he says tended toward "Rodgers and Hart records."[25] It's also significant that he is an avid artist and has written comic books to accompany most of his albums. Kid Koala's musical and artistic upbringing helps explain two of the most distinctive aspects of his work as a turntablist: his emphasis on melody and his interest in creating narrative and song structures in his music.

While a turntable can easily play any melody ever composed, as long as it's been recorded, it's much more difficult for DJs to *create* melodies in performance; most turntables have a limited ability to manipulate pitch, allowing DJs to fashion only the simplest of melodies. These limitations never stopped Koala. Using a combination of the pitch adjust control, the 33 rpm and 45 rpm buttons, and subtle platter-tapping, he manages to create melodies that sound organic and expressive. For "Skanky Panky" (from his 2003 album *Some of My Best Friends Are DJs*) he took a single note and turned it into a trumpet duet. "I found some long-extended horn notes and bent them into what I heard

Figure 7.2 Kid Koala. (Photograph by Corinne Merrell.)

[in my mind], one being the call and one being the response. The melody didn't exist on the record." When I spoke with him in 2009, he was still working to expand his melodic range: "I hear melodies in my head that my hands can't do yet, and it's just a matter of learning to push those intervals out to your fingers. I can kind of hit up to a sixth right now pretty accurately, but any higher than that and, you know, I just need to put in a few more decades of work on it."

Another characteristic of Kid Koala's approach is his focus on musical structure, which he speaks of in terms of narratives and songs. He has described his approach on certain tracks as that of a screenwriter who sets a scene and fashions dialogue among characters. *Carpal Tunnel*'s "Fender Bender," for example, tells the story of a minor car accident. Koala sets the scene with some spoken-word fragments; for example, "Oh yes, if you're driving tonight do be careful," and throws in traffic noise and the sound of a car horn for good measure. The last 1:20 or so is given over to a scratch dialogue representing an argument between the two drivers involved in the fender bender: one pitched lower, the other higher, suggesting a man and a woman. The argument intensifies as traffic piles up behind them (indicated by additional car horns); a police car then arrives and an officer joins the fray as the two drivers tell their sides of the story. "Fender Bender" offers an example of brilliant scratching put at the service of storytelling; at the same time, one can simply enjoy the call-and-response of the scratching completely unaware of the commotion it depicts.

"Skanky Panky" shows how Koala has continued to refine his songcraft since *Carpal Tunnel Syndrome*. The track combines the syncopated rhythms of ska (skanking is a form of dance associated with ska) with jazzy horn solos and duets. The form consists of an intro and outro and several choruses in which the "soloists" shine, singly and in various combinations. He used about forty different records for the piece, almost none of which were actually ska. Some of the records supplied merely a single note, so that what sounds like a funky drum break extracted from a single record might have been "hand-cut," as he describes it, out of half a dozen discs, one each for the kick, snare, toms, and cymbals. It took him half a year to hand-cut this piece. "It's the equivalent of building a [real] house out of Legos," he explains. The marvel of "Skanky Panky"—in my opinion one of his best tracks—is that while we are rightfully astonished at the painstaking work that went into its composition, we listen to it and listen to it again because it is a funky, jazzy, skankalicious tune.

Kid Koala's emphasis on melody, storytelling, and songcraft helps explain his popularity outside of turntablist circles. His mischievous sense of humor only adds to the appeal. As one review of his 2000 album put it, "*Carpal Tunnel Syndrome* . . . is a tour de force of the turntable art, though performed with a rare focus and flair that makes it one of the few DJ-only discs that can be listened to and enjoyed by nonspecialists."[26]

Phantazmagorea

If Qbert's *Wave Twisters* is a psychedelic sci-fi flick and Koala's albums are animated comedies, then *Phantazmagorea*—the 2002 album by California DJ D-Styles—is a horror movie.[27] With a little porn and comedy thrown in. Although there is no visual accompaniment to *Phantazmagorea*, it is a strongly cinematic album, one that evokes images, characters, and action. D-Styles had a keen sense of the visual from the beginning. "When I made this album I wanted to create new soundscapes," he says in the liner notes. "I wanted to introduce the listeners to new colors in sound." The album's very cover hints at this new soundscape, with the word "HORRORPHONIC" replacing the "STEREO-PHONIC" label that used to appear on LPs from the 1960s.

Even if *Phantazmagorea* doesn't tell an explicit story, we can hear it as a sonic exploration of the psychopathic personality. This comes out most obviously in the sixth of nineteen tracks, "Charlie's an Angel," in which the notorious murderer Charles Manson calmly says, "Maybe I should have killed four, five hundred people. Then I would have felt better, felt like I really offered society something." But the subject is intimated as early as the second track, "John Wayne on Acid," which probably refers to the serial killer, John Wayne Gacy. The third track, "Won't You Be My Neighbor," seems to be about David

Figure 7.3 D-Styles, *Phantazmagorea* (2002).

Berkowitz, also known as "Son of Sam," who murdered six people in New York City in 1976 and 1977. Here, the conventions of the horror film become more explicit. It opens with a woman intoning, "His neighbors called him a regular sort of guy," after which we hear in short order: a fast piano line in its lower register (a common trope in horror movie pursuit scenes), a woman screaming, and a low-pitched maniacal laugh created through vinyl manipulation. D-Styles also mixes in a dash of porn—you can't miss the moaning in "Smorgasborg of Sodomy" and he samples one of his favorite adult film stars, Tabitha Cash, in "Clifford's Mustache."[28] (What is it with DJs and porn?[29]) *Phantazmagorea* isn't all sex and/or gore, however. There are some lighter moments, too, as in "F.U.P.M.," where Hervé Villechaize, "Tattoo" from the old TV show *Fantasy Island*, sings a ditty that disses costar Ricardo Montalbán.

Listening to this horror-comedy-porn film "soundtrack" is entertaining (and disturbing) enough to obscure the fact that this is a work of performative DJing, not a digitally created cut-and-paste sound collage. This is a crucial feature of *Phantazmagorea*. D-Styles created everything using a typical turntable setup (Vestax PDX-2000 turntables, Vestax 05-Pro mixer, Shure M44-7 needles), with the addition of a Roland RE-201 Space Echo, a vintage piece of equipment favored by many older DJs. There are also guests on certain tracks, among them Babu, Melo-D, and Qbert, his former crew mates from the Beat Junkies and the Invisibl Skratch Piklz. (D-Styles was a member of both.) But nearly everything we hear on this album was manipulated on vinyl, mostly by D-Styles. The music—which he composed over the course of four years—is often so complex, with multiple layers and seamless transitions, that it's hard to believe it was created as a performance. However advanced the techniques may be, there are also many gestures to the old school. Aside from the echo generator that DJs like Kool Herc often put to good use, D-Styles scratches many of the classic samples, including "ah" and "fresh" (from BeSide's "Change the Beat"), "good" (from Chic's "Good Times"), and "ah yeah" (from Run D.M.C.'s "Here We Go"). Although *Phantazmagorea* was the first of its kind—the first fully scratched solo album—D-Styles was interested not only in making history, but in drawing on it as well.

In a 2002 interview, D-Styles spoke of having "two separate mind frames when work[ing] on music."[30] One focuses on the purely technical (in his case scratching), while the other favors the musical over the technical. On *Phantazmagorea* he tried to strike a balance between the two. As a scratch fanatic, this was difficult for him—"Sometimes I get obsessed with scratching 'ah,' you know. If that's my mood then I'll do that. I had to push myself and mature and stop just scratching 'ah' all day."[31] He succeeded in *Phantazmagorea*, and the result represents the musical maturing of turntablism. Turntablists during this period were seeking to make artistic statements through the long-form structure of the album, hoping to appeal to the musical sensibilities of their audience and not simply impress them with their skills. A final statement by D-Styles captures this new attitude. "If at times you happen to forget that I created these songs solely from scratching, then I've succeeded. Scratch music doesn't have to sound chaotic and busy. It can be as simple and clean as you like."

Endtroducing.....

One of the most acclaimed releases of its time, DJ Shadow's *Endtroducing.....* appears on many lists of the best albums of the 1990s and has been lauded by *Time* magazine and National Public Radio as among the greatest works of the twentieth century.[32] Yet many critics and even devoted fans don't seem to realize that *Endtroducing.....* is a hip-hop album. Listen to tracks like "Midnight in a Perfect World" or "Stem" and certain adjectives may come to mind: airy, contemplative, ethereal, gentle, haunting, mysterious, trippy. None of these are commonly used to describe hip-hop, or at least most of 1990s mainstream hip-hop.

Figure 7.4 DJ Shadow, *Endtroducing.....* (1996). Pictured are Chief Xcel (left) and Lyrics Born (right). (Photograph by B+.)

Yet the first thing DJ Shadow is likely to tell you about *Endtroducing.....* is that it's pure hip-hop.[33] *Endtroducing.....* has been described as acid jazz, ambient, electronica, or trip-hop, but these labels annoy Shadow. "The way that I make music," he explains, "is rooted in the hip-hop paradigm and the hip-hop way of thinking, which is: take what's around you, and subvert it into something that's 100-percent you."[34] For Shadow, hip-hop is defined by attitude and process, not a particular sound. He traces his philosophy to the Bronx era of hip-hop, when the musical eclecticism of the reigning DJs helped define what Grandmixer D.ST describes as the "genreless concept of hip-hop."[35] "Hip-hop," Shadow agrees, "is not a genre of music, but the mind-state in which genres no longer exist. For my mentors—people like Afrika Bambaataa—that was the whole vibe, that hip-hop is actually all forms of music, without genres."[36]

Not only does Shadow consider *Endtroducing.....* a hip-hop album, he thinks of it specifically as a DJ album, despite the fact that he largely created the music with a digital sampler, using his turntables only sparingly.[37] Growing up in Davis, California in the 1980s, Shadow was a bedroom DJ who devoted countless hours trying to cut like his old-school heroes, imitating the solos on Grandmaster Flash's "Step Off" or Davy DMX's "One for the Treble." He cites Cash Money's "Scratchin' to the Funk" as an influence and notes that, "I had been driving around listening to Qbert routines, and Skratch Piklz routines, prior to *Endtroducing.....*"[38] He leaves no doubt about how he conceives of himself as a musician. "One of the most frequent questions I get asked when I do interviews is, 'Do you consider yourself a DJ first, or a producer first?' And I always say a DJ. I mean, *Endtroducing* is categorically a DJ album to me."[39] Although Shadow did all the scratches on the album, he doesn't call himself a turntablist. "This is what I would say. I can scratch good. I just never considered myself a turntablist. I mean, to me, a turntablist, again, is somebody who . . . walk[s] around with that warrior mentality. And you have to go around defending yourself and saying, you know, 'I'm the best.'"[40]

Despite Shadow's demurral, I would argue that *Endtroducing.....* in fact represents an important expansion of the art of turntablism. Two tracks in particular have much in common with the turntablism of the mid-1990s. The first track, "Best Foot Forward," is one of them. In the very first second of the first track of the album we hear scratching, with which Shadow seems to proclaim, "I am a hip-hop DJ." But there's more than just scratches in this short track to make that point. Like a good battle DJ he deploys some boastful wordplay, and puts together what is sometimes called a scratch sentence, a statement stitched together from different records (here indicated by slashes): "Guess who's coming? / DJ / Shadow / back again / who is he? / just your favorite DJ savior."

If "Best Foot Forward" suggests the wordplay that opens a battle routine, the third track, "The Number Song" sounds like a strong DMC routine. Like many a battle routine, it draws from 1970s funk and 1980s hip-hop, and manipulates vocal samples over a fast breakbeat. Another connection to the battle scene of the time is Shadow's manipulation of numbers, like "One, two, three, four, hit it!" from Kurtis Blow's "AJ Scratch" (1984), which has long been popular among battlers.

"The Number Song" isn't a routine, however; Shadow doesn't devote long sections to juggling a single sample, and he uses more records than would be typical. More significantly, he takes what I would call a "composerly" approach to this track, following the time-tested strategy of stating a theme, varying it, departing from it, and then returning to it. After the opening vocal sample, we hear the main beat (or theme) of the track, a fast looped break accompanied by a slow-moving alternation of two low, distorted pitches. After forty seconds, Shadow starts to vary the beat gradually but regularly—just enough to keep things interesting. A jolting transition at 2:05 marks the departure, introducing a completely different beat, texture, and mood. When the opening beat returns (2:42), it's an appealingly familiar sound, which Shadow then varies in new ways. In the last minute the texture thins out and the musical activity decreases, traditional signals that the end of the song is approaching. In the final seconds Shadow stutters the sound, scratching the one record still playing; he then hits the stop button, creating the winding-down sound typical of battle routine codas.

In "The Number Song," Shadow has cannily crafted a track so that it can be enjoyed repeatedly as a song, but without letting listeners forget its roots in the world of the DJ. Moreover, he composed a song without calling attention to the fact that there was no singer. When I asked Shadow about his compositional approach in *Endtroducing.....*, he explained that he wanted to create "instrumental hip hop that wasn't just a beat for someone to rap over. To me, instrumental hip-hop is supposed to have motion and have structure that is different from just a beat."[41]

With their classic samples and kinship to battle routines, "Best Foot Forward" and "The Number Song" evoke both the history of hip-hop and the turntablist scene of the mid-1990s. The gestures were deliberate: "that's my way of showing that I come from someplace legitimate [as a hip-hop DJ]," he says.[42] So what of the other 58 minutes of *Endtroducing.....*, which sound little like these tracks, or most hip-hop for that matter? In their own way they too are just as inextricably connected to the soul of hip-hop and the mindset of the hip-hop DJ.

Consider "Building Steam with a Grain of Salt," which beautifully expresses the philosophy of crate digging, a central activity in the lives of hip-hop DJs. (As Shadow writes in the CD's liner notes, "this album reflects a lifetime of vinyl culture."[43]) The gentle, simple piano loop that sets the track's contemplative mood comes from Jeremy Storch's 1970 song "I Feel a New Shadow," an obscure cut that I suspect initially appealed to Shadow because of its title. On top of Storch's piano line, Shadow layers a spoken-word record that obviously spoke to him. Extracted from a 1974 recorded interview with drummer George Marsh, the passage begins, "From listening to records I just knew what to do—I mainly taught myself." Later in the song, Marsh returns to articulate what might well be Shadow's philosophy of music. "I would like to be able to continue to let what is inside of me, which is, which comes from all the music that I hear, I'd like for that to come out. And it's like, it's not me that's coming. The music's coming through me." To emphasize (and musicalize) this last sentence, Shadow repeats it, rapidly panning it from left to right so it sounds as if the music is truly coming through us as it echoes inside our heads.

Shadow probably found these two records in his favorite digging spot, a record store in Sacramento whose first floor is shown on the cover of *Endtroducing....* This store was the setting of the most memorable scenes in the 2002 documentary *Scratch*. We see Shadow, sitting alone in the dark, claustrophobic basement, as he muses on the spirituality of digging and the ephemerality of music. "This is my little nirvana," he tells us, surrounded by teetering towers of records:

> Being a DJ, I take the art of digging seriously, and this is just a place I've been going for eleven years. . . . And in fact most of my first album [*Endtroducing*] was built off records pulled from here. So it has almost a karmic element of, like, I was meant to find this one on top, or I was meant to pull this out because it works so well with this. So it's got a lot of meaning for me personally.[44]

We can imagine Shadow pulling out the Storch record, deciding it's a keeper because his name is in one of the song titles, and then finding the interview record, which holds the promise of adding a few interesting words to his vinyl vocabulary. The piano line from Storch comes right at the beginning of the 1970 song, so he must have immediately been drawn to it. But the lines from the Marsh interview don't appear until well into the record, and the same is true for many of the samples Shadow uses. Digging is much more than just the acquisition of records—it involves unending hours of listening, ears open to every possibility.

That the two records work so well together is a testament to Shadow's fine ear, but to him there's also a "karmic element" at work. As he sits in the basement of the record store, he elaborates, speaking of the perspective he gains when in the company of countless discs:

> Just being in here is a humbling experience to me because you're looking through all these records and it's sort of like a big pile of broken dreams,

in a way. Almost none of these artists still have a career, really, so you have to kind of respect that in a way. If you're making records and if you're a DJ and putting out releases, whether it's mix tapes or whatever, you're adding to this pile, whether you want to admit it or not. Ten years down the line, you'll be in here—so keep that in mind when you start thinking, like, "Oh yeah, I'm invincible and I'm the world's best," or whatever. Because that's what all these cats thought.[45]

Some might find this a depressing thought, but it needn't be, for crate diggers like DJ Shadow can breathe new life into these forgotten records. Jeremy Storch is a case in point. He had been a member of the 1960s rock group The Vagrants, popular in their Long Island stomping grounds, but never quite a national act. Their closest brush with broader success came in 1967 when they recorded a rock version of Otis Redding's "Respect." Unfortunately for them, just as it started climbing the charts, Aretha Franklin recorded her version of the song, instantly overshadowing the Vagrants' cover (and Redding's original, for that matter). The group broke up in 1968, and Storch went on to make two solo albums, neither of which sold particularly well. Even as his popularity waned, he lived, as his website tells us, "like a typical rock star: experimentation with and heavy use of various drugs and plunging into wild parties and illicit affairs."[46] This lifestyle was unsustainable, and in 1970, his heart stopped on the way to the emergency room after suffering a drug overdose; miraculously, he was revived in the hospital. During his "death experience" he heard the voice of God and found religion.

The one-time philandering addict Jeremy Storch surely thought he was invincible, only to end up largely unknown and nearly dead, his fading musical traces buried in great piles of moldering vinyl. Yet like Storch himself, "I Feel a New Shadow" didn't quite die, and it, too, found redemption. I asked Storch what he thought of being sampled in "Building Steam with a Grain of Salt," and his answer posits a parallel between the two artists: "When I wrote ['I Feel a New Shadow'] I was on a spiritual search. I felt there was something more to life than just being a rock star. I was looking for God. I believe DJ Shadow is in the same position."[47] Storch provides us with one of the innumerable stories hidden inside the vinyl that crate diggers encounter on a daily basis. The elegiac "Building Steam with a Grain of Salt" pays its respects to all those records, the lifeblood of hip-hop. It is, like DJ Shadow's album as a whole, a meta-record, a record about records.

Endtroducing....., of course, is more than simply a meditation on the vicissitudes of vinyl. It's a fine collection of songs, one that demonstrates a composerly approach to turntablism. With a few exceptions, these songs don't sound like the turntable music of the time (or of any time), and to some they don't even sound much like hip-hop. But this is not because Shadow lacks deep roots in hip-hop; on the contrary, he followed in the path of that most revered "Master of Records," Afrika Bambaataa, who sought out music no one else knew. In creating *Endtroducing.....*, Shadow reveals, "I was trying to find a sound different from everybody else's, so the source material had to be different from everybody else's."[48] He clearly achieved his goal. Although most listeners wouldn't put the digitally created *Endtroducing.....* in the same category of the all-analog *Phantazmagorea*, D-Styles's remark about turntablism rings true when applied to Shadow: "[It] doesn't have to sound chaotic and busy. It can be as simple and clean as you like." Or as Shadow himself puts it, "I'm always just trying to say, 'It's bigger than you think it is. DJing is broader than you think it is.' "[49]

The albums by Qbert, Kid Koala, D-Styles, and DJ Shadow offer a study in kinships and contrasts. They differ in mood and sound, but more striking are their similarities. Each album focuses squarely on mixing and scratching—there are no rappers or rock bands in earshot—and demonstrates the artist's musical self-sufficiency. Each draws heavily on spoken-word fragments and sound effects, and each reveals marked visual and cinematic qualities. *Wave Twisters* has its animated film, *Carpal Tunnel Syndrome* was both inspired by cinema and comes with its own graphic novella, and *Phantazmagorea* suggests an experimental soundtrack in search of a film. *Endtroducing.....*, too, is deeply imagistic, its evocative soundscapes giving listeners free rein to conjure up their own personal films. Shadow himself remarked that "[it] was particularly important to articulate a cinematic feeling."[50] The visuality of these albums is no accident, and is an effective strategy in communicating the vitality of a musical form that so often has to be seen to be believed. These were certainly not the only contributions to the turntablist albums of the time—a full list would include works by Craze and Klever, Cut Chemist, Mr. Dibbs, Disk (as Phonopsychographdisk), Faust, Mix Master Mike, Quest, Ricci Rucker and Mike Boo, Shortee, Swamp, and DJ Z-Trip and DJ P[51]—but each of these long-players we've focused on here should be considered landmarks of the art, albums that paved the way for a generation of turntablists whose artistry is flowering at this very moment.

AVANT/ILLBIENT/JAZZ TURNTABLISM ◉

The category of "Avant/Illbient/Jazz Turntablism" may seem to have *miscellaneous* written all over it, but there's good reason to consider, say, Christian Marclay together with King Britt or DJ Logic alongside DJ Spooky, despite the fact that they come from very different musical traditions. And although some of these DJs exist on the fringes of hip-hop—or even completely outside it—their interests and priorities reveal a kinship with the world of Afrika Bambaataa and Grandmixer D.ST: they share an openness to experimentation, they enjoy performing with non-DJs, and they tend to disregard the boundaries of genre. Turntablism, Babu foretold in 1997, "is going to transcend hip-hop. It's going to go way beyond hip-hop where it won't be about using hip-hop records anymore. A real turntablist will flip anything, any record, and express their soul through that."[52] Babu's expansive definition of turntablism most certainly encompasses the work of the artists we'll encounter here.

We can trace what I'll call avant-garde turntablism back to the early part of the twentieth century, when a handful of classical composers in Europe and the United States began experimenting with the turntable as a musical instrument. One of them was the American John Cage, whose *Imaginary Landscape No. 1*, from 1939, was the first published composition to feature the phonograph as a performing instrument. Scored for piano, large Chinese cymbal, and two turntables, the phonograph operators, equipped with test-tone records of single frequencies, pick up and replace the needles on the records in precise rhythms and switch back and forth from 78 rpm to 33 1/3 rpm, creating eerie Theremin-like glissandos. (For the diggers out there, the records are Victor 84519 and 84522.) Today's turntablists should know this haunting music if for no other reason than to hear needle-dropping and tones as they were performed decades before GrandWizzard Theodore and 8-Ball perfected the hip-hop versions of these techniques.[53]

Avant-garde turntablism enjoyed a resurgence starting in the 1980s and has continued to thrive in the underground ever since. Probably the most prominent exponent is Christian Marclay. Although no one would mistake him for a hip-hop turntablist, he shares their artistic perspective—that is, he's not interested simply in the music contained on records, but in using records and turntables to create wholly new sounds and music. He accidentally discovered looping as a college student in Boston in 1978, at about the same time many hip-hop DJs were doing the same:

> While walking to school on a heavily trafficked street a block away from my apartment I found a record on the pavement. Cars were driving over it. It was a Batman record, a children's story with sound effects. I borrowed one of the turntables from school to listen to the record. It was heavily damaged and skipping, but was making these interesting loops and sounds, because it was filled with sound effects. I just sat there listening and some kind of spark happened.[54]

Marclay liked the sound of skipping records so much he put stickers or pieces of tape on his records to force the needle to skip, and so could make loops whenever he wanted. Many a battle DJ has done exactly the same thing. This is one of those stories common in both avant-garde and hip-hop circles. Like John Cage and GrandWizzard Theodore, he heard a record do something that it wasn't supposed to do, or sound like it should not have sounded, and felt compelled to pursue its musical possibilities.

Since the 1980s Marclay has created dozens of turntable works, including *Second Coming* (1982), derived from a pornographic 45 rpm disc; *John Cage* (1988), a kind of mashup created by cutting up several LPs of Cage's music and gluing pieces from different records into a single disc; and *Tabula Rasa* (2003), which involves a blank record and a cutting lathe.[55] In his thirty-year career he has embraced not only sound art but also visual art—much of it deeply linked to music—and is now a celebrated figure in the modern art world.

Christian Marclay is only the best-known of the avant-garde turntablists. The American David Shea, Japan's Otomo Yoshihide, the Canadian Martin Tétreault, and the Englishmen Philip Jeck and Aleksander Kolkowski, among others, have continued to explore the musical capabilities of the phonograph.[56] It may seem that these artists have little direct connection to the world of the hip-hop DJ, but they are never more than one or two degrees of separation away. In 1982 and 1983, Marclay was playing turntables with his band Mon Ton Son in downtown New York clubs like Danceteria and CBGB, moving in the same spaces as hip-hop DJs as well as fellow travelers like Blondie, Bill Laswell, and Kool Lady Blue. He later performed with members of the rock group Sonic Youth, who in turn have performed with DJ Spooky; in 1996, he formed djTRIO, an ensemble with rotating personnel that included Marina Rosenfeld, DJ Olive, Toshio Kajiwara, and Eric M., who all have a strong presence in jazz circles. The connections go on and on, but the point is that the worlds of these DJs are closer to each other than we may at first think, and if they are not all moving in the same direction, they are all pushing the boundaries of turntable music outward.

Since the 1990s jazz musicians have been an increasingly important part of this boundary expansion. In 1994, the jazz saxophonist and bandleader Branford Marsalis formed the group Buckshot LeFonque and released two albums that brought hip-hop into an eclectic mix. The first album, *Buckshot LeFonque* (1994), draws on the talents of DJ Premier, particularly in "Some Shit at 78 BPM (The Scratch Opera)"; the second, *Music Revolution* (1997), enlists DJ Apollo. The next year Apollo teamed up with American trumpeter Russell Gunn for his 1998 album *Ethnomusicology, Volume 1* and then its 2001 sequel; DJ Neil Armstrong took Apollo's place on the third volume, released in 2003. Throughout the second half of the 1990s, British jazzman Courtney Pine collaborated with the successful battler and producer DJ Pogo, who is treated as a sideman as important as any of the others. Another musically adventurous DJ is King Britt. Digable Planets, with whom he toured (as Silkworm), "was just like a jazz band," Britt says, and some of the members were trained in jazz; but he has also worked with prominent jazz performers such as Grover Washington, Jr.[57] In Japan, DJ Krush has been collaborating with jazz musicians since his 1995 debut album, *Krush*, and his sound is often described as "acid jazz," a groove-based genre that mixes jazz, funk, soul, and hip-hop.[58]

Although all of these DJs have collaborated with jazz musicians, they would not actually be considered part of the jazz scene. There is another group of DJs who could well be called jazz turntablists if they were willing to be subjected to such a label. It would at least be accurate to say that they are fully immersed in the world of experimental, freely improvisatory, under-the-radar jazz, what scholar Robin D.G. Kelley has described as "beneath the underground."[59] This circle of jazz turntablists is a small, tight one, and most perform with each other. A few names crop up over and again, in particular DJ Logic, DJ Olive, and DJ Spooky, who have all been active since the late 1990s. Logic, who is more scratch- and breakbeat-oriented than the others, has collaborated with the trio Medeski Martin & Wood (check out the funky "Sugar Craft" from 1999's *Combustication*), as well as the Dirty Dozen Brass Band, Sex Mob, and Uri Caine. He also released a solo album, *The Anomaly*, in 2001, with a backing band of jazz musicians. Like Logic, DJ Olive has performed with Medeski Martin & Wood, Uri Caine, and Dave Douglas; more mixer than scratcher, he tends to favor soundscapes that combine funky grooves and heavy bass with ambient electronics.

Soundscapes that combine funky grooves and heavy bass with ambient electronics. This describes the sound of what is known as illbient, a genre of electronic music that arose in New York in the mid-1990s. The first illbient compilations were released by the Asphodel label—*Crooklyn Dub Consortium Vol. 1* in 1995 and *Incursions in Illbient* in 1996—and Olive was involved with both projects. *Illbient* marries the hip-hop slang *ill* (meaning cool) with *ambient*, the atmospheric electronic music connected with musicians such as Brian Eno and Tangerine Dream. The term and the music are closely associated with both Olive and Spooky, and although there's some debate about who gets credit for the coining the term, they are both indisputably pioneers of illbient, or as Spooky writes it, "ILLbient."

"ILLbient," Spooky wrote in his 2004 book *Rhythm Science*, is "hip-hop turned inside out"; related to hip-hop, but resistant to being pigeonholed.[60] This could well be said of Spooky's music generally. Listen to the opening track of his 1998 album *Riddim Warfare*, the appropriately titled "Pandemonium," and you'll hear dub, orchestral music, 1980s video game sound effects, scratching, and spoken-word fragments, all in close succession. Not every track of *Riddim Warfare* is a manic collage, but all partake of his characteristic eclecticism— with everything from the fast thumping pulse of drum and bass music to a chopped sample of the New World Symphony by Antonin Dvořák. Can all this music be illbient? Yes, according to Spooky, because, he argues, illbient is "the only music in history that isn't defined by a style."[61]

Like Spooky, DJ Singe and DJ Mutamassik were pioneers of illbient but are equally difficult to pin down stylistically—Singe often performs rhythmically intricate free jazz that sometimes recalls Sun Ra, while Mutamassik (whose DJ name can mean *stronghold* or *tenacity* in Arabic) is known for her North African and Middle Eastern–infused beats. (Both DJs are pioneers in another sense as well, in that they are women performing in a still male-dominated world.[62]) If they do have a stylistic home, it would probably have to be jazz, though jazz in the broadest sense that embraces hip-hop, illbient, and experimental classical music.

In many ways, turntablism and jazz are natural partners. Herbie Hancock and Grandmixer D.ST had demonstrated this back in 1983, and the reasons it worked then were the same reasons it worked ten and fifteen years later. For one, the turntable is an extremely versatile instrument in terms of the timbres, textures, and rhythms it can play, and a good turntablist can groove beautifully with a jazz soloist or combo. Robin D.G. Kelley cites their improvisatory flexibility. "DJs have the potential for dramatically altering improvised music because they play an instrument that simultaneously mirrors and deconstructs improvisational practices we associate with jazz. Sonny Rollins' tenor can become a drum, Art Blakey's drum roll a horn or a drone."[63] As an example of this deconstructive practice, consider DJ Sniff, a Japanese experimental turntablist working in the Netherlands. "Instead of using the 'ahh' sound from Fab 5 Freddy's *Change the Beat*," he wrote in the liner notes of his 2011 album *ep*, "I used Anthony Braxton and Max Roach's duo record *Birth and Rebirth* to practice."[64] The title of his album refers to the free-improvising jazz saxophonist Evan Parker, whose served as Sniff's muse and whose records he used in creating what could be called an example of free jazz turntablism.

Rob Swift, who has performed with the great jazz fusion keyboardist Bob James (creator of the oft-sampled "Take Me to the Mardi Gras") as well as saxophonist Dave McMurray and others, also sees a strong affinity between DJs and jazz musicians.

> It's not like when we perform we have a stand with a musical composition in front of us that we're following. We're just playing from the heart, and it's just a self-taught type of music. We learn by watching other people, we teach ourselves, you know what this guy did, and learn this scratch and we figure out how he did it. So I think that's why we compare ourselves to jazz musicians.[65]

As Swift suggests, there's more than a musical connection; both groups tend to learn their craft in the same way and place great importance on knowing the heritage of their music, its geniuses and masterpieces. DJs also draw the comparison because of the cultural legitimacy and stature of jazz. "My mom said jazz is the highest form of music," Qbert told me. "I don't know if it's true or not, but it is pretty damn high, so I started studying jazz musicians."[66] Of course, jazz didn't always enjoy a sterling reputation, and in its early days it was treated like many have viewed hip-hop—more noise than music and a grave threat to the morals and sensibilities of our youth. And not all in the jazz world have embraced hip-hop in general or turntablism in particular. Kid Koala was once barred from registering as a performer for a jazz festival because the organizers didn't recognize the turntable as an instrument.[67] Although the DJ was gaining acceptance in the broader world in the late 1990s, there was—and probably always will be—a certain amount of resistance to an instrument that looks like no other but can sound like them all.

SCRATCHING FOR RESPECTABILITY: CLASSICAL COLLABORATIONS AND TURNTABLATURE ◉

Carnegie Hall is about ten miles south of the birthplace of scratching, but for most of the history of hip-hop that fabled venue of classical music might as well have sat on a distant planet. On October 2, 2005, however, that metaphorical distance closed to zero with something few would have expected to see on that stage: a tuxedo-clad DJ performing on a set of turntables accompanied by a full symphony orchestra. It was the setting of the New York premiere of the *Concerto for Turntables*, by Raúl Yañez with DJ Radar as soloist. Appropriately for this hybrid of popular and art music, the concert was sponsored by the makers of the highly caffeinated drink Red Bull, and the orchestra was made up of college-age performers representing some of the best music schools in the country. Conducted by Constantine Kitsopoulos, they performed together under the banner of the Red Bull Artsehcro—*orchestra* spelled backwards.[68]

At first, the orchestral musicians were not sure what to make of the affair. "It was the first time I ever saw a turntable up close," remembers You-Young Kim, a master's student in viola performance at Juilliard and one of the sixty-four members of the Red Bull Artsehcro. "None of us could imagine what it would sound like, playing with a turntable."[69] But the musicians quickly accepted Radar as a fellow musician. Kim saw Radar as an honorary string player:

Just like stringed instruments, the turntable's technique is also about how to produce the sound and how to shape it. But instead of moving a bow

Figure 7.5 DJ Radar and the Red Bull Artsehcro on the stage of Carnegie Hall, 2005.

across the strings to vibrate the wooden body of the instrument, the D.J. uses his hands to spin the record, so that the stylus vibrates as it passes through musical imprints carved into the vinyl. After that, everything is the same as for any other instrumentalist: controlling articulation, volume, and pitch.[70]

It wasn't clear, though, whether the typical classical music concertgoer would be as accepting. As it turned out, the audience wasn't at all typical. "The hall was full of young people," recalls Kim. "I've never seen this many young listeners at Carnegie Hall! It made us feel so good to play for our own generation, who waved their hands at us and really got into the music."

This was not the first performance of this music—one movement was performed in 2001 at Arizona State University, where Yañez had been a student. But the Carnegie Hall premiere was especially significant for its cultural resonance. Hip-hop DJs have long had a chip on their shoulders, eager to prove themselves to a world that assumes that they are not musicians. There may be no higher validation, then, for a turntablist to command the Carnegie stage just like the most revered musicians of the past century had done before. It may have only been ten miles between Carnegie Hall and the birthplace of hip-hop, but the trip took nearly thirty years.

While DJ Radar never anticipated that he would end up on the Carnegie stage, it was the particular cachet of classical music that led to the *Concerto for Turntables.* In the preface to the score of Radar's 1998 work for turntables, *Antimatter,* legitimacy is foremost on Radar's mind. "This composition," he wrote, "was created for the sole purpose of establishing turntablism as a legitimate form of musical expression through a written and universal musical medium, a score."[71]

While working on *Antimatter,* Radar had the idea of performing with an orchestra, and was urged by a friend to consult Yañez, a graduate student in music at Arizona State. "How cool would it be to have, like, a DJ, or a turntablist, with an orchestra?" Radar asked Yañez.[72] Not very cool, was Yañez's initial reaction: "I'm a jazz musician, and I've played a lot of popular-type music—there's usually no notation for it or anything. So, I'm like, 'What? What are you talking about? You want to do it with the orchestra? Who cares about orchestras?'" But he relented, and one day when Radar was looking at some musical ideas Yañez had sketched, he saw three words scribbled on some staff paper that suggested that his new partner was starting to care about orchestras: "Concerto for Turntables."

The concerto evolved through hours of jamming: Radar on the decks and Yañez on the piano. Yañez would often try to notate what Radar was playing or sketch out a new idea and then Radar would try it, refining it the process, and through this process the piece gradually emerged. Although Yañez is listed as the composer, he happily acknowledges that the *Concerto* was truly a collaborative effort. When they explained the process to me, they unintentionally illustrated the closeness of their working relationship by completing each other's thoughts and sentences:

> YAÑEZ: We agreed as artists that I was going to be the composer and he was going to be the . . .
>
> RADAR: Soloist.
>
> YAÑEZ: . . . the soloist. But in the end, I know I couldn't have written it for another musician. Because everything was a result of us together. He was like, my—I don't know how to—I don't know what words to use, but you can get . . .
>
> RADAR: Lab monkey?
>
> YAÑEZ: Yeah. I was going to say lab monkey.
>
> RADAR: But it was good for me because it made me think of the turntable differently. And it opened up a whole other experimental process for me. So it was definitely a gift. It was like, wow, I didn't realize it could be so . . .
>
> YAÑEZ: Lyrical.
>
> RADAR: Yeah. Lyrical.

It wasn't strictly necessary for Yañez to notate the turntable part—it was written expressly for Radar, and the two could have simply agreed on a general outline of the music, with Radar improvising as necessary. But Radar insisted on a completely notated turntable part, which Yañez at first resisted. "I was like, 'Dude, how the hell are we going to get someone else to play this?' I told him, 'I'm not going to spend the next three years with another turntablist, trying to learn each other's languages.' " But for Radar, the project was bigger than himself. "I just wanted other people to be able to perform it. Basically the whole project is just to communicate . . . what you can do on a turntable. It's an art, you know. It's not just some 'wicki wicki' stuff; there's actually some thought there."

The finished work adheres in many ways to traditional classical concerto conventions. There are three movements, the typical fast-slow-fast ordering, and there's a cadenza, or solo, at the end of the first movement in which the soloist improvises on themes introduced earlier. And as in some nineteenth-century concertos, themes from the first two movements return in the finale. Although much of the solo part is rhythmically intricate, the two musicians felt it was important to bring out the largely unexplored melodic side of the turntable. They did this not only to expand the musical possibilities of the instrument; it was also, like notating the piece and calling it a concerto, a way of legitimizing turntablism, and hip-hop in general. As Yañez observes, many criticize hip-hop for what they believe is a lack of melody, but when people heard Radar they would say, "Look, this guy's really playing melodies."

In the decade following the composition of the *Concerto for Turntables*, Radar and Yañez performed the work for thousands of people across the world. At a time when the first performance of a new composition is often its only performance, this counts as a tremendous success. One of Radar's main goals, however, has not yet been realized: no other turntablist has performed the work. The lack of published score or commercial recording has no doubt contributed to the matter, and the fact that the solo part is so intimately tied to Radar's technique and style may also discourage its spread. But Radar and Yañez are optimistic about the future of the *Concerto*, and see a time when they not only publish the score but create versions for a variety of different skill levels and ensembles, thus disseminating the music—and legitimizing turntablism—on an ever broader scale.

The turn of the millennium saw the beginning of a trend in which turntables came to be incorporated into traditional classical ensembles. The trend began modestly, with a few works sprouting up in North America and, later, in Europe. At about the same time Radar and Yañez were hashing out the *Concerto for Turntables*, another graduate student in music was composing a similar work several thousand miles away in Canada. The composer was Nicole Lizée, and the piece was *RPM for Large Ensemble and Solo Turntablist*, which she wrote in 1999 as a master's student in composition at McGill University in Montreal, a city with a thriving DJ scene.[73] (DJ P-Love was the soloist for the work's premiere.) In addition to *RPM* and the *Concerto for Turntables* there was *sP!t*, for flute, violin, cello, piano, and turntable, a 2000 work by California Institute of the Arts student Nicholas Chase, and *This Present Darkness* for wind ensemble and turntables, premiered in April 2000 by Sean McClowry, then a recent graduate of the Peabody Conservatory in Baltimore. As the decade continued, turntable compositions appeared with greater frequency, contributed by an ever growing list of artists: Mason Bates, Nikitas Demos, Anthony Paul De Ritis, Shiva Feshareki, Paul Leary, Raz Mesinai, Gabriel Prokofiev, Mariam Rezaei, Daniel Bernard Roumain, and Ignaz Schick, among others.[74] Student works continued to appear, but many of these compositions were written by more-established composers. Several more concertos for turntables—by De Ritis, Feshareki, Leary, and Prokofiev—came as well, and more are certainly on the way. Turntable concertos will probably never become as routine as piano or violin concertos, but the day they are no longer regarded as novelties will be a milestone in the battle for legitimacy that many DJs still fight.

For many turntablists, notation is closely tied to this quest for legitimacy. As Radar has written, "The use of a musical notation process for scratching is essential in securing a place within written music history."[75] Around the same time Yañez was notating Radar's part in the *Concerto*, other DJs were starting to develop entire systems of turntable notation—also called "scratch notation" or "turntablature."[76] In the late 1990s and early 2000s, several different systems arose, each illuminating the art of turntablism in different ways.

One of the first turntablists to develop a notation system was A-Trak, at the time a renowned world battle champion. He originally intended it to serve as a memory aid and as a way to spur his creativity.[77] So he started drawing simple pictures, often diagonal lines in a sawtooth-like configuration. Breaks in the lines specified when the sound would be cut off with the crossfader, and hatch marks on the diagonal lines indicated fader "clicks"; that is, a motion all the way to the right or left end of the crossfader track. All of the various lines would be laid over a horizontal axis that showed beats and bars.

A-Trak created this notation as way to keep track of his often complex scratch patterns, but he has also said that it can help turntablists communicate with each other. "We all know how difficult it is to explain a scratch using words," A-Trak points out:

We usually end up resorting to a mix of vocal scratching and awkward midair hand movements. But these antics only refer to the way we personally *feel* a scratch, rather than the way that scratch is actually executed, which is what we're trying to explain. What we're looking for is a common ground in communication where we can accurately break down the given pattern.[78]

Yet whatever advantages it may offer, A-Trak believes that notation is of only limited use to DJs. "The absence of such a system has never stopped deejaying from progressing and 99.9 percent of today's deejays seem to be doing just fine without it." Moreover, he is not concerned with what other musicians or the general public thinks of it: "My purpose in creating this system wasn't to justify scratching in the public eye as a legitimate form of music; to me, this is beside the point."[79] A-Trak's view is that notation is a tool, to be judged by its usefulness.

But for hip-hop filmmaker John Carluccio, legitimacy was a prime motivating force behind the development of his Turntablist Transcription Methodology, or TTM. "TTM," his website explains, "is dedicated to the advancement of the turntable as a musical instrument, and of the turntablist as a musician."[80] TTM had its origins in 1997 as a collaboration among Carluccio, industrial engineer Ethan Imboden (also known as catfish) and Ray Pirtle (a DJ known as Raydawn). They copyrighted their method in 1999, published Version 1.1 in booklet form in 2000, and have maintained a website (www.ttmethod.com) for several years.

The Turntablist Transcription Method works by representing scratches as lines plotted along a rectangular graph in which the horizontal axis represents time and the vertical axis represents record rotation. The notation can also indicate the sample being used, whether the record is sounding or not, the direction of record rotation, and the use and placement of certain percussion sounds: kick, snare, or cymbals. (See Figure 7.6 for a simple TTM transcription of three basic scratches using "fresh.") The TTM website also helpfully includes sound clips coordinated with the notation examples.

Perhaps surprisingly, Carluccio's TTM found its way into the mainstream media. *Time* magazine profiled TTM and Carluccio in 2001; that same year it was written up in the *New York Daily News* and was featured in the documentary *Scratch*. In 2004, it even served as a key plot point in the television show

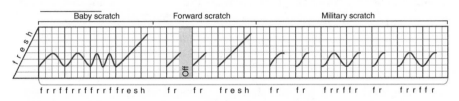

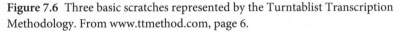

Figure 7.6 Three basic scratches represented by the Turntablist Transcription Methodology. From www.ttmethod.com, page 6.

CSI: NY. Why would audiences care about an obscure tool used by a select few within an already tiny population? At a time when the popular image of hip-hop was dominated by gangstas, their women, and their bling, the whole concept of TTM was irresistibly incongruous; after all, most readers would associate notation with classical music. As Carluccio explains in the *Time* profile, "Putting it on paper elevates the level of the art."[81]

It is difficult to assess the success of TTM. It has certainly helped bring turntablism to the attention of the public, and has perhaps convinced some non-DJs to take turntablism seriously. To my mind, TTM also succeeds to a certain extent as a descriptive tool. TTM transcriptions are capable of providing a clear *visual* analogue of the sounds of scratching. Viewed while listening to the corresponding recording, these transcriptions can clearly convey the extent to which the DJ is manipulating the sound on the records. This may be useful for those unfamiliar with scratching, since it is often difficult to understand how sounds are being manipulated when the listener is hearing but not seeing the performance.

But how successful is TTM as a prescriptive system? How easily could a beginning DJ learn to scratch using the notation and how well could an experienced DJ learn a complex and unfamiliar routine from it? Let's say I take the notation represented in Figure 7.6, and put it on a music stand in front of my turntables with the intention of sight-reading it. What *doesn't* it tell me? It doesn't tell me how fast or loud to scratch, it doesn't say how to turn the sound off or on, and I can't tell how to execute the two differently shaped lines at the beginning of the military scratch example. And if I'm not already familiar with the sample, I don't know what exactly "fresh" sounds like. While this may seem to be damning criticism, Western classical notation is similarly incomplete— much is left to the performer's knowledge and discretion. But the question remains: can TTM succeed as a tool for learning how to scratch? It's fair to say that TTM, like any type of notation, can only be one component of the learning process. At this point, TTM's role in turntablism is as much symbolic as it is pedagogical.

When the French graphic designer Laurent Burte developed a method he calls *scratchgraphique*, he understood that no system of notation can describe or prescribe every detail of a performance. Burte's system is infused with the improvisatory spirit of jazz and is not as prescriptive as a typical classical score. As he explains in his 2003 book, *Scratch Graphique,* "to write out a detailed scratch score is as illusory as trying to capture the spirit of jazz" in notation.[82] He thus sees his notation as a means to provide DJs with the basic principles of scratching while leaving a great deal open to the performer.

Burte's notation is striking—beautiful, even—and is strikingly different from the others I've mentioned. 🌑 Scratchgraphique represents record movements with a combination of flowing curves and straight, bold strokes that Burte explains are derived from the physical gestures of scratching. The immediate impression of many of those who have encountered the notation is that it looks less like notation and more like a written language. "These characters are not notes," Burte writes, "but rather stylized figures that function as an alphabet."[83] Specifically, Burte's calligraphy is reminiscent of Arabic (at least to non-Arabic readers), and this is intentional. "Scratchgraphique characters have an Arabic form. It is important to understand that, contrary to our Latin characters, Arabic characters are by definition malleable, not fixed."[84] By combining the ethos of jazz and the look and structural features of Arabic, Burte avoids comparisons with classical music, but at the same time depicts scratching as something "other," something exotic.

However, like the other systems, scratchgraphique is meant to be a means by which turntablists can learn their art. And it, too, has its strengths and limitations. While it can certainly function as a viable system, its greatest strength may well be in its beauty. Listening to a routine while following Burte's transcription of it (a CD is included with his book for this purpose) may make one admire the subtlety and grace of the DJ's performance more than simply watching a blur of hands.

If turntablist notation systems are in principle no different from the type of notation that countless classical musicians have depended on for centuries, why is it that very few turntablists actually use them to any great extent? Part of the reason may be that there simply hasn't been enough time for them to catch on. But there's a more significant reason connected with the culture and tradition of the hip-hop DJ. For DJing's whole history, practitioners have learned their craft not just by listening to other DJs but by *watching* them, whether in person, on videotapes, or on the Internet. They often learn by seeing exactly where and how others move their hands to manipulate records, tone arms, and mixers. By watching routines they also learn about body tricks and other physical gestures that notation doesn't capture. Graphic representations—however complex or artistic the lines and squiggles—simply don't communicate as much *direct* information. The widespread availability of tutorial videos renders notation merely a useful adjunct to the learning process, but hardly a necessity. As A-Trak put it, most DJs "seem to be doing just fine without it."

The central question about the viability of turntablist notation systems turns not on the limits of notation, but on the need for it in the first place. In 2005, Rob Swift told an interviewer, "It's not something I'd use on stage or anything but I think it's showing people just how far you can take DJing so for that I think it's cool."[85] Here Swift identifies the true significance of turntablature, at least at this point: its value is less in what it can teach turntablists than in what it can teach others about turntablism.

In 1996, five years before the dueling DJ commercial for The Gap, turntablism was at the peak of its creative powers, and the battle scene was flourishing. This was the year of the battle between the Invisibl Skratch Piklz and the X-Men, a summit—both in terms of a peak and a gathering—that demonstrated the artistic heights of turntablism and the intensely competitive but open and amiable atmosphere of the scene. At the time, however, turntablism was still just a blip on the radar of popular culture, and not even well known among fans of the gangsta-rap–dominated world of commercial hip-hop. Gradually, however, the art form that had largely existed beneath the underground started to see more sunlight. Exposure came in many forms, from the popular songs that traded on the cool edginess of scratching, to the turntablature that traded on the respectability of classical music. These "trades" were necessary for achieving the legitimacy that DJs had long craved, and tell the story of turntablism during those years.

In the mid- and late 1990s, turntablism carried crates full of cultural capital. To outsiders it had everything you could want from an underground scene. As an analog art in a digital age, it exuded authenticity and proudly communicated its do-it-yourself mentality. It had a distinctive sound and attitude, and though it was a small scene it didn't exclude outsiders. But many insiders yearned for more. They wanted to reach out to a broader public, they wanted to be respected, and they wanted to be popular. But there was inevitably a tradeoff.

Take the story of the X-Ecutioners' *Built from Scratch*. They got what they wanted—massive crowds, more money than they had ever encountered, and the attention of the mainstream media. Yet there was a price—they were relegated to the role of sidekicks, supplying a dash of hipness and authenticity to a popular rock band. They were neither victims nor sellouts—this was simply the consequence of trying to make their art accessible to the public. There were other tradeoffs as well. Scratch notation gained the attention of the mainstream media, but its admirers outnumber its users. DJ Shadow's *Endtroducing.....* garnered as much respect as any musician could hope for, but for all its acclaim many of its most devoted fans don't realize its connection to turntablism.

"What was our niche?" This is the question Rob Swift asked when looking back at the X-Ecutioners in the wake of their work with Linkin Park. But the question was pertinent to all turntablists during the second half of the 1990s. Was turntablism most at home in the underground, or could it flourish in the mainstream? Taking the long view, the answer is clear: although the art form scratches its way to the surface every so often, much more of its life has been spent out of the spotlight, carrying—often proudly—the status of acquired taste or cult favorite. In a sense, then, this period was an aberration.

In 2008, I put Rob Swift's question of niche to Qbert. Although he has enjoyed more fame than most DJs, and was even named America's Best DJ in 2010,[86] he sees turntablism as essentially incompatible with the mainstream. "It's under-ground, it's like punk rock, it's not commercial. I like it underground, it's always been. We don't want anybody to know about it. It's like, fuck everybody else and just scratch and shit. That's how it was back then, and that's how it is now. And if you think it's dead, then fuck you, get out of here, don't scratch with us."[87]

Kuttin Kandi also sees the return to the underground as inevitable, though she takes a more philosophical outlook. When asked about the evolution of turntablism in 2000, she foretold a decline in its popularity:

Forgotten years ago, suddenly the DJ is popular again. However, the media still lacks the essence of the culture and doesn't fully understand the "art" behind the music. Because of this massive attention to such an "under-ground art" turntablism will become affected in both negative and positive ways. Either way, those who never really cared for it will turn away, and those who truly did will be the ones to stay. So, in the end when the lime-light fades, and the spotlight is turned off . . . the art returns to where it all began and where it belongs.[88]

Kandi's eloquent prediction, as we'll see, turned out to be true.

Falling Barriers: 2002–2011

"Like it or not, *this* is the future!" To some, these were fighting words. The speaker was a representative from the DJ equipment manufacturer, Stanton, who stood sweating under the stage lights at a 2002 DMC battle in New York City as he tried to woo the palpably hostile crowd with his company's new product.[1] *This* was Final Scratch, a hardware/software system that allowed DJs to play digital sound files stored on their laptops using their turntables as controllers. The Stanton rep stood beside DJ B-Side, who had gamely been trying to explain to the crowd of several hundred on that hot summer night that with this new technology you could leave your vinyl at home and simply use two specially made records instead. Hecklers rained abuse on B-Side as he demonstrated the system; some started chanting, "We want vinyl! We want vinyl!" Never mind that Final Scratch *did* use vinyl; the mere presence of a computer plugged into the traditional analog system of two turntables and a mixer was offensive to some. "Many people who were there that night still call me 'That Digital Nigga,'" B-Side recalls with amusement.[2] After B-Side and the Stanton rep retreated from the stage, the battle resumed. A crowd-pleasing showcase by special guest A-Trak capped the night; well into the morning, Kuttin Kandi, MC for the competition, came out to announce that DJ Precision was the winner, with Boogie Blind the runner-up. None of them had used a computer.

Although many DJs resisted digital technology at the time, they were also curious about it. As B-Side pointed out about that night, "The crowd seemed mad and pissed publicly, but half of them came up to me to learn more about what exactly was going on."[3] This combination of resistance and curiosity reveals just how much was at stake: it wasn't just that the tools of the DJ's trade were changing, but their art and their way of life were being challenged as well. In the end, the Stanton representative was right: this technology was the future. Put simply, the introduction of digital technology has been the single biggest development in the history of the hip-hop DJ.

Digital technology has affected the way DJs find, make, and disseminate their music. Moreover, it has influenced not just the *how* of DJing, but also the *who*. These new tools have opened DJing to a broader and more diverse population by simplifying certain aspects of DJ technique and reducing the expense of being a DJ. But technology was not the only factor in the changing demographics of the DJ scene. The same period saw the emergence of the DJ academy, an institution that has changed the way the art is taught, and to whom it is taught. Tied up with digital technology and the DJ academy are other developments, from the growing presence of women in this male-dominated world and the rise of the celebrity disc jockey, to the success of DJ-related games and software applications. All are part of a broader phenomenon that characterized the first decade of the new millennium: a lowering of barriers that gave rise to the notion that anyone can be a DJ.

DIGITAL TECHNOLOGY COMES TO THE DJ: THE CD TURNTABLE ◉

Here's a demonstration that never fails to amaze first-time observers. I put a compact disc in a specially made CD player and press "Play." Then I put my hand on what's called the jog wheel, a simulated record platter about the size of 45 rpm disc. I push it back and forth and . . . out comes the sound of scratching! "But you weren't touching the CD!" onlookers gasp; "How does that work?" they demand. The fact that I can mix and scratch a CD without even touching it seems close to magic. As we'll see, this magical disconnect—digital disconnect may be a better way of saying it—between the music and the DJ's hands was for some artists a great selling point, but a fatal flaw for others.

Digital technology had been in development for much of the twentieth century, but it wasn't until the late 1970s and early 1980s that it entered the market. Although digitally recorded vinyl records were publicly available in 1979, the real impact of digital recordings came in 1982 with a wholly new format, the compact disc. CDs held great appeal: the sound seemed clearer than analog recordings (though some felt and still feel that the sound is "colder"), and they were smaller and often sturdier than records. But for the rest of the 1980s and all of the 1990s, none of this mattered much to hip-hop DJs. CD players were literally and figuratively black boxes, metal monoliths whose inner workings were inaccessible to users. At that time, DJs couldn't mix or scratch with CDs like they could with vinyl records; the machines were simply incompatible with the art of performative DJing. For all the hoopla that accompanied the CD, this technology was not only a step backward for DJs but represented a threat, unceremoniously pushing turntables into near obsolescence.

But starting in 2001, CD technology leapt ahead; or perhaps it's better to say that it finally caught up with DJs. That year, electronics companies began to release players that imitated some of the features of the turntable crucial to performative DJing, including, yes, scratching. First to the market was American Audio's Pro Scratch 1 tabletop CD player, released in January 2001.[4] In July, Pioneer introduced its CDJ-1000, which soon came to dominate the small but growing field; many refer to all CD turntables as CDJs, even though the name refers only to Pioneer products (Figure 8.1). Denon, Technics, and others soon followed with their own models.[5]

Although the various models have slightly different dimensions and features, they generally function in the same ways. They are tabletop units with front-loading CD slots (or trays) and a jog wheel on top; a pitch adjust slider and an array of buttons fill out the interface. Once the CD is inserted into the machine, the DJ does not touch it, but controls its sound through the jog wheel and the various buttons. When the player is in "scratch mode" or "vinyl mode" (the name varies by manufacturer) the DJ can hold the jog wheel down to stop the music or push it forward or back to simulate scratching. I say *simulate* because the CD, safely ensconced in the unit, keeps spinning in its normal fashion even though the DJ may be pushing the jog wheel back and forth.

Figure 8.1 The Pioneer CDJ 1000, first released in 2001. Model pictured is the CDJ 1000 MK3. (Image courtesy of Pioneer Electronics [USA] Inc., © 2011.)

Here is where the digital nature of the CD player comes into play. Handling the jog wheel essentially gives instructions to the machine to manipulate the data—long strings of the digits 0 and 1—representing the sounds contained on the CD. The manipulability of digital sound is the basis for these players' most valuable features. Most notably, cueing and looping are much simpler than on traditional turntables. A DJ can set multiple cue points so that a single tap of a button starts the music at exactly the right spot every time—no hunting for the right groove and gingerly setting the needle down, and no need to deface records with stickers and markers to indicate a particular spot on the vinyl. Looping is also a snap. Just press a button to indicate the beginning and end of a loop, and any segment of a track can be repeated as seamlessly as if Grandmaster Flash were on the wheels of steel. Many other effects—flanging, panning, and echoing, for example—are also possible on these machines. Then there's the convenience factor. CDs hold more music than LPs and are easier to carry, and because a laser rather than a needle is used to play them, record wear isn't a problem. Moreover, with CD burners available on personal computers and laptops, it's a simple matter to make custom discs—it's like being able to press battle records at home.

But these new CD players have their drawbacks, too. Many DJs, particularly hip-hop DJs who perform a lot of complex scratching and mixing, reject the machines. (Electronic dance music DJs, on the other hand, have more readily embraced CD turntables.) Most objectionable is the jog wheel. Instead of the usual twelve-inch record platter, jog wheels are typically between about four and eight inches in diameter, in other words between the size of a small CD and a large 45 rpm record. (Some later models introduced twelve-inch wheels, however.) The smaller size gives DJs less room to move their hands, literally cramping their style. And even on the most robust machines, the jog wheels are light and insubstantial compared to the heavy, solid metal platters of sturdy turntables. Most crucially, jog wheels just don't have the immediacy and tactility of vinyl. As Maseo, longtime DJ and member of the group De La Soul, told me, "I like the feeling of that wax. Licking my fingers so I can get that grip on the record, spin it back and cut it up." "Vinyl is the essence of DJing," he explains; its absence is the CD turntable's "main flaw."[6]

In the earliest of the CD players, latency was also a problem; that is, there was a noticeable lapse in time between moving the jog wheel and hearing the sound, and even the smallest lag can be distracting. Simply put, the feel of these machines is markedly different from that of traditional turntables. Instrumentalists are finely attuned to the size, weight, and texture of their instruments, and even slight changes to these physical properties can have a huge impact. Imagine playing basketball with a volleyball and you get the idea: everything would seem off. For many hip-hop DJs, the physical differences between CD players and the turntables they grew up playing overshadow any of the advantages the digital machines offer.

There are ideological objections to CD players as well. The absence of vinyl is a serious problem for many hip-hop DJs, but not just because they miss its feel. Vinyl is a precious substance in hip-hop. It is authentic, it is elemental, it is fundamental. Vinyl was present at and largely responsible for the birth of hip-hop, and is intimately tied not only to DJing, but to MCing and breaking, for it was the DJ spinning vinyl who made it possible for the b-boys and b-girls to dance and the MCs to rap. There is more than just music inscribed in those black discs; vinyl carries with it the whole history, the DNA, of hip-hop.

Moreover, some DJs oppose these machines precisely *because* they make certain aspects of turntablism so much easier. There is an understandable pride DJs take in being able to loop a break seamlessly or drop the needle quickly and smoothly on a particular groove at will, skills mooted by the CD player's laser-guided accuracy. Some CD players not only make cueing and looping a snap, but can simplify scratching as well by automatically muting the sound of backspinning. This effectively removes the need to use the crossfader on many scratches. On a turntable, even a basic scratch like a stab—a short, repeated forward scratch with the sound of the backspin cut off—demands precise coordination between the record hand and the fader hand to execute cleanly. Not so with these CD players, which allow perfect one-handed stabs every time. For some DJs, eliminating the hard work required to hone their craft cheapens their art. And if a CD player does that much work for the performer, is it an instrument or simply a playback device? When GrandWizzard Theodore derisively remarked that these CD turntables "play themselves," he may have been exaggerating, but his concern was sincere.[7] Speaking for many hip-hop DJs, he categorically stated that using CD turntables "is not *real* turntablism."[8]

In 2005, this anxiety about digital turntablism bubbled to the surface in an online discussion of whether the DMC should allow CD players in its competitions. That January, a DMC representative asked readers of the website djpages. com what they thought of the possibility of changing the rules for the summer 2005 battle season. Many strongly opposed the idea, including a DJ called Furiate:

> This cannot be allowed to happen. The DMC championships are the corner stone of turntablism. It has a historical significance and represents everything good about turntables. It seems these days everyone wants to do things the easy way. The thing I like about turntablism is that it requires genuine skill. Allowing CD DJs to compete with real turntablists is a betrayal.[9]

Some, however, argued that turntablism transcends vinyl, and anything that allows DJs to better realize their musical ideas and to take the art "to the next level" should be embraced. Consider the sentiments of Mixdoctor, a seasoned DJ and battle judge, who responded to Furiate and others:

> The "carrier" does not matter, whether CD or vinyl, it is the skill involved and how innovative the turntablist performance is that is important. I therefore think the inclusion of the CD players can only improve the competition and will finally push forward an art form that has stagnated.
>
> The objections raised above seem to be made by the dinosaurs who want to clutch on to the vinyl disc like it is sacred. IT ISN'T! It is becoming outdated and it is time to move on.[10]

In the end DMC decided not to introduce CD turntables into its 2005 competitions, and is unlikely to try again. DMC founder and director Tony Prince diplomatically explained the decision to me in an e-mail message: "We felt the timing was too controversial to permit digital playback." But he was frustrated by the DJs' resistance, which he felt was shortsighted. "Whether digital playback has a role in turntablism," he argued, depends on whether "the DJs recognise [that] . . . they can express their artistry and creativity digitally."[11] Digital playback did come to have a significant role in turntablism, and battles in particular, but it was not, as we'll see, in the form of CD turntables.

DIGITAL VINYL ◐

There *is* a form of digital DJing that turntablists have turned to in great numbers, a technology that many—even those who wouldn't go near a CD turntable—rave about unashamedly. "Thank God [for it]" Steve Dee testifies. "It has saved my life," gushes Cash Money. "This breaks down the barriers of DJing, and it opens so many doors," say Faust and Shortee. "The best of all worlds," claims DJ Maseo.[12] Even the Master of Records—*analog* records—Afrika Bambaataa, declares, "I love it."[13] These veteran vinyl-loving DJs are all talking about what are known as digital vinyl emulation systems (usually abbreviated DVS).

It wasn't love at first sight, however. DJ B-Side was using a DVS at the battle I described at the opening of the chapter, and was certainly not received well. Some DJs still object to it, and almost all agree that it will not replace hard work and skill. Some veterans criticize the technology for making DJing too easy, for allowing younger DJs to get away without paying their dues. "I loved it when you couldn't mix music unless you had records and turntables. And that's when it was dope," says DJ P, who got his start before digital vinyl hit the scene.

"Those days are over. It's all digital now."[14] Nevertheless, countless DJs who got their start in the vinyl age are using systems by Serato, Torq, Traktor, and others. Why is it that two digital forms of DJing, one that uses a CD player and one that uses a laptop computer, are treated so differently by hip-hop DJs? The answer is simple: vinyl. In short, the DVS allows DJs to keep what they love about vinyl— its feel, look, and authenticity—and avoid what they don't love about it—its weight, cost, and inconvenience.

To understand how digital vinyl systems work, I'll use the popular Serato Scratch Live system as an example, but most of what I say here can be generalized to other products as well.[15] Serato consists of two vinyl records, the proprietary Serato software (to be downloaded to a laptop), a small black metal box with several outputs, and a tangle of red and white RCA cables. At first glance the Serato records seem like any other, but take a closer look. All the bands are exactly the same width, and there are none of the variations in groove density DJs are used to seeing. When played on a turntable *not* connected to a Serato-enabled laptop, this type of record simply emits a long, high-pitched sine wave known as a control signal. But when these records are played on turntables that are wired to a laptop through that black metal box (more on that in a moment) the long *beeeep* disappears. It's replaced by a sound file on the computer, and can now be controlled by manipulating the special records. Scratch a snare hit, loop a bar, juggle a phrase, or needle drop, and you hear just what you would expect. It really does seem like magic.

To make this magic, the control record must convey three basic bits of information to the software: record speed, record direction (backward or forward), and the position of the needle on the record. The control signal is used to convey speed and direction. As anyone who has played around with a turntable knows, when a record slows down, the pitch falls, and when the record speeds up, the pitch rises. The same is true with any DVS record. When the pitch of the control tone increases or decreases, the Serato software interprets this change in frequency as a change in speed, and the speed of the sound file being played changes correspondingly. The control tone is also used to gauge the direction in which the record is spinning. Actually, there are two control tones pressed into each disc, one for the left channel and one for the right, though they are exactly the same frequency, which is why it sounds as if one tone is playing. But the two tones are not sounding at exactly the same time; or more precisely, they are out of phase with each other. The software detects this, and recognizes that if, say, the tone in the right channel is ahead of the left channel tone, then the record is moving forward; if the opposite is true, it's moving backward.

So the software knows the velocity and direction of the record, but how can it tell where exactly the needle is on the record? Here is where the different DVS products differ. Serato tackles this problem by embedding noise into its control records.[16] The noise, which can't be heard above the music, is constantly changing, so at no point is the shape of the waveform exactly like it is before or after it. The Serato software recognizes these changes and uses them to indicate very precisely where on the record the needle is tracking.[17] Other digital vinyl systems, Torq and Ms. Pinky, for example, use a different method called time coding. These records have what are called time stamps, distinct binary numbers encoded into the vinyl. These time stamps correspond to different positions along the record and are mapped onto the sound file playing on the laptop.[18] Whether the records use noise or time stamps, they all recognize needle position. This means that a DJ can needle drop and skip among different parts of a track, just as if it were a typical record.

For control vinyl to do more than simply beep, it has to communicate with the laptop. This is where that black metal box comes in; it's an analog-to-digital converter, or ADC (see Figure 8.2). (Some mixers, like the Rane TTM-57, incorporate an ADC and connect directly to a laptop.) The ADC sends digitized information on changes in the sound of the control record to the software; the software translates the data into corresponding changes in the position, speed, and direction of a digital audio file. The data are then routed into the mixer where they can be manipulated like any analog audio signal. As crucial as the box is, DJs simply plug it in and forget about it; they don't handle it like the control records or monitor it like the software displayed on their laptop.

Figure 8.2 The Serato interface box, an analog to digital converter (ADC) that connects the mixer to the turntables. (Photograph courtesy of Serato Audio Research.)

The software is the final piece to understand.[19] (See Figure 8.3 for a screen-shot of a Serato session.) The bottom half of the screen simply displays track information (artist names, song titles, etc.); the top half is where the action is. The two white circles—"virtual decks," they're called—represent the songs playing on turntable one and two, and indicate beats per minute, the length of the song, and the current position in the song. The black line sweeps around the circle's face, a digital version of the clock system that Grandmaster Flash developed in the 1970s.

Above the white circles are buttons for the different playback modes: absolute (ABS), relative (REL), and internal (INT). Absolute treats the record as if it were normal vinyl, mapping the start of the song to the beginning of the record. Pick up the tone arm and set it down an inch further into the record and it will play the corresponding part of the song. As the Serato manual explains, "ABS mode faithfully reproduces the movement of vinyl control records, including stops, starts, scratching, needle dropping, rubbing and other turntablist techniques."[20] The manual doesn't point out that needle skips are also faithfully reproduced. To avoid skips, use relative mode, which registers the forward or backward movement of the record, but not needle position. If the needle jumps a groove or if the DJ picks up the tone arm and sets it down further into the

Figure 8.3 Screenshot of Serato Scratch Live software, version 2.1. (Image courtesy of Serato Audio Research.)

record, the song will continue playing at the same point. DJs will typically use relative mode in a club setting where advanced turntablist techniques aren't called for; it's especially handy when playing amid curious onlookers or drunken patrons who might bump into the turntables. Finally, internal mode lets the DJ manipulate songs just using the laptop—no turntables or vinyl are necessary. Internal mode is useful if the turntables malfunction during a club set or performance—the music can go on without the vinyl. DJs mostly use either ABS or REL—absolute mode if they want to simulate traditional vinyl as much as possible, and relative if they want to take advantage of the easy looping, cueing, and other effects possible with digital vinyl systems.

Most eye-catching about the Serato screen are the colorful waveform displays that sit in between the virtual decks. Experienced DJs look at a traditional record and can the see variations in the grooves that indicate where in a track the break is. The waveform displays provide a digital analogue, so to speak, of the record grooves, but they offer much more information. The different colors (which do not show on Figure 8.3) indicate frequency—red for low, green for midrange, and blue for the higher end. Even kicks and snares are color-coded, making it easy to line up snares, juggle beats, and match tempos.

I haven't explained all the buttons and features, but we've seen enough to begin to understand how the widespread adoption of digital vinyl has affected the art of the DJ. Talk to a random handful of DJs who had been spinning before they adopted digital vinyl, and you'll get an armful of examples of how the technology has affected their work. Generally, however, there are three areas in which the effect of using a DVS is most pronounced: the transportation of records, the acquisition of records, and the manipulation of records.

The issue of transporting records seems to come up most quickly and often among DJs talking about digital vinyl. "Man, my back feels a whole lot better!" Shortkut says with a laugh when he explains how his life has changed since using digital vinyl.[21] Craze concurs: "Because of all the years of carrying records I've developed lower back arthritis so I am very happy to use Traktor now."[22] When DJs of a certain age—those old enough to have used vinyl for much of their careers—complain about their work-related ailments, they always talk about back pain. This has nothing to do with scratching or mixing records, and everything to do with carrying them. For decades before the advent of digital vinyl, hip-hop DJs spent endless hours hauling crates of records to and from their gigs, loading and unloading, lugging them upstairs and down. Even during their gigs they were constantly bending over to pull discs from their crates or put them back. "We've been carrying records for the last thirty years," GrandWizzard Theodore said of his generation. He doesn't wish that he had had digital vinyl instead of crates for all those years, but as he explains it, "We've paid our dues, so we deserve the right to use Serato."[23]

Vinyl is a particular headache for DJs who travel by plane to gigs or battles. Extra fees, breakage, and theft are a constant reality. Self-described "vinyl fanatic" Afrika Bambaataa "wasn't too keen" on the digital systems when he first encountered them. "But when you travel so much—and I used to come with crazy crates to do my shows, five, six, sometimes—you start to look at expenses."[24] Any jet-set DJ will have a horror story about retrieving crates from baggage claim only to find records missing. Here's one from Shortkut: "I got to the destination where I was supposed to do the gig, and when I got to the baggage claim, half of my records were gone. And that was like three thousand bucks worth of records, you know what I'm sayin'?"[25]

For DJs carrying vinyl, air travel was always difficult. But in the wake of the terrorist attacks of September 11, 2001, flying became a true ordeal, with extra charges and closer scrutiny of baggage. For many DJs, this was the final straw. Rob Swift, for example, started using Serato in reaction to the headaches of traveling in a post-9/11 world.

I started using Serato Scratch Live in April 2005. I made the transition from using strictly vinyl at shows to Serato, primarily, to avoid the hassle of traveling with multiple crates of records. Just before switching over to Serato I went on a ten-day European tour. It was me, my girlfriend, four bags of luggage, three heavy-ass crates of records and absolutely no one to help us carry all of this! What made it worse was paying the excess baggage and overweight penalties airlines charge their customers. So not only was I dealing with the burden of lugging all of these records, I also was being forced to dip into show money in order to pay the excess baggage and overweight charges. By the fifth day of the tour I decided I would never go through that again![26]

Here's a provocative, but unanswerable, question: to what extent did the events of September 11, 2001, hasten the adoption of digital vinyl among hip-hop DJs? Not all DJs travel extensively by air, and those that did might've started using digital vinyl anyway, terrorist attacks or not. Still, digital vinyl didn't become widely popular until certain well-respected DJs started to use it—Jazzy Jeff is often cited as an example. And if flying after 9/11 was the push that those high-fliers needed to leave their crates at home, perhaps the attacks really did have a large-scale impact on the art of the DJ. If so, this would be just another of the countless unforeseen effects of that horrific day.

Digital vinyl systems not only affect how DJs transport their music but how they acquire it in the first place. For many DJs, buying records is a way of life. They make the rounds of their favorite haunts (record stores, thrift shops, library sales) like clockwork and go digging for records in every city they visit.

But with digital vinyl, a DJ really doesn't need more than two records—the control discs that come with the software. Practically speaking, this saves DJs time, energy, and money. For many DJs there's little need to go out digging when it's so simple to find tracks on the Internet, most of which are cheaper than the vinyl versions. The potential savings are tremendous, given that many DJs need multiple copies of records, whether for beat juggling or because they scratch particular discs so much that they quickly wear out. Look at some DJs' libraries and you'll find four, eight, a dozen, or even more copies of an album. With a DVS, only a single file is necessary for beat juggling (just drag the song to both virtual decks and . . . instant doubles!), and the files, unlike vinyl, don't wear out.

Still, DJs haven't given up on traditional vinyl altogether. DJ P speaks for many when he insists that nothing can replace real-world digging. "You can go online and dig. But to me that's not as dope as walking into a flea market downtown and getting dirty and dusty goin' through records."[27] But really, there's no reason that DJs can't have it both ways. "I still go vinyl hunting," Bambaataa told me, but he digitizes everything "to keep my stuff safe." I was surprised to hear Bambaataa—perhaps the king of all diggers—even say that "digging in the digital crates is just as fun as digging in the vinyl."[28] Realistically, however, DJs are almost certainly buying less vinyl in the age of the DVS. When 2011 DMC champion DJ Vajra—who had amassed thousands of discs earlier in his career—was asked how many records he bought in the previous year he answered, "Less than ten." "I dig a lot online," he explained.[29]

Digital vinyl has had an enormous impact on the day-to-day lives of DJs as they acquire music and travel to gigs. But what about the actual practice of DJing—has it changed the way DJs mix and scratch? In the early years of the technology, some DJs wouldn't scratch with a DVS because the lag between movement and sound (i.e., latency) was too much to overcome, and the highly compressed sound files common at the time sounded thin when played on powerful sound systems. These problems have largely disappeared because of advances both in digital vinyl systems and in the quality of sound files. DJ Craze, who knows a thing or two about scratching, barely even notices the difference when he uses Traktor: "There's a tiny li'l difference in how it feels compared to actual vinyl but I already got used to it."[30]

In terms of technique, the simple fact is that a DJ setup with a laptop is a different instrument from one without, and it is impossible to use the two in exactly the same way. How much a digital vinyl system affects a DJ's technique and sound depends on the individual, but the potential influence is great.

Most obviously, the presence of the laptop draws the DJ's attention, and DJs will turn to it if they're searching for a track, dragging a song to the virtual decks, setting loops and cue points, and so on. Most of the best features of a

DVS require close interaction with the laptop. DJs using a DVS will frequently use the track pad and must remember various keyboard commands. DJs also have to learn how to read waveforms and decode the color changes. These are specialized skills that didn't exist in the pre-digital age, but now form part of the digital DJ's techniques.

DJs who scratch, juggle, or needle drop with digital vinyl must frequently divide their attention, toggling quickly from laptop to record and back again. For Qbert, "it's easier to find stuff on vinyl, you know, instead of looking at the computer—that's like an extra thing there, you know, it's like, why do you need that?"[31] Looking at the screen can also be hard on the eyes. Especially in a dark room, the constant shifting of focus between the bright screen two feet away and the darkened room full of dancers beyond the turntables is a recipe for eyestrain.

With a DVS, DJs also risk getting lost in their screens, focusing more on what they see rather than what they hear. This points to what may be the most significant potential change in DJ practice: the transformation of mixing from a largely aural skill to a much more visual skill. Of course, DJs had always used their eyes to help them mix records—they looked at the grooves on the record and added visual cues to guide them, like stickers on the vinyl or lines drawn on labels. Yet none of this would help if they couldn't hear that one song was faster or slower than another or that the kick or snare drums on the two records weren't lining up. Learning to mix two different records so that they segue seamlessly is a painstaking process that requires hearing small differences in tempo and making slight, frequent changes to the pitch adjust sliders or the platter. The waveform displays of digital vinyl systems, however, make the DJ's aural skills less crucial—beat matching can be done purely by lining up different colors and shapes on the display and doesn't necessarily require the ability to hear. When it comes to digital beat matching, the eyes have it.

The presence of a laptop can also affect how DJs interact with a crowd. Some DJs put their laptops on a stand at eye-level above and between the two turntables. This positioning is convenient for the DJ, who simply stares straight ahead to see the display, but the laptop places a barrier between the DJ and the crowd, who may barely even see the man or woman behind the machine. Even if the laptop is off to the side, the DJ could spend more time looking at it than at the crowd. At a dance club this may mean that the DJ misses important cues from the dancers, and at a battle, it might lead to less interaction with the audience, whose cheers could help sway judges about the success of the routines. In his 2008 collaboration with DJ Revolution called "The DJ," rapper KRS-One criticized DVS-dependent DJs for forsaking their audience:

If you got Serato, bravo
But if you can't cut vinyl records you won't be able to follow

Me—a true MC, not a new MC
Fuck the computer, it's you and me
And the crowd, and yes, they want it loud.[32]

On the other hand, using digital vinyl can potentially free a DJ to interact *more* with a crowd. Using a DVS means spending less time flipping through crates, switching records, and cueing them up, and more time gauging and engaging the audience. This is a boon not only to skilled DJs, but to the less skilled as well. Beginners can use the labor-saving features of a DVS and do little more than stand in front of the turntables, pumping up the crowd while the music plays for them. Experienced DJs understandably resent those who get paid for doing very little.

Especially frustrating for many professionals is the phenomenon of the celebrity DJ, which became more prominent in the 2000s with the rise of digital vinyl. DJ P, who had a residency at the Las Vegas casino and resort Palms, often saw celebrities come through and get gigs at the club he usually worked. "You have celebrities who don't even know how to DJ in clubs making five to ten grand playing on a computer." P gave an example of a famous singer: "[Palms] hired her to DJ and she's not a DJ. She didn't know what the crossfader was, she didn't know what the knobs were, she didn't know nothin'."[33] He and the other resident DJ, he reports, had to show her what to do and essentially did her work for her. Using the example of a popular hip-hop producer and rapper who shall go nameless, DJ P explains how he sees digital vinyl as the culprit.

[This rapper] DJs. He sucks, but he gets paid. Why? 'Cause he's [famous]. But he has no business DJing. Let's say there was no such things as Serato or CD players. Do you think [he] would be able to show up at a club with 200, 300 records and rock it? No. He didn't spend his time or his money and go out to a record store and buy these records and take them home and listen to them. Instead he downloaded these files or someone gave them their gig stick so he could put it on his computer and DJ that night. That's the problem I have with Serato.[34]

Many celebrity DJs aren't even musicians of any sort. Actress Lindsay Lohan and socialite Paris Hilton, both of whom are famous mostly for behaving badly, have been paid to DJ parties. It's easy to imagine the disgust and resentment among working-class DJs when they see Hilton making huge amounts of money dancing in front of Serato-run turntables while sporting specially made pink headphones that she was no doubt paid to wear.[35] They may take some comfort, however, in knowing that crowds don't always respond well to celebrity DJs, as happened with Lindsay Lohan's apparently disastrous performance at a London club in early 2010.[36] At this point, at least, no digital vinyl system has yet been devised that eliminates the need for skill.

Finally, digital vinyl can affect song choice and mixing style. DJs carrying crates to a gig may have a few hundred songs with them; with a laptop they will probably have tens of thousands. As Rob Swift points out, "Serato allows me to have my entire library of music at my fingertips. So no matter what the occasion, no matter what the audience demographics, I can take comfort in knowing that I'll always be prepared to play the right music because I've digitized all of my music."[37] Club DJs using digital vinyl can more easily play the latest hits, both because they are cheaper as sound files and because they often appear on the Internet before being released on vinyl. And of course, a great deal of music is never released on vinyl. Some DJs will even download songs while at a dance club in order to meet a request or play a new release.

A DVS also makes mixing songs a much simpler matter than with regular vinyl. Many club DJs don't play whole songs before mixing in a new tune—two verses and chorus, or even just a chorus—so it's crucial to be able to switch quickly and seamlessly between songs. With digital vinyl, there's no chance of fumbling a disc since the control records never need to leave the turntables. As DJ Revolution, who started mixing with vinyl, notes, "If you can save three or four seconds per song just cueing you can spend more time mixing."[38] Deft disc-swapping is also unnecessary in those battles that allow digital vinyl, where a control disc is like a battle record that can be reconfigured endlessly and in real time. The relative ease of quick mixing may actually encourage even quicker mixing, altering the sound and character of DJ sets and routines. DJ A-Minor reports that the dancers he spins for like the quicker mixing style that delivers more songs per hour (or minute). As he puts it, digital vinyl is "good for the ADD crowd."[39]

What about the effect of digital vinyl on the battle scene? It may be too early to tell, since many battles remained analog even years after digital vinyl had become popular. But perhaps a trend we've already seen will only accelerate. With the widespread use of battle records in the 1990s, routines changed from being built around one or two songs to more collage-like compositions created from many short fragments. If we think of control discs as the ultimate in battle records, it seems possible that routines will become denser and more complex.

Some have posited that digital vinyl has already had a profound, but indirect, impact on the battle scene. In a 2007 discussion on the Turntablist Network site, a number of DJs suggested that the technology was hurting battle culture, precisely because it had lowered some of the barriers to becoming a DJ. Enferno, an active club DJ and a former battler, offered this hypothesis:

> Is it possible that Serato has been part of the reason for the battle scene dying? Serato has made club DJing much more accessible to turntablists.

When I was battling, I only knew of a small handful of battle DJs that also DJed for parties, either at clubs or as mobile DJs. Records at $5 to $7 a pop for hiphop, and $9 to $12 for import house was a very expensive business to maintain, so I think that's why there were so few battle DJs that were doing parties. When Serato came on the market, those financial barriers were taken away, and battle DJs could then work on DJing parties, which unlike battling, brings in money. That's just a theory.[40]

DJ Dini, who had competed in more than 100 battles by his count, concurred. "Serato entered my life and everything changed. Now I would much rather spend an afternoon editing music files for a gig I am doing than practicing a battle routine."[41]

Digital vinyl emulation systems are, as I write this, less than a decade old, and few DJs have used any one product for more than five years. There are relatively few seasoned DJs performing today who got their start with digital vinyl, so we don't know what the long-term effect will be. Recently, however, I couldn't help but notice a striking difference between two DJs who use Serato, one older and one younger, whom I've watched multiple times. DJ Bro-Rabb of Durham, North Carolina, has been mixing and scratching for more than fifteen years and is an admitted vinyl fanatic. DJ A-Minor of nearby Chapel Hill is younger and has DJed for only a few years, though he is by now quite accomplished. Bro-Rabb hardly seems to bother with his laptop, stealing occasional sideways glances when he spins. A-Minor, on the other hand, spends much more time than Bro-Rabb interacting with the computer. It's not a crutch, and he knows Serato well enough that the extra attention isn't due to inexperience; the laptop is simply more important for him than for Bro-Rabb. Moreover, A-Minor took the unusual step of avoiding Serato for a year while he learned to mix and scratch using traditional vinyl, logging hundreds of hours on the decks before plugging in. Even so, his relationship with his laptop is noticeably different from Bro-Rabb's. If we can extrapolate from this example, it's possible to imagine a subtle but significant change in technique among hip-hop DJs in the coming years.

Make no mistake: with digital vinyl the function and meaning of the record has fundamentally changed. With vinyl emulation, the disc is not a medium for storing music but a control device. The record has simultaneously been demoted and elevated. It has been relieved of its music, relegated to the role of steering wheel. Yet in losing its distinctiveness—one tone control record is more or less like another—it gains flexibility, and thus power. Ironically, the technology has been enormously successful among hip-hop DJs by disguising the digital as analog. Think for a moment how counterintuitive this approach is. Digital music devices are typically designed to call attention to themselves.

Imagine if Apple had launched the iPod in 2001 not as a sleek, glossy white device with a distinctive screen and jog wheel, but as a black, bulky tape-playing Walkman lookalike complete with protruding stop, play, rewind, and fast forward buttons. It almost certainly would have failed. But this approach is exactly the tactic that Final Scratch and its successors took. And it worked.

Back in 2002, I asked DJ A-Trak what he thought about digital DJing, at the time still a new development:

> I definitely think that vinyl is fundamental to turntablism, but these new technologies can be good tools or good additions to what we do. For a while I wasn't even paying attention to any of them, but now with the Pioneer CDJ and especially with Final Scratch and this new version called Serato Scratch (which is being developed right now) you can't help but want to try it out and see how you can integrate it into what you do. But what you do as a turntablist stays essentially rooted in vinyl.[42]

A-Trak's final sentence tells us everything we need to know about the triumph of digital vinyl over CD turntables. In the end, this is not so much a story about innovation or of features, but of a substance, its physical qualities, and the culture surrounding it.

ACADEMIES OF SCRATCH

The room has that distinctive first-day-of class vibe. Students file in tentatively, and a nervous energy fills the air as they mill about, leaf distractedly through their papers, or introduce themselves to their classmates. The professor and his two teaching assistants, by contrast, are more relaxed as they joke among themselves and make last-minute preparations. The professor then announces that class is to begin, and the chatter stops abruptly as the students turn expectantly toward the front of the classroom.

This could be a scene from almost any American college or university at the dawn of a new semester. Yet this classroom is hardly typical. The main texts in *this* class are twelve-inch vinyl LPs. Instead of sitting at desks and taking notes, the students stand in front of turntables, manipulating records according to the instructor's directions. And this classroom looks nothing like one you would find on a typical campus. This is, in fact, no university course, but the DJ 101 class at the Scratch DJ Academy in New York City, one of dozens of DJ schools scattered throughout the world[43] (Figure 8.4). The goal of lowering barriers is often an explicit part of the missions of these institutions. As the Scratch DJ Academy website states plainly, "In 2002, Rob Principe and the late Jam Master

Figure 8.4 DJ J Smoke teaches at Scratch DJ Academy New York. (Used by permission.)

Jay founded Scratch DJ Academy with the goal of lowering the barrier of entry to the art form of the DJ."[44] Or consider the mission statement of Dubspot, another school in Manhattan: "We believe that everyone can make music, regardless of past training and experience. We are focused on helping students of all ages achieve their music and personal enrichment goals."[45] All schools make equipment accessible to their students and many offer financial aid or free workshops. Collectively, these academies are teaching hundreds of thousands of students and in the process are changing the way DJing is taught and are expanding the demographics of the art.

To understand how these academies are teaching the art of the DJ, consider a representative class, one that took place in November 2006 at the Los Angeles branch of the Scratch DJ Academy.[46] The Academy shares space with a record store called Rehab, which sits in the shadow of Interstate 405 in an industrial area of the city. Records and DJ supplies are sold in the front half of the store; the classroom occupies the rear. The space holds ten DJ set-ups, each of which consists of two turntables, a mixer, and a set of small speakers. Instead of traditional turntable stands, however, the equipment rests on two rows of oil drums. Together, the oil drums, the graffiti, and the faux-brick wallpaper decorated with razor wire are intended to impart the sense that one has stepped into a gritty inner-city alley.

I attended the second ninety-minute session of an eight-week course for beginners called DJ 101. The class was taught by DJ Hapa, a thriving LA club

DJ who established the Los Angeles branch of Scratch in 2004; his assistants were DJ Slim and DJ Puffs, both former Academy students. (Hapa referred to Puffs and Slim as his TAs, and to himself as the professor.) Other than myself, there were seven students in the class ranging in age from about fourteen to twenty—they were Asian American, black, Latino, and white. Puffs, the teaching assistant, was the lone woman in the room. In this one way, the class was unusual—in many academies women make up a sizable minority and sometimes even a majority of the students in any given class.

We started the class by introducing ourselves—using our DJ names, not our so-called government names. After some friendly chit-chat, the bulk of the session was devoted to a mixture of theory and practice. In the theory segments, we gathered in front of a whiteboard on which Hapa drew various diagrams. He discussed measures and time signatures—"beats and bars" as he called it—as well as common popular song structures. Hapa emphasized the importance of "the 1," by which he meant the first beat of a four- or eight-bar phrase, explaining that in order to mix records it is crucial to be able to identify "the 1." Hapa's discussion of "the 1" verged on the mystical—it was fine and important for beginners to count beats, he said, but eventually they would need to *feel* it, to be one with "the 1." ◐

In between our forays to the whiteboard we practiced various scratches. We started with the baby scratch; we all had stickers on our records to identify the "tip" of the sound (a snare hit) we were to scratch. Hapa often exhorted us to "watch our marks" while we were scratching and emphasized the importance of correct body position—fingers relaxed, wrist locked, and elbow low. He also emphasized the importance of bobbing one's head to the beat while scratching (and really, at all times). The music, he told us, had to be not just in our ears, but in our bodies.

Let's follow a bit of the next part of the class, when Hapa put on a record with a strong beat and then had us slowly work up to a baby scratch: ◐

> HAPA: Remember, the keys to scratching: fingers straight, nine o'clock. First thing—fingers straight, not necessarily flat but straight. Third thing, no fingers, no wrist, full arm. OK, and then, fourth thing. Move to the beat. You are the metronome. Move to the beat. OK?
>
> STUDENT: [inaudible]
>
> HAPA: Yeah, if you're on the left turntable, left hand at nine, if you're on the right turntable, right had at nine. OK? Here we go. I'll start off—you guys come in when you're ready.
>
> [From here Hapa and Slim are shouting to be heard over the music.]
>
> HAPA: Watch your mark! Watch your mark!
>
> HAPA: Whole notes!

Hapa and Slim: Forward two three four, back two three four. Forward two three four, back two three four.

Hapa: Half notes, half notes!

Hapa and Slim: Forward two, back two, forward two, back two, forward two, back two, forward two, back two.

Hapa: Quarters!

Hapa and Slim: Forward, back, forward, back, forward, back. . . .[47]

We learned a few more basic scratches, and later in the class Hapa had each student take turns improvising a four-bar scratch solo. This was the most nerve-wracking part of the session; some students didn't come in at the right time or were simply at a loss for what to do. Hapa, Slim, and Puffs were admirably supportive, however, heaping praise when we succeeded and encouraging us when we didn't. We ended the class with more discussion of song structure, and then Hapa left us with an assignment. We were to listen attentively to all types of music over the next week, both familiar and unfamiliar, and try to feel "the 1" in each song.

When people unfamiliar with the phenomenon of the DJ academy learn that I have taken scratching lessons, two questions often follow. "You can take classes on that?" and, "Were you the only white guy there?" The questions actually aren't unreasonable, given that for the first quarter-century of hip-hop's history, few if any formal DJ courses were available, and that at one time most hip-hop DJs were black or Latino. Moreover, most DJs learned by observing friends, relatives, or neighbors and developed their skills largely through trial and error. However, DJing has changed profoundly over the course of the past three decades. The DJ academy is a perfect symbol of this change, and of the growing pains that have accompanied it. Hip-hop DJs have long yearned for mainstream respectability, but they also revere the roots of their art in the streets of the Bronx, and talk solemnly about the importance of "paying dues" and "keeping it real." The DJ academy not only symbolizes but also embodies this tension, which comes out in the form of two competing discourses—the discourse of the street and the discourse of the university.

It's no surprise that DJ academies aim for street credibility and try to "keep it real." Vinyl is the most obvious symbol of realness. Although most academies also teach digital DJing, for many the use of vinyl is central to their mission. In class, the names and stories of the pioneering DJs are repeated with reverence, and teachers stress the importance of learning the history of the art. Every DJ 101 student at the Scratch DJ Academy is taught Grandmaster Flash's clock theory and learns the story of GrandWizzard Theodore and the invention of scratching (sometimes straight from the source). In many academies, students assume DJ names, a practice that connects them to the very earliest days of hip-hop.

I've also mentioned the visual links to the inner city in the Los Angeles academy with its graffiti, oil drums, and razor wire. When I asked DJ Hapa what he was going for when he decorated that space, his answer was simple and clear: "The Bronx, 1973."[48] In the New York branch of Scratch a stylized mural depicts graffiti-covered subway cars, also a signifier of 1970s New York.

Keeping it real also means hiring instructors who are well known and respected in the DJ community. Scratch DJ Academy was co-founded by the late Jam Master Jay, practically a hip-hop saint. Among Scratch's other instructors are GrandWizzard Theodore and former champion DJs such as ie.MERG, Craze, and Rob Swift. Across town, Dubspot employs DMC champ DJ Shiftee, veteran DJ Neil Armstrong, and Precision, the youngest member of the X-Ecutioners. Most DJ academies, wherever they are, tend to enlist the best known DJs in the area.

While DJ academies strive to stay close to the street, they also reach out to what might be seen as its polar opposite: the university. If the street is supposed to be gritty, dangerous, and real, the university is the ivory tower—safe and set apart from the real world. Yet what is so striking about the DJ academies is how heavily they borrow from the jargon of the American university. "Professors" and their "TAs" teach courses with titles such as DJ 101 and DJ 201, and employ syllabi and "course packs." ◗ The academies also administer quizzes, tests, and final exams (sometimes known as "vinyl exams"), and present diploma-like certificates at graduation ceremonies. I, in fact, am the proud holder of diploma awarded me upon completing a DJ 101 course. Below the image of the baseball cap wearing DJ, it states, "This certifies that Mark Katz, having satisfactorily completed the DJ 101 Course of Studies prescribed by the Scratch DJ Academy-Miami, is therefore awarded this certificate of accomplishment. In testimony in hereof," etc., etc. All it lacks is Latin. ◗ And of course the fact that many of the schools I have encountered use the word "academy" as part of their name is significant. Michael Cannady, the Chief Strategy Officer and Chief Operating Officer at Scratch DJ Academy in New York, explained that the use of this terminology "was to make this place seem as professional as possible. When we started everyone thought we would be out of business in a year. So we were . . . concerned with having that professional appeal so that when people would go online they would see the terminology and realize that this was a *real* school where you could learn *real* things."[49]

Cannady's emphasis on the word "real" shows that academic language is more than just part of a sales pitch. Hip-hop DJs have long been defensive about their art. Although they consider turntables musical instruments and themselves musicians, outsiders are often dismissive, and believe that these DJs simply play records, something anyone can do. It's not surprising, then, that the first sentence in one DJ 101 course pack solemnly explains, "Before you learn to

DJ, it is important to realize that you are about to learn an instrument."[50] So while the university may be in short supply of "street cred," it represents a seriousness of purpose and embodies mainstream respectability. The association with the discourse and values of higher education sends the message that DJing is both serious and respectable and, by extension, a *real* art.

In striving to embody a kind of street sensibility and simultaneously achieve mainstream respectability, DJ academies seem to be driven by nearly contradictory impulses. This sense of contradiction characterizes turntablism as a whole. At the turn of the millennium, it was a musical art in flux, flush with the promise of broader public acceptance and fraught with anxiety about alienation from its roots. Between about 1999 and 2001, turntablism was hot. DJs were featured in commercials and were performing with popular rock groups and in films. The technical skill of battle DJs was generally agreed to be much higher than it was ten or even five years earlier. New digital technologies were expanding the musical possibilities for DJs and making it easier to become a DJ. Moreover, there came to be a greater diversity among DJs in terms of race, age, and gender than ever before.

Some of these developments can be traced to the proliferation of DJ classes. DJing has for much of its history been taught informally and privately. Academy classrooms, however, are public, professional, and open to all comers. Rob Swift, who occasionally teaches in the New York branch of Scratch, suggests that this openness is one of the main virtues of the DJ academy. "I think DJ schools [are] positive for the art of DJing [and] Turntablism," he explained. "The more people that come to understand what it takes to be a DJ [or] Turntablist, the more people will get involved with the movement. This in turn can only help the art continue to grow."[51] Montreal DJ Killa-Jewel sees the academies as especially encouraging of women. As she told me, "by having these schools where you have teachers that are very respectful you can be a girl and not have to risk feeling uncomfortable around guys. I think it's an excellent way for girls to start learning."[52] The Scratch DJ Academy has a high percentage of women in its classes; it also sponsored the women-only battle, "She's My DJ," in 2005 and 2006.[53] Many DJs also praise the academies for flattening out the learning curve. For example, DJ Immortal, my teacher in Miami, told me that it took him years to learn through trial and error what I learned in five classes. These schools are furthermore helping DJs navigate their way through the ever-expanding array of musical and technological possibilities, especially digital vinyl systems and mixing software. Finally, the academies are employing DJs, helping them earn a regular income and avoid the hand-to-mouth existence common in the profession. GrandWizzard Theodore told me very frankly that one of the reasons he started teaching at Scratch was because it finally allowed him to have dental insurance.[54]

Yet there is a flip slide to all of these positive changes. While the demographics in the scene have broadened in general, there are proportionally fewer
African Americans among the ranks of DJs. Some argue that the academies
will marginalize the traditional approaches to the art by promoting newer
systems, like the new digital technologies. Others believe that the higher
skill level among DJs has come at the expense of musicality and imagination.
And while new DJs can learn more quickly in the academies than in their basements, the sense of "paying dues," traditionally a core value in hip-hop, may
become a quaint notion. Moreover, it's an open question as to whether it's even
possible for the academies to "keep it real." DJ Pone (Travis Rimando), who
taught for several years at the Norcal DJ Academy in Berkeley, California, has
expressed this worry. As he mused,

> [DJ academies seem] inconsistent with our underground hip-hop philoso-
> phy, like the whole "keeping it real" philosophy, I'd say, for the reason
> that hip-hop, at its heart, is supposed to be anti-institutional, right?
> The fact that it's kind of become institutionalized also parallels the
> commercialization of hip-hop, the commodification of it.[55]

Perhaps Pone shouldn't worry. I've found a good deal of flexibility and an
absence of dogmatism among veteran DJs when it comes to DJ academies.
Some are pragmatists, teaching because they need to make ends meet, and
some are idealists, teaching because they see it as a calling. Yet others, like
DJ Quest, started as pragmatists and became idealists. He initially resisted the
idea of teaching his art in any formal way: "I never thought DJing belonged in
the classroom." But in 2004 he had the opportunity to teach. He needed the
money, so he took the gig. When he started he was reluctant to "give away the
secrets" that he had struggled to learn on his own. Then something changed.
"This is what happened," he said. "As soon as I started showing people how to
do it I absorbed it so much more. It opened up my understanding." When
I spoke to Quest in 2010, he had established a studio called DJ Quest's School
of DJ Arts, and was happily teaching several days a week, "giving back to my
culture."[56]

Even many self-admitted purists have no objections to DJ academies. I asked
Qbert whether a DJ could get a diploma in scratching and still keep it real. He
said all he cared about was the end result—the music—and then he offered this
bluntly worded definition of keeping it real: "If . . . it's fucking kicking ass, then
you're fucking keeping it real."[57] In fact, a year after he told me this, in May
2009, he launched his own school, Qbert Skratch University. QSU is an online
academy that allows students to watch tutorials streamed over the Internet,
submit film of their routines, and receive individualized feedback from Qbert

in the form of video commentary. Its goal is much like that of its bricks-and-mortar cousins. "This is a community of DJs," Qbert explains in a video posted at the site—"it is a safe and encouraging place to jump in."[58]

What should we make of the DJ academy? On one hand, it's an unlikely phenomenon that opens itself to charges of exploiting and diluting hip-hop culture. Kool Herc and Afrika Bambaataa didn't need professors, TAs, and syllabi to create hip-hop. And maybe it's not such a good thing to let just anyone in on the secrets of the art, especially to those who don't appreciate its history and culture. On the other hand, the DJ academy is perfectly consistent with an ideal that is as important to most DJs as paying dues and keeping it real: legitimacy. As long as DJs have been mixing and scratching records, they have been characterized as little more than button pushers and record wreckers. And as long as these mischaracterizations have been made, DJs have sought to demonstrate their musicianship and defend their very existence as musicians. DJ academies symbolize and further this quest for legitimacy. Here, then, is another way to understand the phenomenon. DJs who teach in these academies, who earn a regular paycheck while doing what they love and giving back to their culture, are *not* selling out. They're doing exactly the opposite, and engaging in an honorable pursuit as old as hip-hop: they're getting paid.

DJ Hero

The hype was over the top, and the mainstream media reviews were almost equally breathless: "The most anticipated game of the year," "Best party game," "The most innovative and immersive music experience of 2009," "Put[s] the power of the DJ and the artistry of hip hop music into the hands of consumers around the world."[59] The subject was *DJ Hero*, a video game developed by FreeStyleGames and released in October 2009 by Activision, home of the immensely popular *Guitar Hero* franchise. Though not a blockbuster on par with its guitar-driven cousins, *DJ Hero* sold 1.2 million copies in less than a year and spawned a sequel, *DJ Hero 2*, in October 2010.[60] It was not the first DJ-centered video game—that distinction goes to Konami's *Beatmania*, first released in Japan in 1997—but *DJ Hero* has been the most popular of its kind, introducing DJing to a broad public and shaping the way many view DJs and their art.

The game's concept is fairly straightforward. The player is the DJ, and scores points by mixing and scratching according to the game's instructions. Using a specially designed controller in the form of a turntable (see Figure 8.5), the player presses buttons and operates the simulated platter, crossfader, and

Figure 8.5 DJ Hero controller. (Photograph by Jacob Metcalf.)

tone-control knob to mix and scratch two songs that are playing at the same time. Essentially, gameplay consists of manipulating one of several dozen mash-ups of popular songs that make up the game's soundtrack. On the screen at all times are three glowing neon lines stretching into the distance from the perspective of the player. The lines correspond to the left, center, and right positions of the crossfader; the colors match the green, red, and blue buttons on the controller. For the most part, players do one of three things: move the crossfader to change between songs, or play both together; press the buttons to activate different samples that are added to the mix; or push the platter back and forth to create scratching sounds. ◉

For first-timers the game can be tricky and a bit confusing—the player operates a variety of controls in various combinations and in rapid succession while being bombarded by an almost seizure-inducing barrage of flashing lights. (The setting of any game session is one of several fantasy dance clubs.) It doesn't take long to master the basic movements, yet that initial hurdle leads many players to appreciate the difficulty of *real* DJing. Here's one player's experience, related shortly after the game was released:

> Now if you want to learn real DJing this won't help you, it WILL though help you appreciate what DJ's do. . . . I must say I thought DJ[s] just stood there and looked cool, but they have to pay attention and really listen to what they are doing. They are artist[s] and I appreciate them now after playing the game.[61]

The first impression of many real DJs was less positive. Here's a sample of (unedited) comments culled from the DJ Geometrix online forum:

> I've never seen a bigger pile of absolute shit than this game. Not even anywhere near how the real co-ordination works.
>   this is the epitome of fake djing.
>   This game is strictly for gaming nerds who know absolutely nothing about dj'ing or turntablism. No dj in their right mind would ever think this game could be comparable to the real thing.[62]

Playing *DJ Hero*, they rightly point out, is almost nothing like actual DJing. The crossfader has only three positions, the turntable is small and insubstantial, and the colored buttons on the platter make it clear that the controller is a toy. What's more, the player's movements simply activate sounds rather than create and finely control them.

Many DJs were also insulted by the way the game was marketed. The two most prominently featured names in the initial *DJ Hero* campaign were not even DJs, but rather the rappers Eminem and Jay-Z.[63] There was good reason for this—their songs were featured on the game's soundtrack and they were much more famous than any DJ. Still, the omission of DJs from the campaign was remarkable. As one DJ wrote in an online forum, this was "just another example of how the industry ignores the contribution of DJs."[64]

But it would be fair to say that the game gets the DJ *concept* right. *DJ Hero*, like actual DJing, involves real-time sound manipulation and requires fine motor control and a good sense of rhythm. And once the player advances beyond the manic button-mashing phase it's possible for players to achieve that immersive engagement with the music that good DJs often feel while they're spinning. The game disabuses players of the notion that DJs simply dance or pose in front of a pair of turntables, and it does this without requiring them to spend months practicing. *DJ Hero* will not prepare players to get on a pair of 1200s and cut some vinyl, but it can reward them with the sense of being part of the music that accomplished DJs know well.[65]

Although the initial marketing campaign for *DJ Hero* left DJs out in the cold, the game itself involved well-respected figures from the community. Grandmaster Flash narrates the tutorials in the first *DJ Hero*, and Flash as well as Cut Chemist, J. Period, Jazzy Jeff, DJ Shadow, and Z-Trip contributed mixes to the soundtrack; in *DJ Hero 2*, Qbert and Shadow are playable avatars. Shadow, who was consulted during the game's development, saw his role in this way: "This was an opportunity for me to give my opinions about the art of DJing . . . and you know, try and tone down some of the cheesier aspects that were being discussed. [I wanted to] see what I could do to steward a reasonable representation to the masses."[66] Where it mattered—in the game itself—real DJs played a central role in *DJ Hero*.

DJ Hero was part of the mainstreaming of mixing and scratching, a phenomenon that, in its most recent incarnation, dates back to the X-Ecutioners' collaboration with Linkin Park in 2002. The game has generated a broader appreciation for the art, yet the attention *DJ Hero* brought—as we saw in the X-Ecutioners' case—came at the expense of the nuances and complexity of actual DJing. *DJ Hero* may well be part of a gradual simplification of a rich art form. In an intriguing Internet forum post from 2010, German DJ Frogstar posited that, with the widespread use of digital technologies that simplify aspects of DJing, "there is a very thin line between dj hero and what is happening in the dj booth."[67] The gap between digital vinyl systems like Serato and *DJ Hero* may in fact not be very wide, and it's possible that it will shrink to the point that game controllers and digital DJ interfaces do largely the same thing. In fact, there is already a well-established performance art known as controllerism, defined by one of its foremost practitioners, Moldover, as "the art of manipulating sounds and creating music live using computer controllers and software."[68] 🎧 Controllerism extrapolates from turntablism by replacing analog turntables and vinyl with instruments that often look like overgrown DJ mixers or small MIDI keyboards with extra knobs and faders. Video game controllers hardly stand up to the instruments Moldover and other controllerists use, but they belong to the same family, and can be modified to expand their musical capabilities. It can even be argued that digital vinyl systems collapse the distinction between turntables and controllers. "The moment you drop control vinyl on your deck," argues veteran DJ and technology expert, Gizmo, "you've converted your turntable into a controller. Make a loop or hit a cue point . . . well, you're a controllerist."[69]

Perhaps "modded" *DJ Hero* consoles will become capable of creating sophisticated new music. After all, something will have to be done with all those millions of controllers. In 2011, the *DJ Hero* series was put on "hiatus"—apparently sales were not robust enough to justify a *DJ Hero 3*.[70] The game survived for less than two years, and perhaps will be recalled as a symbol of one of those brief moments when the hip-hop DJ captured the imagination of a broad public. But more DJ games are surely on the horizon, and *DJ Hero* may come to be seen as part of a broader trend, one that sees the continuing blurring of boundaries between turntable and controller, between DJ and gamer, between professional and enthusiast.[71] There's another way, too, to interpret the short life of *DJ Hero*, and perhaps these interpretations are not mutually exclusive. The ultimate lesson of the game's demise may be a simple but powerful one: DJing is hard. With all the blurring of boundaries that the future will bring, we can take comfort in the enduring truth that talented, hard-working musicians will always stand apart.

DJ HEROINES

Look at the selection of *DJ Hero* avatars or at the photos on DJ academy web-sites, and it's hard not to notice all the women—women scratching, women mixing, women with headphones cupped to their ears, women rocking crowds. There are certainly marketing reasons to depict women so prominently, but these images also reflect reality. Although they still make up a tiny minority of battle DJs, women have become more prominent in every other way. They are showcasing, playing clubs, hosting radio shows, teaching classes, forming crews, and releasing records and instructional videos. Women have played a role in hip-hop since the beginning—DJ Wanda Dee, DJ RD Smiley, DJ Baby Dee and others were cutting it up decades ago in the Bronx. But the surge of women DJs is more a phenomenon of the 2000s, and is another example of how barriers started falling away in that decade. There is no one reason for this change, no catalyzing event that started it all. The gender dynamics of DJing evolved because of the hard work of several pioneering women, because of advances in technology, and because of developments in DJ pedagogy.

Even in the 1990s, women DJs were rare enough in hip-hop that most of them were introduced to their craft by men, often their DJ boyfriends. Two artists in particular, Kuttin Kandi and Shortee, helped change this, and paved the way for the next generation of women. A native of Queens, New York, Kuttin Kandi became a DJ in the early 1990s when she was sixteen, learning how to mix and scratch on other people's turntables. She acquired her own equipment at eighteen, which was when she met DJ Roli Rho, whom she describes as "the main influence in my love for DJing."[72] She soon became a member of the 5th Platoon crew, joining Rho, Daddy Dog, Do Boy, ie.MERG, Neil Armstrong, and Vinroc as its first and still only female member. Kandi started battling in 1996, and in 1998 was a finalist in the DMC U.S. Championship battle, a feat still unequaled by any woman. Virginia native DJ Shortee, who had been a drummer since the age of seven, started DJing in 1995 after seeing her future boyfriend (and later husband) DJ Faust perform.[73] As a duo, she and Faust toured the world, and as a solo artist she was the first woman to release a DJ album, *The Dreamer* (1999) and the first to release an instructional video, *Shortee's DJ 101* (2002). Kandi and Shortee were not the only trailblazers, but they, as much as anyone, inspired, encouraged, promoted, and taught the next generation of women DJs.

In 1997, Kandi co-founded Anomolies, a collective that represents women throughout hip-hop—DJs, MCs, and b-girls alike. Its purpose is "to provide a space for women to: develop themselves as artists, make a living through their art while maintaining personal and professional integrity, [and] build a strong support and resource network of other committed and passionate artists."[74]

Figure 8.6 Kuttin Kandi in 2010. (Photograph by Peter Macapugay.)

Its mission is feminist and activist: the collective, whose name contains the words "no mo[re] lies," seeks to expose the "misrepresentations of women as two-dimensional stereotypes."[75] But at the same time it works to generate business for their members. Anomolies led the way for other similar collectives, and a decade later groups such as Chicks with Decks, Dutty Girl, Females wit' Funk, Octopussy, Queens of Noize, Shejay, and Sister SF were promoting the careers of perhaps hundreds of women DJs around the world.[76]

Kandi has also encouraged women directly through her performances. To give one example, Killa-Jewel saw Kandi give a showcase at the 1999 DMC battle in New York City. Kandi, she says, "was the first woman to inspire me when I started out. I felt like I could relate to her because . . . we were in it for the same reasons, and that was primarily because we love to do it."[77] Killa-Jewel, in turn, has inspired many other women, like Tyra from Saigon, a Vietnamese-born, Canadian-bred DJ now living in California. Tyra "was just floored" when, in 2004, she saw a video of Killa-Jewel scratching. "I can't explain the feeling I had when I saw that. You know, I'd seen guys do that but I'd never seen a girl tear it up like that. So from that moment on I just locked myself in a room and practiced."[78] Only a few months later she was performing publicly and soon won the hard-earned respect of some of the world's best turntablists. (To quote Shortkut: "That girl, Tyra from Saigon—she's sick. Wow!"[79]) For Killa-Jewel, Tyra, and many others touched directly or indirectly by Kandi, it mattered that they were watching a *woman* tearing it up. On some level they might have known that women could perform as DJs at such a high level, but for them and others, it took seeing it to truly believe it.

Even Shortee, who had already been an accomplished DJ by the time she saw a video of DJ Symphony of the Beat Junkies deftly mixing two records, didn't realize that women could beat-juggle.[80] Shortee understands that the best way to inspire is to lead by example, and she has done this not only through her years of touring, but through her teaching. For several years Shortee (often teaming up with Faust) was one of the head instructors at Scratch DJ Academy in Los Angeles, teaching classes on mixing, scratching, and beat juggling. Her biggest impact as a teacher, however, comes from her instructional videos.

Shortee's DVDs, *DJ 101* and *DJ 202*, start with the basics of equipment setup and lead through progressively more advanced lessons on mixing, scratching, and beat juggling. A third video, *Turntable Tune-Up*, is entirely devoted to turntable maintenance and repair, and more recently she has been sharing her knowledge on the Web, joining the faculty of the online school TurntableU. com. These videos are not explicitly directed at women, but women may benefit from them more than men. Although beginning DJs, whether men or women, might be equally clueless about ground wires and potentiometers, men are more likely to have a network of DJs they can observe without asking too many questions that would reveal their ignorance. A woman DJ, however, may be the only female in her circle, and might be reluctant to consult men about equipment or techniques for fear of being ridiculed or stereotyped. Shortee's videos answer all the questions women (and men) may be afraid to ask. Videos in general have been tremendously important for women for the same reason, and are often central to their development as DJs. Annalyze, a successful DJ from Rochester, New York, cites Shortee's first video as crucial. "Once I saw her DJ 101 video my world was rocked. I would just nerd-out on that and try to learn to flare—I had that video memorized. Bottom line: she holds it down for all the ladies—a true pioneer in my mind."[81] It may be no coincidence that we've seen more and more women coming up through the ranks since the rise of DVDs and Internet video sites.

Kandi and Shortee have collectively influenced women DJs across the globe and are rightfully considered pioneers. Though their backgrounds, styles, and philosophies differ, their contribution to DJing is, in one way, the same: they made it possible for a generation of women to learn from other women. In the future maybe it won't matter how a DJ learns her craft; if so, we can give due credit to these two artists.

Although female representation in the world of the hip-hop DJ is on the rise in general, there is one area of DJ life that has changed relatively little in this regard: the battle. Aside from Jazzy Joyce, DJ Symphony, and Kuttin Kandi, or more recently Asif, Beverly Skillz, DJ Courtney, and Lazy K, very few women have succeeded or even competed in battles, and when they do, they are almost always the lone female. One solution is the all-female DJ battle, which has generated heated debate among those it is intended to promote. Perhaps the first such battle was the Woman of Steel DJ Battle, sponsored by *Vibe* magazine and held in New York City in 2001. DJ MK took the prize; Jazzy Joyce and Kuttin Kandi were among the judges.[82] Other women-only battles came in 2005 and 2006 (She's My DJ, New York City), 2008 (Put Da Needle On Da Record, Brooklyn), 2009 (Battle Royale, Boracay, Philippines), and 2010 (Bragging Rights, Fullerton, California). There have been others, but in comparison to the traditional type of battle, they are few and far between.

The central question about all-female battles is whether they actually help women. Tachelle Wilkes and Danielle Brantley, who organized She's My DJ in 2005 and 2006, believe they do. According to Wilkes, She's My DJ is a way to "bring back the love to hip-hop and bring back respect for women."[83] Their decision to follow a showcase format—where each DJ plays for the judges and crowd individually—was significant:

> We wanted to give women that room to breathe, just a bit, so they could come out and feel a little bit more comfortable with competing. Competition itself can be a little bit abrasive. Women are capable of doing the head-to-head, but . . . we just felt that the showcase would be best just to bring women out of the woodwork.[84]

It was not just prizes or bragging rights that the winners received, but "support" and "nurturing," to use Wilkes's words; and among other things, battle winners were given scholarships to the New York Scratch DJ Academy. She's My DJ provided an alternative to the conventional model, offering competition but not confrontation, and rewarding winners with the means to improve, and not simply prove, themselves.

Not all women embrace the idea of single-sex battles. Some worry that separation will never promote equality. DJ Tina T, a popular West Coast club DJ, is ambivalent, offering these words to fellow women:

> I don't think there is anything wrong with all-female DJ battles. I have competed in one myself and will be there to support in any way I can when they happen. Decide for yourself why you are entering an all-female DJ battle: the prize money, experience, exposure, fun? I truly hope that you gain all of this and more, but keep in mind that until you are on an even playing field, respect in a male-dominated industry might not be included.[85]

DMC battle organizer Christie Z-Pabon is less equivocal: "I have never sup-ported all-female DJ battles in general, no matter who is throwing them. . . . There is nothing," she insists, "physically keeping girls/women from winning the nationally recognized battles that include men."[86] DJ Syentiffic came out even more decisively in an Internet discussion. "Do I want a female competi-tion? No. I'm equal to any man, and if he has a problem with it . . . BRING IT ON!!"[87]

Kuttin Kandi has seen how, if organized for the wrong reasons, these compe-titions can do great harm. She was once involved with a battle as a consultant and judge that turned out merely to be a means of promoting a brand of alcohol rather than promoting women DJs. The organizers were apparently less inter-ested in the contestants' skills than in their looks, and to Kandi's horror many of the women didn't even know how to operate a mixer. "This was a complete insult to the DJ culture and an upset to women overall, because this could have potentially made those beginner female DJs not want to continue learning. . . . This could also give the wrong message to the audience," who, she worried, might assume that "women did not know how to DJ." But instead of rejecting women-only battles outright, she decided to become more active in the scene. "After this failure of a competition, I realized that it is important that I continue to be involved in what ways I can to either offer my advice to those who organize female DJ battles, even though I might not like the idea . . . because organizers will do their battles anyway, with or without us."[88]

It's easy to see both sides of the debate. On one hand, these competitions open battling to women who might not have considered it otherwise, and offer support and professional opportunities to participants. Some see these battles as steppingstones to mixed-gender competitions, as was the case with DJ Vtech. Her first battle was only for women. "I didn't win but it gave me a little confi-dence and motivated me to enter another battle." She then entered a battle in 2010 as the only woman, and won.[89] On the other hand, some find the very concept offensive and argue that separate can never be equal. At this point, it's an open question as to whether the all-female DJ battle is lowering barriers, creating new ones, or doing a bit of both.

One development that seems unequivocally to have lowered barriers for women is the rise of digital DJing. CD turntables and especially digital vinyl systems have reduced the need to dig in the crates or to carry crates of records from gig to gig. In both cases these advantages may have a stronger impact on women than men. Digging in the crates is often spoken of by male DJs as phys-ically demanding and even adventurous, more like hunting than gathering. So although anyone can shop for records, the macho culture of digging helps rein-force the sense that DJing is a masculine pursuit. Many male DJs say similar things about the heavy lifting that was necessary in earlier days, and some have speculated to me that perhaps this is one reason there have been so few women DJs. I doubt that the need to lug heavy crates would actually stop any motivated woman, but again, there is the perception that DJing is a manly activity, and this perception may be stronger than any reality in creating barriers to women. But with CDJs and digital vinyl systems, these perceptions may be disappearing. The point here is that digital technologies have simply made it easier for anyone to become a DJ, and this is as true for women as for men.

Women DJs have always been treated differently from their male counterparts. Their abilities are questioned, and they endure condescending and sexist remarks. Sometimes even their existence is doubted. Many women DJs have had the following experience: they are carrying records or gear into a club or are even standing behind a set of turntables when a man comes up and asks them if they know where the DJ is.[90] And when they're not invisible, they're all too visible. Look at the comments section of any Internet video featuring a woman DJ and with depressing predictability there will be at least one remark about her breasts. Highly skilled women are sometimes asked to pose or even DJ nude, without regard to their musical talents.

Yet at the same time, many women DJs say that their looks—and simply the novelty of being a woman behind the decks—can serve their careers well. Killa-Jewel knows that as a woman she gets more attention than men. "People want to see something that they don't see every day. So in that respect I do have an edge. It's just the way it is."[91] Or as Tyra from Saigon explains, "I know that because I'm a girl, I can attract more attention, obviously. Of course I'm going to use that to my advantage." But every woman DJ has to decide if, when, and exactly how to use her femininity, a complicated and ever-changing calculus that has no real counterpart for men. "I wouldn't want to wear a revealing top in a promo shot," Tyra offers as an example. "I'm not about selling myself physically."[92] (She is one of those women who received—and declined—an offer to pose nude for a magazine.) Not all women agree about how far is too far, as Killa-Jewel has pointed out. "There are a lot of female DJs out there who . . . DJ with their breasts hanging out. They DJ in their bikinis and that's not how I want to be represented as a female DJ."[93]

The day may never arrive when gender is no longer a factor in the DJ world—after all, gender differences, though they may evolve, will never disappear. But as changes in the scene over the past decade suggest, the time is coming when a DJ can be described as "dope" or "sick"—or whatever future slang comes to mean *good*—without anyone feeling the need to add the words, "for a girl."

* * * * *

As I was drafting this chapter in the fall of 2010, two events took place, just a day apart, that I took as a sign that it was time to finish *Groove Music*. On the first of these two days a new era began; the next day, one came to an end.

On October 19, 2010, Tony Prince, founder of the DMC battle, the series of competitions that had been shaping the world of DJing for more than a quarter century, made an announcement that was both shocking and seemingly inevitable: the DMC had gone digital. Here is part of the text that was posted on the DMC website:

> DMC, the preeminent showcase for DJ talent around the world, are pleased to announce that Serato and Rane have come on board as major sponsors of the DMC World DJ Championships, a collaboration which DMC believes will take DJ creativity to an entirely new level with the ability to use Serato's Scratch Live. In order to balance traditional mixing and the popularity of digital vinyl playback, DMC have confirmed that from 2011 the 26-year-old event will, like the DMC DJ TEAM CHAMPIONSHIP, permit the use of the software-based system Serato Scratch Live in addition to traditional vinyl.[94]

The Team Championship, dominated in recent years by France's C2C and Japan's Kireek, had already allowed crews to use laptops. This change disturbed some, but at least the centerpiece of the DMC, and of battle culture in general—the Battle for World Supremacy—was still pure. No longer. Starting in 2011, vinyl emulation systems would be allowed in the six-minute solo routines of the Battle for World Supremacy. (Serato and Rane, however, did not demand exclusivity—competitors were allowed to use any DVS.[95]) Within a few days thousands of words of commentary from DJs around the world poured into various turntablist sites. To some, this was a welcome development; to others it was a sign of the apocalypse.[96] And then, as if one shocking development was not enough, in December 2010, DMC made another technologically driven change. In February 2011, they would launch a completely new battle: the DMC Online DJ Championships, in which DJs would post their routines to a DMC website to be judged both by the public and by expert DJs. (Germany's DJ Unkut won the inaugural twelve-round competition.) For the DMC, the twenty-first century officially arrived in 2011.

But let's return to October 2010. On the 20th of that month, the day after DMC issued its press release, the Japanese electronics giant Panasonic made an equally momentous announcement: it was discontinuing production of its legendary Technics 1200 turntables. As a representative explained to the *Tokyo Reporter*, "Panasonic decided to end production mainly due to a decline in demand for these analog products and also the growing difficulty of procuring key analog components necessary to sustain production."[97]

In late 2010, the analog era officially ended for DJs. Of course, DJs will continue to use old-style vinyl records with traditional turntables. And the indestructible Technics 1200 will continue for years as the turntablist's favored instrument. More and more, however, DJs will learn their craft using digital technologies; they will encounter these technologies in DJ academies, and they will use them in battle. Video games and the digital technologies that professional DJs use may well become harder to distinguish from one another, as will amateurs and professionals; distinctions between men and women DJs may become less pronounced as well.

This new era will bring both positive and negative change. There is a finite amount of talent in the world, and adding more DJs to the world will not alter that. There will simply be more bad DJs overwhelming the proportionally small number of good ones; hardworking professionals may lose jobs to poseurs and imposters, their craft devalued and underappreciated. The expanding demographics of the DJ world, on the other hand, is welcome. And the prospect of new techniques, new approaches to DJing, and new forms of creativity is tremendously exciting. A revitalized DJ scene may well await us.

"Anyone can be a DJ" is a phrase that was probably uttered more often on any given day in the 2000s than in all the decades before. Sometimes it's spoken with contempt by experienced DJs who have lost gigs to newcomers. Sometimes it is spoken with a sense of optimism and enthusiasm by the managers and teachers of DJ academies. Often it is spoken as part of a breathless marketing campaign to sell electronic gadgets or video games. Whatever the perspective, it represents a world in which barriers to becoming a DJ have surely fallen away.

Conclusion: Full Circle

It's a classic Bronx park jam. A few hundred people occupy a playground in Crotona Park, just south of the Cross-Bronx Expressway. The DJs and MCs stand with their backs to the chain-link fence, the sound system set up on folding tables. A small area in front of the performers has been roped off to keep troublemakers and the overcurious at a distance. A few rows of people crowd in to admire the skills of the DJs and MCs, cheering and nodding their heads to the beat. Behind them are the dancers, mostly grooving in place singly or in couples. Further back a circle has formed around a six-by-six foot square of linoleum duct-taped to the blacktop. This is the b-boy cipher, and a group of young men, most of them sporting Adidas, take turns showing off their moves as the tunes boom from the speakers seventy-five feet away.

The crowd is mostly black and Latino young adults, but there are also whites and Asians, babes in arms, and older folk leaning on canes or sitting on benches. It's a peaceful event; a few cops mill around on the periphery, though that's about all they do. It's a warm summer evening, and most people wear jeans and T-shirts or halter-tops. But some are dressed to impress, peacocking in their polyester outfits, gold chains, and perfectly blown-out Afros.

Back at the DJ table, Grandmaster Caz is stirring up the crowd. He's an expert with the vinyl—as we know, he started out as part of a DJ duo with Disco Wiz—but he quickly became better known as an MC. He doesn't let anyone forget his roots, though, and he spins and raps simultaneously. The people standing in front of the DJ area stare in amazement or rap along with him. Other DJs come and go as well, supplying a steady stream of hot funk. Everyone has a good time, even though the power source gives out a few times. The music occasionally falls silent, but no one gets too worked up—the tunes keep coming back.

This was the scene at a park jam I attended in July 2010. Everything I noted could have taken place more than thirty years earlier, and although this wasn't the hip-hop equivalent of a Civil War battle reenactment, the idea behind this jam was to enjoy the music, dance, and spectacle of an earlier time. Run by Christie Z-Pabon and her husband, the hip-hop dance pioneer Jorge "Fabel" Pabon, the Tools of War summer park jams were established in 2003 with the intention to "restore true Hip Hop culture and the legends who kicked it off back to the NYC Parks where they first rocked."[1] Not everything I saw was 1970s vintage, however, the most conspicuous difference being technology. The turntables were analog, but they spun Serato control records and were tethered to a shiny silver Apple laptop computer. The crowd was technologically up-to-date as well, with many using their phones as digital cameras to capture the action. The event seemed to exist in two different eras at the same time.

The Tools of War Park Jam series is hardly unique in this way. As I worked on *Groove Music*, especially in the last few years of the 2000s, over and again I encountered evidence of this simultaneous embrace of past values and sounds, and current technologies and lifestyles. Here are two more examples.

June, 2008: I'm in a Philadelphia club listening to Rich Medina preside over the decks—in this case a pair of CD turntables. When I walk in, only a few are dancing on the small floor. But then Medina puts on the b-boy classic, "It's Just Begun," a 1972 tune by the Jimmy Castor Bunch older than anyone on the floor. At the first sound of the dissonant horns and a double hi-hat flourish, a cheer erupts. Bodies pack the floor as the vocals enter: "Watch me now / Feel the groove / Into something / Gonna make you move." Suddenly a space opens, and a slim black woman in a stylish tracksuit starts toprocking. A young white man in a sweaty tuxedo T-shirt and trilby hat takes up the challenge and crowds her with equally fancy footwork. A battle breaks out, as the music continues: "Day or night / Black or white / Dance or sing / You gotta do your thing." Though the times have changed and the technologies are new, these b-boys and b-girls happily take part in a tradition that others their age would consider ancient history.

September, 2010: I'm standing in a light rain watching Public Enemy perform in Raleigh, North Carolina. At one point in the show, MCs Chuck D and Flavor Flav pause to praise their DJ and step to the side of the stage. The spotlight shines on the DJ standing at the turntables, who then proceeds to perform a hard-rocking solo to the cheers of the crowd. The song is "Terminator X to the Edge of Panic," one of the scores of DJ tracks hip-hop groups released in the 1980s. But it's not 1988, the year the song was released on *It Takes a Nation of Millions to Hold Us Back*. (And actually it's DJ Lord, not Terminator X, on the decks.[2]) For a moment, though, I convince myself that I've returned to a time when just about every hip-hop show had a moment like this, a time when DJs regularly enjoyed the spotlight and their MCs publicly praised those bringers of beats. At the end of the show, Flavor Flav starts to wax political and demands that the crowd chant, "Fuck separatism!" He's talking about blacks and whites, Christians, Jews, and Muslims, but he could also be talking about hip-hop and the separation between DJs and MCs.

At the beginning of *Groove Music* I promised to tell stories, stories about the people, places, events, music, and objects that created and shaped the art and culture of the hip-hop DJ. Now at the end, we can look back and see some broader narratives as well. In one way, the story of the hip-hop DJ has been the story of a family drifting apart and then coming together again. In the beginning there was the DJ and the dancer, and soon after that, the MC. These three formed a tightly knit unit, each one hardly conceivable without the other. The first fault lines began to show at the end of the 1970s, when MCs started getting recording deals, some ditching the DJs who had gotten them to that point. Even so, DJs and MCs continued to make great music together throughout the 1980s, producing classic DJ tracks like "AJ Scratch," "Go Cut Creator Go," "He's the DJ, I'm the Rapper," "King Cut," and "Peter Piper."[3] Cuts like these became rarer at the end of the 1980s as DATs came to prominence, and DJs once again felt that they were being shoved aside. Aided by new technologies of their own, especially in terms of improved mixer capabilities, many DJs started to go their own way. The self-contained art of turntablism arose in the 1980s, continued to evolve through the 1990s, and hit its peak of popularity at the turn of the millennium. But as my earlier anecdotes suggest, a decade later, the three musical elements of hip-hop seemed to be growing closer.[4] Here I'll return to the wise words of Kuttin Kandi who, in 2000, at the height of turntablism's mainstream popularity, correctly predicted what would happen once the DJ's fleeting fame passed. When "the spotlight is turned off," she said, "the art returns to where it all began and where it belongs."[5] We now come full circle; the needle tracking this groove music has traveled 360 degrees. Yet when a record returns to twelve o'clock, the needle is no longer in exactly the same spot; likewise, even though the world of the hip-hop DJ has come full circle, it has changed in the process. But in the end, as it was in the beginning, the art of the hip-hop DJ is part of a broader culture, one that expresses itself through the combined forces of beats, rhymes, and dance.

There are other important stories to tell beyond this tale of the hip-hop family—stories about technology, innovation, competition, identity, self-invention and reinvention. A recurring theme in *Groove Music* is the intimate and complex relationship between DJs and technology. DJs would not exist without turntables, records, mixers, headphones, speakers, and their various incarnations and successors; at the same time, hip-hop DJs have never accepted the limitations of these technologies. In the process of repurposing and re-creating their tools, they transformed the turntable and mixer into a musical instrument. With this instrument they pushed the boundaries of their art, continually "taking it to the next level" by creating new sounds, new songs, and new techniques. Innovation, both technological and musical, has always been at the center of the art of the hip-hop DJ.

The hip-hop DJ's imperative to "take it to the next level" not only reveals the crucial role of innovation but also the central place of competition, the force that powers the art's motor. DJ battles have been fought as long as hip-hop has existed, and they are the reason DJing has grown and changed for nearly forty years. It may seem odd that the battle is so important given that most hip-hop DJs do not compete, or do so only for short periods. But it has had an outsized influence, because it is in battles that techniques emerge, technologies are tested, artists are developed, and legends are born. For decades battles have been captured on tape and film, and these documents travel the world, spreading the art and influencing future generations.

The fact that innovation and competition are central to the art and culture of the hip-hop DJ is no accident. Both are closely bound up with issues of identity, specifically the identity of the Bronx pioneers. It matters that the first generation of hip-hop DJs were, for the most part, young men, most of them black, some Latino. It matters that these DJs lived in precarious circumstances; they were not born with silver spoons in their mouths but chips on their shoulders. As young men everywhere, they were told, whether directly or implicitly, that they needed to show power in order to command respect. At this time and place, they could have easily looked to guns or drugs for this power. They chose music. This choice meant that they had to prove themselves through their artistry and personality. They also had to be resourceful. Because they had little disposable income, they had to be creative in the way they acquired, assembled, and used their sound systems. Poverty did not, however, dictate their use of turntables. Their use of these technologies and the music they played was also shaped by their heritage, whether coming in the form of funk grooves, the timbres and rhythms of salsa, or the tradition of Jamaican-style sound systems and clashes. Change any of these initial conditions of hip-hop—its time, place, and socioeconomic conditions, or the race or gender of its creators—and hip-hop itself would be a very different phenomenon, if it existed at all. In time, however, those conditions did change. Women came to play a larger role; Asians and whites started to participate in ever more crucial ways. The art expanded geographically and economically, moving beyond New York, beyond depressed urban areas, beyond cities and the United States altogether. In the process the art changed, and will continue to change.

In their innovative uses of technology, hip-hop DJs can be likened to inventors, but they are also inventors in a more abstract way: they invented themselves. Although there were some precedents in disco, the Bronx pioneers of the 1970s created a new category of musician, what I call the performative DJ.

Recall GrandWizzard Theodore's words: "Hip-hop came from nothing. The people that created hip-hop *had* nothing. And what they did was, they created *something* from *nothing*."[6] The hip-hop DJ also went through a series of reinventions, moving (or being pushed) from the center of hip-hop to the periphery, and then becoming the center of the rather hermetic world of turntablism before renewing and strengthening ties with MCs and b-boys and b-girls.

Reinvention has been essential to the art's survival. Consider some alternate histories of the hip-hop DJ. In one version, Kool Herc starts spinning at parties in the Bronx in 1973, but his fragmented style never catches on, never attracts what would have become b-boys, b-girls, and MCs. Hip-hop is stillborn, dying before it is even named. In another version, Kool Herc, Afrika Bambaataa, Grandmaster Flash, GrandWizzard Theodore, and the other pioneering DJs enjoy local success for a few years in the 1970s, but hip-hop never develops beyond a fad. It is never recorded commercially and lives on only in the aging memories of those who experienced it first-hand. Or maybe hip-hop does make it onto records and becomes an international phenomenon in the late 1970s and early 1980s. But the huge success of rapping completely overshadows the art that helped bring the MC into existence. Hip-hop DJs are simply those who play rap records; the art of turntablism never emerges. None of these possibilities are farfetched. But as many times as hip-hop DJing could have died out, it never did. The art evolved, adapting to new times, circumstances, and technologies. There's nothing to say that the hip-hop DJ won't once again face extinction. Today the threat might come, ironically, from the lowered barriers that have relaxed technical demands and opened the art to all comers. DJing might become so diluted that it's hardly recognizable as a distinct art at all. But given its nearly forty-year track record of survival, it's a good bet that it will continue to reinvent itself, and more than that, thrive.

The themes I've explored here are not unique to the stories I've been telling in *Groove Music*. And this is why the story of the hip-hop DJ matters beyond that relatively small world. It matters because the DJ is at the core (if no longer the center) of a global artistic, cultural, and economic phenomenon: hip-hop. It matters because the broad strokes of the DJ's story illuminate the condition of modern musicians in general, who must invent and reinvent themselves in order to make their way in a world of rapidly changing technologies, media, and tastes. And at its broadest, the story of the hip-hop DJ is the story of contemporary America, so strongly defined by the shifting dynamics of race, gender, and class, so deeply shaped by entrepreneurship, innovation, and technology.

So many stories, all contained within a spiral groove.

Appendices

The DJ's Instrument

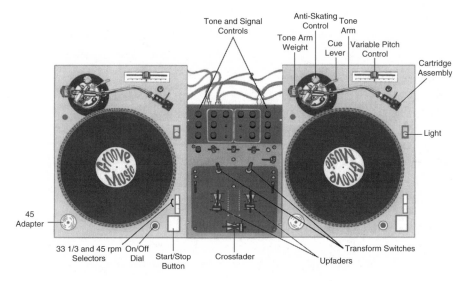

Appendix 1.1 The DJ's Instrument: two turntables and a mixer. (By Nicole M. Havey.)

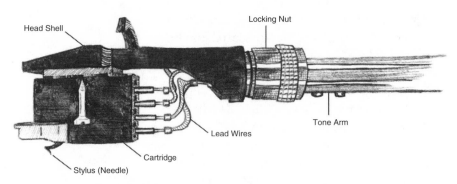

Appendix 1.2 Close-up of the cartridge assembly. (By Nicole M. Havey.)

Raw Materials and Finished Products:
Breaks, Tracks, and Albums

(See the discography for the complete citations of the songs and albums cited here.)

20 Classic Breaks ◉

For more breaks, see the Crate Kings, "300 Classic Hip Hop Drum Breaks, Samples, and Loops."
www.cratekings.com/300-classic-hip-hop-drum-breaks-samples-and-loops/

"Amen Brother" by The Winstons (1969)
"Apache" by The Incredible Bongo Band (1973)
"Ashley's Roachclip" by The Soul Searchers (1974)
"Assembly Line" by The Commodores (1974)
"The Big Beat" by Billy Squier (1980)
"Dance to the Drummer's Beat" by Herman Kelly (1978)
"Funky Drummer" by James Brown (1970)
"Funky President" by James Brown (1974)
"Get Out of My Life, Woman" by Lee Dorsey (1966)
"I Just Want to Celebrate" by Rare Earth (1971)
"Impeach the President" by The Honey Drippers (1973)
"It's Just Begun" by The Jimmy Castor Bunch (1972)
"Johnny the Fox Meets Jimmy the Weed" by Thin Lizzy (1976)
"Mary Mary" by The Monkees (1967)
"Rock Steady" by Aretha Franklin (1971)
"Super Sporm" by Captain Sky (1978)
"Synthetic Substitution" by Melvin Bliss (1974)
"Take Me to the Mardi Gras" by Bob James (1975)

"Walk This Way" by Aerosmith (1975)
"You'll Like It Too" by Funkadelic (1981)

Five Classic Samples used by DJs ◈

"Good," from Chic, "Good Times" (1979)
"Ah," from BeSide, "Change the Beat" (1982)
"Fresh," from BeSide, "Change the Beat" (1982)
"It's Time," from Hashim, "Al-Naafiysh (The Soul)" (1983)
"Ah Yeah," from Run D.M.C., "Here We Go (Live at the Funhouse)"
   (1985)

12 Classic Solo DJ Tracks ◈

Grandmaster Flash: "The Adventures of Grandmaster Flash on the
   Wheels of Steel" (1981)
Grandmixer D.ST: "Crazy Cuts" (1983)
G.L.O.B.E. and Whiz Kid (featuring Whiz Kid): "Play that Beat Mr. DJ"
   (1983)
Davy DMX: "One for the Treble (Fresh)" (1984)
2 Live Crew (featuring Mr. Mixx): "What I Like (Scratch Version)"
   (1985)
DJ Cash Money (as Dr. Funnkenstein): "Scratchin' to the Funk" (1986)
Mixmaster Gee and the Turntable Orchestra (featuring Mixmaster Gee):
   "The Manipulator" (1986)
Eric B. and Rakim (featuring Eric B.): "Eric B. is on the Cut" (1987)
Schoolly D (featuring DJ Code Money): "It's Krack" (1987)
DJ Jazzy Jeff and the Fresh Prince: "DJ on the Wheels" (1988)
Gang Starr (featuring DJ Premier): "DJ Premier in Deep Concentration"
   (1989)
Tuff Crew (featuring DJ Too Tuff): "Behold the Detonator" (album
   version) (1989)

16 MC Odes to their DJs ◈

Kurtis Blow (featuring Kool DJ AJ): "AJ Scratch" (1984)
Marley Marl and MC Shan (featuring Marley Marl): "Marley Marl
   Scratch" (1985)

Word of Mouth (featuring DJ Cheese): "King Kut" (1985)

Run D.M.C. (featuring Jam Master Jay): "Peter Piper" (1986)

Steady B (featuring Grand Dragon KD): "Bring the Beat Back" (1986)

DJ Jazzy Jeff and the Fresh Prince (featuring DJ Jazzy Jeff): "The Magnificent Jazzy Jeff" (1987)

LL Cool J (featuring Cut Creator): "Go Cut Creator Go" (1987)

Big Daddy Kane (featuring Mister Cee): "Mister Cee's Master Plan" (1988)

Biz Markie (featuring Cool V): "Cool Vs Tribute to Scratching" (1988)

Cash Money and Marvelous (featuring Cash Money): "The Music Maker" (1988)

Kool G Rap (featuring DJ Polo): "Butcher Shop" (1988)

Public Enemy (featuring Terminator X/Johnny "Juice" Rosado): "Terminator X to the Edge of Panic" (1988)

Sway and King Tech (featuring King Tech): "King Tech" (1988)

Low Profile (featuring DJ Aladdin): "The Dub B.U. Just Begun" (1989)

EPMD (featuring DJ Scratch): "Funky Piano" (1990)

The Lords of the Underground (featuring DJ Lord Jazz): "Lord Jazz Hit Me One Time (Make It Funky)" (1993)

25 Turntablist Albums

The Beat Junkies: *The World Famous Beat Junkies*, Vol. 1 (1997)

Birdy Nam Nam: *Birdy Nam Nam* (2005)

DJ Craze and DJ Klever: *Scratch Nerds* (2002)

Cut Chemist: *The Audience's Listening* (1996)

D-Styles: *Phantazmagorea* (2002)

DJ Faust: *Man or Myth* (1998)

Kid Koala: *Carpal Tunnel Syndrome* (2000)

DJ Krush: *Krush* (1995)

DJ Logic: *The Anomaly* (2001)

Mix Master Mike: *Anti-Theft Device* (1998)

Mr. Dibbs: *Primitive Tracks* (2000)

Phonopsychographdisk (aka DJ Disk): *Ancient Termites* (1998)

Qbert: *Wave Twisters–Episode 7 Million: Sonic Wars Within the Protons* (1998)

DJ Quest: *Questside (Untold Tales)* (2001)

Return of the D.J. Vol. 1 (1995)

DJ Revolution: *King of the Decks* (2008)

Ricci Rucker and Mike Boo: *Sketchbook (An Introduction to Scratch Music)* (2003)

DJ Shortee: *The Dreamer* (1999)
DJ Sniff: *ep* (2011)
DJ Swamp: *Never Is Now* (1998)
Urban Revolutions: *The Future Primitive Sound Collective* (2000)
X-Ecutioners: *X-Pressions* (1997)
DJ Yoda: *The Amazing Adventures of DJ Yoda* (2006)
DJ Z-Trip: *Shifting Gears* (2005)
DJ Z-Trip and DJ P: *Uneasy Listening Vol. 1.* (1999)

Major Battle Winners, 1981–2011

The following was compiled with the generous assistance of Christie Z-Pabon and Doc Rice.

New Music Seminar Battle Champions, 1981–1994

The New Music Seminar was founded in New York by Tom Silverman, and was the first major annual battle for DJs.
   (*Note*: Beginning in 1992, Supermen Productions sponsored the battle.)

1994	DJ Noize (Denmark)
1993	DJ 8-Ball (USA)
1992	Mix Master Mike (USA)
1991	DJ Supreme (USA)
1990	Steve Dee (USA)
1989	DJ Miz (USA)
1988	DJ Scratch (USA)
1987	DJ Cash Money (USA)
1986	DJ Jazzy Jeff (USA)
1985	Easy G Rockwell (USA)
1984	DJ Cheese (USA)
1983	Afrika Islam (USA)
1981	Whiz Kid (USA)

DMC, 1985–2011

The Disco Mix Club was founded in England in 1983 by Tony Prince, and has been organizing battles annually since 1985.

DMC World Champions (Showcase Style)

2011   DJ Vajra (USA)
2010   DJ LigOne (France)
2009   DJ Shiftee (USA)
2008   DJ Fly (France)
2007   DJ Rafik (Germany)
2006   DJ Netik (France)
2005   ie.MERG (USA)
2004   ie.MERG (USA)
2003   DJ Dopey (Canada)
2002   DJ Kentaro (Japan)
2001   DJ Plus One (UK)
2000   DJ Craze (USA)
1999   DJ Craze (USA)
1998   DJ Craze (USA)
1997   DJ A-Trak (Canada)
1996   DJ Noize (Denmark)
1995   Roc Raida (USA)
1993   The Dream Team (Mix Master Mike and DJ Qbert) (USA)
(Note: The 1993 battle actually took place on January 18, 1994)
1992   The Rock Steady DJs (DJ Apollo, Mix Master Mike, and DJ Qbert)
       (USA)
1991   DJ David (Germany)
1990   DJ David (Germany)
1989   Cutmaster Swift (UK)
1988   DJ Cash Money (USA)
1987   Chad Jackson (UK)
1986   DJ Cheese (USA)
1985   Roger Johnson (UK)

Battle for World Supremacy (Head-to-Head Style)

2011   DJ Nelson (France)
2010   DJ Switch (UK)
2009   DJ Switch (UK)
2008   DJ Switch (UK)
2007   DJ Shiftee (USA)
2006   DJ Co-ma (Japan)
2005   DJ Pro Zeiko (Germany)
2004   DJ Akakabe (Japan)

2003   DJ Tigerstyle (UK)
2002   DJ Netik (France)
2001   DJ Netik (France)
2000   DJ Kodh (France)

DMC World Team Champions

2011   Kireek (Japan)
2010   Kireek
2009   Kireek
2008   Kireek
2007   Kireek
2006   C2C (France)
2005   C2C
2004   C2C
2003   C2C
2002   Birdy Nam Nam
2001   Perverted Allies (Canada/UK/USA)
2000   The Allies (Canada/USA)
1999   Scratch Perverts (UK)

DMC USA Team Champions

2011   Battle Star
2010   Battle Star
2009   Battle Star
2008   The Angry Exs
2007   [no team entry]
2006   Animal Crackers
2005   Battle Star
2004   [no team entry]
2003   Evolution DJs
2002   Evolution DJs
2001   Perverted Allies
2000   The Allies
1999   The Allies

DMC American Battleground Champions (Showcase style)

2011   DJ Vajra
2010   DJ Etronik
2009   DJ Shiftee
2008   DJ Slyce
2007   DJ Precision

2006   DJ Fred Funk
2005   DJ Kico
2004   ie.MERG
2003   DJ Enferno
2002   DJ Perseus
2001   DJ Klever
2000   DJ Klever
1999   DJ P-Trix
1998   DJ Craze
1997   DJ Slyce
1996   DJ Swamp
1995   Roc Raida
1993   DJ Rectangle
1992   DJ Apollo, Mix Master Mike, DJ Qbert
1991   DJ Qbert
1990   DJ Baby G
1989   DJ Aladdin
1988   DJ Cash Money
1987   Joe Rodriguez
1986   DJ Cheese

DMC U.S. Supremacy Champions (Head-to-Head Style)
2011   DJ Fascinate
2010   DJ Solo
2009   Grandmaster Supreme
2008   DJ SPS
2007   DJ Shiftee
2006   DJ Etronik
2005   DJ I-Dee
2004   ie.MERG
2003   ie.MERG
2002   DJ Kico
2001   DJ Snayk Eyez
2000   DJ Snayk Eyez and Supa Dave

ITF, 1996–2005

The International Turntablist Federation was founded 1996 in San Francisco by Alex Aquino. The advancement battle crowned the all-around best DJ in head-to-head competitions, but there were also battles for juggling, scratching, and teams.

ADVANCEMENT BATTLE

2005	DJ Pro Zeiko (Germany)
2004	DJ Rafik (Germany)
2003	DJ Tigerstyle (England)
2002	DJ Kodh (France)
2001	DJ Woody (England)
2000	A-Trak (Canada)
1999	A-Trak (Canada)
1998	Vinroc (USA)
1997	Vinroc (USA)
1996	Total Eclipse (USA)

INTRODUCTION

1. This story was told to me by GrandWizzard Theodore. GrandWizzard Theodore, interview with the author, Chapel Hill, NC, 25 October 2007. I use the term *hip-hop* in this book to refer to the broad cultural movement comprising the four "elements" of DJing, MCing (rapping), b-boying and b-girling (called *breakdancing* by outsiders, but not practitioners), and graffiti art. Often "hip-hop" is used to mean rap, or rap + DJing. For the sake of clarity I avoid this kind of usage, though I sometimes speak of "hip-hop music," by which I mean the combination of the DJ's beats and the MC's rhymes. In general, my discussion of hip-hop in this book is limited to DJing, MCing, b-boying and b-girling. Although graffiti is an important part of hip-hop culture, it is not as directly connected to the art of the DJ as are the other two elements, and will come up only occasionally.

2. According to the *Oxford English Dictionary*, the term was first used in its modern sense by journalist Walter Winchell in a 1941 issue of *Variety*. *Oxford English Dictionary*, 3rd ed., s.v. "disc." For more on the origins of the disc jockey, see Marc Fisher, *Something in the Air: Radio, Rock, and the Revolution That Shaped a Generation* (New York: Random House, 2007). See also Bill Brewster and Frank Broughton, *Last Night a DJ Saved My Life: The History of the Disc Jockey*, rev. ed. (London: Headline, 2006).

3. *Oxford English Dictionary*, 3rd ed., s.v. "disc."

4. "Radio: Thank You, Mr. Husing," *Time Magazine*, 11 November 1946, online at www.time.com/time/magazine/article/0,9171,854234-2,00.html. The article reports that the well-known radio announcer, Edward Britt "Ted" Husing, was taking a position as a DJ at the New York station WHN. The unnamed author notes that "Ten years ago he [Husing] would not have sat at the same bar with a disc-jockey," and quotes from Husing's 1935 autobiography in which Husing proudly explains, "We never played phonographs into our mikes, but always gave the public genuine acts."

5. Some radio DJs and producers also mix and scratch, and on those occasions they can be considered performative DJs. For more on hip-hop radio DJs, and in particular the pioneers Mr. Magic, Kool DJ Red Alert, Funkmaster Flex,

and the KDAY Mixmasters, see Dan Charnas, *The Big Payback: The History of the Business of Hip-Hop* (New York: New American Library, 2010). For more on hip-hop producers, see Joseph G. Schloss, *Making Beats: The Art of Sample-Based Hip-Hop* (Middletown, CT: Wesleyan University Press, 2004), and chapter 4 of this book.

6. Mark Katz, "The Phonograph Effect: The Influence of Recording on Listener, Performer, Composer, 1900–1940" (Ph.D. diss., University of Michigan, 1999).

7. Mark Katz, *Capturing Sound: How Technology Has Changed Music* (Berkeley: University of California Press, 2004). A revised and expanded edition was published in 2010.

8. *Groove Music* actually began life as a collaborative project with the historian Rayvon Fouché, and grew out of a grant we received from the National Science Foundation in 2005.

9. Jim Fricke and Charlie Ahearn, *Yes Yes Y'all: The Experience Music Project Oral History of Hip-Hop's First Decade* (New York: Da Capo, 2002); Jeff Chang, *Can't Stop, Won't Stop: A History of the Hip-Hop Generation* (New York: Picador, 2005); Brewster and Broughton, *Last Night a DJ Saved My Life*.

10. GrandWizzard Theodore, quoted in *Scratch* (2001), Palm DVD, 3046-2.

11. David Nye, *Technology Matters: Questions to Live With* (Cambridge, MA: MIT Press), 3.

12. For more on these topics, see Ronald Kline and Trevor Pinch, "Users as Agents of Technological Change: The Social Construction of the Automobile in the Rural United States," *Technology and Culture* 37 (1996): 763–95; and Nelly Oudshoorn and Trevor Pinch, "Introduction: How Users and Non-Users Matter," in *How Users Matter*, edited by Nelly Oudshoorn and Trevor Pinch (Cambridge, MA: The MIT Press, 2003), 1–25.

13. DJ Cash Money, telephone interview with the author, 23 June 2008.

CHAPTER 1

1. Grandmaster Flash and David Ritz, *The Adventures of Grandmaster Flash: My Life, My Beats* (New York: Broadway Books, 2008), 241–42.

2. "Funky Drummer" was recorded on November 1969 and released as a seven-inch single, King 6290, in March 1970.

3. Steinski, telephone interview with the author, 28 February 2008.

4. For more on terms *breakdancing* and *b-boying*, see Joseph G. Schloss, *Foundation: B-Boys, B-Girls, and Hip-Hop Culture in New York* (New York: Oxford University Press, 2009), 58–67.

5. Flash and Ritz, *The Adventures of Grandmaster Flash*, 37–38.

6. Although most breaks are tantalizingly brief, some songs offer long stretches of unaccompanied (or largely unaccompanied) percussion, for example, "It's Just Begun" or The Incredible Bongo Band's "Apache." Both are still heard in b-boy and b-girl ciphers, or dance circles.

7. DJ Breakout, quoted in Fricke and Ahearn, *Yes Yes Y'all*, 96.

8. The national infant mortality rate in 1973 was 17.6 per 1,000. Ann Golenpaul, ed., *Information Please Almanac, Atlas, and Yearbook, 1976* (New York: Simon

& Schuster, 1976), 76. Bronx mortality rate and all other statistics and examples mentioned here come from Martin Tolchin, "South Bronx: A Jungle Stalked by Fear, Seized by Rage," *New York Times*, 15 January 1973, pp. 1, 19.

9. The statistic of 30,000 fires is cited in Chang, *Can't Stop, Won't Stop*, 10. See also Jonathan Mahler, *Ladies and Gentlemen, the Bronx Is Burning: 1977, Baseball, Politics, and the Battle for the Soul of a City* (New York: Farrar, Straus and Giroux, 2005).

10. GrandWizzard Theodore, telephone interview with the author, 19 December 2006.

11. Quoted in Tolchin, "South Bronx: A Jungle Stalked by Fear, Seized by Rage," p. 1. The other articles in this series, also by Tolchin, are "Gangs Spread Terror in the South Bronx," *New York Times*, 16 January 1973, pp. 1, 28; "Rage Permeates All Facets of Life in the South Bronx," *New York Times*, 17 January 1973, pp. 1, 22; and "Future Looks Bleak for the South Bronx," *New York Times*, 18 January 1973, pp. 1, 50.

12. Hip-hop first arose in the West and South Bronx, and generally in the most blighted areas of the borough. The DJs operated within a fairly small area in the early years—Jeff Chang calls it a "seven-mile world"—largely south of Fordham Rd. and west of White Plains Rd. Chang, *Can't Stop, Won't Stop*, 109. Some influential DJs did live somewhat further out, like Baron and Breakout, who represented the northeast Bronx around Gun Hill Rd. and Co-op City. Grandmixer DXT has said that as early as the mid 1970s, he was DJing at clubs in Westchester County, north of the Bronx. Grandmixer DXT (formerly D.ST), interview with the author, New York, NY, 30 July 2010.

13. Kool Herc, quoted in Fricke and Ahearn, *Yes Yes Y'all*, 26.

14. Flash quotes from Flash and Ritz, *The Adventures of Grandmaster Flash*, 47–48.

15. Ibid., 46–47.

16. For a detailed and insightful account of Bambaataa's early career, see Chang, *Can't Stop, Won't Stop*, 89–107. For more on the influence of the film *Zulu* on Bambaataa, see David Toop, *Rap Attack 3* (London: Serpent's Tail, 2000), 56–57.

17. Afrika Bambaataa, quoted in Fricke and Ahearn, *Yes Yes Y'all*, 49.

18. Grandmixer DXT (formerly D.ST), interview with the author.

19. The Zulu Nation exists to this day, and has chapters across the globe: it is, as its website explains, an "International Hip Hop Awareness Movement." Universal Zulu Nation, www.zulunation.com.

20. See Fricke and Ahearn, *Yes Yes Y'all*, 44, 52.

21. Sha-Rock, quoted in Fricke and Ahearn, *Yes Yes Y'all*, 50.

22. All Disco Wiz quotes in this paragraph come from DJ Disco Wiz, interview with the author, Stamford, CT, 4 February 2008.

23. DJ Baby Dee, telephone interview with the author, 22 July 2010.

24. Typically, Grandmaster Flash is grouped with Kool Herc and Afrika Bambaataa as the third member of a hip-hop "trinity." Flash, however, came a bit later, and his style of DJing is built on the work of Herc and Bam, so I have decided to address Flash's contributions separately in the next chapter.

25. In September 2008, the building was sold, sparking fears that rents would rise, and perhaps that the building would be razed to make way for a more upscale housing development. See David Gonzalez, "Will Gentrification Spoil the Birthplace of Hip-Hop?" *New York Times*, 21 May 2007, online at www.nytimes.com/2007/05/21/nyregion/21citywide.html. The building was not razed, but conditions deteriorated under the new owners. The building was sold again in 2010, this time with considerable financial support from city agencies. See Sam Dolnick, "Hope for a Bronx Tower of Hip-Hop Lore," *New York Times* 6 September 2010, online at www.nytimes.com/2010/09/07/nyregion/07sedgwick.html.

26. Afrika Bambaataa, telephone interview with the author, 19 July 2011.

27. Grandmaster Caz, interview with Scott Preston, *Cincy Groove*, 7 October 2008, online at www.cincygroove.com/?q=node/622.

28. DJ Shadow, quoted in Kodwo Eshun, *More Brilliant Than the Sun: Adventures in Sonic Fiction* (London: Quartet, 1998), 14.

29. Anne Danielsen, *Presence and Pleasure: The Funk Grooves of James Brown and Parliament* (Middletown, CT: Wesleyan University Press, 2006), 155. For more on rhythm in funk breaks, see chapter 2 of Mark J. Butler, *Unlocking the Groove: Rhythm, Meter, and Musical Design in Electronic Dance Music* (Bloomington and Indianapolis: Indiana University Press, 2006).

30. For further information, see Jim Payne's book, *Give the Drummers Some!* (New York: Face the Music Productions, 1996).

31. Junior Lincoln, quoted in Dick Hebdige, *Cut 'N' Mix* (London: Comedia, 1987), 63. Hebdige's book also includes a chapter (see pp. 136–48) comparing reggae and hip-hop.

32. For a history of sound systems in Jamaica and detailed descriptions of sound system clashes, see Norman C. Stolzoff, *Wake the Town and Tell the People: Dancehall Culture in Jamaica* (Durham, NC: Duke University Press, 2000), 41–64 and 193–226.

33. Kool Herc, quoted in Fricke and Ahearn, *Yes Yes Y'all*, 25.

34. DJ Disco Wiz, interview with the author.

35. Wayne Marshall, "Kool Herc," in *Icons of Hip Hop*, ed. Mickey Hess (Westport, CT: Greenwood, 2007), 12; Michael E. Veal, *Dub: Soundscapes and Shattered Songs in Jamaican Reggae* (Middletown, CT: Wesleyan University Press, 2007), 247.

36. Kool Herc, quoted in Amir Said, *The Beat Tips Manual*, 5th ed. (Brooklyn, NY: Superchamp, 2009), 41.

37. Alan Hines, "Brooklyn's Mighty Mobile Jocks," *Discothekin'* (June 1976): 14.

38. Juan Flores, "Puerto Rican and Proud, Boyee!: Rap, Roots and Amnesia," in *The Hip Hop Reader*, ed. Tim Strode and Tim Wood (New York: Pearson Longman, 2008), 32.

39. Ivan Sanchez and Luis Cedeño, *It's Just Begun: The Epic Journey of Disco Wiz, Hip Hop's First Latino DJ* (Brooklyn, NY: powerHouse, 2009).

40. All quotes in this paragraph come from DJ Disco Wiz, interview with the author.

41. Sanchez and Cedeño, *It's Just Begun*.

42. Juan Flores, *From Bomba to Hip-Hop: Puerto Rican Culture and Latino Identity* (New York: Columbia University Press, 2000), 119.

43. Charlie Chase, quoted in Fricke and Ahearn, *Yes Yes Y'all*, 165.

44. Flores, *From Bomba to Hip-Hop*, 119–20.

45. Ibid., 123.

46. Johnny "Juice" Rosado, quoted in Russell Myrie, *Don't Rhyme for the Sake of Riddlin': The Authorized Story of Public Enemy* (New York: Canongate, 2008), 45. For more on Rosado's role in Public Enemy, see the chapter "Johnny Juice in the House," pp. 45–49.

47. Rob Swift, e-mail message to the author, 21 March 2011.

48. Craze's first name was originally "Aristh," but now "Arist" is correct. As he explains, "When I became a U.S. citizen I took off the h . . . was too hard to pronounce." DJ Craze, e-mail message to the author, 3 July 2011.

49. For more, see John Storm Roberts, *The Latin Tinge: The Impact of Latin American Music on the United States*, 2nd ed. (New York: Oxford University Press, 1999) and Roberta L. Singer and Elena Martínez, "A South Bronx Latin Music Tale," *Centro* 16 (Spring 2004): 177–201.

50. Allen Jones, *The Rat That Got Away: A Bronx Memoir* (New York: Fordham University Press, 2009), 19.

51. Interview with Renee Scroggins, Bronx African American History Project, 3 February 2006. My sincere thanks to Mark Naison for supplying me with the Allen Jones and Renee Scroggins quotes.

52. Disco Wiz, telephone conversation with the author, 10 June 2008.

53. "Juice," from *Tough*, Mercury LP 1505.

54. Kool DJ AJ, quoted in Fricke and Ahearn, *Yes Yes Y'all*, 35.

55. GrandWizzard Theodore, telephone interview with the author, 19 December 2006.

56. Grandmaster Flash, quoted in Fricke and Ahearn, *Yes Yes Y'all*, 28.

57. This information comes from Tim Lawrence, *Love Saves the Day: A History of American Dance Music Culture, 1970–1979* (Durham, NC, and London: Duke University Press, 2003), 34, 62, 84, 110, 152, 178.

58. Bambaataa, telephone interview with the author.

59. Flash and Ritz, *The Adventures of Grandmaster Flash*, 58.

60. Sheri Sher, *Mercedes Ladies* (New York: Vibe Street Lit, 2008), 106.

61. Steinski, telephone interview with the author.

62. François Kevorkian, quoted in Tim Lawrence, "Disco Madness: Walter Gibbons and the Legacy of Turntablism and Remixology," *Journal of Popular Music Studies* 20 (September 2008): 281.

63. John "Jellybean" Benitez, quoted in Lawrence, *Love Saves the Day*, 217.

64. My thanks to Tim Lawrence for alerting me to the looping of Siano and Luongo. Tim Lawrence, e-mail message to the author, 24 May 2011.

65. Bambaataa, telephone interview with the author.

66. Disco Wiz, quoted in Fricke and Ahearn, *Yes Yes Y'all*, 25.

67. GrandWizzard Theodore, interview with Troy L. Smith, Summer 2005, online at www.jayquan.com/gwtheodore.htm.

68. For reprints of many early hip-hop flyers, see Johan Kugelberg, ed., *Born in the Bronx: A Visual Record of the Early Days of Hip Hop* (New York: Rizzoli, 2007).

69. My thanks to Sureshot La Rock for sharing these flyers from his personal collection.

70. Tim Lawrence, "Disco Madness," 277.

71. I agree with Tim Lawrence, who argues that "an analysis of the relationship between disco/dance and hip hop/rap should begin not with the assumption of difference and opposition, as has been the case so far, but instead with the recognition of their shared roots and perspectives." Tim Lawrence, "Disco Madness," 321.

72. Murray Forman, *The 'Hood Comes First: Race, Space, and Place in Rap and Hip-Hop* (Middletown, CT: Wesleyan University Press, 2002), xvii.

73. See, for example, Theresa A. Martinez, "Popular Culture as Oppositional Culture: Rap as Resistance," *Sociological Perspectives* 40 (1997): 265–86; Daniel Fischlin and Ajay Heble, ed., *Rebel Musics: Human Rights, Resistant Sounds, and the Politics of Music Making* (Montreal: Black Rose Books, 2003); Ian Peddie, ed. *The Resisting Muse: Popular Music and Social Protest* (Aldershot, England: Ashgate, 2006).

74. "The Breaks" was released on Blow's 1980 album *The Breaks*, Mercury 6337137.

75. Robert Caro, *The Power Broker: Robert Moses and the Fall of New York* (New York: Vintage, 1975), 840–41.

76. Chang, *Can't Stop, Won't Stop*, 10.

77. Caro, *The Power Broker*, 889.

78. Ibid.

79. Grandmaster Flash, quoted in Forman, *The 'Hood Comes First*, 69.

80. Caroline Polk O'Meara, "New York Noise: Music in the Post-Industrial City, 1978–1985" (Ph.D. diss., University of California, Los Angeles, 2006), 200. Chapter 4 offers a provocative exploration of the connections between hip-hop and the urban spaces of New York City.

81. Langdon Winner, "Do Artifacts Have Politics?" *Daedalus* 109 (Winter 1980): 121–36.

82. Grandmixer DXT (formerly D.ST), interview with the author.

83. Afrika Bambaataa, interview with Nardwuar, no date, online at www.nardwuar.com/vs/afrika_bambaataa/print.

84. Sher, *Mercedes Ladies*, 13.

85. Flash and Ritz, *The Adventures of Grandmaster Flash*, 46.

86. As historian Robin D.G. Kelley rightly points out, academics writing about hip-hop often fail to "acknowledge that what might also be at stake here are aesthetics, style, and pleasure." Robin D.G. Kelley, *Yo' Mama's Disfunktional!: Fighting the Culture Wars in Urban America* (Boston: Beacon, 1997), 17.

87. Kool Herc, quoted in Fricke and Ahearn, *Yes Yes Y'all*, 43.

88. Afrika Bambaataa, quoted in Fricke and Ahearn, *Yes Yes Y'all*, 310.

89. GrandWizzard Theodore, telephone interview with the author, 19 December 2006.

90. See, for example, Veal, *Dub: Soundscapes and Shattered Songs in Jamaican Reggae*, 245.

91. DJ Disco Wiz, interview with the author.

Chapter 2

1. Ralph Ellison, *Invisible Man* [1952] (New York: Modern Library, 1994), 7.

2. Rahiem, quoted in Fricke and Ahearn, *Yes Yes Y'all*, 107.

3. Though not a DJ, Sha-Rock, a woman and an MC, had an all-female security team called the Sisters Disco. This was an exceptional case. See Fricke and Ahearn, *Yes Yes Y'all*, 104.

4. DJ Disco Wiz, interview with the author.

5. Nelson George, "Hip-Hop's Founding Fathers Speak the Truth," *Source*, no. 50 (November 1993): 47. This interview was reprinted in *That's the Joint: The Hip-Hop Studies Reader*, ed. Murray Foreman and Mark Anthony Neal (New York: Routledge, 2004), 50–62.

6. Afrika Bambaataa, quoted in "The Knights of the Turntables," *Rap Pages* 5 (April 1996): 53–54. The tapes Bambaataa mentions continue to circulate. Harlem-based hip-hop historian Troy L. Smith, for example, has a collection of more than 200 tapes capturing live shows between 1977 and 1983. For a description of this important collection, see http://respectthearchitects.blogspot.com/2009/06/troy-l-smith-live-old-school-hip-hop.html.

7. Charlie Chase, quoted in Fricke and Ahearn, *Yes Yes Y'all*, 167.

8. For more on the business of hip-hop, see Charnas, *The Big Payback*.

9. DJ Disco Wiz, interview with the author.

10. Rahiem, quoted in Fricke and Ahearn, *Yes Yes Y'all*, 107. These two crews also featured MCs who normally would have battled each other in a rapping contest. In this case, however, the battle was decided by a DJ.

11. DJ Baron, quoted in Fricke and Ahearn, *Yes Yes Y'all*, 99.

12. Mark McCord, "Kool DJ Herc vs. Pete DJ Jones: One Night at the Executive Playhouse," *Wax Poetics*, no. 17 (June–July 2006): 87.

13. DJ Disco Wiz, interview with the author.

14. DJ Steve Dee, interview with the author, Harlem, NY, 17 July 2007.

15. Grandmaster Caz, quoted in the documentary *NY77: The Coolest Year in Hell*, originally broadcast on VH1, 11 August 2007. This segment can be viewed online at www.vh1.com/video/misc/167259/caz-vs-bam.jhtml#id=1566482. Disco Wiz confirmed the story and related what happened after they lost. Disco Wiz, conversation with the author, Chapel Hill, NC, 3 February 2009.

16. Jazzy Jay, quoted in Chairman Mao, "The Knights of the Turntables," *Rap Pages* 5 (April 1996): 51.

17. Tony Tone, quoted in Fricke and Ahearn, *Yes Yes Y'all*, 101.

18. DJ Disco Wiz, interview with the author.

19. Kevie Kev, quoted in Chairman Mao, "The Knights of the Turntables," 53.

20. Chang, *Can't Stop, Won't Stop*, 114.

21. Ibid., 113–14.

22. Afrika Bambaataa, quoted in Fricke and Ahearn, *Yes Yes Y'all*, 65.

23. Rahiem, quoted in Fricke and Ahearn, *Yes Yes Y'all*, 87.
24. Van Silk, quoted in Fricke and Ahearn, *Yes Yes Y'all*, 49.
25. Flash and Ritz, *The Adventures of Grandmaster Flash*, 53–55.
26. Ibid., 8.
27. Grandmaster Flash quotes from Flash and Ritz, *The Adventures of Grandmaster Flash*, 28. For more on his early technical interests and work, see pp. 25–28.
28. Flash and Ritz, *The Adventures of Grandmaster Flash*, 64.
29. "New Meteor Mixer for Discos Bared," *Billboard* 81 (22 February 1975): 74. The mixer was pictured in several ads in *Billboard*, and clearly shows the crossfader, labeled "Turntable Fader."
30. Disco Wiz, interview with the author.
31. DJ Disco Wiz, quoted in Fricke and Ahearn, *Yes Yes Y'all*, 131–33.
32. Afrika Bambaataa, quoted in Fricke and Ahearn, *Yes Yes Y'all*, 45.
33. DJ Breakout, quoted in Fricke and Ahearn, *Yes Yes Y'all*, 95.
34. GrandWizzard Theodore, lecture at the University of North Carolina at Chapel Hill, 24 October 2007.
35. Grandmaster Flash quotations from Flash and Ritz, *The Adventures of Grandmaster Flash*, 76, 79.
36. GrandWizzard Theodore, telephone interview with the author, 9 November 2011.
37. See Pete DJ Jones, interview with JayQuan, October 2001, online at www.thafoundation.com/pete.htm. Flash discusses Jones in Flash and Ritz, *The Adventures of Grandmaster Flash*, 87–93.
38. Flash and Ritz, *The Adventures of Grandmaster Flash*, 86.
39. Theodore has claimed that he introduced the needle drop when he was ten-and-a-half years old, which would date it to the summer of 1973. Given that Kool Herc gave what is widely considered the first hip-hop party in August 1973, it seems more likely that Theodore was a bit older, perhaps eleven-and-a-half, when he first needle dropped. GrandWizzard Theodore, telephone interview with the author, 19 December 2006.
40. GrandWizzard Theodore, quoted in Fricke and Ahearn, *Yes Yes Y'all*, 63.
41. Charlie Chase, quoted in Fricke and Ahearn, *Yes Yes Y'all*, 119.
42. GrandWizzard Theodore, telephone interview with the author, 19 December 2006.
43. Ibid.
44. Theodore describes this incident in Fricke and Ahearn, *Yes Yes Y'all*, 63. He was underage at the time, but apparently was still able to perform in The Sparkle.
45. Rahiem, quoted in Fricke and Ahearn, *Yes Yes Y'all*, 87.
46. Grandmaster Flash, quoted in Fricke and Ahearn, *Yes Yes Y'all*, 63.
47. GrandWizzard Theodore, interview with the author, 19 December 2006. Theodore also uses the term "rubbing" in Fricke and Ahearn, *Yes Yes Y'all*, 63.
48. Flash and Ritz, *The Adventures of Grandmaster Flash*, 86.
49. GrandWizzard Theodore, quoted in Brewster and Broughton, *Last Night a DJ Saved My Life*, 247.

50. Theodore's identification of "Passport" and "Jam on the Groove" come from GrandWizzard Theodore, interview with Troy L. Smith, summer 2005, online at www.jayquan.com/gwtheodore.htm. Theodore's identification of "Johnny the Fox" in Fricke and Ahearn, *Yes Yes Y'all*, 63. Theodore's birth date and age when he first scratched come from a telephone interview with the author, 19 December 2006. Release dates for "Johnny the Fox" in M.C. Strong, ed., *The Great Rock Discography*, 5th ed. (Edinburgh: Mojo, 2001), 984.

51. GrandWizzard Theodore, telephone interview with the author, 9 November 2011.

52. GrandWizzard Theodore, interview, Red Bull Music Academy, Berlin, 1998, online at www.redbullmusicacademy.com/TUTORS.9.0.html?act_session=32.

53. Johnny "Juice" Rosado, telephone interview with the author, 11 March 2008.

54. Online at www.oreillynet.com/pub/a/oreilly/digitalmedia/2004/11/24/dxt.html.

55. Joseph Schloss cites (but disagrees with) a number of such statements in *Making Beats*, 28–30.

56. Schloss, *Making Beats*, 28.

57. Rayvon Fouché, "Say It Loud, I'm Black and I'm Proud: African Americans, American Artifactual Culture, and Black Vernacular Technological Creativity," *American Quarterly* 58 (2006): 647.

58. Ibid., 642.

59. Fricke and Ahearn, *Yes Yes Y'all*, 130.

60. This is just one example of Rodriguez's technological creativity. Among other things, he wired two receivers together so he could mix records and created homemade disco lights by putting Christmas lights inside an upturned umbrella, cutting holes in it, and hanging it from the ceiling. Ivan "Doc" Rodriguez, telephone interview with the author, 9 March 2008.

61. DJ Baby Dee, telephone interview with the author, 22 July 2010.

62. Flash and Ritz, *The Adventures of Grandmaster Flash*, 61.

63. DJ Disco Wiz, interview with the author.

64. Ibid.

65. "Flash Demonstrates Analog vs. Digital!" online at www.youtube.com/watch?v=jJZPKJcZG-Y, posted 15 July 2009.

66. GrandWizzard Theodore, quoted in Fricke and Ahearn. *Yes Yes Y'all*, 63.

67. DJ Steve Dee, interview with the author.

CHAPTER 3

1. For an excellent collection of flyers, see Kugelberg, ed., *Born in the Bronx*.

2. Grandmaster Caz, quoted in Fricke and Ahearn, *Yes Yes Y'all*, 79.

3. Cowboy, quoted in Fricke and Ahearn, *Yes Yes Y'all*, 209.

4. Grandmaster Flash, quoted in Fricke and Ahearn, *Yes Yes Y'all*, 74.

5. Afrika Bambaataa, quoted in Fricke and Ahearn, *Yes Yes Y'all*, 76.

6. Robert Palmer, "Pop Jazz," *New York Times*, 3 September 1982, online at www.nytimes.com/1982/09/03/arts/pop-jazz.html.

7. Sha-Rock, quoted in Fricke and Ahearn, *Yes Yes Y'all*, 222.

8. DJ Baron, quoted in Fricke and Ahearn, *Yes Yes Y'all*, 222.

9. Jazzy Jeff, quoted in Fricke and Ahearn, *Yes Yes Y'all*, 215.
10. "Rappin' and Rocking the House" was released in 1979 on Enjoy Records; the label can be viewed at www.discogs.com/viewimages?release=87107.
11. "Good Times" was first released in 1979 as a 12-inch single on Atlantic Records, DSKO 192. A shorter version (the single is 8:14) was later released on Chic's album *Risque*.
12. Sher, *Mercedes Ladies*, 79.
13. Bambaataa, telephone interview with the author.
14. Nile Rodgers, interview at Canadian Music Week, Toronto, March 2007, online at www.youtube.com/watch?v=t-SCGNOieBI.
15. Flash and Ritz, *The Adventures of Grandmaster Flash*, 133.
16. Sanchez and Cedeño, *It's Just Begun*, 73–74.
17. For fuller accounts of the genesis of "Rapper's Delight," see Fricke and Ahearn, *Yes Yes Y'all*, 181–96 and Chang, *Can't Stop, Won't Stop*, 129–34. A good deal of the information in this section is drawn from these two invaluable sources. See also Charnas, *The Big Payback*, 28–42.
18. Sanchez and Cedeño, *It's Just Begun*, 74.
19. Rodgers told an interviewer that he and co-composer Bernard Edwards "threatened a lawsuit [and] our names were added to the copyright, so if you look at a copy of 'Rapper's Delight,' it says right there that I'm the co-writer." Nile Rodgers, interview at Canadian Music Week.
20. Chang, *Can't Stop, Won't Stop*, 133.
21. Flash and Ritz, *The Adventures of Grandmaster Flash*, 150.
22. Chuck Miller, "Two Turntables and a Microphone: The Story of Grandmaster Flash," *Goldmine* 22 (6 December 1996): 74.
23. Michael Hill, "The Clash at the Clampdown," *Village Voice* (10–16 June 1981): 74. Hill notes that Flash is using two turntables, but he might have had three machines at his disposal when recording the track. Flash sometimes mixed on three decks, as in the famous kitchen scene in the film *Wild Style*.
24. "Rapture" was released on Blondie's 1980 LP, *Autoamerican*, Chrysalis CHE 1290. It was also released as a single in January 1981.
25. In a 1981 Village Voice review of a Grandmaster Flash show, Vince Aletti writes, "Flash comes out first complete with rousing introduction, takes off a black cape and—plays records. He goes to the double turntables at the back of the stage and cuts and blends bits of 'Good Times' and 'Another One Bites the Dust.'" Quoted in Miller, "Two Turntables and a Microphone."
26. Robert Ford, Jr., "B-Beats Bombarding Bronx: Mobile DJ Starts Something with Oldie R&B Disks," *Billboard* (1 July 1978): 65. Reprinted in *That's the Joint: The Hip-Hop Studies Reader*, ed. Murray Foreman and Mark Anthony Neal (New York: Routledge, 2004), 41.
27. Nile Rodgers, interview at Canadian Music Week.
28. See Fricke and Ahearn, *Yes Yes Y'all*, 285–95 for interviews with Freddy, Ahearn, and others about *Wild Style*.
29. Chang, *Can't Stop, Won't Stop*, 186.
30. Fricke and Ahearn, *Yes Yes Y'all*, 295.

31. "First Person: Kool Lady Blue," BBC World News America, 17 November 2008, online at http://news.bbc.co.uk/2/hi/programmes/world_news_america/7734647.stm. Additional information on Blue comes from Chang, *Can't Stop, Won't Stop*, 168–70.

32. For more on "Buffalo Gals," see Timothy Warner, *Pop Music: Technology and Creativity: Trevor Horn and the Digital Revolution* (Aldershot, England: Ashgate, 2003), 50–61.

33. Ruza Blue, e-mail message to the author, 12 June 2011.

34. "First Person: Kool Lady Blue."

35. Jazzy Jay, quoted in Chang, *Can't Stop, Won't Stop*, 170.

36. Ruza Blue, e-mail message to the author.

37. Anna Quindlen, "Where to Roller Skate to a Disco Beat," *New York Times*, 20 March 1981, online at www.nytimes.com/1981/03/20/arts/where-to-roller-skate-to-a-disco-beat.html. The opening of the Roxy was chronicled in Ron Alexander, "Stars Spin In to Open Roxy Roller Disco," *New York Times*, 6 December 1979, p. C1.

38. Brewster and Broughton, *Last Night a DJ Saved My Life*, 271.

39. Steinski, telephone interview with the author.

40. Chang, *Can't Stop, Won't Stop*, 173.

41. Afrika Bambaataa, quoted in Fricke and Ahearn, *Yes Yes Y'all*, 310.

42. Ann Marie Boyle, telephone interview with the author, 30 May 2010.

43. Ruza Blue, e-mail message to the author.

44. Phase II: "The Roxy," Celluloid 12-inch single, CEL 159.

45. Blue left the Roxy involuntarily in August 1983. According to Blue, "I was ousted from the club by the owner . . . at the same time as the *Beat Street* movie deal was being made with the club. He wanted me out of the way so that he could reap all the credit and the rewards." Parts of the early hip-hop film, *Beat Street* (1984), were shot in the Roxy, though it "did not reflect the scene I had created there," says Blue. Ruza Blue, e-mail message to the author.

46. For a contemporary account of the tour, see David Hershkovits, "London Rocks, Paris Burns, and the B-Boys Break a Leg," *Sunday News Magazine*, 3 April 1983, reprinted in *And It Don't Stop?: The Best American Hip-Hop Journalism of the Last 25 Years*, ed. Raquel Cepeda (New York: Faber and Faber, 2004), 27–34.

47. "Change the Beat," Celluloid 12-inch single, CEL 156.

48. My thanks to Catherine Hughes for translating the lyrics.

49. Bernard Zekri, telephone interview with the author, 12 July 2010. Subsequent quotations from Zekri come from the same source.

50. Roger Trilling, telephone interview with the author, 24 May 2010.

51. Boyle, telephone interview with the author.

52. Michael Beinhorn, e-mail message to the author, 23 May 2010.

53. Boyle, telephone interview with the author.

54. Fab 5 Freddy, telephone interview with the author, 4 August 2011.

55. Beinhorn, e-mail message to the author, 23 May 2010.

56. My thanks to Akitsugu Kawamoto and Makiko Kawamoto for the translations.

57. For a discussion of the Vocoder in hip-hop (and modern culture generally), see Dave Tompkins, *How to Wreck a Nice Beach* (Chicago: Stop Smiling, 2010).
58. Many sources incorrectly state that it is Fab 5 Freddy uttering these words.
59. DJ Apollo, interview with the author, 29 March 2008, Berkeley, CA; liner notes to DJ Shadow, *Endtroducing.....*, Mo Wax CD 697–124 123–2.
60. See www.whosampled.com for a list of songs that sample "Change the Beat."
61. Grandmixer DXT (formerly D.ST), interview with the author.
62. For a discussion of "ah" and "fresh" among DJs, see "Ahhh—What's Your View," online at www.skratchlounge.com/index.php?showtopic=349, 1 September 2005.
63. DJ Miyajima, interview with the author, Tokyo, Japan, 2 June 2008.
64. DJ Qbert, interview with the author, Burlingame, CA, 27 March 2008.
65. Bill Laswell, telephone interview with the author, 28 May 2010.
66. Bambaataa, telephone interview with the author.
67. Qbert, interview with the author.
68. Mix Master Mike, quoted in *Scratch*.
69. Grandmixer DXT (formerly D.ST), interview with the author.
70. Bill Laswell, interview with Skizz Fernando, in *WS50: The Video Album*, Word Sound DVD, WSCD050, 2004.
71. Laswell, interview with Skizz Fernando.
72. I am indebted to Michael Beinhorn for his detailed explanation of the compositional process, which I summarize here. Beinhorn, e-mail message to the author, 23 May 2010.
73. Laswell, telephone interview with the author.
74. There have been differing accounts of the records D.ST used. In the 2004 documentary *WS50* cited earlier, Laswell said that he had given D.ST a 1969 Nonesuch record of the Balinese monkey chant to scratch. Beinhorn says that the monkey chant was used on "Earthbeat," another track from the album *Future Shock*, but not on "Rockit." (Beinhorn, e-mail message to the author, 23 May 2010.) When I asked Laswell for clarification, he answered that this was probably correct. (Laswell, telephone interview with the author.)
75. Grandmixer DXT (formerly D.ST), interview with the author.
76. Beinhorn, e-mail message to the author, 23 May 2010.
77. Information on the Led Zeppelin sample comes from Martin Bisi, telephone interview with the author, 14 August 2011 and Michael Beinhorn, e-mail message to the author, 15 August 2011. The two worked together using a Lexicon M93 Prime Time digital delay unit to capture the sound, a cutting-edge technology at the time.
78. Laswell, telephone interview with the author.
79. Ibid.
80. Rob Swift et al., interview with Bevan Jee (1997), online at www.bombhip.hop.com/xmen.htm.
81. Grandmixer DXT (formerly D.ST), interview with the author.
82. Rosado, telephone interview with the author.
83. The Grammy performance can be seen at www.youtube.com/watch?v=o4EhaQklWqA.

84. Robert Christgau, "The Magnificent Seven," *Village Voice* (2 November 1982): 59. For another review see Hill, "The Clash at the Clampdown."

85. For more on the life of Jam Master Jay, see David E. Thigpen, *Jam Master Jay: The Heart of Hip Hop* (New York: Pocket Star Books, 2003).

CHAPTER 4

1. For an account of hip-hop's growing prominence in the early 1980s, see Chang, *Can't Stop, Won't Stop*, chapters 8 and 9.

2. Lefty Banks, review of *Return of the DJ*, in *Classic Material: The Hip-Hop Album Guide* (Toronto: ECW Press, 2003), 140.

3. Donald Janson, "Spray Paint Adds to Graffiti Woes," *New York Times*, 25 July 1971, p. 31.

4. See Grand Wizard Rasheen, interview with James G. Spady, *The Global Cipha*, 15 December 2008, online at www.thaglobalcipha.com/Rasheen.html.

5. For more on Philadelphia's contributions to hip-hop, see Mickey Hess, *Hip Hop in America: A Regional Guide*, Volume 1: East Coast and West Coast (Santa Barbara, CA: ABC-CLIO, 2010), 143–75.

6. King Britt, interview with the author, Philadelphia, PA, 19 June 2008.

7. A.D. Amorosi, "Made from Scratch," *Philadelphia City Paper*, 22–28 August 2002, online at http://citypaper.net/articles/2002-08-22/cover.shtml.

8. Cash Money, telephone interview with the author.

9. Ibid.

10. Ibid.

11. Ibid. Cash Money demonstrates rhythm scratching in a scene filmed for (but not included on) John Carluccio's *Battle Sounds* documentary, which can been seen at www.youtube.com/watch?v=-BPk_dISsJQ.

12. Cash Money, telephone interview with the author.

13. Ibid.

14. Ibid.

15. Online at www.youtube.com/watch?v=7E0BXv99PQs.

16. Audio recordings of the routines, consolidated into one track, can be heard at www.youtube.com/watch?v=3IbVXHvb7mI and www.soundclick.com/bands/page_songInfo.cfm?bandID=247179&songID=1713458.

17. Cash Money, telephone interview with the author.

18. Online at http://blogs.myspace.com/index.cfm?fuseaction=blog.view&friendId=205867087&blogId=295844370, 5 August 2007.

19. DJ Ta-Shi, interview with the author, Tokyo, Japan, 2 June 2008.

20. Qbert, interview with the author.

21. Tony Prince, interview with the author, London, England, 14 April 2008.

22. DJ Cash Money, quoted in Paul Sullivan, "Three Times Deep: DJ Cash Money Is Deep Into Everything," *Wax Poetics*, no. 15 (2007): 22–25. Also available online at http://paul-sullivan.com/words/interviews/107-dj-cashmoney-wax-poetics-2007.html.

23. Jazzy Jeff, quoted in Amorosi, "Made from Scratch."

24. Jazzy Jeff, interview with Butch Mayo, 10 August 2008, online at www.youtube.com/watch?v=-Vi74l3sl14.

25. See, for example, Phil White, Luke Crisell, and Rob Principe, *On the Record: The Scratch DJ Academy Guide* (New York: St. Martin's Griffin, 2009), 291.
26. The album was originally released on two LPs; the second disc, which included the cuts that featured Jazzy Jeff, is labeled "Bonus Scratch Album."
27. Jazzy Jeff, interview with Butch Mayo.
28. Inexplicably, Cash Money was omitted from the proclamation's list of important Philadelphia DJs. The mayor's office subsequently issued an amended document. For images of both versions, see www.myspace.com/djcashmoney 12/photos/54393701.
29. Chang, *Can't Stop, Won't Stop*, 172. For more on Silverman's contributions to hip-hop, see Charnas, *The Big Payback*.
30. "Jazzy Sensation" is credited to Afrika Bambaataa and the Jazzy Five, while "Planet Rock" was released by Afrika Bambaataa and the Soulsonic Force.
31. Robert Christgau, "Rock 'n' Roller Coaster: The Music Biz on a Joyride," *Village Voice* (7 February 1984). Reprinted at www.robertchristgau.com/xg/rock/musicbiz-84.php.
32. S.H. Fernando, *The New Beats: Exploring the Music, Culture, and Attitudes of Hip-Hop* (New York: Anchor, 1994), 15.
33. Battle information comes from a flyer from the personal collection of Sureshot La Rock.
34. Malcolm McLaren, quoted in Jonathan Takiff, "Will New Music Stick Around?" *Philadelphia Daily News*, 28 July 1982, Features section, p. 27.
35. Grandmixer D.ST is often credited with winning the 1982 New Music Seminar, but he has said that he had never even attended the NMS. Grandmixer DXT (formerly D.ST), interview with the author.
36. Tony Prince and Sally McLintock, interview with the author, Slough, England, 27 May 2011.
37. Tony Prince, interview with the author, London, England, 14 April 2008. Subsequent quotations from Prince are from the same interview.
38. An amateur video of the routine can be seen on YouTube at www.youtube. com/watch?v=K_Wn-eWxsXU.
39. DJ Craze, quoted in White, Crisell, and Principe, *On the Record*, 149.
40. John Carluccio, telephone interview with the author, 16 October 2001.
41. DJ A-Trak, e-mail message to the author, 26 August 2002.
42. Christie Z-Pabon, e-mail message to the author, 16 November 2002.
43. For a demonstration, see DJ Angelo, online at www.youtube.com/watch?v= w3ozzXEzWbI. See also *DJ Qbert's Complete Do-It Yourself, Vol. 1 Skratching*, Thud Rumble DVD, 2003.
44. Qbert, quoted in Brewster and Broughton, *Last Night a DJ Saved My Life*, 283.
45. Cash Money, telephone interview with the author.
46. DJ Jazzy Jeff, quoted in White, Crisell, and Principe, *On the Record*, 150–51.
47. Grand Wizard Rasheen, interview with James G. Spady, *The Global Cipha*, 15 December 2008, online at www.thaglobalcipha.com/Rasheen.html.
48. DJ Jazzy Jeff, quoted in *Turntablist Transcription Method*, online at www. ttmethod.com/. See page 9 under "Chapters."
49. Steve Dee, interview with the author.

50. Ibid.
51. Roc Raida, quoted in Brewster and Broughton, *Last Night a DJ Saved My Life*, 283.
52. Online at www.youtube.com/watch?v=v8sUBhB9wwA.
53. For footage of Aladdin's DMC routine, see www.youtube.com/watch?v=BkqInUBGZcc.
54. Steve Dee, interview with the author.
55. DJ Aladdin, e-mail message to the author, 10 July 2011.
56. For footage of Cutmaster Swift's copycat filmed in 1989, see "Cutmaster Swift: The Best-Kept Secret, Part 1," online at www.youtube.com/watch?v=5rt0tI0NNVE. See 2:35–4:35, especially in the second half of the excerpt. His routines at the 1988 New Music also featured the copycat, which can be heard at http://soundcloud.com/cutmaster_swift/cms-new-music-seminar-1988, esp. following 0:52.
57. Cutmaster Swift, interview with the author, Slough, England, 27 May 2011.
58. Cash Money, telephone interview with the author.
59. As an indication of the centrality of innovation, a 1999 survey of the best turntablists includes a section in each entry designated "Innovation." Charles Aaron, "Mix Masters: The Top 13 Turntablists in the World," *Spin* (April 1999): 128–32.
60. Bambaataa, telephone interview with the author.
61. Brewster and Broughton, *Last Night a DJ Saved My Life*, 282; and *DJ Qbert's Complete Do-It Yourself, Vol. 1*.
62. Pete Rock, quoted in *Beat Kings: The History of Hip Hop*, Nature Sounds DVD, 2006. This segment is also accessible on YouTube at www.youtube.com/watch?v=aparc-DPN3o.
63. Chang, *Can't Stop, Won't Stop*, 256.
64. Chairman Mao, "The Legacy of Marley Marl," *Ego Trip* 3, no. 3 (1998): 88–89.
65. Brian Coleman, *Check the Technique: Liner Notes for Hip-Hop Junkies* (New York: Villard, 2007), 238. In the early days recording studio engineers assisted producers a great deal, sometimes even becoming (usually uncredited) producers themselves. See Andre Torres, "Give the Engineer Some," *Wax Poetics*, no. 1 (Winter 2001), reprinted in *Wax Poetics Anthology*, vol. 1 (Brooklyn, NY: Wax Poetics Books, 2007), 140.
66. DJ Shortkut, interview with the author, Colma, CA, 28 March 2008.
67. Evil Dee, quoted in *Deep Crates: Documentary Film Dedicated to the Art of Beatdiggin'*, Beatdawg DVD, n.d.
68. Craze, e-mail message to the author.
69. Hank Shocklee, interview at the Red Bull Music Academy, Seattle, 2005, online at www.redbullmusicacademy.com/video-archive/transcript/hank_shocklee__art_brut/transcript.
70. Prince Paul, interview at the Red Bull Music Academy, Cape Town, 2003, online at www.redbullmusicacademy.com/video-archive/transcript/prince_paul__prince_of_thieves/transcript. He talks about his experience as a DJ and his love of records at greater length in Prince Paul, "The Memoirs of Prince

Paul," *Wax Poetics*, no. 2 (Spring 2002), reprinted in *Wax Poetics Anthology*, vol. 1 (Brooklyn, NY: Wax Poetics Books, 2007), 117–25.

71. See www.the-breaks.com/search.php?term=impeach + the + president& type=4.
72. Rodriguez, telephone interview with the author.
73. Cut Chemist, interview with Agent B, 13 December 2006, online at http://archive.ohword.com/features/543/cut-chemist-interview.
74. DJ Premier, interview with DJ Monk One, no date [post-2006], online at www.scion.com/broadband/index.html?ch=0&sh=1&ep=18.
75. DJ Kool Akiem, quoted in Schloss, *Making Beats*, 157. For more on the relationship between producing and DJing, see Schloss, *Making Beats*, 51–57.

CHAPTER 5

1. DJ Babu, with D-Styles and Melo D, "Turntablism," *Beat Junkies Classic Material*, Vol. 1, Beat Junkie Sound CD, 2001.
2. DJ Babu, quoted in Neva Chonin, "An Itch to Scratch: The New School Turntablists," *Option*, no. 77 (November–December 1997): 60. See also DJ Babu, interview with K-Per, 26 June 2005, www.ukhh.com/elements/turntablism/babu/index.html.
3. Babu wasn't actually the first to use these terms. According to Grandmixer DXT, Herbie Hancock called him a turntablist when they were performing "Rockit" in concert in 1984. "When people would come up to Herbie and go, 'What do you call him?,' he would say, 'He's a turntablist.'" Grandmixer DXT (formerly D.ST), interview with the author. In the documentary *Scratch*, Babu in fact identifies DXT as the original turntablist.
4. D-Styles, liner notes to *Phantazmagorea*, Beat Junkie Sound CD, PHAN-001, 2002.
5. DJ Disco Wiz, interview with the author.
6. Cutmaster Swift, e-mail message to the author, 3 June 2011.
7. Advertisement for Stanton 500AL in *High Fidelity* 20, no. 7 (1970): 25. The same ad ran in *DB: The Sound Engineering Magazine, Journal of the Audio Engineering Society*, and *Stereo Review*.
8. DJ Craze, e-mail message to the author.
9. Ibid.
10. See www.stantondj.com/cartridges.html.
11. Kjetil Falkenberg Hansen, "The Basics of Scratching," *Journal of New Music Research* 31 (2002): 358.
12. Ibid. The higher tracking force and narrower frequency range are functions of the spherical shape of the tip of the stylus. Styli also come in elliptical shapes, which have a better frequency response but a lower tracking force. John Steventon explains the differences between the two shapes in *DJing for Dummies*, 2nd ed. (West Sussex, England: John Wiley & Sons, 2010), 104.
13. *Billboard* 75 (30 November 1963): 43.
14. DJ Rhettmatic, interview with the author, Los Angeles, CA, 14 June 2008.

15. Online at www.shure.com/americas/products/phono/m44-7-turntablist-record-needles, viewed 6 June 2011.
16. For a demonstration of the crab scratch, see *DJ Qbert's Complete Do-It Yourself, Vol. 1.*
17. Qbert, interview with the author.
18. Ibid.
19. According to audio engineer Rick Jeffs, the first documented use of the word "crossfade" was in 1973. (Although he suggests that the first crossfader control dates to about 1977, I have seen examples of crossfaders from 1975. See footnote 29 on p. 272.) Rick Jeffs, "Evolution of the DJ Crossfader," *RaneNote*, no. 146 (1999), online at www.rane.com/note146.html. See also David Cross, "A History of the Development of DJ Mixer Features: An S&TS Perspective," (B.A. thesis, Cornell University, 2003). Available online at www.zenknee.com/DJ_Mixer_History.pdf.
20. The earliest crossfaders also tended to come in the form of knobs instead of horizontal sliders; knobs kept the machine's innards better sealed from the elements than a slider, whose open track exposed the mixer's electronics to dust and liquid.
21. Cash Money, telephone interview with the author.
22. Shortkut, interview with the author.
23. The gun oil solution is often mentioned on DJ Internet forums. See, for example, the comment made by DJ Ginsu D on the *Scratchworx* website on 3 February 2005, online at www.skratchworx.com/news3/comments.php?id=223. The Jazzy Jeff example is discussed in chapter 4.
24. http://djquest.com/index.php?page=biography.
25. DJ Quest, telephone interview with the author, 10 August 2010. DJ Focus's innovative equipment designs include a mixer, crossfader, and slipmat he developed for Stanton.
26. See "DJ Technology Timeline," online at www.rane.com/pdf/djtimeline.pdf.
27. Jeffs, "Evolution of the DJ Crossfader."
28. Shortkut, interview with the author. All other quotes from Shortkut in this section come from this interview.
29. DJ Rhettmatic, interview with the author. All other quotes from Rhettmatic in this section come from this interview.
30. This and other quotes in the paragraph from Qbert, interview with the author.
31. The original statement was in Japanese. Quoted in Rayvon Fouché, "Following the Artifacts: Hip Hop, Japan, and Technological Knowledge," in *Studies of Urban International Society: Compilation of Seminar Papers* (Osaka: Urban Culture Research Center, Osaka City University, 2009), 83. Online at http://educa.lit.osaka-cu.ac.jp/~ggp/nakami/2009/Studies_of_International_Urban_Society_2009.pdf.
32. Vernacular technological creativity, which I also discuss in chapter 2, comes from the work of historian Rayvon Fouché. Fouché, "Say It Loud, I'm Black and I'm Proud." Of particular interest here is Fouché's discussion

of Grandmaster Flash's work with Rane on designing the Empath mixer; see pp. 656–657.

33. Kid Koala, interview with Mark Katz, David Hutcheson, Sara Soltau, and Reed Turchi, Carrboro, NC, 18 April 2009.

34. DJ Disk, who was a member of the ISP for a time, is not Filipino.

35. Oliver S. Wang, "Spinning Identities: A Social History of Filipino American DJs in the San Francisco Bay Area (1975–1995)" (Ph.D. diss., University of California, Berkeley, 2004), 72. For more on the Go-Go's, see pp. 154–60. A book version of Wang's dissertation is forthcoming from Duke University Press.

36. Wang, "Spinning Identities," 18.

37. DJ Qbert, interview with the author.

38. Quoted in Wang, "Spinning Identities," 114.

39. Quoted in ibid., 120. See pp. 121–24 for more on the tension between scratching and mixing in the Bay Area DJ scene.

40. This discussion of Qbert's early scratching draws on DJ Qbert, interview with the author.

41. See www.youtube.com/watch?v=1trx1-9sub8.

42. Apollo, interview with the author.

43. Mix Master Mike, undated interview, interviewer not identified, online at www.djsunited.com.au/Mix Mastermike.html.

44. Apollo, interview with the author.

45. See www.youtube.com/watch?v=X90KpaSwVuA. My thanks to Ryan Ebright for identifying *Street Fighter II* as the source of "You Lose!" The routine also includes other phrases (e.g., "sonic boom") taken from the game.

46. Billy Jam, interview with the author, New York, N.Y., 4 February 2008.

47. See Hip Hop Slam's website for information on other releases, www.hiphopslam.com.

48. *The Wire*, nos. 221–26 (2002): 71.

49. I draw my information on Dave Paul largely from an interview from 2008 with an unidentified interviewer. See www.bombhiphop.com/newbomb/bombpages/dpint.html.

50. *Spin* magazine ranked Volumes 1 and 2 of the series as the 25th best album of the 1990s. *Spin* 15 (September 1999): 131. Volume 6 was released in 2009.

51. Alex Aquino, quoted in Chonin, "An Itch to Scratch," 60.

52. These terms come from the text on the box holding the VHS tape of the second ITF competition. My thanks to Travis Rimando for this text, as well as for general information on the ITF.

53. DJ Pone (Travis Rimando), e-mail message to the author, 8 July 2010.

54. Todd S. Inoue, "Beats Generation," *San Jose Metro*, 7–13 (November 1996), online at www.metroactive.com/papers/metro/11.07.96/scratch-pickles-9645.html.

55. Ibid.

56. Apollo, interview with the author.

57. Inoue, "Beats Generation."

58. Rhettmatic, interview with the author.

59. Wang, "Spinning Identities."
60. Elizabeth H. Pisares, "Do You Mis(recognize) Me: Filipina Americans in Popular Music and the Problem of Invisibility," in *Positively No Filipinos Allowed: Building Communities and Discourse*, ed. Antonio T. Tiongson, Jr., Edgardo V. Gutierrez, and Ricardo V. Gutierrez (Philadelphia: Temple University Press, 2006), 191.
61. Oliver Wang, e-mail message to the author, 1 November 2011.
62. GrandWizzard Theodore, telephone interview with the author, 19 December 2006.
63. Shortkut, interview with the author.
64. *As the Tables Turn*, Red Line Music DVD, no label number, 2007.
65. At various times, Diamond J, DJ Boogie Blind, and DJ Precision were members as well.
66. *As the Tables Turn*.
67. For an appreciation, see Ronnie Reese, "Roc Raida, 1972–2009: The Grand Master" *Wax Poetics*, no. 38 (2009): 24.
68. See, for example, Qbert and Mix Master Mike's comments in the film *Scratch*.
69. DJ Aladdin, e-mail message to the author, 10 July 2011.
70. Rhettmatic, interview with the author. For more on the KDAY Mixmasters, see Charnas, *The Big Payback*.
71. Rhettmatic, interview with the author.
72. Andrew Bernal, interview with the author, Los Angeles, CA, 14 June 2008.

CHAPTER 6

1. Sun-Tzu, *The Art of War*, quoted in http://en.wikipedia.org/wiki/The_Art_of_War.
2. Rob Swift, interview with the author, Roslyn, VA, 6 July 2001.
3. Ibid.
4. "Gong DJ Battle Info & Rules," online at www.myspace.com/thegongdjbattle/blog/242145843, posted 1 May 2010.
5. Shortkut, quoted in "Tones, Beats, and Biting," an excerpt from John Carluccio's *Battle Sounds* documentary, online at www.battlesounds.com/CLIP5_8BALL.html. DJ Disk, Steve Dee, Qbert, and others also address biting in this segment.
6. DJ Rectangle, quoted in "Tones, Beats, and Biting."
7. See www.youtube.com/watch?v=UV8562B-1lY. See the accompanying comments for debates about the merits of the routine.
8. See www.youtube.com/watch?v=KkoQOupR0CE, starting at 1:10.
9. DJ Craze, e-mail message to the author.
10. See www.youtube.com/watch?v=khgy9bA_mSU, starting at 3:22, for this routine. For an excellent account of the battle, see Neil Strauss, "Battle of the Needle Freaks," *Spin* (April 1999): 125–26.
11. DJ Craze, e-mail message to the author.
12. A-Trak, e-mail message to the author.

13. DJ Fatfingaz, in "The Death of Battling," *DJ Geometrix* forum discussion, 8 August 2007, www.djgeometrix.com/message_board/topic.asp?TOPIC_ID=8834.

14. Online at www.youtube.com/watch?v=H_QQ1Kqc59s.

15. Tony Prince, interview with the author, 14 April 2008.

16. See www.youtube.com/watch?v=H_QQ1Kqc59s and www.youtube.com/watch?v=39BEkgkCX-c.

17. There were other series as well, such as the Octopus series and Paul Winley's *Super Disco Brakes*, but UBB was the best known and most influential. For more on the various breakbeat compilations, see John Leland and Steve Stein, "What It Is," *Village Voice* 33 (19 January 1988): 24–30; and Andrew Mason, "Building Blocks," *Wax Poetics*, no. 1 (Winter 2002): 44–50.

18. DJ Shadow, quoted in Eliot Wilder, *Endtroducing. . . . .* (New York: Continuum, 2005), 54.

19. Prince Paul, "The Memoirs of Prince Paul," 119.

20. Grandmixer DXT (formerly D.ST), interview with the author. Subsequent quotations in this paragraph come from the same interview.

21. As we saw in Chapter 2, in 1977 Grandmaster Caz and DJ Disco Wiz used what may have been the very first battle record with their "plate," a privately pressed 10-inch acetate record that only they used. Dan the Automator's 1989 record *Music to Be Murdered By* had several "Bonus Noise" tracks filled with sounds intended to be scratched and mixed, though whether this is a battle record is open to debate. My thanks to Travis Rimando (DJ Pone) for pointing this out.

22. Bullet Proof Space Hamsters, *Hamster Breaks* Volume 1, Funky Stupid Dope Shit LP, BPSH 001; Psychedelic Skratch Bastards, *Battle Breaks*, Dirt Style LP, BB 001. The Psychedelic Skratch Bastards, identified as DJ Twirlz, Darth Fader and Zodiak Tweaker, are likely aliases for Apollo, Mix Master Mike, and Qbert, given that the cartoon figure on the cover has a hat with "Rocksteady" and a ring with FMH20 on it; the three DJs belonged to both groups mentioned.

23. Cash Money, telephone interview with the author.

24. Swift, e-mail message to the author, 10 January 2008.

25. Qbert, interview with the author.

26. DJ Pone (Travis Rimando), interview with the author, Berkeley, CA, 8 November 2006.

27. *As the Tables Turn*, Red Line Music DVD, no label number, 2007.

28. A video of the team battle can be viewed at www.youtube.com/watch?v=EnAF8ehFRiE. This was the only film easily available—the sound and picture quality are unfortunately of poor quality.

29. The Piklz released a version of this routine on a 12-inch single for Asphodel called "Invisibl Skratch Piklz Vs. Da Klamz Uv Deth."

30. The individual battles of the ISP vs. X-Men exhibition can be seen on *As the Tables Turn* and *The Best of I.T.F.*, Volume. 1, DJ Honda DVD, DHBA-9, 2006. The former DVD has better sound quality.

31. My thanks to Travis Rimando (DJ Pone) for pointing this out to me.

32. Shortkut, interview with the author.

33. Ibid.
34. Qbert, interview with the author.
35. Ibid.
36. Shortkut, interview with the author.
37. Qbert, interview with the author.
38. Rob Swift, e-mail message to the author, 11 January 2008.
39. Ibid.
40. Note: the DJ names in this story are not intended to refer to actual DJs. If you are DJ X, DJ Boddicker, DJ Krassen, or DJ Velvel, this is not about you. Unless you want it to be.
41. Quoted in "DJ Slyce Interview," *Dirty Waters*, 6 September 2008, online at http://dirtywaters.blogspot.com/2007/09/dj-slyce-interview.html.
42. DJ Swamp, telephone interview with the author, 18 November 2009. The routine can be viewed at www.youtube.com/watch?v=0KsQvPS1dWA.
43. Steve Dee, interview with the author.
44. 8-Ball explains that tones were first heard in a 1988 DMC battle, and cites as his inspiration Qbert's fashioning of "Mary Had a Little Lamb" in a 1989 battle. *Skratchcon 2000*, Thud Rumble DVD, SC2000. For interviews with 8-Ball, Qbert, Mista Sinista, and others about tones, see "Tones, Beats, and Biting," an excerpt from John Carluccio's *Battle Sounds* documentary, online at www. battlesounds.com/CLIP5_8BALL.html. For a review of 8-Ball's victory at the 1993 New Music Seminar battles, see Hal Espen, "Jockey Club," *New Yorker*, 9 August 1993, pp. 26–28.
45. At the Skratchcon 2000 gathering, 8-Ball provided the formula for playing the melody from Black Sabbath's "Iron Man," with the speeds in brackets: [33 rpm] -8, 8, 8 [45 rpm], -8, -8, 4, 0, 4, 0, 4, 0 [33 rpm] 8, 8 [45 rpm] -8, 8. *Skratchcon 2000*.
46. Steve Dee, interview with the author.
47. *As the Tables Turn*.
48. DJ Beware, "How to Be a Scratch DJ," *Soundpark: Your Place for Homegrown Music*, 2 October 2003, online at http://fm4.orf.at/spinfo/108354/main.
49. Steve Dee, interview with the author.
50. Espen, "Jockey Club," 28.
51. Shortkut, interview with the author.
52. Babu, quoted in Brian O'Connor, "Career Decknician," *DJ Times* 19 (March 2006): 27.
53. Cash Money, telephone interview with the author.
54. Steve Dee, interview with the author.
55. DJ Immortal, interview with the author, Miami, FL, 14 December 2006.
56. I explore this issue in more detail in my article, "Men, Women, and Turntables: Gender and the DJ Battle," *Musical Quarterly* 89 (Summer 2006): 580–99. The present discussion is drawn in part from this article.
57. DJ Tigerstyle (Alvin Seechurn), interview with the author, London, England, 14 April 2008.
58. DJ Quest, telephone interview with the author, 11 August 2010.
59. Johnny "Juice" Rosado, telephone interview with the author.

60. Quoted in Pete Miser, "Viva La Nerd Hip Hop Revolution," *Theme*, no. 1 (Spring 2005): 60–61. Online at www.thudrumble.com/images/headlines/ThemeIssue.pdf.

61. Ken-One, interview with the author, Tokyo, Japan, 5 June 2008. For a discussion of otaku and hip-hop in Japan, see Ian Condry, *Hip-Hop Japan: Rap and the Paths of Cultural Globalization* (Durham and London: Duke University Press, 2006), 124–28.

62. Kid Koala, interview with Mark Katz, David Hutcheson, Sara Soltau, and Reed Turchi.

63. Shortkut, interview with the author.

64. Peanut Butter Wolf, quoted in Chonin, "An Itch to Scratch," 61.

65. Hard data on the gender of DMC battlers seems not to exist; however, when I consulted two of DMC's battle organizers in 2007 together the two could only name five women who had battled in their competitions. To be on the safe side, I more than doubled that estimate. Christie Z-Pabon, e-mail message to author, 23 March 2007; Sally Mclintock, e-mail message to author, 29 March 2007.

66. According to the U.S. Bureau of Labor Statistics, women made up 216,000, or 2.5%, of the 8,522,000 who worked in these occupations in 2004. "Employed Persons by Major Occupation and Sex, 2003–2004 Annual Averages," U.S. Bureau of Labor Statistics, online at www.bls.gov/cps/wlf-table10-2005.pdf. My estimate of women battlers is necessarily rough. However, if we assume that 2.5% of the approximately 200 DJs who entered DMC battles in the U.S. in 2005 were women, there would have been five women competing that year. Given that the two DMC organizers I cited in the previous note could only name five women who had ever battled in their competitions, 2.5% seems to be a generous figure.

67. Christie Z-Pabon, e-mail message to the author, 1 January 2007.

68. DJ Revolution, telephone interview with the author, 19 May 2009.

69. DJ Z-Trip, quoted in *Scratch*.

70. DJ Quest, telephone interview with the author.

71. Apollo, interview with the author.

Chapter 7

1. The video can be viewed at www.youtube.com/watch?v=Oh6Q8dDVjlM.

2. This text comes from the back of the *Skratchcon 2000* DVD case.

3. The Beastie Boys worked with DJ Hurricane and then Mix Master Mike; DJ Muggs scratched (and produced) for Cypress Hill; King Britt (a.k.a. Silkworm) supported the MCs of Digable Planets; Qbert partnered with Dr. Octagon (a.k.a. Kool Keith) on the excellent 1996 album *Dr. Octagonecologyst* (esp. "Blue Flowers"); Diamond J, DJ K La Boss, and DJ Scratch worked with EPMD at various times; Eric B. was half of Eric B. and Rakim, just as DJ Premier was half of Gang Starr; Jurassic 5 worked with Cut Chemist and Nu-Mark; Public Enemy had Johnny "Juice" Rosado and Terminator X, and so on.

4. See Pop Will Eat Itself's 1989 album *This Is the Day. This Is the Hour. This Is This!* and Living Colour's 1991 cover of James Brown's "Talking Loud and

Saying Nothing." For one of many Laswell examples, listen to the 1992 Praxis album, *Transmutation (Mutatis Mutandis),* with the DJ Afrika Baby Bam, along with virtuoso guitarist Buckethead, funk bassist Bootsy Collins, and others.

5. Charles Aaron, "What the White Boy Means When He Says Yo," *Spin* 14 (November 1998): 114.

6. "MMMbop," Wikipedia, http://en.wikipedia.org/wiki/MMMBop.

7. In neither case is a DJ credited with the scratches; "Where It's At" actually samples GrandWizzard Theodore's "Military Cut" from the *Wild Style* soundtrack. Beck did start using and crediting actual DJs beginning with DJ Swamp, who toured with him and performed on his 1998 album *Midnite Vultures.*

8. "Tom Morello Guitar Lessons 03 Bulls on Parade," www.youtube.com/watch?v=kyxKJLgfT7A.

9. DJ P, telephone interview with the author, 22 April 2009.

10. Brian Coleman, "Turntablists: Return of the DJ," *CMJ New Music Monthly,* no. 55 (March 1998): 14.

11. *As the Tables Turn,* Red Line Music DVD, no label number, 2007.

12. Ibid.

13. Ibid.

14. Tony Prince, interview with the author, Slough, England, 27 May 2011.

15. For a discussion of these factors and the differences between live and recorded music in general, see my book *Capturing Sound: How Technology Has Changed Music,* rev. ed. (Berkeley: University of California Press, 2010), 10–55.

16. The X-Ecutioners, *Built from Scratch,* Loud compact disc, 501563 2, 2002. Mista Sinista left the group shortly after the release of the album, and the group toured in support of the album as a trio. See *As the Tables Turn* for comments from all the members of the group on Sinista's departure.

17. Quoted in Noah Callahan-Bever, "The Spinners," *Vibe* (August 2002): 128.

18. *As the Tables Turn.*

19. Ibid.

20. Ibid.

21. Quoted in Callahan-Bever, "The Spinners," 128.

22. Swift, interview with the author.

23. Rob Swift, quoted in *As the Tables Turn.*

24. DJ Qbert, *Wave Twisters, Episode 7 Million: Sonic Wars Within the Protons,* Galactic Butt Hair compact disc, GBH0007-2, 1998. The album also features beats and scratches by DJ Disk, D-Styles, DJ Flare, Mix Master Mike, DJ Shortkut, Vinroc, and Yogafrog, and guitar work by Buckethead.

25. Kid Koala, interview with Mark Katz, David Hutcheson, Sara Soltau, and Reed Turchi, Carrboro, NC, 18 April 2009. Other quotations from Kid Koala in this section also come from this interview.

26. *The New Rolling Stone Album Guide,* 4th ed., ed. Nathan Brackett and Christian Hoard (New York: Fireside, 2004), 450.

27. D-Styles, *Phantazmagorea,* Beat Junkies Sound compact disc, PHAN-001, 2002.

28. D-Styles mentions the Tabitha Cash sample in DJ Pone, "Waxing That Wax: The Porn/Turntablism Connection Part 2, D-Styles Interview," 12 March 2002, online at www.hiphopslam.com/articles/artic_porntablism_pt2.html.

29. See the three-part series on "porntablism" by DJ Pone, online at www.hiphopslam.com/articles/artic_avn_awards_2002.html; www.hiphopslam.com/articles/artic_porntablism_pt2.html; and www.hiphopslam.com/articles/artic_porntablism_pt3.html. See also Mr. Dibbs, "Porntablist," from his 2003 album *The 30th Song*.

30. D-Styles and Shortkut, interview with Mr. Trick and Laurent Fintoni, Turntable Radio, 2002, online at www.turntableradio.com/2008/07/18/turntable-radio-the-mr-trick-years-show-2.

31. Ibid.

32. See the Wikipedia entry for *Endtroducing.....* for references to the many accolades it received. Online at http://en.wikipedia.org/wiki/Endtroducing.

33. DJ Shadow, *Endtroducing.....*, Mo Wax compact disc MW 059 CD.

34. DJ Shadow, quoted in Eliot Wilder, *Endtroducing.....* (New York: Continuum, 2005), 89.

35. Grandmixer DXT (formerly Grandmixer D.ST), interview with the author.

36. Jason Fine, "Revolutions per Minute: DJ Shadow, Hip-Hop Militant," *Option*, no. 73 (March–April 1997): 62.

37. For a good discussion of DJ Shadow's use of the digital sampler in *Endtroducing.....*, see Michael A. D'Errico, "Behind the Beat: Technical and Practical Aspects of Instrumental Hip-Hop Composition," (M.A. thesis, Tufts University, 2011), 19–38.

38. DJ Shadow, telephone interview with the author, 10 January 2011.

39. Ibid.

40. Ibid.

41. Ibid.

42. Ibid.

43. DJ Shadow, *Endtroducing.....*, liner notes, Island Records CD, 1996.

44. DJ Shadow, quoted in *Scratch*.

45. Ibid.

46. Online at http://jeremystorch.net/jeremystorch/jeremy_storch_biography.htm.

47. Jeremy Storch, e-mail message to the author, 25 August 2010.

48. DJ Shadow, quoted in Wilder, *Endtroducing.....*, 71.

49. DJ Shadow, telephone interview with the author.

50. DJ Shadow, quoted in Wilder, *Endtroducing.....*, 77.

51. See the discography for a list of these artists' albums.

52. DJ Babu, quoted in the liner notes to *Deep Concentration: The Future of Experimental Hip Hop*, Om CD, no label number, 1997.

53. A good recording of *Imaginary Landscape No. 1* is on *Early Modulations: Vintage Volts*, Caipirinha Productions compact disc, CAI-2027-2. For further discussion of avant-garde turntablism, see Katz, *Capturing Sound*, 109–23.

54. Douglas Kahn, "Christian Marclay's Early Years: An Interview," *Leonardo Music Journal* 13 (2003): 19.

55. *Second Coming*, on Christian Marclay, *Records, 1981–1989*, Atavistic compact disc, alp62cd; *John Cage*, on Christian Marclay, *More Encores*, ReR compact disc, CM1. *Tabula Rasa* seems not to have been recorded for a commercial release, and has been performed only a handful of times (with sound artist Flo Kaufmann) since 2003.

56. See the discography for selected albums by these artists.

57. Britt, interview with the author. See the discography for selected albums by the artists mentioned in this paragraph.

58. See in particular his 1996 album with Japanese trumpeter Toshinori Kindo, *Ki-Oku*. Krush and bassist Bill Laswell have collaborated frequently in recent years.

59. Robin D.G. Kelley, "Beneath the Underground: Exploring New Currents in 'Jazz,'" in *Uptown Conversation: The New Jazz Studies*, ed. Robert G. O'Meally, Brent Hayes Edwards, and Farah Jasmine Griffin (New York: Columbia University Press, 2004), 404–16.

60. Paul D. Miller, *Rhythm Science* (Cambridge, MA: MIT Press, 2004), 48.

61. DJ Spooky, quoted in Greg Tate, "Adventures in Illbient," *Vibe* (April 1998): 54.

62. For more on DJ Singe and DJ Mutamassik, see Tate, "Adventures in Illbient," and Kelley, "Beneath the Underground."

63. Kelley, "Beneath the Underground," 407.

64. The notes are also accessible at www.djsniff.com/ep.html.

65. Swift, interview with the author.

66. Qbert, interview with the author.

67. Kid Koala, interview with Mark Katz, David Hutcheson, Sara Soltau, and Reed Turchi.

68. For a brief documentary on the concert, see www.youtube.com/watch?v=5SRIjZjeg3w.

69. You-Young Kim, "An Orchestral Project Is 'Bullish' on Innovation," *The Juilliard Journal Online* 22 (November 2005), www.juilliard.edu/update/journal/j_articles712.html.

70. Ibid.

71. DJ Radar, *Antimatter* (San Francisco: Om Records, 2000), 1. Radar composed the work, but was assisted by Yañez in the transcription into musical notation.

72. Raúl Yañez and DJ Radar, interview with the author, Guadalupe, AZ, 13 June 2008. All subsequent quotes from the two in this section come from this joint interview.

73. Nicole Lizée, "RPM for Large Ensemble and Solo Turntablist," (Master's thesis, McGill University, 2000). A recording is available on *This Will Not Be Televised*, Centredisques CD, CMCCD 13508, 2008.

74. See the discography for selected albums by these artists. (Some of the artists' works for turntables have not been commercially released, however.)

75. DJ Radar, *Antimatter*, 1.

76. For an excellent study of the subject, see Felicia M. Miyakawa, "Turntablature: Notation, Legitimization, and the Art of the Hip-Hop DJ," *American Music* 25 (Spring 2007): 81–105. See also Doc Rice, "Transforming Notation:

Pioneering the Hieroglyphics of the Scratch." *Rap Pages* (August 1999): 32. Rice, who has also developed a notation system, notes that Qbert, Icue1200, and DJ Enema have as well. In his instructional books on DJing, Stephen Webber uses traditional and largely unmodified notation for rhythm exercises for DJs. See his *DJ Skills: The Essential Guide to Mixing and Scratching* (Burlington, MA: Focal, 2007) and *Turntable Technique: The Art of the DJ*, 2nd ed. (Boston: Berklee Press, 2010).

77. A-Trak, "Scratchnotation," *Tablist*, no. 1 (March 2002): 34. A-Trak publicly introduced his system at Skratchcon 2000, and his presentation can be seen on the *Skratchcon 2000* DVD.

78. Ibid., 35.

79. Ibid.

80. See www.ttmethod.com, "About TTM" (no separate URL).

81. Josh Tyrangiel, "Turntablist Expert: Now Every Night He Saves a DJ's Life," *Time*, 28 May 2001, online at www.time.com/time/magazine/article/0,9171,999984,00.html. Other discussions in the press (including a video clip from *CSI: NY*) can be found in the News section of the TTM website, www.ttmethod.com.

82. Laurent Burte, *Scratch graphique: une recherche typographique au plus profond du son* (Paris: Pyramyd, 2003), 62. Original in French. Burte also discusses his work in his blog, http://laurentburt.wordpress.com/category/scratch-graphique/.

83. Ibid., 64.

84. Ibid., 68.

85. Rob Swift, interview with Belly and DJ Void, (2005), online at www.superhappywax.com/robswift.php.

86. See www.americasbestdj.net/bestdj/2010.htm.

87. Qbert, interview with the author.

88. Kuttin Kandi, interview with MarWax, 30 January 2000, online at www.5thplatoon.com/articles/kuttinkandiinterview.htm.

CHAPTER 8

1. Unidentified speaker, 5 June 2002, New York City. The event was the 2002 DMC regional battle held at the B.B. King Blues Club and Grill in Manhattan.

2. B-Side, e-mail message to the author, 9 November 2010.

3. Ibid.

4. Jim Tremayne, "Dance & Electronic Music: Great Gear!," *Billboard*, 5 October 2002, p. 34.

5. For a helpful early survey of DJ CD players, see Todd Souvigner, *The World of DJs and the Turntable Culture* (Milwaukee: Hal Leonard, 2003), 223–57.

6. DJ Maseo, telephone interview with the author, 17 November 2011.

7. GrandWizzard Theodore, conversation with the author, Baltimore, MD, 3 May 2005.

8. Ibid.

9. Comment by user Furiate, http://forum.djpages.com/topic.asp?TOPIC_ID=5653&#25144, posted 20 January 2005.

10. Comment by user Mixdoctor, http://forum.djpages.com/topic.asp?TOPIC_ID=5653&#25144, posted 20 January 2005.

11. Tony Prince, e-mail message to the author, 25 April 2005.

12. Steve Dee, interview with the author; Cash Money, telephone interview with the author; DJ Faust, quoted in Stephen Webber, *DJ Skills: The Essential Guide to Mixing and Scratching* (Burlington, MA: Focal Press, 2008), 123; DJ Maseo, telephone interview with the author.

13. Bambaataa, telephone interview with the author.

14. DJ P, telephone interview with the author.

15. For Serato Scratch Live data sheets and manuals, see www.rane.com/scratch.html#gpm1_11.

16. Specifically, Serato adds pink noise, which is somewhat like white noise in that there is no single detectable pitch but rather a wash of frequencies. Perhaps the most noticeable difference between white and pink noise is that the latter is stronger in the lower frequencies.

17. My thanks to Steve Macatee of the Rane Corporation for explaining the basics of the tone control record to me. Steve Macatee, telephone conversation with the author, 17 December 2010.

18. Information on time stamps comes from Chad Carrier, "Technical Information and Tips on Torq's Vinyl Control System," undated PDF available at www.mspinky.com/Some_Technical_Info_on_VInyl.pdf.

19. My thanks to DJ A-Minor for walking me through the Serato Scratch Live software.

20. *Rane SL 1 for Serato Scratch Live: Operator's Manual 2.0* (Serato Audio Research, 2010), available for download at www.rane.com/pdf/sl1manual20.pdf.

21. Shortkut, interview with the author.

22. Craze, e-mail message to the author.

23. GrandWizzard Theodore, interview with the author, Chapel Hill, NC, 23 October 2007.

24. Bambaataa, telephone interview with the author.

25. Shortkut, interview with the author.

26. Swift, e-mail message to the author, 10 January 2008.

27. DJ P, telephone interview with the author.

28. Bambaataa, telephone interview with the author.

29. DJ Vajra, interview with unidentified interviewer, 10 October 2011, www.youtube.com/watch?NR=1&v=uZEJ3agzb-8.

30. DJ Craze, e-mail message to the author.

31. DJ Qbert, interview with the author.

32. DJ Revolution, featuring KRS-One, "The DJ" from King of the Decks, 2008.

33. DJ P, telephone interview with the author.

34. Ibid.

35. "Paris Hilton Is Becoming a DJ and Has Custom Designed Pink Headphones Built for Her Debut," Hollywood Giants, available at http://hollywoodgiants.

com/2010/11/06/paris-hilton-is-becoming-a-dj-and-has-custom-designed-pink-headphones-built, 6 November 2010.

36. "Exclusive: DJ Lindsay Lohan Fails to Wow in London," Radar Online, available at www.radaronline.com/exclusives/2010/03/exclusive-dj-lindsay-lohan-fails-wow-london, 5 March 2010.

37. Swift, e-mail message to the author, 10 January 2008.

38. DJ Revolution, telephone interview with the author, 19 May 2009.

39. DJ A-Minor, conversation with the author, Chapel Hill, NC, 3 December 2010.

40. DJ Enferno, "The Death of Battling," Turntablist Network discussion, 10 August 2007. Online at www.djgeometrix.com/message_board/topic.asp?TOPIC_ID=8834.

41. DJ Dini, "The Death of Battling," Turntablist Network discussion, 10 August 2007. Online at www.djgeometrix.com/message_board/topic.asp?TOPIC_ID=8834.

42. A-Trak, e-mail message to the author.

43. The first DJ school was probably the United DJ Mixing School in Sydney, Australia, which opened in 1993. See www.djsunited.com.au/school.html.

44. Online at www.scratch.com/about.

45. Online at www.dubspot.com/about.

46. Between 2003 and 2008, I observed and participated in classes in New York City, Miami, Los Angeles, Berkeley, and Tokyo, and conducted interviews with academy instructors, managers, and students as well as DJs unaffiliated with any academy. Between 2008 and 2011, I continued to interview DJs and others about the phenomenon.

47. Scratch DJ Academy, Los Angeles, 4 November 2006. Recorded with permission.

48. DJ Hapa, telephone interview with the author, 23 February 2011.

49. Michael Cannady, interview with the author, New York, NY, 2 July 2007.

50. "DJ101 Course Pack," unpublished text (New York: Scratch DJ Academy, 2005), 2.

51. Swift, e-mail message to the author, 10 January 2008.

52. Killa-Jewel, telephone interview with author, 22 December 2006.

53. Tachelle Wilkes, telephone interview with the author, 20 December 2006.

54. GrandWizzard Theodore, interview with author, Chapel Hill, NC, 23 October 2007.

55. Pone, interview with the author, 8 November 2006.

56. All quotes from DJ Quest from DJ Quest, telephone interview with the author, 10 August 2010.

57. Qbert, interview with the author, 27 March 2008.

58. Online at www.qbertskratchuniversity.com.

59. Sources: http://multivu.prnewswire.com/mnr/djhero/40706/; www.time.com/time/specials/packages/article/0,28804,1945379_1944169_1944175,00.html; www.usatoday.com/tech/columnist/marcsaltzman/2009-12-03-games-2009_N.htm; http://multivu.prnewswire.com/mnr/djhero/40706/.

60. For a collection of DJ Hero-related statistics and references, see http://en.wikipedia.org/wiki/DJ_Hero.

61. J.N. Gillespie, posted 29 October 2009, online at www.amazon.com/review/ R3P872G25J01SP/ref=cm_cr_pr_viewpnt#R3P872G25J01SP.

62. Comments posted by Druboogie, Marcus, and Shmeeze, online at www.dj geometrix.com/message_board/topic.asp?TOPIC_ID=12646, 8–9 November 2009.

63. Yasmine Richard and Gil Kaufman, "Eminem, Jay-Z Share Stage for 'DJ Hero' Party," online at www.mtv.com/news/articles/1613079/eminem-jayz-share-stage-dj-hero-party.jhtml, 2 June 2009.

64. Comment by user Jojosribshack, online at www.denondjforums.com/forum/ index.php?f=15&t=11356&rb_v=viewtopic, 2 November 2009.

65. For a study of music video games (though not DJ Hero) that explores the distinctive musical engagement players have with those games, see Kiri Miller, "Schizophonic Performance: Guitar Hero, Rock Band, and Virtual Virtuosity," *Journal of the Society for American Music* 3 (November 2009): 395–429. See also Tero Karppi and Olli Sotamaa, "Methodological Observations from Behind the Decks," in *Games as Services: Final Report*, ed. Tero Karppi and Olli Sotamaa (Finland: University of Tampere, 2010), 56–72.

66. DJ Shadow, telephone interview with the author.

67. Comment by user Frogstar, online at www.djtechtools.com/forum/showthread. php?t=17499, 29 August 2010.

68. Moldover, quoted in http://moldover.com/wordpress/. Moldover also explains controllerism in two videos, "Moldover's Approach to Controllerism (1 of 2)," www.youtube.com/watch?v=L2McDeSKiOU and "Moldover's Approach to Controllerism (2 of 2)," www.youtube.com/watch?v=dznjQIarboY.

69. This statement was made in the comment section of his own article, "Controller Battle? Watch Out DMC," 22 June 2011, online at www.skratchworx.com/ newspage.php4?fn_mode=comments&fn_id=1735.

70. "Activision Potentially Ends Guitar Hero and DJ Hero," 9 February 2011, online at http://theherofeed.com/2326/activision-potentially-ends-hero-series/.

71. As of early 2012 a competing game, "Scratch: The Ultimate DJ," remains in development; its release date held up because of legal troubles. See http://en. wikipedia.org/wiki/Scratch:_The_Ultimate_DJ.

72. Kandi, interview with MarWax. For more information on Kandi, see her website, www.kuttinkandi.com. Kuttin Kandi and Eunice Parks, "Kuttin' Kandi," *Asian Week*, 27 July–2 August 2001, online at www.asianweek.com/2001_07_27/ arts_kuttinkandy.html.

73. See Stephen Webber, "Faust and Shortee: Two Turntablists Mix Music and Life," in *DJ Skills*, 115–23.

74. See www.myspace.com/anomolies.

75. Ibid.

76. For more on women's DJ collectives, see Sîan Norris, "Turning the Tables," The *Guardian*, 28 November 2007, sec. G2, p. 16; online at www.guardian.co.uk/ lifeandstyle/2007/nov/28/women.electronicmusic.

77. Killa-Jewel, telephone interview with the author.

78. Tyra from Saigon, interview with the author, North San Jose, CA, 28 March 2008.

79. Shortkut, interview with the author, Colma, CA, 28 March 2008.

80. DJ Shortee, undated interview, online at www.dogsonacid.com/showthread. php?threadid=556952. Kuttin Kandi, in an interview with music scholar Ellie Hisama, also cited Symphony as an inspiration. Ellie Hisama, "'B-Girl Stance in a B-Boy's World': DJ Kuttin Kandi, Hip Hop Activist," paper presented at the Society for American Music, Cleveland, OH, 13 March 2004.

81. DJ Annalyze, quoted in Jim Tremayne, "Annalyze: Turntablist on the Rise," *DJ Times* 20 (January 2007), online at www.djtimes.com/issues/2007/01/_ samplings_index_01_2007.htm.

82. Advertisement in *Vibe* (January 2002): 51.

83. Wilkes, telephone interview with the author.

84. Ibid.

85. DJ Tina T, "Female DJ Battles," online at http://beezoblog.com/main/?p=9957, 8 September 2010.

86. Z-Pabon, e-mail message to author, 1 January 2007.

87. "Discussion: Where the Ladies At?" Scratchworx.com, posted 3 May 2005. Online at http://www.skratchworx.com/news/comments.php4?id=271.

88. Kuttin Kandi, e-mail message to the author, 8 July 2011.

89. DJ Vtech, quoted in "Interview: Inside the Mind of a Beezo Battle DJ" (Part 2), 29 September 2010, online at http://beezoblog.com/main/?p=12345. The Beezo Battle is a series of competitions held in southern California.

90. See Yara Sellin, "DJ: Performer, Cyborg, Dominatrix" (Ph.D. diss., University of California, Los Angeles, 2005), 153.

91. Killa-Jewel, telephone interview with the author.

92. Tyra from Saigon, interview with the author.

93. Killa-Jewel, telephone interview with author.

94. DMC World DJ Championships, online at www.dmcdjchamps.com, 19 October 2010.

95. Tony Prince and Sally McLintock, interview with the author, Slough, England, 27 May 2011.

96. See, for example, "Oh wait… DMC is going digital after all," Skratchworx, 18 October 2010, online at www.skratchworx.com/news3/comments.php? id=1562.

97. "Dead Spin: Panasonic Discontinues Technics Analog Turntables," *Tokyo Reporter*, 20 October 2010, online at www.tokyoreporter.com/2010/10/28/ dead-spin-panasonic-discontinues-technics-analog-turntables.

CONCLUSION

1. Tools of War Facebook page, www.facebook.com/group.php?gid=101115026613. See also David Gonzalez, "Park Jam Series Brings Hip-Hop to New Generation," *New York Times*, 5 June 2009, online at http://cityroom.blogs.nytimes.com/ 2009/06/05/park-jam-series-brings-hip-hop-to-new-generation.

2. Johnny "Juice" Rosado has said that he and Terminator X scratched on that track. See Myrie, *Don't Rhyme for the Sake of Riddlin'*, 110.

3. See the Appendix for a list of classic DJ tracks and the companion website for recordings of selected tracks.

4. As I mentioned in the Introduction, graffiti, though considered one of the four elements of hip-hop artistic culture, has not played a central role in the history of the hip-hop DJ, which is why I have focused on the DJ's role within hip-hop *music*, meaning beats (DJs), rhymes (MCs), and dance (b-boys and b-girls).
5. Kandi, interview with MarWax.
6. GrandWizzard Theodore, telephone interview with the author, 19 December 2006.

2 Live Crew. "What I Like (Scratch Version)." *What I Like*. Fresh Beat Records 12-inch single FBR 002 (1985).

311. "Down." *311*. Capricorn Records compact disc CXK 42041 (1995).

Aerosmith. "Walk This Way." Toys in the Attic. Columbia LP PC 33479 (1975).

Afrika Bambaataa and the Soul Sonic Force. "Planet Rock." *Play at Your Own Risk/ Planet Rock*. Polydor 12-inch single 2141 675 (1982).

Altered Beats: *Assassin Knowledges of the Remanipulated*. Axiom LP 162-531 046-1 (1996).

A-Trak. *Gangsta Breaks*. Ammo Records LP AM-04 (2000).

Automator (a.k.a. Dan the Automator). *Music to Be Murdered By*. HomeBass Records 12-inch single hB 88365.

Babe Ruth. "The Mexican." *First Base*. Harvest LP SW 11151 (1972).

DJ Babu. *Super Duck Breaks: The Saga*. Stones Throw Records compact disc STH 2046 (2002).

The Beat Junkies. *The World Famous Beat Junkies Vol. 1*. PR Records compact disc PRR54280 (1997).

The Beat Junkies. *The World Famous Beat Junkies Vol. 2*. Blackberry Records compact disc BLK 005 (1998).

The Beat Junkies. *The World Famous Beat Junkies Vol. 3*. Blackberry Records compact disc BLK 72018 (1999).

Beck. "Loser." *Mellow Gold*. Geffen Records compact disc DGCG-24634 (1994).

Beck. "Where It's At." *Odelay*. Geffen Records compact disc DGCG-24823 (1996).

BeSide. "Change the Beat." Celluloid 12-inch single, CEL 156 (1982).

Big Daddy Kane. "Mister Cee's Master Plan." *Long Live the Kane*. Cold Chillin' LP 9 25731-1 (1988).

Birdy Nam Nam. *Birdy Nam Nam*. Uncivilized World compact disc UWECD 6 (2005).

Biz Markie. "Cool V's Tribute to Scratching." *Goin' Off*. Cold Chillin LP 25675-1 (1988).

Bliss, Melvin. "Synthetic Substitution." *Reward/Synthetic Substitution*. Sunburst Records 7-inch single SU-527 (1973).

Blondie. "Rapture." *Autoamerican*. Chrysalis LP CHE 1290 (1980).

Blow, Kurtis. "AJ Scratch." *Ego Trip*. Mercury LP 822 420-1 M1 (1984).

Blow, Kurtis. "The Breaks." *The Breaks.* Mercury LP 6337137 (1980).

Blow, Kurtis. "Juice." *Tough.* Mercury LP 1505 (1982).

Brown, James. "Funky Drummer, Part 1 and 2." King 45 rpm disc 6290 (1970).

Brown, James. "Get on the Good Foot." *Get on the Good Foot.* Polydor LP PD-2-3004 (1972).

Buckshot LeFonque (featuring DJ Premier). "Some Shit at 78 BPM (The Scratch Opera)." *Buckshot LeFonque.* Columbia LP C2 57323 (1994).

Buckshot LeFonque (featuring DJ Apollo). *Music Revolution.* Columbia LP CK 67584 (1997).

Bullet Proof Scratch Hamsters. *Hamster Breaks Volume 1.* Bullet Proof Records LP BPSH 001 (1993).

Busy Bee. "Jazzy on the Mix." *Running Thangs.* UNI Records LP UNI-2 (1988).

Cage, John. "Imaginary Landscape No. 1." *Early Modulations: Vintage Volts.* Caipirinha Music compact disc CAI 2027-2 (2000).

Captain Sky. "Super Sporm." *The Adventures of Captain Sky.* AVI Records LP AVI 6042 (1978).

Cash Money (orig. released as Doctor Funnkenstein and D.J. Cash Money). "Scratchin' to the Funk." *Scratchin to the Funk.* Sound Makers Records 12-inch single TTED-3014 (1986).

Cash Money and Marvelous. *Where's the Party At?* Sleeping Bag Records LP TLX 42016 (1988).

Chic. "Good Times." *Good Times.* Atlantic 12-inch single DK4801 (1979).

Commodores. "The Assembly Line." *Machine Gun.* Motown LP M6-798S1 (1974).

Courtney Pine (featuring DJ Pogo). *Underground.* Antilles compact disc 537 745-2 (1997).

DJ Craze and DJ Klever. *Scratch Nerds.* Counterflow Recordings compact disc 25 (2002).

Crooklyn Dub Consortium. *Certified Dope Vol. 1.* WordSound compact disc WSCD003 (1995).

Cut Chemist. *The Audience's Listening.* Warner Bros. compact disc 48559-2 (1996).

D-Styles. *Phantazmagorea.* Beat Junkie Sound compact disc PHAN-001 (2002).

Davis, John, and the Monster Orchestra. "I Can't Stop." *Night and Day.* Sam Records LP LP700 (1976).

Davy DMX "One for the Treble (Fresh)." *Tuff City.* CBS Associated Records 12-inch single 4Z9 04955 (1984).

Deep Concentration: The Future of Experimental Hip Hop. Om compact disc 4 IMW2 39506-2 01 (1997).

DJ Disk. *See* Phonopsychographdisk.

Dorsey, Lee: "Get Out of My Life, Woman." *The New Lee Dorsey.* Amy LP AMY 8011 (1966).

The Egyptian Lover. "What is a D.J. If He Can't Scratch?" *On the Nile.* Egyptian Empire Records LP DMSR-0663 (1984).

EPMD. "Funky Piano." *Business as Usual.* Def Jam Recordings LP C 47067 (1990).

Eric B. and Rakim. "Eric B. Is on the Cut." *Paid in Full.* 4th and Broadway LP BWAY 4005 (1987).

Eric B. and Rakim. "I Know You Got Soul." *Paid in Full.* 4th and Broadway LP BWAY 4005 (1987).

Fab 5 Freddy. "Change the Beat." *Change the Beat.* Celluloid 12-inch single CEL 156 (1982).

DJ Faust. *Man or Myth.* Bomb Hip-Hop compact disc BOMB 2009 (1998).

DJ Flare. *Hee Haw Brayks.* Dirty Style Records LP HHB 001 (1999).

Franklin, Aretha. "Rock Steady." *Young, Gifted, and Black.* Atlantic LP SD-7213 (1972)

Funky Four Plus One. "Rappin' and Rocking the House." *Rappin' and Rocking The House.* Enjoy Records 12-inch single 6000 (1979).

Gang Starr. "Code of the Streets." *Hard to Earn.* Chrysalis LP F1 28435 (1994).

Gang Starr. "DJ Premier in Deep Concentration." *No More Mr. Nice Guy.* Wild Pitch Records compact disc WPD 2001 (1989).

G.L.O.B.E. and Whiz Kid. "Play That Beat Mr. D.J." *Play That Beat Mr. D.J.* Tommy Boy Music 12-inch single TB 836 (1983).

Grandmaster Flash. "The Adventures of Grandmaster Flash on the Wheels of Steel." *The Adventures of Grandmaster Flash on the Wheels of Steel.* Sugar Hill Records 12-inch single SH-557 (1981).

Grandmaster Flash and the Furious Five. "The Birthday Party." *The Birthday Party.* Sugar Hill Records 12-inch single SH 555 (1981).

Grandmaster Flash and the Furious Five. "Freedom." *Freedom.* Sugar Hill Records 12-inch single SH-549 (1980).

Grandmixer D.ST. "Crazy Cuts." *Crazy Cuts.* Island Records 7-inch single 7-99803 (1983).

Grandmixer D.ST. & The Infinity Rappers. "Grandmixer Cuts It Up." *Grandmixer Cuts it Up.* Celluloid 12-inch single CEL 158 (1982).

GrandWizzard Theodore. "Military Cut." *Wild Style.* Animal records LP APE 6005ST (1983).

DJ Grazzhoppa. *DJ Big Band + AKA Moon.* Cypres Records 0606 (2010).

Gunn, Russell (featuring DJ Apollo). *Ethnomusicology, Volume 1.* Atlantic CD 83165-2 (1998).

Gunn, Russell (featuring DJ Apollo). *Ethnomusicology, Volume 2.* Justin Time CD JUST 172 (2001).

Gunn, Russell (featuring DJ Neil Armstrong). *Ethnomusicology, Volume 3.* Justin Time CD JUST 189-2 (2003).

Hancock, Herbie. "Rockit." *Future Shock.* Columbia LP FC 38814 (1983).

Hanson. "MMMbop." *Middle of Nowhere.* Mercury compact disc 534 615-2 (1997).

Hashim. "Al-Naafiysh (The Soul)." *Al-Naafiysh (The Soul).* Cutting Records 12-inch single CR-200 (1983).

The Hellers. "Life Story." *Singers. . . Talkers. . . Players. . . Swingers. . . and Doers.* Command LP RS 934 SD (1968).

Herman Kelly and Life. "Dance to the Drummer's Beat." Percussion Explosion. Electric Cat LP ECS-225 (1978).

The Honeydrippers. "Impeach the President." *Impeach the President/Roy C's Theme.* Alaga records 7-inch single AL-1017 (1973).

ie.MERG. *Audiocide.* Inside Records LP IRG-10-001 (2005).

Ill Insanity. *Ground Xero.* The Ablist Productions compact disc TAP510 (2008).

Incubus. "Battlestar Scralatchtica." *Make Yourself.* Epic compact disc EK 63652 (1999).

Incursions in Illbient. Asphodel LP ASP 0968-1 (1996).

Invisibl Skratch Piklz. "Invisibl Skratch Piklz Vs. Da Klamz Uv Deth." *Invisibl Skratch Piklz Vs. Da Klamz Uv Deth*. Asphodel 12-inch single ASP 0106 (1996).

James, Bob. "Take Me to the Mardi Gras." *Two*. CTI Records LP CTI 6057 (1975).

DJ Jazzy Jeff and the Fresh Prince. "DJ on the Wheels." *He's the DJ, I'm the Rapper*. Jive LP 1091-1-J (1988).

DJ Jazzy Jeff and The Fresh Prince. "The Magnificent Jazzy Jeff." *Rock the House*. Word-Up LP WDLP 0001 (1987).

DJ Jazzy Jeff and The Fresh Prince. "Jazzy's Groove." *And in This Corner. . . .* Jive compact disc 1188-2-J (1989).

Jimmy Castor Bunch. "It's Just Begun." *It's Just Begun*. RCA LP 4640 (1972).

Jive Rhythm Trax. "122 BPM." *Mix-Trix #4*. Kut-Up Records LP MT 004 (1984).

Kid Koala. *Carpal Tunnel Syndrome*. Ninja Tune LP ZEN 34 (2000).

Kid Koala. "Tricks 'n' Treats." *Scratchappyland*. Ninja Tune 10-inch promo ZEN 10KK (1997).

Kid Koala. *Some of My Best Friends Are DJs*. Ninja Tune compact disc ZEN CD82 (2003).

Kid Rock. "Bawitdaba." *Devil Without a Cause*. Atlantic LP 83119 (1999).

King Tech and M.C. Sway. "King Tech." *Flynamic Force*. All City Records 12-inch single K88020 (1988).

Knights of the Turntables. "Techno Scratch." *Techno Scratch*. JDC Records 12-inch single JDC 0034 (1984).

Kool G Rap and DJ Polo. "Butcher Shop." *Road to the Riches*. Cold Chillin' LP 25820-1 (1989).

DJ Krush. *Krush*. Shadow Records compact disc SDW-004-2 (1995).

DJ Krush and Toshinori Kindo. *Ki-Oku*. Sony compact disc SRCS 8093 (1996).

Leary, Paul. "Concerto for Trumpet, Turntables and Orchestra." *4 World Premieres*. Contemporary Youth Orchestra compact disc (2010).

Lightnin' Rod. "Hustlers Convention." *Hustlers Convention*. United Artists Records LP UA-LA156-F (1973).

Linkin Park. "One Step Closer." *Hybrid Theory*. Warner Bros. Records compact disc 9 47755-2 (2000).

Live Human. *Monostereosis: The New Victrola Method*. Fat Cat compact disc FATCD03 (1999).

Lizée, Nicole. "RPM for Large Ensemble and Solo Turntablist." *This Will Not Be Televised*. Centredisques compact disc CMCCD 13508 (2008).

LL Cool J. "Go Cut Creator Go." *Bigger and Deffer (BAD)*. Def Jam Recordings LP C 40793 (1987).

DJ Logic. *The Anomaly*. Ropeadope Records compact disc RCD 16004 (2001).

The Lords of the Underground. "Lord Jazz Hit Me One Time (Make It Funky)." *Here Come the Lords*. Pendulum Records LP 61415-1 (1993).

MacDonald, Ralph. "Jam on the Groove." *Sound of a Drum*. Marlin LP 2202 (1976).

DJ Magic Mike and The Royal Posse. "Magic Mike Cuts the Record." *DJ Magic Mike and the Royal Posse*. Cheetah Records compact disc TCRC 9401 (1989).

Mandrill. "Fencewalk." *Composite Truth*. Polydor LP PD 5043 (1973).

Mantronik, Kurtis. "Fresh Is the Word" and "Needle to the Groove." *Mantronix: The Album*. Sleeping Bag Records LP TLX-6 (1985).

Marclay, Christian. "John Cage." *More Encores*. No Man's Land 10-inch disc NML 8816 (1989).

Marclay, Christian. "Second Coming." *Records, 1981–1989*. Atavistic compact disc ALP062CD (1997).

Marley Marl Featuring MC Shan. "Marley Marl Scratch." *Marley Marl Scratch*. NIA Records 12-inch single NI1248 (1985).

McLaren, Malcolm. "Buffalo Gals." *Buffalo Gals*. Island Records 12-inch Single 0-99950 (1982).

Medeski Martin & Wood (featuring DJ Logic). "Sugar Craft." *Combustication*. Blue Note compact disc 4 93011 2 (1998).

Incredible Bongo Band. "Apache." *Bongo Rock*. MGM LP 2315 255(1973).

Mixmaster Gee and the Turntable Orchestra. "The Manipulator." *The Manipulator*. MCA Records 12-inch single MCA 23631 (1986).

The Monkees. "Mary Mary." *More of The Monkees*. Colgems LP COM-102 (1967).

Mr. Dibbs. *Primitive Tracks*. Cease and Desist compact disc CND001-1 (2000).

Passport. "Ju-Ju Man." *Infinity Machine*. Atlantic LP SD 36-132 (1976).

Phase II. "The Roxy." *The Roxy*. Celluloid 12-inch single CEL 159 (1983).

Prokofiev, Gabriel. *Concerto for Turntables and Orchestra*. Nonclassical compact disc NONCLSS005 (2009).

Psychedelic Skratch Bastards. *Battle Breaks*. Dirt Style LP, BB 001 (1992).

Phonopsychographdisk (aka DJ Disk). *Ancient Termites*. Bomb Hip-Hop compact disc BOMB 2009 (1998).

Public Enemy. "Terminator X to the Edge of Panic" *It Takes a Nation of Millions to Hold Us Back*. Def Jam Recordings compact disc CK 44303 (1988).

Qbert. *Superseal Breaks*. Dirty Style Records LP SEAL 002 (2000).

Qbert. *Wave Twisters–Episode 7 Million: Sonic Wars Within the Protons*. Galactic Butt Hair Records LP GBH 0007-1 (1998).

Queen. "Another One Bites the Dust." *The Game*. Elektra LP 5E-513 (1980).

Queen. "We Will Rock You." *News of the World*. Elektra LP 6E-112 (1977).

DJ Quest. *Questside (Untold Tales)*. Hip Hop Slam compact disc HHS027 (2001).

Rage Against the Machine. "Bulls on Parade." *Evil Empire*. Epic compact disc EK 57523 (1996).

Rare Earth. "I Just Want to Celebrate." *One World*. Rare Earth LP RS520 (1971).

DJ Rectangle. *The Ultimate Battle Weapon*. Twist-N-Tangle LP TNT 004 (1997).

Return of the D.J. Vol. 1. Bomb Hip-Hop compact disc BOMB 2002 (1995).

DJ Revolution, featuring KRS-One. "The DJ." *King of the Decks*. Duck Down compact disc cd-DDM2085 (2008).

Rob Swift. "Salsa Scratch." *Sound Event*. Tableturns compact disc TBL-001 (2002).

Roc Raida. *Hater Breaks*. AdiarCor Records LP AC 730 (2002).

Rucker, Ricci. *The Utility Phonograph Record 1*. Sound In Color LP SICBRK100 (2003).

Rucker, Ricci, and Mike Boo. *Sketchbook (An Introduction to Scratch Music)*. Sound In Color compact disc SICCD099 (2003).

Run D.M.C. "Here We Go (Live at the Funhouse)." *Here We Go (Live at the Funhouse)*. Profile Records 12-inch single PRO-7079-0 (1995).

Run-DMC. "Jam Master Jay." *Run D.M.C.* Profile Records LP PRO-1202 (1984).

Run DMC. "Peter Piper." *Raising Hell.* Profile Records LP PRO-1217 (1986).

Schoolly-D. "It's Krack." *The Adventures of Schoolly-D.* Schoolly-D Records LP SD117 (1986).

Scratch Attack, vols. 1–3. Hip Hop Slam compact discs HHS 032, 037, 040 (2002-2003).

DJ Shadow. *Endtroducing.....* Mo Wax compact disc MW 059 CD (1996).

DJ Shortee. *The Dreamer.* Bomb Hip-Hop compact disc BOMB 2042 (1999).

DJ Shortee and Step 1. *Bikini Wax.* 5 Star Records LP (2007).

DJ Sniff. *ep.* PSI compact disc 11.02 (2011).

DJ Spooky That Subliminal Kid. *Riddim Warfare.* Outpost Recordings compact disc OPRD-30031 (1998).

The Soul Searchers. "Ashley's Roachclip." *The Salt of the Earth.* Sussex LP SRA 8030 (1974).

Spoonie Gee Meets The Sequence. "Monster Jam." *Monster Jam.* Sugar Hill Records 12-inch single SH550 (1980).

Squier, Billy. "Big Beat." *The Tale of the Tape.* Capitol Records LP ST-12062 (1980).

Steady B. "Bring the Beat Back." *Bring Back the Beat.* Jive LP 1020-1-J (1986).

Steinski. *What Does It All Mean: 1983–2006 Retrospective.* Illegal Art compact disc IA116.

Storch, Jeremy. "I Feel a New Shadow." *From a Naked Window.* RCA LP LSP-4447 (1970).

Sublime. "What I Got." *Sublime.* Gasoline Alley Records compact disc GASD 11413 (1996).

Sugar Ray. "Every Morning" and "Someday." *14:59.* Lava, Atlantic LP 83151-1 (1999).

The Sugar Hill Gang. "Rapper's Delight." *Rapper's Delight.* Sugar Hill Records 12-inch single SH-542 (1979).

Super Disco Brakes Vol. 1. Paul Winley Records LP P.W. L.P. 133 (1979).

DJ Swamp. *Never Is Now.* Lakeshore Records compact disc LAK 33685-2 (1998).

Thin Lizzy. "Johnny the Fox Meets Jimmy the Weed." *Johnny the Fox.* Mercury LP SRM-1-1119 (1976).

Trouble Funk. "Pump Me Up." *Drop the Bomb.* Sugar Hill Records LP SH 266 (1982).

Tuff Crew. "Behold the Detonator" *Back to the Wreck Shop.* Warlock Records LP WAR-2712 (1989).

Tuff Crew. "Deuce, Ace, Housin.'" *Danger Zone.* Warlock Records LP WAR-2705 (1988).

Turntables by the Bay. Hip Hop Slam compact disc HHS 023 (2001).

Ultimate Breaks and Beats, vols. 1–25. Street Beat Records LPs SBR 501-525 (1986–1991).

Urban Revolutions: The Future Primitive Sound Collective. Future Primitive Sound compact disc and LP FPS 005 (2000).

UTFO. "Roxanne Roxanne." *UTFO.* Select Records LP SEL 21614 (1985).

The Winstons. "Amen Brother." *Color Him Father.* Metromedia Records LP MD 1010 (1969).

Word of Mouth. "King Kut." *King Kut.* Beauty and the Beast Records 12-inch single BAB 100 (1985).

The Wreckin Cru. "Surgery." *Surgery*. Kru-Cut Records 12-inch single KC-002 (1984).

X-Ecutioners. "It's Goin' Down." *Built from Scratch*. Loud Records compact disc 501563
    2 (2002).

X-Ecutioners. *X-Pressions*. Asphodel LP ASP 0977 (1997).

DJ Z-Trip. *Shifting Gears*. Hollywood Records compact disc 2061-62503-2 (2005)

DJ Z-Trip and DJ P. *Uneasy Listening Vol. 1*. Self-released LP (1999).

BIBLIOGRAPHY

INTERVIEWS AND PERSONAL COMMUNICATIONS

DJ A-Minor. Conversation with the author, 3 December 2010.
DJ A-Trak. E-mail message to the author, 26 August 2002.
DJ Aladdin. E-mail message to the author, 10 July 2011.
DJ Apollo. Interview with the author, Berkeley, CA, 29 March 2008.
Bisi, Martin. Telephone interview with the author, 14 August 2011.
DJ B-Side. E-mail message to the author, 9 November 2010.
DJ Baby Dee. Telephone interview with the author, 22 July 2010.
Bambaataa, Afrika. Telephone interview with the author, 19 July 2011.
Beinhorn, Michael. E-mail message to author, 23 May 2010.
Beinhorn, Michael. E-mail message to the author, 15 August 2011.
Bernal, Andrew. Interview with the author, Los Angeles, CA, 14 June 2008.
Boyle, Ann Marie. Telephone interview with the author, 30 May 2010.
Blue, Ruza. E-mail message to the author, 12 June 2011.
Cannady, Michael. Interview with the author, New York, NY, 2 July 2007.
Carluccio, John. Telephone interview with the author, 16 October 2001.
DJ Cash Money. Telephone interview with the author, 23 June 2008.
DJ Craze. E-mail message to the author, 3 July 2011.
Cutmaster Swift. Interview with the author, Slough, England, 27 May 2011.
DJ Disco Wiz. Interview with the author, Stamford, CT, 4 February 2008.
DJ Disco Wiz. Telephone interview with the author, 10 June 2008.
DJ Disco Wiz. Conversation with the author, Chapel Hill, NC, 3 February 2009.
Fab 5 Freddy. Telephone interview with the author, 4 August 2011.
Fintoni, Laurent. Interview with the author, Tokyo, Japan, 5 June 2008.
Grandmixer DXT (formerly D.ST). Interview with the author, New York, NY, 30 July 2010.
GrandWizzard Theodore. Conversation with the author, Baltimore, MD, 3 May 2005.
GrandWizzard Theodore. Telephone interview with the author, 19 December 2006.
GrandWizzard Theodore. Interview with the author, Chapel Hill, NC, 23 October 2007.

GrandWizzard Theodore. Interview with the author, Chapel Hill, NC, 25 October 2007.

GrandWizzard Theodore. Telephone interview with the author, 9 November 2011.

DJ Hapa. Telephone interview with the author, 23 February 2011.

Immortal. Interview with the author, Miami, FL, 14 December 2006.

J. Dayz. Interview with the author, New York, NY, 28 July 2007.

Jam, Billy. Interview with the author, New York, NY, 4 February 2008.

Jones, Pete DJ. Telephone interview with the author, 22 July 2010.

Ken-One. Interview with the author, Tokyo, Japan, 5 June 2008.

Kid Koala. Interview with Mark Katz, David Hutcheson, Sara Soltau, and Reed Turchi, Carrboro, NC, 18 April 2009.

Killa-Jewel. Telephone interview with the author, 10 January 2008.

King Britt. Interview with the author, Philadelphia, PA, 19 June 2008.

Kuttin Kandi. E-mail message to the author, 8 July 2011.

Laswell, Bill. Telephone interview with the author, 28 May 2010.

Macatee, Steve. Telephone conversation with the author, 17 December 2010.

DJ Maseo. Telephone interview with the author, 17 November 2011.

McLintock, Sally. E-mail message to the author, 29 March 2007.

McLintock, Sally. Interview with the author, Slough, England, 27 May 2011.

Mista Donut. Interview with the author, Tokyo, Japan, 6 June 2008.

DJ Miyajima. Interview with the author, Tokyo, Japan, 2 June 2008.

DJ P. Telephone interview with the author, 21 April 2009.

DJ Pone (Travis Rimando). Interview with the author, Berkeley, CA, 8 November 2006.

DJ Pone (Travis Rimando). Interview with the author, Berkeley, CA, 27 March 2008.

DJ Pone (Travis Rimando). E-mail message to the author, 8 July 2010.

Prince, Tony. E-mail message to the author, 25 April 2005.

Prince, Tony. Interview with the author, London, England, 14 April 2008.

Prince, Tony. Interview with the author, Slough, England, 27 May 2011.

DJ Qbert. Interview with the author, Burlingame, CA, 27 March 2008.

DJ Quest. Telephone interview with the author, 10 August 2010.

DJ Radar. Interview with the author, Guadalupe, AZ, 13 June 2008.

DJ Revolution. Telephone interview with the author, 19 May 2009.

DJ Rhettmatic. Interview with the author, Los Angeles, CA, 14 June 2008.

Rodriguez, Ivan "Doc." Telephone interview with the author, 9 March 2008.

Rosado, Johnny "Juice." Telephone interview with the author, 11 March 2008.

DJ Sarasa, aka Silverboombox. Interview with the author, Tokyo, Japan, 6 June 2008.

DJ Shadow. Telephone interview with the author, 14 January 2011.

DJ Shadow. E-mail message to the author, 7 December 2010.

DJ Shortkut. Interview with the author, Colma, CA, 28 March 2008.

Steinski. Telephone interview with the author, 28 February 2008.

DJ Steve Dee. Interview with the author, Harlem, NY, 17 July 2007.

Storch, Jeremy. E-mail message to the author, 25 August 2010.

DJ Swamp. Telephone interview with the author, 18 November 2009.

Swift, Rob. Interview with the author, Roslyn, VA, 6 July 2001.

Swift, Rob. E-mail message to the author, 10 January 2008.

Swift, Rob. E-mail message to the author, 11 January 2008.

Swift, Rob. E-mail message to the author, 21 March 2011.
DJ Ta-Shi. Interview with the author, Tokyo, Japan, 2 June 2008.
DJ Tigerstyle (Alvin Seechum). Interview with the author, London, England, 14 April 2008.
Trilling, Roger. Telephone interview with the author, 24 May 2010.
Tyra from Saigon. Interview with the author, North San Jose, CA, 28 March 2008.
Wilkes, Tachelle. Telephone interview with the author, 22 December 2006.
Yañez, Raúl. Interview with the author, Guadalupe, AZ, 13 June 2008.
Z-Pabon, Christie. E-mail message to the author, 16 November 2002.
Z-Pabon, Christie. E-mail message to the author, 1 January 2007.
Z-Pabon, Christie. E-mail message to the author, 23 March 2007.
Z-Pabon, Christie. E-mail message to the author, 6 June 2011.
Zekri, Bernard. Telephone interview with the author, 12 July 2010.

Books, Articles, and Films

Aaron, Charles. "What the White Boy Means When He Says Yo." *Spin* 14 (November 1998): 114–129.
Aaron, Charles. "Mix Masters: The Top 13 Turntablists in the World." *Spin* 15 (April 1999): 128–132.
Ahearn, Charlie. "Interview with Jay Smooth", part 2. *Ill Doctrine*. 24 October 2007. Online at www.illdoctrine.com/2007/10/charlie_ahearn_interview_part.html.
Alperts, Randy. "Interview: GrandMixer DXT Scratches Deep into Digital." *O'Reilly Digital Media*, 24 November 2004. Online at http://digitalmedia.oreilly.com/2004/11/24/dxt.html.
Amorosi, A.D. "Made from Scratch." *Philadelphia City Paper*, 22–28 August 2002. Online at http://citypaper.net/articles/2002-08-22/cover.shtml.
As the Tables Turn. Red Line Music DVD, no label number, 2007.
A-Trak. "Scratchnotation." *Tablist*, no. 1 (March 2002): 34–35.
A-Trak. *Sunglasses Is a Must*. Audio Research Records, Inc., DVD, ARDVD-01, 2006.
Babbitt, Milton. "Interview with Frank J. Oteri." *New Music Box*, 1 December 2001. Online at www.newmusicbox.org/page.nmbx?id = 32fp04.
DJ Babu. "Interview with K-Per." 26 June 2005. UKHH.com. Online at www.ukhh.com/elements/turntablism/babu/index.html. (Link inactive.)
Bambaataa, Afrika. "3 Questions: Afrika Bambaataa." *Minneapolis City Pages*, 17 January 2007. Online at http://blogs.citypages.com/gimmenoise/2007/01/ 3_questions_afrika_bambaataa.php.
Bambaataa, Afrika. "Interview with Nardwuar." No date. Online at www.nardwuar.com/vs/afrika_bambaataa/print/.
Banks, Lefty. "Return of the DJ." In *Classic Material: The Hip-Hop Album Guide*, edited by Oliver Wang, pp. 140–41. Toronto: ECW Press, 2003.
Beat Kings: The History of Hip Hop. Nature Sounds DVD, 2006.
Bell, Paul. "Interrogating the Live: A DJ Perspective." Ph.D. diss., Newcastle University, 2009.
The Best of I.T.F., Vol. 1. DJ Honda DVD, DHBA-9, 2006.

Brewster, Bill, and Frank Broughton. *Last Night a DJ Saved My Life: The History of the Disc Jockey*, rev. ed. London: Headline, 2006.

Burte, Laurent. *Scratch graphique: une recherche typographique au plus profond du son*. Paris: Pyramyd, 2003.

Butler, Mark J. *Unlocking the Groove: Rhythm, Meter, and Musical Design in Electronic Dance Music*. Bloomington and Indianapolis: Indiana University Press, 2006.

Callahan-Bever, Noah. "The Spinners." *Vibe* (August 2002): 124–28.

Caro, Robert. *The Power Broker: Robert Moses and the Fall of New York*. New York: Vintage, 1975.

Chairman Mao, "The Knights of the Turntables." *Rap Pages* (April 1996): 48–54.

Chang, Jeff. *Can't Stop, Won't Stop: A History of the Hip-Hop Generation*. New York: Picador, 2005.

Charnas, Dan. *The Big Payback: The History of the Business of Hip-Hop*. New York: New American Library, 2010.

Chonin, Neva. "An Itch to Scratch: The New School Turntablists," *Option*, no. 77 (November–December 1997): 56–61.

Christgau, Robert. "The Magnificent Seven." *Village Voice*, 2 November 1982, p. 59.

Coleman, Brian. "Turntablists: Return of the DJ," *CMJ New Music Monthly*, no. 55 (March 1998): 14–15, 47.

Coleman, Brian. *Check the Technique: Liner Notes for Hip-Hop Junkies*. New York: Villard, 2007.

Cook, Dave. "Filipino DJs of the Bay Area: Why Are They So Successful?" Davey D's Hip Hop Corner. October 1995. Online at www.daveyd.com/filipinodjs.html.

Cross, David. "A History of the Development of DJ Mixer Features: An S&TS Perspective." B.A. thesis, Cornell University, 2003. Online at www.zenknee.com/DJ_Mixer_History.pdf.

D-Styles. Liner notes to *Phantazmagorea* [2002]. Beat Junkie Sound CD, PHAN-001.

Danielsen, Anne. *Presence and Pleasure: The Funk Grooves of James Brown and Parliament*. Middletown, CT: Wesleyan University Press, 2006.

"The Death of Battling." *DJ Geometrix* forum discussion. Online at www.djgeometrix. com/message_board/topic.asp?TOPIC_ID = 8834.

Deep Crates: Documentary Film Dedicated to the Art of Beatdiggin'. Beatdawg Films DVD, no label number, 2004.

D'Errico, Michael A. "Behind the Beat: Technical and Practical Aspects of Instrumental Hip-Hop Composition." M.A. thesis, Tufts University, 2011.

Diss Miss. "Interview with Safe Soul." UKHH.com. 2 June 2006. Online at www.ukhh. com/features/interviews/diss_miss/index.html. Link inactive.

DJ Cash Money. "Interview with DJ Sake." 27 August 2007. Online at www.brightcove. tv/title.jsp?title = 1155199964&channel = 1137939859.

DJ Qbert's Complete Do-It Yourself, Vol. 1 Skratching. Thud Rumble DVD, DIY001DVD, 2003.

DJ Qbert's Scratchlopedia Breaktannica: 100 Secret Skratches. Thud Rumble DVD, SECRT001, 2007.

"DJ Slyce Interview." *Dirty Waters*, 6 September 2008. Online at http://dirtywaters. blogspot.com/2007/09/dj-slyce-interview.html.

Ellison, Ralph. *Invisible Man*. New York: Modern Library, 1994.

Eshun, Kodwo. *More Brilliant Than the Sun: Adventures in Sonic Fiction.* London: Quartet, 1998.

Espen, Hal. "Jockey Club." *New Yorker,* 9 August 1993, pp. 26–28.

Fernando, S.H. *The New Beats: Exploring the Music, Culture, and Attitudes of Hip-Hop.* New York: Anchor, 1994.

Fine, Jason. "Revolutions per Minute: DJ Shadow, Hip-Hop Militant." *Option,* no. 73 (March–April 1997): 58–63, 70–73.

Flores, Juan. *From Bomba to Hip-Hop: Puerto Rican Culture and Latino Identity.* New York: Columbia University Press, 2000.

Flores, Juan. "Puerto Rican and Proud, Boyee!: Rap, Roots and Amnesia." In *The Hip Hop Reader,* edited by Tim Strode and Tim Wood, pp. 30–40. New York: Pearson Longman, 2008.

Ford, Robert Jr. "B-Beats Bombarding Bronx: Mobile DJ Starts Something with Oldie R&B Disks." *Billboard* (1 July 1978): 65. Reprinted in *That's the Joint: The Hip-Hop Studies Reader,* edited by Murray Foreman and Mark Anthony Neal, p. 41. New York: Routledge, 2004.

Forman, Murray. *The 'Hood Comes First: Race, Space, and Place in Rap and Hip-Hop.* Middletown, CT: Wesleyan University Press, 2002.

Fouché, Rayvon. "Following the Artifacts: Hip Hop, Japan, and Technological Knowledge." In *Studies of Urban International Society: Compilation of Seminar Papers,* pp. 59–85. Osaka: Urban Culture Research Center, Osaka City University, 2009. Online at http://educa.lit.osaka-cu.ac.jp/~ggp/nakami/2009/Studies_of_International_Urban_Society_2009.pdf.

Fouché, Rayvon. "Say It Loud, I'm Black and I'm Proud: African Americans, American Artifactual Culture, and Black Vernacular Technological Creativity." *American Quarterly* 58 (2006): 639–61.

Frederikse, Tom, and Phil Benedictus. *How to DJ: The Insider's Guide to Success on the Decks.* New York: St. Martin's Griffin, 2006.

Fricke, Jim, and Charlie Ahearn. *Yes Yes Y'all: The Experience Music Project Oral History of Hip-Hop's First Decade.* New York: Da Capo, 2002.

George, Nelson. "Hip-Hop's Founding Fathers Speak the Truth." *Source,* no. 50 (November 1993): 43–50. Reprinted in *That's the Joint: The Hip-Hop Studies Reader,* edited by Murray Foreman and Mark Anthony Neal, pp. 50–62. New York: Routledge, 2004.

Goldberg, David Albert Mhadi. "The Scratch Is Hip-Hop: Appropriating the Phonographic Medium." In *Appropriating Technology: Vernacular Science and Social Power,* edited by Ron Eglash, Jennifer L. Croissant, Giovanni Di Chiro, and Rayvon Fouché, pp. 107–44. Minneapolis: University of Minnesota Press, 2004.

Gonzalez, David. "Will Gentrification Spoil the Birthplace of Hip-Hop?" *New York Times,* 21 May 2007. Online at www.nytimes.com/2007/05/21/nyregion/21citywide.html.

Grandmaster Flash. "Interview with Davey D." *Davey D's Hip Hop Corner,* September 1996. Online at www.daveyd.com/interviewgmflashchronicle.html.

Grandmaster Flash and David Ritz. *The Adventures of Grandmaster Flash: My Life, My Beats.* New York: Broadway Books, 2008.

Grandmixer D.ST. "Interview with JayQuan." *Tha Foundation,* 11 January 2004. Online at www.thafoundation.com/dst.htm.

Grand Wizard Rasheen. "Interview with James G. Spady." *The Global Cipha*, 15 December 2008. Online at www.thaglobalcipha.com/Rasheen.html.

GrandWizzard Theodore. "Interview, Red Bull Music Academy." Berlin, 1998. Online at www.redbullmusicacademy.com/TUTORS.9.0.html?act_session = 32.

GrandWizzard Theodore. "Interview with Troy L. Smith." Tha Foundation. Summer 2005. Online at http://www.thafoundation.com/gwtheodore.htm

Hager, Steven. *Hip Hop: The Illustrated History of Break Dancing, Rap Music, and Graffiti.* New York: St. Martins, 1984.

Hansen, Kjetil Falkenberg. "The Acoustics and Performance of DJ Scratching: Analysis and Modeling." Ph.D. diss., University of Stockholm, 2010.

Hansen, Kjetil Falkenberg. "The Basics of Scratching," *Journal of New Music Research* 31 (2002): 357–65.

Hebdige, Dick. *Cut "N" Mix.* London: Comedia, 1987.

Hershkovits, David. "London Rocks, Paris Burns, and the B-Boys Break a Leg." *Sunday News Magazine*, 3 April 1983. Reprinted in *And It Don't Stop?: The Best American Hip-Hop Journalism of the Last 25 Years*, edited by Raquel Cepeda, pp. 27–34. New York: Faber and Faber, 2004.

Hess, Mickey. *Hip Hop in America: A Regional Guide*, Vol. 1: East Coast and West Coast, pp. 143–75. Santa Barbara, CA: ABC-CLIO, 2010.

Hines, Alan. "Brooklyn's Mighty Mobile Jocks." *Discothekin'* (June 1976): 14–17.

Inoue, Todd S. "Beats Generation." *San Jose Metro*, 7–13 November 1996. Online at www.metroactive.com/papers/metro/11.07.96/scratch-pickles-9645.html.

Jacobs, Justin. "Catching Up With... *DJ Hero* Producer Will Townsend." Paste Magazine, 29 October 2009. Online at www.pastemagazine.com/articles/2009/10/catching-up-with-dj-hero-producer-will-townsend.html.

Jeffs, Rick. "Evolution of the DJ Crossfader." *RaneNote*, no. 146 (1999). Online at www.rane.com/note146.html.

Jenkins, Willard. "Fab 5 Freddy: The Max Roach Influence." *Jazz Times*, 26 May 2011. Online at http://jazztimes.com/articles/27743-fab-5-freddy-the-max-roach-influence.

Kahn, Douglas. "Christian Marclay's Early Years: An Interview." *Leonardo Music Journal* 13 (2003): 17–21.

Karppi, Tero, and Olli Sotamaa. "Methodological Observations from Behind the Decks." In *Games as Services: Final Report*, edited by Tero Karppi and Olli Sotamaa, pp. 56–72. Finland: University of Tampere, 2010.

Katz, Mark. *Capturing Sound: How Technology Has Changed Music*, rev. ed. Berkeley: University of California Press, 2010.

Katz, Mark. "Men, Women, and Turntables: Gender and the DJ Battle." *Musical Quarterly* 89 (Summer 2006): 580–99.

Kelley, Robin D.G. "Beneath the Underground: Exploring New Currents in 'Jazz.'" In *Uptown Conversation: The New Jazz Studies*, edited by Robert G. O'Meally, Brent Hayes Edwards, and Farah Jasmine Griffin, pp. 404–16. New York: Columbia University Press, 2004.

Kelley, Robin D.G. *Yo' Mama's Disfunktional!: Fighting the Culture Wars in Urban America*. Boston: Beacon, 1997.

Kid Koala. "Interview with Scott Thill." *Morphizm*. 22 January 2007. Online at www.morphizm.com/recommends/interviews/kidkoala.html.

Kim, You-Young. "An Orchestral Project Is 'Bullish' on Innovation." *The Juilliard Journal Online* 22 (November 2005) . Online at www.juilliard.edu/update/journal/j_articles 712.html.

Krims, Adam. *Music and Urban Geography*. New York: Routledge, 2007.

Kugelberg, Johan, ed. *Born in the Bronx: A Visual Record of the Early Days of Hip Hop*. New York: Rizzoli, 2007.

Kuttin Kandi. "Interview with Marwax." 30 January 2000. Online at www.5thplatoon. com/articles/kuttinkandiinterview.htm.

Laswell, Bill. "Interview with John Doran." *The Quietus*, 15 July 2009. Online at http:// thequietus.com/articles/02185-bill-laswell-interviewed-bass-how-low-can-you-go.

Lawrence, Tim. "Disco Madness: WALTER Gibbons and the Legacy of Turntablism and Remixology." *Journal of Popular Music Studies* 20 (September 2008): 276–329.

Lawrence, Tim. *Love Saves the Day: A History of American Dance Music Culture, 1970–1979*. Durham, NC, and London: Duke University Press, 2003.

Leland, John, and Steve Stein. "What It Is." *Village Voice* 33, 19 January 1988, pp. 24–30.

Lizée, Nicole. "RPM for Large Ensemble and Solo Turntablist." Master's thesis, McGill University, 2000.

Lomax, Alan. "Saga of the Folksong Hunter." In *Alan Lomax, Selected Writings 1934–1997*, edited by Ronald Cohen, p. 173. New York: Routledge, 2003. Originally published in 1960. Quoted in Anthony Seeger, "Lost Lineages and Neglected Peers: Ethnomusicologists Outside Academia," *Ethnomusicology* 50 (Spring—Summer 2006): 217.

Mahler, Jonathan. *Ladies and Gentlemen, The Bronx Is Burning*. New York: Farrar, Straus, and Giroux, 2005.

Marshall, Wayne. "Kool Herc." In *Icons of Hip Hop*, edited by Mickey Hess, pp. 1–25. Westport, CT: Greenwood, 2007.

Martinez, Theresa A. "Popular Culture as Oppositional Culture: Rap as Resistance." *Sociological Perspectives* 40 (1997): 265–86.

Mason, Andrew. "Building Blocks." *Wax Poetics*, no. 1 (Winter 2002): 44–50.

Matos, Michaelangelo. "All Roads Lead to 'Apache.'" In *Listen Again: A Momentary History of Pop Music*, edited by Eric Weisbard, pp. 200–207. Durham, NC: Duke University Press, 2007.

McCord, Mark. "Kool DJ Herc vs. Pete DJ Jones: One Night at the Executive Playhouse." *Wax Poetics*, no. 17 (June–July 2006): 85–94.

Michel, Sia. "Spins: DJ Shadow, *Endtroducing. . . . . .*" *Spin* (January 1997): 81.

Miller, Chuck. "Two Turntables and a Microphone: The Story of Grandmaster Flash and the Furious Five." *Goldmine* 22 (6 December 1996): 72–74, 88, 90.

Miller, Kiri. "Schizophonic Performance: Guitar Hero, Rock Band, and Virtual Virtuosity." *Journal of the Society for American Music* 3 (November 2009): 395–429.

Miller, Paul D. *Rhythm Science*. Cambridge, MA: MIT Press, 2004.

Miyakawa, Felicia M. "Turntablature: Notation, Legitimization, and the Art of the Hip-Hop DJ." *American Music* 25 (spring 2007): 81–105.

Montano, Ed. "'How Do You Know He's Not Playing Pac-Man While He's Supposed to Be DJing?': Technology, Formats and the Digital Future of DJ Culture." *Popular Music* 29 (2010): 397–416.

Myrie, Russell. *Don't Rhyme for the Sake of Riddlin': The Authorized Story of Public Enemy*. New York: Canongate, 2008.

Naison, Mark. "From Doo Wop to Hip Hop: The Bittersweet Odyssey of African-Americans in the South Bronx." *Socialism and Democracy* 18 (2004): 37–49.

Norris, Sîan. "Turning the Tables," *The Guardian*, 28 November 2007, sec. G2, p. 16. Online at www.guardian.co.uk/lifeandstyle/2007/nov/28/women.electronicmusic.

NY77: The Coolest Year in Hell. Originally broadcast on VH1, 11 August 2007.

O'Connor, Brian. "Career Decknician." *DJ Times* 19 (March 2006): 26–28.

O'Meara, Caroline Polk. "New York Noise: Music in the Post-Industrial City, 1978–1985." Ph.D. diss., University of California, Los Angeles, 2006.

Parks, Eunice. "Kuttin' Kandi." *Asian Week*, 27 July–2 August 2001. Online at www.asianweek.com/2001_07_27/arts_kuttinkandy.html.

Payne, Jim. *Give the Drummers Some!: The Great Drummers of R&B, Funk & Soul*, edited by Harry Weinger. Katonah, NY: Face the Music Productions, 1996.

Perry, Imani. *Prophets of the Hood: Politics and Poetics in Hip Hop*. Durham, NC: Duke University Press, 2004.

Pisares, Elizabeth H. "Do You Mis(recognize) Me: Filipina Americans in Popular Music and the Problem of Invisibility." In *Positively No Filipinos Allowed: Building Communities and Discourse*, edited by Antonio T. Tiongson, Jr., Edgardo V. Gutierrez, and Ricardo V. Gutierrez, pp. 172–98. Philadelphia: Temple University Press, 2006.

Poschardt, Ulf. *DJ Culture*. Translated by Shaun Whiteside. London: Quartet, 1998.

Potter, Russell A. *Spectacular Vernaculars: Hip-Hop and the Politics of Postmodernism*. Albany: State University of New York Press, 1995.

Prince Paul. "The Memoirs of Prince Paul." *Wax Poetics*, no. 2 (Spring 2002). Reprinted in *Wax Poetics Anthology*, Vol. 1, pp. 117–25. Brooklyn, NY: Wax Poetics Books, 2007.

Reese, Ronnie. "Roc Raida, 1972–2009: The Grand Master" *Wax Poetics*, no. 38 (2009): 24.

Rice, Doc. "Transforming Notation: Pioneering the Hieroglyphics of the Scratch." *Rap Pages* (August 1999): 32.

Roberts, John Storm. *The Latin Tinge: The Impact of Latin American Music on the United States*, 2nd ed. New York: Oxford University Press, 1999.

Rock, Pete. "Interview with Andrew Friedman." *Guitar Center* catalog, April 2008, L08–L11.

Rodgers, Nile. Interview at Canadian Music Week, Toronto, March 2007. Online at www.youtube.com/watch?v = t-SCGNOieBI.

Rose, Tricia. *Black Noise: Rap Music and Black Culture in Contemporary America*. Hanover, NH: Wesleyan University Press, 1994.

Said, Amir. *The Beat Tips Manual*, 5th ed. Brooklyn, NY: Superchamp, 2009.

Sanchez, Ivan, and Luis Cedeño. *It's Just Begun: The Epic Journey of Disco Wiz, Hip Hop's First Latino DJ*. Brooklyn, NY: powerHouse, 2009.

Sanneh, Kalefa. "Spin Doctorate." *New York Times*, 8 August 2004, 2:1, 25.

Schloss, Joseph G. *Foundation: B-Boys, B-Girls, and Hip-Hop Culture in New York*. New York: Oxford University Press, 2009.

Schloss, Joseph G. *Making Beats: The Art of Sample-Based Hip-Hop*. Middletown, CT: Wesleyan University Press, 2004.

Scratch. Palm DVD, 3046-2, 2001.

Sellin, Yara. "DJ: Performer, Cyborg, Dominatrix." Ph.D. diss., University of California, Los Angeles, 2005.

Sher, Sheri. *Mercedes Ladies*. New York: Vibe Street Lit, 2008.

Singer, Roberta L., and Elena Martínez. "A South Bronx Latin Music Tale." *Centro* 16 (Spring 2004): 177–201.

Skratchcon 2000. Thud Rumble DVD, SC2000, 2000.

Slovick, Sam. "The Fil-Am Invasion." *LA Weekly*, 8 August 2007. Online at www.laweekly.com/news/features/the-fil-am-invasion/16965.

Smith, Sophy. "Compositional Processes of UK Hip-Hop Turntable Teams." Ph.D. diss., De Montfort University, 2006.

Smith, Sophy. "The Process of 'Collective Creation' in the Composition of UK Hip-Hop Turntable Team Routines." *Organised Sound* 12, no. 1 (2007): 79–87.

Snapper, Juliana. "Scratching the Surface: Spinning Time and Identity in Hip-Hop Turntablism." *European Journal of Cultural Studies* 7 (2004): 9–23.

Souvigner, Todd. *The World of DJs and the Turntable Culture*. Milwaukee: Hal Leonard, 2003.

Steventon, John. *DJing for Dummies*, 2nd ed. Chichester, England: John Wiley and Sons, 2010.

Stolzoff, Norman C. *Wake the Town and Tell the People: Dancehall Culture in Jamaica*. Durham, NC: Duke University Press, 2000.

Strauss, Neil. "Battle of the Needle Freaks." *Spin* (April 1999): 125–26.

Sullivan, Paul. "Three Times Deep: DJ Cash Money Is Deep Into Everything." *Wax Poetics*, no. 15 (2007): 22–25.

Tai, James. "Science Friction." *URB*, no. 57 (January–February 1998): 42–47.

Tate, Greg. "Adventures in Illbient," *Vibe* (April 1998): 54.

Thigpen, David E. *Jam Master Jay: The Heart of Hip Hop*. New York: Pocket Star Books, 2003.

Tiongson, Antonio T., Jr. "Filipino Youth Cultural Politics and DJ Culture." Ph.D. diss., University of California, San Diego, 2006.

Tolchin, Martin. "South Bronx: A Jungle Stalked by Fear, Seized by Rage." *New York Times*, 15 January 1973, pp. 1, 19.

Tompkins, Dave. *How to Wreck a Nice Beach*. Chicago: Stop Smiling, 2010.

Toop, David. *Rap Attack 3*. London: Serpent's Tail, 2000.

Torres, Andre. "Give the Engineer Some." *Wax Poetics*, no. 1 (winter 2001). Reprinted in *Wax Poetics Anthology*, Vol. 1, pp. 139–41. Brooklyn, NY: Wax Poetics Books, 2007.

Tremayne, Jim. "Dance & Electronic Music: Great Gear!" *Billboard*, 5 October 2002, pp, 34, 42.

Tremayne, Jim. "Interview with Jam Master Jay." *DJ Times* (June 2000). Online at www.djtimes.com/original/djmag/jun00/JamMasterJay.htm.

Tyrangiel, Josh. "Turntablist Expert: Now Every Night He Saves a DJ's Life." *Time*, 28 May 2001. Online at www.time.com/time/magazine/article/0,9171,999984,00.html.

Van Veen, Tobias. "The Art and Craft of Turntablism: The DJ School." *Discorder* (March 2002). Online at http://www.quadrantcrossing.org/papers/Vinyauralism02-Discorder-tV.pdf.

Veal, Michael E. *Dub: Soundscapes and Shattered Songs in Jamaican Reggae*. Middletown, CT: Wesleyan University Press, 2007.

Wang, Oliver S. "Spinning Identities: A Social History of Filipino American DJs in the San Francisco Bay Area (1975–1995)." Ph.D. diss., University of California, Berkeley, 2004.

Webber, Stephen. *DJ Skills: The Essential Guide to Mixing and Scratching*. Burlington, MA: Focal, 2007.

Webber, Stephen. *Turntable Technique: The Art of the DJ*, 2nd ed. Boston: Berklee Press, 2010.

Weheliye, Alexander G. *Phonographies: Grooves in Sonic Afro-Modernity*. Durham, NC: Duke University Press, 2005.

"Where the Ladies At?" *Scratchworx.com*, forum thread, posted 3 May 2005. Online at www.skratchworx.com/news/comments.php4?id = 271.

Whipper Whip. "Interview with Troy Smith." *The Foundation* (winter 2006). Online at www.jayquan.com/whip.htm.

White, Phil, and Luke Crisell. *On the Record: The Scratch DJ Academy Guide*. New York: St. Martin's Griffin, 2009.

Wilder, Eliot. *Endtroducing. . . .* New York: Continuum, 2005.

Wilkes, Tachelle. "Killa Jewel: Proceed with Caution." *Femmixx.com*. Online at www.femmixx.com/killajewelinterview.html.

Williams, H.C. "Grandmaster Flash." In *Icons of Hip Hop*, edited by Mickey Hess, pp. 27–48. Westport, CT: Greenwood, 2007.

Winner, Langdon. "Do Artifacts Have Politics?" *Daedalus* 109 (Winter 1980): 121–36.